NEW YORK DAYS

Books by Willie Morris

North Toward Home

Yazoo

Good Old Boy

The Last of the Southern Girls

James Jones: A Friendship

Terrains of the Heart

The Courting of Marcus Dupree

Always Stand in Against the Curve

Homecomings

Good Old Boy and the Witch of Yazoo

Faulkner's Mississippi (with William Eggleston)

After All, It's Only a Game

New York Days

NEW YORK DAYS

WILLIE MORRIS

LITTLE, BROWN AND COMPANY
BOSTON · NEW YORK · TORONTO · LONDON

FIRST PAPERBACK EDITION

Library of Congress Cataloging-in-Publication Data

Morris, Willie.
New York days / Willie Morris. — 1st ed.
p. cm.
ISBN 0-316-58421-5 (hc) 0-316-58398-7 (pb)
1. Morris, Willie — Homes and haunts — New York (N.Y.) 2. New York (N.Y.) — Social life and customs — 20th century. 3. New York (N.Y.) — Intellectual life — 20th century. 4. Authors, American — 20th century — Biography. 5. Editors — United States — Biography. 6. Harper's magazine. I. Title.
PS3563.O8745Z474 1993
813'.54 — dc20
[B] 93-13244

10 9 8 7 6 5 4 3 2 1

MV-NY

Designed by Jeanne Abboud

Published simultaneously in Canada by Little, Brown & Company (Canada) Limited

PRINTED IN THE UNITED STATES OF AMERICA

To JoAnne,
who wasn't there, but should have been

and to Bob Kotlowitz,
who *was* there and I'm glad

Over the great bridge, with the sunlight through the girders making a constant flicker upon the moving cars, with the city rising up across the river in white heaps and sugar lumps all built with a wish out of non-olfactory money. The city seen from the Queensboro Bridge is always the city seen for the first time, in its first wild promise of all the mystery and the beauty in the world. . . .

"Anything can happen now that we've slid over this bridge," I thought; "anything at all. . . ."

— F. Scott Fitzgerald,
The Great Gatsby

~ CONTENTS

Preface

I would like this book to be considered a sequel to my *North Toward Home,* which was published a quarter of a century ago.

Two or three of my friends and colleagues from our time together suggested I focus tightly on the events surrounding *Harper's Magazine* itself. Although this stormy and thrilling experience was central to these New York days, I concluded after much thought, and in the spirit of the earlier book, to make this memoir deliberately less rigid in framework and more allusive and eclectic and broad-ranging: the city itself in the Sixties, the diversity of its people (some famous, some not), the social and literary and political worlds, the sweeping events enveloping the city and the nation, my own personal life.

With the passing of the years, memory merges and entwines all these for me. My proud hope is that both volumes can be read as a continuing entity.

W. M.

New York Days

~ I Came to the City

1

I CAME TO THE CITY and it changed my life.

I was exalted by it, exulted in it. I was a young man at a great personal threshold in a place and a moment throbbing with possibility, observing America from here in its extravagant peaks and turmoils, giving myself to the town and it to me: a most American covenant. I had arrived in 1963 from the provinces eventually to become editor-in-chief of *Harper's*, America's oldest magazine, at the age of thirty-two. Is it surprising that in time I grew to deem myself more a New Yorker than a Mississippian? New York was my patron city, crux and apogee of our national experience, matrix and pinnacle for me then of all the human artifacts.

The New York days! They seem faraway now, back again in the hinterland as I have been for more than ten years, and yet oddly near, surely only a fortnight ago, and they lifted me far out of myself: the stunning cosmos of the city at a time in which everyone seemed to know everyone else and where everything of importance seemed to happen first, its magic and majesty as epicenter of the nation and the world, its interlocking literary and cultural and political and social milieux, its glamorous parties and beautiful women and dialogue sparkling with adroit repartee, its clever *bon mots* and full-blooded lunacies, its teeming adventure and perilous fun, its monumental ambition, its aura then of idealism and titillation and tempestuous feasibility, the hard work and the gratification. I was part of all that. We were going to re-make literary America.

Not for me Mencken's "third-rate Babylon." The unbenighted metropolis comprehended the outlander who had immemorially come here in quest and odyssey; there was world enough and time for the Dixie exile. Life pullulated for me. I was young, from the South, wanted to know everyone and live everything. Roaming the city in the random hours, my psyche working so with ideas and feelings, I thought sometimes I would die of my own heat and curiosity and cunning. Tinder-dry I was then for the great town, and therefore inflammable. "I'll introduce you to every wit, halfwit, and nitwit in New York," the drunken poet told Frank Capra's Mr. Deeds, and that too was the city's voice whispering sedulously in my ear.

There were eight million telephone numbers in the Manhattan directory, and every one of them would have returned my calls. I knew the writers, the poets, the intellectuals, the editors, the actresses, the tycoons, the homicide detectives, the athletes, the *belle figure,* and not a few *fakirs* and reprobates and charlatans. I wined with Sinatra and eavesdropped in the *trattorias* on the Mob. I sat next to DiMaggio in the Garden ringside seats and addressed literary matrons in hats in the Waldorf-Astoria. I danced with Scarlett O'Hara's younger sister and Scott Fitzgerald's only daughter. I grew familiar with the palatial townhouses and high-rise penthouses on the Upper East Side with marble staircases, wide and steep and long, and Steinway grands which Gershwin had played on right in these rooms, and Cole Porter of Peru, Indiana, and Johnny Mercer of Savannah, Georgia, and I talked with the people who had known them all: George would play for us at the drop of a hat. As if he needed an excuse! Johnny drank too much, you know, but he was an amusing fellow. Cole was crippled by that frightful accident, but what a dear he was! And on any such evening if it were an entertainment or theatrical crowd ("How are you, dahling?" punctuated with moist profuse kisses) Comden and Green might be trying one of their new tunes around a piano in a parlor, or Lena Horne singing "Stormy Weather," or Bobby Short up from a night off at the Carlyle, or the Texas boys of the Fantasticks playing all those years on Sullivan Street in the Village, diverting such a bedazzled gathering. One could in these moments stand on the outside balconies and absorb the music from the distance and tinkle the ice in your glass and watch the great lights of Manhattan come on. Or think nothing at all of sighting Leonard Bernstein briefly alone in some sumptuous alcove there and engaging him in dexterous city chatter, then withdrawing from one's pocket a ballpoint pen some politician from home had sent you with its inscription *"I'm a Yellow Dog Democrat"* and presenting it to Leonard Bernstein, as I most certainly did one evening or another. "What in heaven is a Yellow Dog Democrat?" he asked. "A Southern Democrat who will vote for a yellow dog over a Republican," I replied. "How very clever! Eminently logical!" he responded, accepting the gift with deft metropolitan alacrity, then wandering the salon in the dappling glitter showing it to the others.

I liked Manhattan in the rain, when you could sit near the window of a bar in midtown and watch how *contained* it seemed under the elements, the raindrops bouncing on the tops of the vehicles and dissolving surrealistically in the night, the people scurrying by, or seeking shelter, the mighty facades enveloped in a dim soft mist: who are these souls hastening away under the rain, and where might they be going? I even grew to like it in the snow, the light, dervishing snowfalls like veils against the dimming lamps, the way the snowflakes swirled along the cross streets as in snowy tunnels and caught in the branches of the lonely little trees. I liked its seasons. Except for its blazing heat waves, when little phantasmic mists shimmered on the asphalt and concrete and steel, I liked the brassy blue-gray of New York summer dawns, liked too the summer afternoons when everyone was away, its supple and seductive whispers.

"I shall never forget the weekend Laura died," one of my favorite movies of New York begins. "A silver sun beamed through the sky like a huge magnifying glass. It was the hottest Sunday in my recollection. I felt as if I were the only human being left in New York City." Those big movie houses around Fiftieth Street were cool. There was something sensuous about the summer there — "overripe," Fitzgerald found it, "as if all sorts of funny fruits were going to fall into your hands." The city in summer was hot, hot as one's boyhood when you left your own cool moviehouse and its honeyed conjurings and were out again in the lush baking cauldron of reality that had been waiting there all along for you while you sat in the darkness with dreams, living the moments of life yet to be lived. "Far down the street a hydrant burst into a fountain of silver water," William Styron had observed in *Lie Down in Darkness,* "and three boys in shorts scampered in and out and darted and retreated like slick brown bees toward a silver blossom." On some nights the city, Saul Bellow knew, was hot as Bangkok, the whole continent seeming "to have moved from its place and slid nearer the equator, the bitter gray Atlantic to have become green and tropical, and the people, thronging on streets, barbaric fellaheen among the stupendous monuments of their mystery, the lights of which, in dazzling profusion, climb upward endlessly into the heat of the sky."

I liked the early springtime when the small scraggly trees in the heart of the city were trying so hard to burst into life, their modest limbs reaching beseechingly upward, the drafty wind along streets like breezeways, the trembling clouds in new shafts of sun. I liked the high shifting cloudbanks way beyond the Hudson River at the farthest western horizon, as if the whole nimbus of the American continent were somehow waiting expectantly out there under those very cloudbanks.

I liked Christmas in the city before the coming of the January murk, the twinkling of lights in avenue windows in the wintry nights, a gossamer touch of virgin snow, roasting chestnuts and the carols from Rockefeller Plaza and St. Patrick's, and Tiffany's and F.A.O. Schwarz and B. Altman's and Bloomingdale's, and Luchow's for the ceiling-high tree and the brass band playing "O, Tannenbaum," and the streetcorner Santa Clauses, some of them more than a little drunk.

On a burnished morning of New York springtime, 1967, I had moved my things into the editor-in-chief's rooms of *Harper's.* The editorship of this venerable national institution mattered to me greatly, for I had perused so many of its old back issues, and had worked for it for more than four years, and felt in my deepest heart the sweeping efficacy of its lineage and its possibilities in a heightened age, and now its owners had given my colleagues and me a mandate to revitalize it. It had been some time now since the magazine had crossed East Thirty-third Street from the old Harper & Brothers building to more substantial quarters at Two Park Avenue, and the editor's office occupied a considerable corner suite with a precipitous view of Park and the animated lower Murray Hill neighborhood, and if you peered long enough between the skyscrapers across the way, you might catch a hasty little finger of the East River, somnolent and tawny in the early sun. The walls of the office were decorated with framed covers of the magazine from the nineteenth century, and a graceful portrait of William Dean Howells, and wonderfully illustrated posters of Mark Twain's *Personal Recollections of Joan of Arc,* which had been serialized in *Harper's* in 1896 and which the author considered his finest book, though in this instance I believed he had misjudged. I sat for a moment in the leather swivel chair and pondered the clean immaculate oaken desk, the last time for several years it would be *that* clean, and I recalled Twain's own self-admonition: "If I ever get up there, I'll stick if I can."

Sitting there momentarily alone, with the massed whine of Park Avenue rising tremulously up from below and the Manhattan sunlight reflecting on the facades of the neighboring buildings, I thought of the cluttered composing room of the *Yazoo Herald* when I was a boy, and the dusty corner behind the linotypes where I once wrote my stories on a vintage Smith-Corona my father had given me for a Christmas long ago, and I remembered our offices of the *Texas Observer* off the Drag in Austin on the ground floor of a diminutive wooden building with a bare slanting floor and nocturnal roaches and insects splattering against the window panes in summer. I recalled all the deadlines come and gone since those times, the hard work and sleepless nights with burning tongue from the cigarettes and No-Doz. In this morning hush I felt as fulfilled as I was the day I was awarded the American Legion Citizenship Award in junior high school, or when I was sixteen and we won the state championship in baseball. I remembered, too, the counsel of my high school basketball coach, Hardwood Kelly, before an important game: "Hang loose as a goose." Was I afraid?

In the instant I may even, I confess, have had sentiments similar to those of the ballplayers from the tiny town in the locker room before the state finals in the movie *Hoosiers:* "Let's win this one for all the small schools who never got a chance to play here." On the bulletin board behind the desk I thumbtacked the clarion in Joseph Pulitzer's will, still reprinted every day on the editorial pages of the *St. Louis Post-Dispatch* and which I had put on the wall of every office where I had ever worked: "That it will always fight for progress and reform, never tolerate injustice and corruption, always fight demagogues of all parties, never belong to any party, always oppose privileged classes and public plunderers, never lack sympathy for the poor, always remain devoted to the public welfare, never be satisfied merely with printing news, always be drastically independent, never be afraid to attack wrong, whether by predatory plutocracy or predatory poverty." Would *that* apply to my magazine in the onrushing Sixties?

In the midst of these ruminations John Fischer, the departing editor, suddenly came in. He looked thin and tired. He was leaving that day to go abroad. Two days previously we had had a meeting with the owners on finances, and the magazine was still working under a strong deficit.

"I feel badly about leaving you with that situation," he said.

"I'll take it ten years, Jack," I said.

"Five's enough. I did it too long. Well, I'll be going."

I thanked him. We shook hands, then in a skitterish haste he was away. Now, from the pinnacle of the years, I wish I had said more in that moment, that I would not so much have been there had it not been for him, that I cared for him — as with my own father on his deathbed in the King's Daughters' Hospital back home long before, when I had wanted to tell him that if I ever had a son I would name him after him, but could not say it. Perhaps it had something to do with being young and not knowing much about such things, and thinking you will live forever.

On that day I became the eighth editor of *Harper's* since 1850, the youngest in its 117-year history. I never gave much thought to my age then. That would only come with time. There was too much to be done to dwell upon such an idle question. I was too busy.

When people brought up the matter I suggested that the magazine profession by the nature of its demands should be a young person's calling, and that most baseball players had already hung up the spikes by then anyway.

But who was I? What did I *expect?* Mary McCarthy wrote, citing Orwell, that an autobiography which does not tell something bad about the author cannot be any good. I was not, as Margot Channing said of Eve Harrington in *All About Eve,* "a lamb in our big stone jungle." I was "long-headed," as my grandmother in Mississippi used to call me for being the boy who jumped highest out of the tree into the water. Like my contemporary and *paisano* Elvis, I was close in those days to being nothing if not a Mississippi hothead, and when anyone inquired of my politics I said Jefferson Democrat, and with a suspicion of absolutes and "ideological truth," yet a Jeffersonian with certain emphatic notions about a historic magazine amid the clashing American cultures of the day. Our public statement promised the magazine would try to be lively and relevant if sometimes irreverent in attitude and would have "a stronger appeal for younger readers — young in age, young at heart." I had written down some other thoughts and gave them to my colleagues: "The country badly needs a truly *national* magazine, unidentified with any intellectual clique or with any region, or city, or slice of a city, willing to fight to the death the pallid formulas and deadening values of the mass media. It needs a magazine young and courageous enough to carry the language to its limits, to reflect the great tensions and complexities and even the madnesses of the day, to encourage the most daring and imaginative and inventive of our writers, scholars, and journalists — to help give the country some feel of itself and what it is becoming." These were dramatic words, perhaps, and more than a shade self-righteous, but I believed them. Privately, more surreptitious than loose and sweeping public statements, my vision was of a magazine that *had* to be read, that would take on the "Establishment," assume the big dare, move out to the edge, make people mad, edify and arouse and entertain, tell the truth. I had faith in sturdy empirical reporting buttressed by good writing and never fretted too much about length if the writing itself were strong and brave and evocative. And I believed in the challenge of writers and reporters to give subjective responses to the events they confronted when this was called for, even to participate at times in those events, using the techniques of the novelist and the first-person so long as the facts and the mood were treated with the utmost truth. And to be outrageous if need be, as if sometimes a magazine, like a person, must be reckless in behalf of the qualities it passionately cares for. Above all, I believe I wanted to get *Harper's* back to its roots, its own literary heritage. Only those things, that's all. I believed, too, Frank Crowninshield's editorial creed in the maiden issue of *Vanity Fair* just before World War I that "we, as a nation, have come to realize the need for more cheerfulness, for hiding a solemn face, for a fair measure of pluck and for great good humor." All this would be difficult, if not impossible, of course. But was it not worth a try? The magazine business itself was in a condition of flux, growing more and more difficult economically — increased printing costs, a damaging policy on the part of the federal government on postal rates, many other things. The general interest magazine was going into decline, while there was a corresponding upsurge of specialized magazines such as those aimed at doctors who flew their own planes and liked to ski in Aspen.

The year 1967 marked the 150th anniversary of Harper & Brothers Publishers. For those indulgent of political prophecy, it was also the year the Washington clairvoyant Jeanne Dixon predicted many Republican victories ahead beginning in 1968, Governor Ronald Reagan of California becoming destined for greatness despite having to guard himself against the Eastern Establishment, Richard Nixon growing more important to his country and party, nothing but trouble for Lyndon Johnson, Mao Tse-tung and Ho Chi Minh soon to be gone from the arena of world power, and Vietnam only a bonfire compared to battles yet to come. There, too, lay an editorial agenda.

In those exhilarating days my contemporaries and I, as in Lord Lindsay's eulogy to his fellow Cambridge Olympians in *Chariots of Fire,* had "hopes in our hearts and wings on our heels." And the energy, God, the energy we had — we vibrated with it. We were in the spirit of the 1960s in the freedoms we enlarged and explored.

The Empire Chinese Restaurant would be our neighborhood nexus: on Madison Avenue, just north of Thirty-fourth and south of the old J. P. Morgan mansion, a gloomy, opaque establishment with a substantial bar and lounge, and restaurant tables all around, and drifting everlastingly over these the mingling cachet of chop suey and moo-shoo and roasting duck. Why we had chosen this saturnine place among the dozens in this particular vicinity for our after-work gossip and plotting — editors and writers and contributors from the American provinces and novelists and poets and wives and girlfriends and intrepid hangers-on — was one of those New York conundrums: it merely happened. One of our fellow habitués was a handsome young Texas woman, John Steinbeck's sister-in-law, who worked for the television game shows, and the inscrutable yet benevolent *maître d'* always gave us the most secluded tables on the understanding that someday he would be a guest on "To Tell the Truth." Many was the magazine issue conceived here over our interminable cocktails in the dying late afternoons, and the dilemmas of the turbulent nation of that era assessed and dissected, and alliances forged and dissolved, and the florid courting of the finest writers of America for their disparate assignments. I can close my eyes now and absorb the vanished voices there. Is that Norman Mailer moving about there? Bernard Malamud? Is that my colleague Larry L. King promising Mr. Suey Han a brief appearance on "To Tell the Truth"? David Halberstam in *contretemps* with a Freudian existentialist on Bobby Kennedy? Arthur Miller talking about Soviet intellectuals with Bob Kotlowitz? Bill Moyers fresh from the heartland on the things most troubling to Americans? Joan Didion illumining the *angsts* of Southern California for a *New York Post* sportswriter? Dandy Don Meredith of the Dallas Cowboys describing for Marshall Frady his days as an SMU Mustang? Irwin Shaw recounting events at the Cannes Film Festival to the *Village Voice* man? Ed Koch in lengthy soliloquy with the bearded columnist Pete Hamill on New York reform politics? Turner Catledge in conversation with a college editor on his first press runs on the *Neshoba Democrat*? George Plimpton and José Torres assaying a championship bout in the Garden? Seymour Hersh and Neil Sheehan just back from Saigon? Sara Davidson telling of her travels with Jacqueline Susann? Dick Schickel talking movies with a verbose Yalie? Sterling Lord counselling a young novelist on where best to publish? Jean Stein inviting everyone to a party at her place that very night for Aaron Copland, or was it Lauren Bacall? William Styron discussing human slavery in Virginia, circa 1831, for an intellectual from Vanderbilt? Senator Harris of Oklahoma edifying Bennett Cerf on the Choctaw Indians? James Dickey reciting W. B. Yeats to a Bronx fireman who wrote verse?

Those early finished issues of our magazine came from the marrow of our bones, reflecting, as the old *Texas Observer* once had for me, not just our gratifications, but our errors and shortcomings and sins. On the day the first shiny new monthly issues were delivered to our office, those maiden copies just off the presses with their clean fresh *smell*, I would wait until late afternoon, then take one to the Empire Chinese and sit alone at a booth in a corner and read it cover to cover, and pondering what was right in it and what was wrong. I remember now those solitary moments as if they were yesterday, the whole world ahead and the nation out there beyond the chrome-and-glass towers and the gathering Manhattan shadows waiting breathlessly for these words.

Once in these years I was on a commercial airliner from New Orleans to New York. We were half an hour or so south of Memphis; I was looking out my window in a haphazard reverie when I suddenly saw something far below which seized me in deepest recognition. I knew what it was immediately from the familiar contours of the river, and from the outline of its streets, and from the smoke spiraling eerily upward from the chemical plant out on Highway 49-E. From the high heavens in the moment's apparition there was my hometown all unexpectedly laid out for me, remote and translucent and clear as a revelation. I was transfixed there by its hallucinatory yet commonplace images, the wilderness and bluffs and flatland encompassing it all around. There was my old high school, and beyond it the neighborhood where I grew up. I knew there were people down there dying in the King's Daughters' Hospital, and teenagers driving around in cars, and cotton coming out on the powerful land. It all looked very small. I recognized the broad boulevard where my house was — somewhere down there my backyard where all the dogs of my boyhood lay buried — the street where we once strolled along on Friday nights of school in our blue-and-yellow Cub Scout caps on the way to a war movie downtown, *First Yank in Tokyo,* or *The Fighting Sullivans,* or *Purple Heart.* The radios from the big houses blared the war news from North Africa or London or the South Pacific, or the words of Roosevelt or Churchill echoing out into the springtime darkness. There was something in this, I sensed, just a shred of youthful emotion and memory, that from the echoes of the radios in the boulevard domiciles lay something of the fragile beleaguered fate of us. How to know this then? It was there somehow in the trees and the lawns, the birds and the windchimes, the clouds and the shadows. That war was not like this Vietnam one.

In my clandestine God's view of my place, I could almost feel the past rising up to me and asking: where on earth, fast-moving boy, are you going now?

On that day it was to New York City that I was going, after some magazine jaunt or other pertaining to facets of that decade, and the sudden glimpse of my town from thirty-five thousand feet brought back my father's shambling motion as he fungoed me a baseball down there, my mother playing Mozart on the baby grand in the front room, my dog trying to climb the elm tree after squirrels, the slow begrudging change of its seasons, the sound of the Illinois Central whistle and of the hounds barking mournfully from far away. Where else but to New York City was I going? There was much to do there, and things accumulating, and I had been three days away.

Who indeed *was* I then in those bright optimistic days, those high, windy, incandescent days, I ask myself anew, before the scrim of age, the miasma of regret, the dangers, toils, and snares of my childhood hymns? "There are two tragedies in life," George Bernard Shaw wrote. "One is not to get your heart's desire. The other is to get it." All of us struggle; all of us *respond* to struggle. In our secret being we are all tormented by the uncertainty, seldom more than in the glowing victories of youth: What if I fail? What do I do when they find out I'm me? Was my own burgeoning success all smoke and mirrors, all ambition's tally, or in those flamboyant, troubled times for America was there something in this that would be true and brave and enduring?

Years later and very far away, reading the compendious monthly numbers of our magazine of that time, I ponder with a kind of bemused tenderness what it all meant, the office hours, the deadlines, the telephone calls, the mountains of manuscripts, the business lunches, the editorial crises, the people and the power and the glamour. As with many strange and long-ago things in a person's life, one wonders, did it ever mean anything at all? If Henry James is correct and we hold in our souls and egos and beings the seeds of every event that happens to us, then is it not the odyssey itself that lives in our core? I will try to comprehend in the passage of the years that own especial past for me, evanescently, and of the emotions, and in the service of memory, for memory is all any of us has. Perhaps in this solitary quest the reader will find himself too, a coming to terms with the randomness of life and experience, the bittersweetness of all of it: the eternal troth.

~ Early Days

2

THE LETTER was unexpected.

My wife and I were having breakfast in our house on Bridle Path in Austin when the postman arrived with the morning's mail. It was early in 1962. I was editor of the *Texas Observer*, a statewide political and literary weekly. I had just turned twenty-eight.

I had been writing for *Harper's Magazine* and had recently finished a piece on the radical right in the Southwest, so the envelope was not an unfamiliar one: the impressive old *Harper's* crest with the lighted torch above the "1817," a sight which never failed to thrill me when I got a fine and serendipitous letter from one of its editors. I opened it. It was from John Fischer, the editor-in-chief of the magazine. I do not have that letter now, irretrievably lost as it must have been among the heedless debris of moving about America with a family in that time, but I can fairly well quote it from memory, since it was not the sort of letter one easily forgets:

> I'm writing this in confidence. I've been editor for ten years. It's been a gratifying but debilitating job, and I want to spend more time on my own work. Quite frankly I'm looking around for a successor. I don't know if you're the man, but I have a hunch you are. You write pretty well and I notice you've put some humor into *The Observer*. You could try it up here for a while and see what you think. I'll do the same. It's premature now. I won't have an opening for three or four months. But get in touch with me in a couple of weeks.

I handed the letter to Celia. She read it, then put it on the breakfast table. "Good God!" she said.

The little long-ago tale I am about to tell is rooted in one of the most passionate and tempestuous periods in American experience, one that still elicits vehement controversy, and likely always will: "The most decisive decade in its long history," as John F. Kennedy predicted of these years in the nation. Kennedy, himself, of course, did not live to see them out, and many others did not either.

"Oh, no!" James Earl Jones in the role of the burnt-out writer, the Salinger-type recluse, confronts Kevin Costner in *Field of Dreams*. "You're from the Sixties!" and proceeds to douse him with insect repellent. "Back to the Sixties! No place for you in the future. Get back while you still can!" I have often thought it hazardous to draw on decades as unerring historical measurements — "decadology" some detractors have called it — as if decades have now supplanted *centuries* as social and intellectual imperatives, but in this instance permit me that reasonable liberty, and not the least, I beg, for one's own selfish purposes; this is a personal memoir, and the Sixties were by far the most flamboyant and stimulating and despairing and keenly delineated interim in this memoirist's lifetime: best of times, worst of times. In the sweep of the Twenties, the Thirties, the Forties, the Fifties, in the way Americans look back on these arbitrary entities, each of these eras represents something palpable in the popular memory, compasses of the national life and not mere vagrant whims — compasses which ultimately suggest real priorities, fashions, ideals, fears, triumphs, failures, transgressions. To try to capture a decade, Tom Wolfe writes, also means "You're hitting on something that resonates with other people's impressions." I intend to take the Sixties on their own terms, and my own investment in them on more or less those terms, too.

To me the Sixties were not a literal, sequential reality, but a nearly metaphorical one, shaped in good dimension by the hot retrospection of feeling. For some they coincided with the Vietnam years. For others they commenced on November 22, 1963, and concluded with the Kent State killings in mid-1970. For me, in the most vivid idiosyncratic way, they began in the public library in Palo Alto in December 1962 and ended in New York City in March 1971.

Vitality and violence and upheaval are not infrequent handmaidens at certain historical moments. From the summit of the cultural capital and in my extensive travels as a writer and editor I bore witness to a broader America sundered with its internecine tensions and angers and extremes, its enveloping conflicts, and I had a consuming ache and fear for my country then, for its dire tempers and unravelling excesses, all the incredible prodigal clashing voices of a crazy mass democracy, and for "the fragility of the membranes of civilization," as Arthur Schlesinger, Jr., wrote then, "stretched so thin over a nation so disparate in its composition, so tense in its interior relationships, so cunningly enmeshed in underground fears and antagonisms." *Harper's Magazine* itself with its roster of distinguished contributors was to reflect much of this, interpret it, shape it, criticize or goad it: the youth rebellion, the counter-culture, the alienation of the generations, the cresting of the civil rights movement, the great domestic reforms of the Johnson administration, the assassinations, the radical chic, the sexual revolution, the wreckage of the cities, the conservative backlash and the armed reaction, and above all — undergirding all these and profoundly inflaming them — the deepening folly and tragedy of the Vietnam War.

Between the parental generation shaped by the Depression and World War II and their 1960s middle-class offspring, the world sometimes seemed to have broken in two. Between the church-oriented and nonviolent black civil rights activists of the South and the later ghetto revolutionists of the North rose another fatal hiatus. Between the Vietnam "hawks" and "doves" lay a subterranean abyss that threatened the fabric of civilized debate, even of society itself, in an America enervated and splintered more than any period since the Civil War: black versus white, rich versus poor, urban versus suburban, a balkanization of emotions and fealties and dependencies. And there were about two dozen other chasms, political, social, cultural, rivaling themselves in wildness and acridity.

The American Sixties began in considerable faith and idealism for most of us, but at their worst would evoke some of the deepest crevices of our soul, the most nihilistic and self-destructive: "its violence," Irving Howe would write of the decade in *Harper's*, "its coarseness, its jabbery, its sexual cult." In Saul Bellow's *Mr. Sammler's Planet* the old Jewish exile who had seen everything looks out at the Sixties from the Upper West Side:

> . . . the dreams of nineteenth-century poets polluted the psychic atmosphere of the great boroughs and suburbs of New York. Add to this the dangerous lunging staggering crazy violence of fanatics, and the trouble was very deep. Like many people who had seen the world collapse once, Mr. Sammler entertained the possibility it might collapse twice. He did not agree with refugee friends that this doom was inevitable, but liberal beliefs did not seem capable of self-defense, and you could smell decay. You could see the suicidal impulses of civilization pushing strongly.

I telephoned John Fischer at *Harper's* in New York. My wife Celia had just received a Woodrow Wilson for graduate study at Stanford. The bone-wearying work at the *Texas Observer* had caught up with me, and I wanted to go to California for a while. "Go out there," Fischer advised: "read, reflect." I could join the magazine in three or so months. I had also been offered a job with the *New York Times*. Tom Wicker and Homer Bigart, stellar *Times* men whom I had gotten to know in their reporting trips to Texas, arranged for me to talk with the *Times*'s James Reston. I told him I was going to *Harper's*. He discouraged me. "It's an old man's calling," he said. Strange to understand how set one's ambitions were; I see now that for a young writer with all of life ahead of him it was a big decision, fraught with consequence, full of pitfall. What if, I ask myself now, I had taken the *Times*?

Stanford was too golden, the patina of privilege. Yet even there, as at the University of Texas during my declining *Observer* days, young people were responding to the challenge of the Kennedy takeover: protest meetings, debates, much talk among the students of new commitments, of the Peace Corps, of government service.

The tone of public discourse, the willingness in the new circles of power to acknowledge the very existence of real problems, the youthful *feel* of Washington, were having a salutary effect. There was the example of the courageous mass nonviolent protests sweeping the South — and, of course, the image of Jack Kennedy himself. I am not sure the 1960s in all their flowering and complexity could have happened without JFK. What if Richard Nixon had gotten the 16,500 more votes in the key places in '60 and been elected instead? Who knows? Norman Mailer's widely read piece in *Esquire* on the 1960 Democratic Convention had described the "cold liberation" that emanated from Kennedy and predicted that he would help to release "a host of energies and impulses long storing up in the psychic underground." You could not help but like Jack Kennedy, especially if you were young. He was *ours*. He was my kind of fellow: he was funny, innovative, ironic, loved whimsy and history and women, and was a tough and consummate Boston pol. I liked the way he pronounced *Cuber, yayer, National Gaahd, hemispheah*. In somber suit and tie, disguised more or less as a Baptist pastor, I had sat amidst the Protestant preachers in the plush, green-carpeted ballroom of the Rice Hotel in Houston during the '60 campaign and observed him in his famous confrontation as he declared why a Catholic should be eligible for the Presidency; my view was from the side of the podium, and under the lectern, during his eloquent testimonial, I noticed his hands were trembling: he was human. Later, watching his inaugural address, I actually thought he was speaking straight to me.

Three things pleased me in my sojourn at golden Stanford: My two-and-a-half-year-old son running the olympian literary critic Yvor Winters off a campus sidewalk with his tricycle. Sitting in the centerfield bleachers at Candlestick Park watching Willie Mays of the San Francisco Giants and talking with him two or three times between innings of one-sided games. And the garden of the Palo Alto public library.

I began going to the library to peruse the back issues of *Harper's Magazine*. The winter on the peninsula that year was splendid, a succession of warm dazzling windless days, and the accommodating young librarian allowed me to sit at a table in an herbaceous courtyard with those bound volumes, seven or eight hours a day sometimes, and absorb the magazine's past. I loved the faint musty smell of those worn volumes in the dappled sunlight: How I wanted to be its editor someday! But why, indeed, me? The world of aspiration and accomplishment in the fabled city seemed an eternity away on those dallying secret afternoons, and I a presumptuous and callow imposter. Yet I returned day after day, thumbing the pages in a supple lethargy, reading long-forgotten essays and articles by forgotten people, and wonderful pieces and stories by remembered ones, and after a while I would be in the engrossing thrall of another world entirely, and another America. Once the librarian came out for an amiable chat. "If you don't mind my asking," she said, "why do you sit out here all by yourself reading these old magazines?" "I'm going to work for this magazine," I replied. "Oh, wow!" she said. *"Harper's!* How did you manage *that?"*

Harper & Brothers Publishers, established shortly after the Battle of Waterloo when New York City was essentially a big overgrown Dutch village of gables and steeples and hogs roaming the streets, had founded the magazine in 1850 to go along with its slightly more venerable sibling publication, *Harper's Weekly.* Its first editor, in fact, later founded the *New York Times.* The pioneers, I learned there in Palo Alto, had carried its bound volumes across the continent in their covered wagons. It had been the great "family" magazine of the nineteenth century. In its early years its distinction largely lay as a showpiece of English fiction: Dickens, Thackeray, Hardy, Trollope, the Brontës, George Eliot. From this transatlantic emphasis it gradually began to transform itself into an influential American journal on wide-ranging subjects, both articles and fiction for an authentic national audience: "the reflex of current movements and institutions," an editor declared, "reflecting the developing interests and concerns of those who are directly involved in shaping the realities of American life." It published portions of Melville's *Moby Dick.* Henry James's *Washington Square* ran serially beginning in 1881. William Dean Howells, Bret Harte, William Gilmore Simms, Stephen Crane, even Horatio Alger. And, of course, Mark Twain. And did anyone know, as I was to learn in that library out at the Western littoral, that on that fateful morning in 1892 in Fall River, Massachusetts, Lizzie Borden was actually reading a *Harper's* before Mr. and Mrs. Borden fell to the axe?

It was a durable and resilient old institution that had seldom hesitated to change as the times had changed, to speak in the accents of its own age. I searched out the issue which was published the month of my birth. It included pieces on the dangers of federal crime control, the Russian economy, population increases, and racism in America. The grand centennial number of 1950 included Thomas Mann, William Faulkner, W. H. Auden, Eleanor Roosevelt, and Katherine Anne Porter, and even had a congratulatory essay by the President of the United States. This was heady stuff indeed! There was one story from those early days that oddly touched and gratified me, recounted in the centennial issue by the editor of that day, Frederick Lewis Allen:

> For a time, the power to run the presses was provided by a fine white horse which was harnessed to a beam projecting from a vertical shaft, which revolved; by a system of gears the motion of this shaft was translated into power for the presses. Every day, from seven o'clock in the morning until twelve, and then from one till six, the horse walked round and round the vertical shaft. At last he grew old and was retired to a farm to enjoy a leisurely old age. For a few days he pranced light-heartedly about the fields. But then, it seems, he began to feel that sense of frustration which often afflicts the elderly. At any rate, one morning at seven the old horse heard a factory whistle blow, left his shed, went out to the middle of the field where there was a large tree, and dutifully walked round and round the tree till he heard the twelve o'clock whistle. For an hour he rested; from one o'clock till six he walked round the tree again; and this thereafter became his daily routine.

I admired that old horse. He seemed to be telling me something about the institution for which he had labored, and about tenacity and pride and endurance.

The morning came that I arrived for my first day's work, after a solitary bus ride on a Greyhound across the breadth of America, at the old *Harper's* building at 49 East Thirty-third, just behind the Vanderbilt Hotel, once an elegant society hotel, on Park Avenue. The magazine and the publishing house had both been quartered here since 1923, when the older building on Franklin Square, which had been there since 1854, had burned to the ground. It was a somber and imperturbable red-brick structure of some six stories, dwarfed by the lofty Vanderbilt. Yet there was something honorable about its gaunt, narrow facade, its decorous sufficiency, as if proud ancestry itself would yet carry the contemporary day. My office in the corner of the top floor was minuscule, approximately the dimensions of a good-sized dining room table, which I shared with a secretary and reader, a young college graduate from the Midwest who was usually obscured from my view behind tall stacks of unsolicited manuscripts balanced precariously between her in and out trays, so imposing that when she wished to communicate with me she had to stand to her full height. The desk I inherited had belonged to Robert B. Silvers, who had just departed *Harper's* to establish the *New York Review of Books,* the cubbyholes and drawers of which contained outdated memoranda and several pairs of old socks. I recalled a bit of doggerel from Ogden Nash: *"I sit in an office at 244 Madison Avenue / And say to myself, You have a responsible job, havenue?"*

My wife and child were still out West, not to arrive for several weeks, and despite one's inflated Balzacian ambitions, or perhaps because of them, those early days were often unutterably lonely. Many was the time I would remain in the deserted offices late at night, or come down to work on rainy Manhattan weekends. On those first summer weekends the magazine office on that top floor of the fine, settled building was utterly silent, suspended, perhaps, waiting for something, or remembering, a place of monumental ghosts, while outside its windows the abandoned city and its million lairs lay dumb and torpid in the summer *ennui.* There was a splendid old catalogue file in the office, a prodigious oaken Victorian cabinet that took up the best part of a wall, which held the records, card by card, of each story, article, or poem published since 1850, these arranged alphabetically both by the title and the surname of the author, with the dates of submission, acceptance, and publication, the length of the manuscript, and the amount of money paid. I adored that magic cabinet, that trove of sequestered riches, and could pore over it in these muted quarters for hours on end as I had the bound volumes in Palo Alto: C: *Clemens, Samuel.* J: *James, Henry.* A: *Adams, Henry.* S: *Sartre, Jean Paul.* D: *Dreiser, Theodore.* R: *Roosevelt, Theodore.* K: *Kennedy, John F.* D: *Dickens, Charles.* K: *Kipling, Rudyard.* D: *Dickinson, Emily.* L: *Lewis, Sinclair.* W: *Wilson, Woodrow.* B: *Brontë, Emily.* So a magazine became a living thing to me.

On one such nocturnal retreat in that hushed chamber of the literary spirits I remember going to the magazine rack and reading back issues of *The New Republic* and *The Nation,* for there was nothing like those dusty ideological numbers to make you feel guilty when you were out of sorts. Then I turned to *Esquire.*

There was a special issue of that journal just out, about writing in America, with a full-page color drawing of a party at George Plimpton's house overlooking the East River, and convivial New York people in lean and spirited discourse. There in the middle was the lanky host Plimpton conversing at a makeshift bar with Willem de Kooning, and Peter Duchin at a piano, and scattered here and there James Baldwin and Larry Rivers and Ava Gardner and Jules Feiffer and Allen Ginsberg and Kim Novak and Richard Condon and Lillian Hellman and Dwight Macdonald and Budd Schulberg and a dozen or so others. In the lonely weekend office I stared hard at that picture: why, Plimpton's house as reported in *Esquire* was on Seventy-second Street, a trifling three or four subway stops from where I now sat, and there might be a party like that going on right now! If I knocked on the door, would they let me in? Would I ever be part of all that? Elsewhere in the *Esquire* was a double-page "chart" of the New York literary world of the early 1960s, ranking writers, agents, publishers, magazines, beginning with the "red hot center" and moving away from that in calibrated hues to the remote, insignificant fringes. I searched for my own magazine. There it was, way out on the most forlorn fringe, in an emasculated neutral tint above the category "Squaresville."

I learned the rudiments of the new job during the day, and often wandered the city in the nighttime just as the countless young writers from the provinces had always done, absorbing its raw turmoils and mysteries, the impervious play of dusk and dark on its concrete and glass, its hard swift thrusts of life. New York City in those very first moments was all radiance and adumbra for me, all swirling light and blending shadow. I would dine alone at some parsimonious spot in the vicinity of the office. I preferred the darker, more uninhabited places, with cheap Mediterranean murals on the walls, and cheap frescoed mirrors, and the metallic sound of drinks being shaken behind a half-empty bar, and candlelight on checkered cloths, and the words of lovers at some corner table, their alien accents even in the tenderest conversations as metallic to me as the bartender's shaker. I remembered in such moments my Scott Fitzgerald and his Lost City: "At the enchanted metropolitan twilight I felt a haunting loneliness sometimes, and felt it in others — poor young clerks who loitered in front of windows waiting until it was time for a solitary restaurant dinner — young clerks in the dusk, wasting the most poignant moments of night and life."

I stalked the ghosts of my literary heroes, sometimes out to the Brooklyn Bridge — "How could mere toil align thy choiring strings!" — to Battery Park to imagine the now inaccessible sea of *Moby Dick,* to Chelsea and the shabby old hostelry where Wolfe wrote *You Can't Go Home Again,* to the patternless streets of the Village resonant with Henry James and Edna St. Vincent Millay and Willa Cather and e. e. cummings, to Chomondely's bar on Bedford Street to see if its regular J. D. Salinger himself might be there, to the stretches of Saul Bellow's Upper West Side along the Hudson and the upper windows of the tall buildings where no one ever seemed to be inside (Bellow's rich detail of streets, subways, ferries — his Manhattan topography — was a map on the consciousness of the Anglo-Saxon arrival), to Fifth Avenue and the bars around the Scribner's Building itself, where Ernest Hemingway had once hit Max Eastman in the nose and where Maxwell Perkins consumed his martinis while assuaging the torrid Hemingway or the affrighted Fitzgerald or the unmanageable Wolfe, to the Manhattan stretches made vivid by Philip Roth, to the Upper East Side whose townhouses in rows like sentinels had once played host to Sherwood Anderson of Clyde, Ohio (who had said: "When an American stays away from New York too long, something happens to him. Perhaps he becomes a little provincial, a little afraid"); to Sinclair Lewis of Sauk Center, Minnesota; Thomas Wolfe of Asheville, North Carolina; William Faulkner of Lafayette County, Mississippi. I conjured Faulkner here in obscure corners at highball parties drawing on his pipe and observing the New York species, or telling lies about his war wounds and the steel plate in his skull, or passing out on sofas in crowded *bourgeois* salons, or writing barefooted in rich friends' apartments, or telling people as indeed he had done: "Why, in New York even the dogs look inhuman." I thought of Faulkner whenever I passed the Doubleday store on Fifth Avenue where he had worked as a clerk and captivated the old ladies. I thought of him whenever I descended into the subways, the letter he wrote home to his mother and father about getting to Stark Young's house: "I can nip down a hole in the ground, take a subway to the Grand Central Terminal, take a shuttle train from there without ever seeing day light, go to Times Square and — still without coming into the world, take another train and pop out of a hole at Mr. Stark's door, all for a nickel. It's marvelous, but you're just like a rat." I thought of him too in the Village where he dwelled in a dingy room serving his apprenticeship to Melville, Conrad, Balzac, and Dickens, and pondered the Mississippi he saw from the ample metaphoric distance of the city. Most of all it was Thomas Wolfe, the phantasmagoric presence from Old Catawba, insomniac wanderer, poet of the city for three generations of fledgling romantic outlanders, who had actually visited my very floor of the Harper & Brothers building in conferences with the book editor who succeeded Max Perkins and whom I sometimes half-expected to come upon in my own more diffident ramblings in the great web and jungle of his Enfabled Rock these sixty years later, "that distant Babylon, cloud-capped and rosy-hued there in the smoke of his imagination," and of which before his own latter embitterment he had rhapsodized, "There is no place like it, no place with an atom of its glory, pride, and exultancy. It lays its hand upon a man's bowels; he grows drunk with ecstasy; he grows young and full of glory, he feels that he can never die."

As with Joan Didion in her early days in New York, when in the dusks of the East Seventies she "would look in the bright windows of brownstones and see cooks working in clean kitchens and imagine women lighting candles on the floor above and beautiful children being bathed on the floor above that," I grew a voyeur to the city's private and public facsimiles. Sometimes I would drift down to Union Square; as the derelicts drowsed on the benches, and young Puerto Ricans frisked like squirrels under the forsaken trees, I would wander alone among the debates and perorations. Most of them were cranky anomalies from the Depression, but there were more hostile modern intonations here and there: blacks in flimsy suits excoriating the impoverishments of the ghettos, elfin young men in agitated disquisition on homosexual rights, and others of them in shrill assault against their massed adversaries, and here and there volatile soliloquies on Red China, Africa, civil rights in the South, Vietnam. In the threadbare nighttime cacophony in this faded quarter of old and clashing doctrines, I sensed something inchoate rising in America.

Amid the eddying chaos of the streets outside, and the deepening disaffections of the Great Republic beyond, the offices of *Harper's* in those days seemed a warm, secure little island, a cozy honeycomb of quiet and civility — if one discounted the Irish office manager pouncing on the young secretaries in tantrum — of unhurried courtesies and solicitudes. Many of the older people with me there have gone now the way we all go. They seemed so much older to me then. At noontimes in the eternal Manhattan dance they waited in the reception room for the creaky elevator to go to their lunches at Ten Park or the Cedars of Lebanon, the ritual carried out unto death. It would take me some time to realize how easy it was to go stale in the magazine business. "He has a kind of infantile dependence on the magazine," Wilfrid Sheed described one of his characters in his engaging novel *Office Politics,* "which he mistakes for love." I liked them and pray to be gentle with them.

John Fischer at age fifty-three had been editor-in-chief for ten years. He was born and brought up in one of the most astringent and desolate stretches of America, the High Plains, a lofty plateau lying in the Texas and Oklahoma Panhandles, by geographical quirk one of the last sections of the United States to be settled; his grandfather was a friend of Geronimo. He was either a Texan or an Oklahoman, he said, because he was born on a farm which straddled the line and was not certain which side he was on at birth. It is a country of whining winds and sandstorms and brutal winter snows, harsh and strident ground marked by one of the nation's most relentless strains of political archconservatism. Jack Fischer was a graduate of the University of Oklahoma and Oxford, where he was a Rhodes Scholar. After World War II, where he served in India, he worked for the wire services, then joined the publishing firm of Harper, from which he contributed to the magazine. When Frederick Lewis Allen retired in 1953, he assumed the editorship; he also wrote "The Easy Chair," the nation's oldest journalistic column.

He was a tall, slender man with dark shaggy eyebrows, the head of a macaw, and a deep rapid voice without the slightest trace of the Southwest, a terse, neutral kind of American tongue. There was a shy gentleness to him, and when he laughed it was often punctuated by a sudden brief grin, less a laugh than a hasty snort. He was by no measure a humorous or comic man and was one given to punctilio, but he could come out with bizarre things. Of the Jews in the office saying farewell for Rosh Hashanah or Yom Kippur, he observed to me, "Do you notice they take the *Christian* holidays too?" Once an office secretary took off the top half of her little finger while cutting the edges of a galley proof for paste-up. After they whisked her away to the hospital, Jack Fischer came into my office. "That'll teach a woman not to handle a knife," he said. Yet, withal, he may have been the *tensest* man I ever knew. With his abrupt gestures and his unceasing interrogations in normal conversation he seemed wracked with unabating tension; even his ears looked nervous. I could never quite comprehend this jittery tautness. Had the city done this to him? The magazine calling? Once, after I got to know him well and to hold him in warm and honest affection, I almost asked: "Jack, why are you so damned *nervous?*" I did not: some you can ask such questions, and others not. Beneath that austere facade there had to have been turmoil; it was a long way from the fierce winds of the Panhandle to the dining rooms of the Century. He was squeamish about words, both in and out of print. Often I wished he would just once have exclaimed, "Well, *fuck* that!" but this was less likely than Henry Kissinger performing with the Grateful Dead at halftime of a Sugar Bowl. In our years together I only once saw him disarranged. One day a secretary rushed to me and reported something odd transpiring in Mr. Fischer's office. I hastened down there to investigate. Some strange visitor was jabbing at Jack Fischer with his umbrella, smiting him irritably with it about the chest and neck and shoulders. What *contretemps* had incited *this?* I took the umbrella away from the truant, while a disheveled Jack Fischer, hair awry, glowered at him and encouraged him to leave.

He was a professional of the old school. He knew the pitfalls of magazine publishing, its tacts and diplomacies, its workaday risks, its delicacies. Once in those early days Joseph Fox, a ranking editor at Random House, approached me about my doing a book for that firm every year, myself choosing the twenty-five best magazine articles of each year and editing those volumes with an introduction. This was a pleasing possibility. I went to Jack and told him of it. "I wouldn't do it under any circumstances," he said. "What about your own writers who don't make the book? They won't be too gratified." I thought this irrelevant advice, but as I learned more of the trade I saw how right indeed he was.

The High Plains notwithstanding, Jack Fischer was to the core Eastern Establishment. He relished its perquisites, its modulations, its containments. The men he introduced me to at the Century Club and elsewhere in my first weeks were a veritable roster of that Establishment: John J. McCloy, Walter Lippmann, General Gruenther, Kingman Brewster, Thomas Finletter, Hamilton Fish Armstrong, DeWitt Wallace, Winthrop Aldrich, a number of others; once he took me to lunch on Wall Street with the president of the Stock Exchange. He did not know nor care very much about the major American writers of the day. I believe he considered the

American novel more or less dead and most of its best practitioners wanton and destructive. When I was becoming acquainted with Norman Mailer, for instance, he asked me, "Is he crazy? Does he drink as much as they say?" His favorite American novelist was James Gould Cozzens.

He was kind to me, and thoughtful; I grew to care for him very much. The two of us spent countless lunches together in the Murray Hill neighborhood — a little fish place at Lexington and Thirty-fourth, a diffident hotel restaurant down the way, tiny Italian spots around Park or Lex or Madison — talking endlessly of the magazine profession. Many of these establishments were so crowded, the tables squeezed so tightly together, that sometimes I was afraid I would sneeze all over some woman almost in my lap at the next table — unlikely spots for private talks, but people never seemed to notice since they were obliviously chattering away too. I know now that he was "grooming" me. The talk between us was direct, specific, circumscribed, involving deadlines, office personalities, contributors, the magazine deficit, agents, editors of the publishing house — no emotion here, largely facts and logistics. He had Celia and my son to dinners at his house in White Plains, introduced us to his lovely wife and daughters. Once his wife genially took me aside. "He needs you," she said. "He's worked too hard all his life. You've taken a lot of the burden off him. I want to thank you." There is a secret little crevice in the wall of an isolated corridor in Grand Central where, when one puts his ear to it, he can hear all the sounds and echoes of the immense and vaulted and tumultuous Grand Central lobby. Going out to White Plains for a visit, he led my son to this enigmatic spot and demonstrated its usages. Once, during a conversation in his office, I mentioned to him that I was trying to give up cigarettes; he left and returned fifteen minutes later with an expensive pipe and a package of Dunhill.

The Century Club was noted for its copious and authoritative martinis. A "Century martini" among the male elite in the city of that time was a familiar appellation, for it was in every way a stupendous concoction. At our lunches Jack always had one martini. One day I ordered myself a second. "Well, why not?" he said.

"I will too." It was difficult to talk from the heart with him: there was his incredible tension, and with it, I sensed, an inmost reluctance to go beyond forms. He reminded me in that regard of my own dead father. But on this day he relaxed a little, talked about his Panhandle origins, about how much he cared for his daughters. I felt drawn to him in that moment as never before, in every way as a son is to a father. I am now the age he was then, and in the rueful perspective of the years I know that he must have shared my feeling. He cared for me and helped me. Which of us on that mellow afternoon in the Century could have foreseen that one day long hence we would fall out over the very magazine that had brought us together? Was this fated in the complexity and affection of our relationship: son versus father, father versus son? The stresses of the Sixties? The city itself? I am sorry, Jack. Did I let you down?

The magazine had a circulation then of roughly 260,000, with an annual deficit averaging $125,000 to $150,000, depending on what bookkeeping method one looked at, which each year the publishing house satisfied, doing so out of storied in-house tradition, the magazine's national prestige, and the not-infrequent possibility of arranging a book contract with a contributor. Jack Fischer was known throughout publishing circles in the city, and among contributors around the country, for his parsimony, which may have been one reason why a disproportionate number of *Harper's* articles were written by rich people, diet faddists, housewives, dilettantes who indulged in quaint foreign travel, and verbose retired professors and diplomats, too often grindingly arid. Larry L. King, the flamboyant and outspoken novelist and playwright who was just then getting a risky start free-lancing for magazines, was asked by Jack Fischer to fly from Washington to New York to discuss a writing assignment. They went to an inexpensive restaurant in the East Thirties. King described the occasion in his book *None But a Blockhead*:

> When the bill came he carefully added it, quibbled with the waiter over fifteen cents, wrote in a small tip and then — after more pencil work — said to me, peering over his glasses, "Your

share will be eight thirty-two." Since it is normal for editors to pay for lunch when they confer with writers, I laughed at his little joke. But Mr. Fischer was not joking; I had to come up with my share. Perhaps it was my punishment for refusing the writing assignment he had offered: "We'll pay four hundred dollars plus a hundred toward your airline ticket," he had said of a story that would require my going to Texas. "Christ, Mr. Fischer," I had answered, "my round-trip ticket would cost more than that! What am I supposed to do when I get there, live in an open field and eat bush berries?" Mr. Fischer's lips pursed as if he had just sampled a green persimmon and he said, shortly, that that was his best offer. I declined it. Later, when I billed *Harper's* for my expenses to New York for that discussion, Jack Fischer refused to pay because I had rejected the assignment.

The other editors of that time were exceedingly nice, good and honorable people, all considerably older than I, whose accumulated service to *Harper's* amounted to a stunning number of years. The best known was Russell Lynes, the managing editor, a gracious and spirited New Englander, Berkshire School and Yale, author of books including *Highbrow, Lowbrow, Middlebrow* and *The Tastemakers,* who also wrote the long-running "After Hours" column. He had been a protegé of Frederick Lewis Allen's, and as office prattle suggested had expected the appointment as his successor, hence his personal relationship with Jack Fischer, though on the surface congenial, did not go deep. (I can recall only one altercation with Russell Lynes in those maiden days, and I did not even get in a word. He came into my office carrying a manuscript and laughing. "You put a critical op [magazine jargon for *opinion*] on a John Betjeman poem? We don't criticize John Betjeman around here," and was instantly gone again.) Katherine Gauss Jackson had been the fiction and book editor for many years. Catharine Meyer, curatorial in her motherly efficiencies, handled the flow of copy, galleys, deadlines, and was also the principal researcher and copyreader. Marion K. Sanders, writer and political specialist, was the wife of a New York doctor. Joyce Bermel, wife of a playwright, was several years older than I but the closest to me in age.

It was a small staff, and manuscripts and memoranda were directed to the various editors by their individual initials, and those initials are engraved to this day in my memory, and bring back those youthful times: JF, RL, CM, KGJ, MKS, JB, and the newest, WM. I have seldom known any group of people who so loved meetings, which I hated. In the weekly or twice-weekly editorial conferences I would sometimes grow dizzy, have hot flashes, and took to asking outsiders to telephone me with bogus long-distance calls, anything to get me out of those meetings. And then there were the secretaries, God bless them one and all! There were dozens of them who came and went in my *Harper's* tenure. Invariably they were college graduates, Wellesley or Vassar or the big state universities and almost never New York natives, who wished to go into publishing, and they were starting at the lowest level as typists and first readers in the hope of advancement. They too were absorbed in the vigor and excitement of the city in their first arrival, and yearned to be part of its alluring rituals, and they worked very hard. A draconian Irishwoman from Queens, soon mercifully to retire, who had been the office manager for years, dealt with them in alternating dispositions of tenderness and wrath, nothing in between, and her apoplectic tempers sent these young women, like birds flushed from the cover, scurrying into the cage-like cubbyholes or behind the filing cabinets. New York was our literary and journalistic marketplace, and there would be thousands of them clustered around the immense axis of publishing, newspapering, and broadcasting, having come in from the heartland in the old American ritual on Greyhound busses and trains like the Century Express, the Spirit of St. Louis, the Empire Builder, the Crusader. Most of them would not "make it"; the more resourceful and talented might. To this day I hold them dear — where on earth, I wonder, are you now?

It was a good job, a great deal easier, I thought then, than the *Texas Observer* had ever been, because the pace was so languid and because I was still in apprenticeship. My early assignments involved much of everything, including reading all the voluminous "over the transom" unsolicited submissions which came in on the

Wednesdays of each week, and passing along to the others with a typed comment pasted on the envelope anything with the vague glimmer of promise. "For some time now my wife has been telling me I should be a writer." . . . "Enclosed is an article on my Persian cat Isabelle, who passed away eight years ago but by me is not forgotten." . . . "I am submitting to you a Neo-Zunilian approach to ancient vessels." At first, as with any newcomer to any new job, I was concerned about committing some sort of egregious underestimation, some terrible *faux naif.* Had not the young Stingo, likewise the true autobiographical William Styron, up from the South as a junior first reader at McGraw-Hill in *Sophie's Choice,* appended his assessment of the future monumental best-seller, *Kon-Tiki:* "a long, solemn, and tedious Pacific voyage best suited, I would think, to some kind of drastic abridgement in a journal like the *National Geographic.*" From these first readings I grew to suspect there were more writers of poetry in America than there were readers of poetry. Further, an impressive number of submissions arrived from prisons and mental hospitals. Not a few manuscripts were squalid, and not especially in the literal sense. Strands of old spaghetti, for instance, might be stuck between pages. One morning I was startled when my resourceful secretary, who shared my undersized office with me, began to squeal. She was opening a manilla envelope and a roach crawled out; she and I took to washing our hands twice a day. This was the beginning of a long period when manuscripts dominated my life, manuscripts stacked man-high on tables, crammed in my old black leather briefcase, spilling off bookcases. Manuscripts from every humble corner of the Great Republic. Immaculate manuscripts, greasy manuscripts. Literate and semi-literate and illiterate manuscripts. *"I hear American singing. . . ."* Words, words, words: words that mattered, words that half-mattered, words that did not matter at all. How to judge the flawed and funny and lonely American words?

One assignment, I recall, took me to Wall Street to assist the prominent New Dealer David Lilienthal, the first director of the TVA, with a magazine piece. One afternoon the octogenarian Upton Sinclair came unannounced to the office to discuss his contributing an article on a complicated diet which kept him youthful and fit. There he was, sitting across from my desk: Upton Sinclair!

There were a number of other assignments similar to the Lilienthal: a frightened monsignor who wished to tell about certain things going on in the Church, a soldier from the North in the 82nd Airborne posted at Ole Miss during the Meredith crisis, a U.S. Congressman who had trouble putting together declarative sentences.

One assignment in particular stands out in memory, and because it so captures the mood of those first *Harper's* days for me, I wish to describe it in some detail. In 1965 Arthur Schlesinger, Jr., and Theodore Sorenson had just published, in two reputable mass-circulation magazines which are now no longer with us, the chapters on the Bay of Pigs from their forthcoming books on the slain President Kennedy. Allen Dulles, the former director of the Central Intelligence Agency who had been out of power since late 1961, had told Jack Fischer that he wanted to write a rebuttal to Schlesinger and Sorenson, a defense of the CIA in the Bay of Pigs operation. Jack Fischer sent me down to Washington to help Mr. Dulles put his piece together, to interview him and get his thoughts down, encourage him to write and edit — in short to summon a piece out of him.

I arrived on an Indian summer afternoon, one of those delicate and elusive late September days when the white facades of the official town seem to swim in the sadness of its memories. The old man who greeted me at the door of his mansion on Q Street in Georgetown was legendary long before, surely not at all an ordinary mortal. The CIA was, after all, our secret government, the shadowy crucible of our political establishment and American Empire, and God only knows what cabalistic secrets and puzzles, stealthy enigmas, underhanded confidences, occult and deceitful anathemas lay shrouded in his American patriciate's cerebrum. I myself had been secretly recruited by the CIA as a senior in college, and took its battery of tests in Washington en route to a scholarship in England, and on suddenly returning home to the States a year and a half later on the illness of my father, soon received a plain white envelope with an ordinary Louisiana address and the cryptic message: "We know you are in Mississippi for a while. Contact us if you need us." That was the CIA.

"It's hard to operate with legendary figures," Jack Kennedy had said of Allen Dulles, when the consequences of the Bay of Pigs were finally in, and from which Kennedy was to learn much that would hold him in good stead in the fearful Cuban missile crisis several months later, and I was afraid that he might be as cold and rigorous as his brother John Foster had been — a Calvinistic personage to me when he was Secretary of State under Eisenhower, with his unbending rhetoric on massive retaliation and brink-of-war — or as forbidding as his own occasional photographs in the magazines and newspapers. But from the moment we sat down to our long work days in a study overlooking a sedate walled-in terrace with its luxuriant ivy, with no one else about except a servant or two, I felt I was in the company of a courtly and civilized man, curious and feeling about his fellow creatures, a casual and entertaining host, and, best of all, an engrossing raconteur, especially with stories about spies. We worked hard, he with his sleeves rolled up at the table where we met each morning, I with a small pile of notes gleaned from much of what had been published up to then on the Bay of Pigs. He relied on me to pose the right questions for his answers to Schlesinger and Sorenson.

His family was at the Dulles compound near Watertown, New York, on Lake Ontario, and in the lingering twilights, after my questions and his soliloquies, the two of us took walks around Georgetown, which gave to me in its supple fluency and patinas of time the sense of a rich, downy old Southern town. The first lamps flickered above the rusty brick sidewalks and on the branches of the great leafy trees, and I looked into the enormous lower rooms of those mysterious dwellings and saw the elegant furnishings and chandeliers and the bookcases lined deep with books. As with my first New York explorations among the tall buildings along the Hudson on Riverside Drive, I never saw real people stirring around inside, although I felt they had to be in there somewhere. Here the two of us were, the old gray eminence and the ambitious young editor, chattering about the Cuban Brigade or those early meetings with President Kennedy and his new men in the Cabinet Room of the White House. In one such talk in the lordly vicinity around Dumbarton Oaks he stunned me with an abrupt comment. "That little Kennedy," he said, ". . . he thought he was a god." Even now these words leap out at me, the only strident ones I would hear from my unlikely collaborator.

Then back to the terrace behind his house for two or three drinks before our lonely dinner, where I asked him what Europe was like during the war, and he entertained me in fine particulars.

That was more than a quarter of a century ago. We never got the piece from him. The client is dead, and the junior editor is not so junior anymore. The Bay of Pigs, for all the regrets and acrimony, has long receded into a footnote to the Kennedy years. What I remember most from that time is not the complexities of adequate air cover or the inaccessibility of the Escambray, but the tales over whiskey of spying against Hitler in the 1940s, and Georgetown unfolding sensually for me in an autumn's dusk.

As an associate editor, I had begun corresponding with a good number of writers and journalists of my age whom I had yet to meet, including David Halberstam, then in Vietnam for the *New York Times*; his brilliant dispatches from there would soon win him a Pulitzer. Halberstam and I were almost exact contemporaries and had a great deal in common, including many mutual acquaintances all across America, and in the not-distant future we would become close friends and allies, sharing in the momentous hope of our enterprise, in the hard work to come, in the vitality and variety of New York City and its people. He wrote me from Saigon: "It looks like you've made the big leagues. I'd like to write for you." For an early issue of '65 I obtained from him a piece on the Vietcong — "tough, indoctrinated, and ready to die, and in this endless, relentless war of revolution the misery of the people was the Vietcong's constant source of strength" — which later formed a chapter in his *The Making of a Quagmire.* These were prophetic and realistic words for early 1965, and augured more to come.

More often than not a magazine is, and always has been, as indeed it should be, a reflection of its editor: his personality and concerns, tastes and foibles. Jack Fischer's *Harper's* was decent, responsible, quiet, fastidious. Certain matters disturbed me. Fischer for a time began inviting Robert Manning, the new editor-in-chief of *The Atlantic Monthly,* who over the years I grew to like and respect very much, to an occasional weekly *Harper's* editorial meeting to inform him of the content of future issues in order to avoid conflict and overlap. Since I personally considered *The Atlantic* a major rival, despite the two magazines' using the same advertising agency, I thought this practice appalling, and said so. Too, a staff decision was made to delete this sentence from a piece by Larry L. King on Washington lobbyists: "As one who attended several of Billie Sol Estes's Washington dinner parties, I am sure they had more fun at the Last Supper." The offending sentence was later restored at the last minute after I requested a protest editorial meeting, but Mencken among others had been writing infinitely more outrageous things in the magazines forty years before, and without wishing to sound self-serving the incident, certainly in symbolic regard, was revealing of the long-standing reluctance of *Harper's* to be in the least wanton or wicked or sinful, or to offend any of a broad range of ticklish or entrenched sensibilities.

Things were happening in America. I very much liked my older colleagues, but it had not taken me long to sense that our magazine was somewhat remote and docile and safe, wanting in enthusiasm, too lacking in *quirks* and emotional commitments, removed from the restless and excessive contemporary civilization it served. I longed for the chance to try to make it more responsive.

3 ~ The Sixties Unfold

I WAS A CHILD of the 1950s, having graduated from high school almost precisely seven years after the end of World War II, a relatively placid and decorous time in our national life: "the silent generation," I think we were called, a time of rules and obedience and the proprieties, not risk-taking, a somnolent and very prosperous crossing — or so the collective memory has it.

The cars of the era had huge wheels, sun visors, elaborate appurtenances, so that they resembled tanks with fins, the gas-guzzling behemoths of the Motown genius. In college, on any whim, I would drive my black-and-white Chevy with dual exhausts hundreds of miles into the nighttime, up to Memphis or down to the Gulf, watching an autumn moon above the sea of dead stalks, the bare trees silhouetted against a sweep of skyline. Once we drove all the way to New Orleans without a stop for Saturday night in the Quarter, then turned around and came back, and the next week drove up to Asheville to see Thomas Wolfe's grave with the angel on the tomb, where the caretaker said, "Tom Wolfe never amounted to much." We never failed to stop for hitchhikers when the mood was right — wandering Negroes and soldiers and dirt farmers. One learned a great deal about America from these meanderers of the Southern night: the passions that sweep across it, its loneliness, its jubilations and uncertainties. I developed a mystic longing for the Southland in these journeys, feeling its history in acutely visual terms: Jefferson dwelling on governance in the gardens of Monticello. Lincoln striding the doomed streets of Richmond with a ragtail bodyguard wary of snipers. Lee in nightfalls after the war riding Traveller over the gutted lands of old battlefields. All the years of politicians and preachers prancing the countryside.

The summer before I went away to college I was in the Sears store in my hometown, browsing among its counters, surveying the harvest of the American bounty on display there, this bonanza of latter-day riches in the poorest of its commonwealths. I was attracted by flickering images. Drawn there trance-like, I stood before a row of tiny television screens set in hefty maple cabinets, about a dozen of them, all of them turned on, the blurred, snowy images of a wrestling match as magnetic as a hypnotist, all this brought in mysteriously from faraway Memphis on cumbersome mile-high antennas. Then the action switched to a baseball game, and "Muscles" Upton of the St. Louis Browns was at bat in the man-made blizzard — my virginal glimpse of the new and horrific phenomenon, so destined to come into its own to such effect in the 1960s, and on this day it transfixed me. I watched as Muscles Upton struck out on a wide sweeping curveball. "They just came in yesterday," the clerk said. "Ain't they somethin'?"

Everyone in the Fifties seemed to decry the *ennui* of American life: the encroaching suburbia, the deadening hand of television, the materialism and acquiescence of the young. How soon this divination would change! Yet my colleagues and I in the mid-1950s on the *Daily Texan,* the distinguished student daily at the University of Texas, in that phantasmagoric and fractured Texas society, were anything but tidy conformists, challenging and carrying the day against a know-nothing governing board on freedom of expression, integration, and other issues which with a small handful of notable exceptions lay largely dormant on the docile college campuses of the time. I remember with pride the first story I sold to a national magazine, to the old *Nation* under Carey McWilliams for thirty-five dollars. (The *Nation* paid high in the double figures, someone once said.) Back home during a summer Joe McCarthy's voice boomed out from a hundred radios, merging with the hot heavy heat on the drowsing thoroughfares, superseding even Gordon McLendon's perfervid baseball broadcasts.

The last four years of that decade I was at Oxford University, immersed in history at a fourteenth-century college, far removed from certain things which were simmering beneath the reticent surfaces back home in America, yet that exotic interlude in all its muted isolation was a coda, giving me a rare perspective on my native ground poised as it was then at the juncture of engrossing and important events.

I had been peremptorily dispatched to Oxford with my American contemporaries by Cecil Rhodes as one of "the best men for the world's fight." There is an extant photograph of the thirty-two of us Rhodes Scholars, on a golden autumn's forenoon on the deck of the *Flandre* in our crossing, the purple, sun-crossed Atlantic breakers as background. These were the Eisenhower years, and America was doing fine. Ike was an emotionally tranquil influence on America under the pervasive fear of the great weaponry of obliteration, and he wears well now with age. It was the time of Suez, Budapest, and Adlai Stevenson's second defeat. Ike had ileitis. The dollar lasted a long time. The hegemony of the big green passport swept all before it.

We encountered there an England still in the ruin of war. And in Oxford we confronted one of the preeminent universities of the world, if not *the* foremost, in its inwardness and nuance, a nexus far removed from our home soil, where the measure was more languid and the aspect more subtle, a repository of the complexities of mankind. The sacrosanct privacy of the place, the almost studied eccentricities, the enervating fogs and rains, at first elicited a loneliness, an *angst* and melancholia such as I had never known before. The advanced civility of our new milieu, the weight of its history, where every blade of grass had known a dozen drops of blood, the Old World tensions, seemed cloying and troublesome, and the mementos of mortality were everywhere, in the lugubrious graveyards, in the interminable rolls of the war dead in the college chapels, in the dampened dusks and spooky midnights. Had any single place on earth of comparable size produced such an august array of human beings? The catalog was endless; to try to list them, and the stupendous accomplishments they shaped there, would be futile, but imagine the oppressiveness of their footfalls as their spirits stalked a young American a generation or so ago.

The essence of the Oxford system was the tutorial, in which the student, after intensive reading, wrote weekly or twice-weekly essays and defended them in private sessions with his college tutor, or don. Examinations were comprehensive and came at the end of three years, six hours a day for more than two weeks. Lectures were optional, one of the English students having explained to me that they had gone out of fashion with the invention of the printing press in the fifteenth century. With the weekly tutorial essay the only formal requirement, one might do as he pleased: read novels, write poetry, go to London, sleep till noon, or devote sixteen hours a day reading for the next tutorial There was an abiding homage to independence and self-sufficiency, and to the paths one's mind took. I would be reading in my rooms in my college, about the Hundred Years War, perhaps, or the pressures on Lincoln to issue the Emancipation Proclamation, and, under the allure of the ancient quadrangle out my window or of the Latin psalms of the boys' choir in the chapel, lapse into endless reveries about home, or the past. It was not an uncommon malaise. "If the people at Annapolis knew how much I daydreamed in this place," a U.S. Naval Academy man in my group confessed to me, "I'd be up for a court-martial."

Yet, slowly, the spell of Oxford grew, until one was suffused with it, with its majesty and largesse. We became Oxford men, and the high and elegiac mosaic of it would be part of us forever. During our first term there a friend from the Upper Midwest confided to me, "I look out my bedroom every morning, across Merton's front quad, just to make sure the chapel, which was built around 1290, is still standing. I think I expect to find it transmuted overnight into the Farmers' Cooperative grain elevator in Freeman, South Dakota." He would later tell me the chapel had become more real to him than the grain elevator, an admission I comprehended.

Every first of May for hundreds of years, the choristers of Magdalen had sung carols and lavish madrigals in Latin at dawn from the top of the college tower. In the strenuously bilious Oxford setting, May Morning occasioned a traditional drinking *fête* that began the previous evening and intensified with the coming of the light. Dawn came in the raw gloom. Under the magnificent Magdalen Tower with its great, wise pinnacles, the disheveled students in tuxedos and tight skirts, one youngster's trousers ripped open from ankle to waist, were drinking from their champagne bottles, and town chaps and their glassy-eyed consorts from their cider magnums — a social amalgam across the divide — and below the Magdalen Bridge the river was lined with punts, and from an arched Gothic roof above a queue of gargoyles, three or four Magdalen men poured champagne down upon the crowd, all of it reminding me of nothing if not an Ole Miss–Mississippi State football game, or an Oklahoma–Texas. Then, in a moment against this piebald backdrop all was hushed. The bells rang, and from the tall, serene tower etched against the melancholy dawn the Latin hymn wafted out above the celebrative young, suddenly stilled, and floated across the tiny green river, and gently over the spires and meadows of the haunted old town, as if the town might be saying in solicitude: "We have seen all this before." In that instant, my comrades and our English girls were launching our punts northward on this river, champagne in hand, for a miniature river island named Mesopotamia, where we stayed till dark and got gloriously drunk. It was, after all, May Morning, and time was passing, and, like ourselves, also merely mortal.

Dennis Potter, destined to become one of Britain's finest writers with his BBC epics such as *The Singing Detective* and *Pennies from Heaven,* became one of my best Oxford friends. His father was a coalminer in Gloucestershire, in the Forest of Dean, where sons usually ended in the pits too, but he was in Oxford on a state scholarship. He was a good-hearted and warm-spirited young man, but bitterly caustic toward Tory Britain. He was a left-wing activist, spry in debate and repartee, and in our first terms at Oxford always seemed torn between politics and writing. He and I often talked about future political careers. He borrowed my Scott Fitzgerald paperbacks; he was intrigued by why Fitzgerald wrote two versions of *Tender Is the Night.* His interest in the American South, its inward mores and wild humor and destructive racial climate, was boundless — and especially about its literature; I see now this had much to do with language. He was also fascinated by movies; I had already seen my share of them, but he had seen considerably more. There was a tenacious establishment in Oxford in those days called the Scala, a dim little movie house on Walton Street in a working class neighborhood fifteen minutes' walk from our college. Often was the darkening winter afternoon I sat in my rooms reading for the next tutorial as the boys' choir sang its madrigals from the chapel across the greensward and I surrendered to the Oxford melancholia, when with a vehement knock on the door Dennis would appear from nowhere. "Let's go to the Scala! It's got *The Third Man.*" "This is my kind of neighborhood," he might say as we walked along Walton Street, past a big gloomy cemetery and the gas works and the drab, miniature brick dwellings. Inside the cinema there would only be a handful of students, in equal escape from the fog, books, and madrigals. Here I saw *Anna Karenina* for the first time, and *The Fallen Idol,* and Kubrik's *The Killing,* and *A Yank at Oxford, The Man Who Never Was,* and Hitchcock's original *The Thirty-Nine Steps,* and all sorts of others, including more than a few Grade B ones. Dennis sometimes enigmatically whispered to himself during these showings, and smirked, snickered, laughed. Adjacent to the Scala was a small Indian restaurant with no more than six or seven tables. When the movie was over, Dennis and I would detour to a hushed, morbid little pub and buy two quarts of ale and take them into the Indian place, there to dine for not more than a half-crown on Madras curry and parathas and discuss in considerable detail the film we had just seen, first in Marxist terms, then Freudian or Jungian or Christian Existentialist. "I want to make a *Malthusian* interpretation of this one," he remarked on one such day. I did not know what that was, having never once heard of Malthus in Mississippi or Texas. He gave me a small, edifying lecture on Malthus.

One day he persuaded me to come give a talk to the members of the college Labor Club. "What will I talk about?" I asked. "Oh, it doesn't matter. Perhaps the Anglo-American Alliance. They're anti-American but secretly like Americans. Or you can attack the Nazis. Anything critical of Hitler will go over well." The president of the Oxford University Communist Club was also a guest, the first flesh-and-blood Communist I ever saw. Later, in my monthly transatlantic telephone call to my parents back home, I reported that I had just given a talk to the Young Socialists. "Please, son," my mother said, "don't have your picture taken with any of them!"

The Warden of Rhodes House was E. T. Williams. He had been a history don at Oxford on the outbreak of World War II, then became a major in intelligence. General Bernard Montgomery discovered him in the Whitehall labyrinth and promoted him overnight to brigadier. He was the G-2 throughout the war for Montgomery, who credited him with the strategy that routed the Germans at El Alemein. He was seldom without a brandy and a cigar, often inviting Ed Yoder of Chapel Hill and me to join him in these nourishments in his private quarters of Rhodes House. This grand and flamboyant exemplar of the British establishment told us to call him "Bill." There was an American from the Midwest in our group named Winston. In conversation Bill Williams kept citing Winston, his personal habits, the things he said and did. "Warden," Yoder asked him one night, "why do you keep talking about Winston?" "I'm not talking about *your* Winston," he replied. "I'm talking about Churchill." Shortly after that I asked him what were his politics. "I'm right-wing Tory," he responded, "which I understand is considerably farther to the left of anything you have in the United States."

Rich American tourists were ubiquitous in Europe in those years. In the summers college students from the States shouted and embraced in extravagant recognition on the streetcorners of Paris. On an evening boat tour down the Rhine I heard my compatriots sing "The Moon Shines Bright Tonight Upon the Wabash," and there was something vaguely frightening about this. The American military was everywhere too. Brightly beribboned NATO officers and airmen in crew cuts from the SAC bases around Oxford walked the High in swarms on weekends. I was arrested three times by MP's right there in Oxford until I learned to let my hair grow long. Anti-Americanism was in acute flourish. "Yanks Go Home!" was painted on many of the walls. British students marched on the nuclear installations. Our Oxford basketball team, consisting mostly of Americans and captained by Paul "Tike" Sarbanes of Baltimore and Balliol College, one day to be a U.S. Senator, and including Ed Yoder of Chapel Hill and Jesus College, later Pulitzer winner ("What a friend we have in Jesus," we said of him) was invited to play the team at a nearby SAC base. The Air Force dispatched a bus for us. When we entered that gigantic installation, we were in another world entirely — the America of the late 1950s: trim houses with mothers in hair-curlers tending their children, Buicks and Chevrolets, a baseball diamond, gum-chewing airmen tossing footballs, voices from the mountains and ghettos and swampbogs and prairies, all of this embued with an affluence we had nearly forgotten. Immense silver airships sat far out on the runways, guarded by figures wearing holsters. I knew that H-Bombs were stored there somewhere. We entered the glass doors of the PX, passing a stern-visaged sergeant who examined us warily until the colonel explained we were his guests. Inside we were greeted by recorded Elvis tunes. Air Force wives in slacks and sneakers roamed among the booze and groceries — the pyramidal stacks of chicken a la king, Hormel chili, Uncle Ben's Rice, macadamia nuts, Kleenex — and there was a cornucopia of textiles and synthetics and twills, gadgets and knick-knacks and titillating apparati: radios and record players and tape recorders, deep fryers and refrigerators and battery-charged carving knives and freezers and mixers and rotating blenders, toasters and vacuums and electric shakers. One huge set of counters was filled with children's toys of every description, another with cameras and Kodachrome film, and the frozen-food section was large as a warehouse; to remind me of home I bought a quart of sourmash and some baseball bubblegum cards.

When our basketball team won the national championship we received a formal invitation from the Soviet government to represent England in the Moscow Games that summer. The Soviets would pay our way to Berlin, and fly us from there to Moscow on a special plane. An exhibition tour of the Russian provinces was suggested. But the *realpolitik* of the day intervened. The State Department, soon followed by the Foreign Office, advised us it was not in the "best interests" of the United States for us to go. It was the height of the Cold War; not until the *Porgy and Bess* troupe two years later would there be a significant cultural exchange. We protested. It was our responsibility as scholars to see Russia. Finally, the venerable university itself refused to let us go. This, too, was a small lesson to be discovered of one's own country and the breadth of certain of its fears and apprehensions.

An American student told me he was in a large group of people the year before along the grim ravine called New College Lane when Harry Truman, who was getting an honorary degree from Oxford University, came walking jauntily along in gown and mortarboard toward the Sheldonian, preceded by all the Oxford eminences looking much like peacocks in their colorful academic regalia, including the gnome-like figure who carried the ceremonial mace. As Truman came abreast my friend knew he must shout something to him. "Give 'em hell, Harry!" Truman looked right at him, removed his mortarboard and flourished it. "Thank you, sir!" he said, and the simple tale of this seemly little exchange made me strangely homesick. As president of the American students, it was my responsibility to accompany John Hay Whitney, our ambassador to the Court of St. James's, in his limousine to Rhodes House, where he was to give a speech. Jock Whitney turned to me with piercing seriousness and said, "I hope you'll like my talk tonight. I intend to attack the Red Chinese."

One arrived at the Turf Tavern, *my* pub, through a maze of medieval alleys, bordered by tall, half-timbered lodgings. Situated unprepossessingly at the end of a widening cobbled lane only a few yards from a gaunt stone wall of New College, it was a small, sedate medieval establishment described by Thomas Hardy in *Jude the Obscure;* I believe Hardy was secretly infatuated with his own character, Arabella the barmaid. It was a quiet, mellow sanctuary, presided over by an elderly brother and sister, whose homely yellow cat sometimes perched on our table as we took our infinite pints of bitter. Here we Yanks talked endlessly of what was happening back home: the National Guard at Little Rock and acts of racial oppression in the South and the Elvis phenomenon, and John Foster Dulles's "massive retaliation," Sputnik, the U-2. It was from the Turf Tavern, shortly after the Soviets launched Sputnik with the dog inside, that we telephoned the offices of the British Society for the Prevention of Cruelty to Animals to voice our support of their national protest. Where and when would the little dog finally land on earth? we asked. We wished to send a delegation to welcome him back. "I'm afraid the little dog will never come home," the official said. "He's up there forever."

Here we answered ceaseless interrogations from the English students about the United States, for the curiosity among them about our country, its politics, its foreign policy, its literature, its music, its sexual mores, was interminable. It was in itself valuable to see how obsessed foreigners were with us. Was it because we ruled the world, and set its standards? What kind of man was Senator Kennedy? Lyndon Johnson? They wanted to know why the college students in America were so *docile*. "You will never have a revolution, will you?" one of them asked. I even debated in the Oxford Union on the question: "Resolved: This House Deplores the Coca-Colonialization of the World," arguing before the quizzical British as a Mississippian in favor of the motion. There were intimate teas with travelling Americans such as Robert Frost, and also Adlai Stevenson, who patiently and with graceful wit responded to our questions about the Eisenhower times, and cozy evenings at the house of George Kennan, who had a visiting Oxford chair, during which he told stories of diplomacy in the American Century. An English friend in my college was dating Julia Gaitskell, a student in one of the Oxford women's colleges; she was the daughter of Hugh Gaitskell, head of the Labor Party and shadow prime minister, the opposite number of Anthony Eden; I had often heard Gaitskell in lively debate in the House of Commons, supported rhetorically by his shadow foreign minister Nye Bevan, the greatest orator outside of Theodore G. Bilbo and Martin Luther King, Jr., I have ever heard. My friend invited me to come with him to London during the term break and go out on the town with him and his date. We went to her house in Hampshire where I sat on a terrace with the brilliant Hugh Gaitskell and talked about America. "It's your turn now," he said. "I'm afraid we're a weary nation. I hope you can do it."

Sitting one day in the Strangers' Gallery in the House of

Commons for the debate on Suez and the stresses in the Anglo-American Alliance, I saw a large figure emerge onto the floor from the entrance beneath us and laboriously make his way to his seat on a Tory back-bench. There was a carnation in the lapel of Winston Churchill.

New College, my college, had been new in 1379. It was founded by one William of Wykeham, Bishop of Winchester, to ameliorate the ravages to the clergy of the Black Death, and to produce "men of good learning, fruitful to the Church of God and to the King and Realm." How did an American boy of the 1950s fit into *that?* The concrete stairs leading to the dining hall were deeply grooved with the footsteps of the two-score generations. In the medieval hall itself where we dined on kipper and oatmeal at breakfast, and vintage roast beef and potatoes the rest of the time, the portraits of warriors and ecclesiastics and parliamentarians gazed gloomily down on the long dark tables; at one of them a young Englishman once asked me to describe the precise odor of a skunk, and the physiognomy of armadillos, and whether rattlesnakes could bite through boots. The porters locked the gates to the college at eleven P.M., securing them with padlocks and iron, and the only way to get in, or out for that matter, was to climb a treacherous stone salient behind the library, over spikes and broken glass embedded in the stone. Locked inside, we peregrinated these monastic confines in the late hours. A mystic from New Delhi with obscure eyes claimed to communicate with the college spirits. I once ran into him in the gardens at two A.M. kneeling in the grass, his arms spread to the heavens in supplication; I got away from there fast. In the farther corner of our quadrangle, on a luminous day of '57, as a mucilaginous band of American tourists watched in disbelief, we used a Coca-Cola bottle to christen a 1934 Buick touring car we had purchased for fifty pounds to take us to Rome. We had christened it "Foster," after John Foster Dulles, but Foster did not even make it to Dover. On this swathe of quadrangle lawn, Neil Rudenstine of Connecticut once hit me fly balls with my own baseball bat and ball. Using the Old City Wall as an outfield fence, I patrolled it against his audacious flies and drives. He dispatched a long, towering fly that barely missed the Joshua Reynolds stained-glass windows of the chapel. "That's it!" Rudenstine yelled petulantly. "That's the last time I'll do this!" And the future president of Harvard retired to his essay paper on Roman Britain and the threat to it of the Picts and Scots.

Sitting alone there in my rooms so many hours each day with the great ancient quadrangle and the Old City Wall before me, and with my history books, Clarendon's *History of the Great Rebellion,* perhaps, and Gibbon's *Decline and Fall,* my brain awhirl with the falterings of civilization, including my own country, and my own secret view of the human race as masses in flight or in rapine, biblical swarms fleeing ruin or wreaking it, always trying to survive, or to destroy. Yet the timeless beauty from my window always mocked my dismal theory. I was baffled even then that the Rhodes Scholarships, with all their prestige and power, had in their half-century of existence yet to produce an American President—Senators, yes, and Congressmen, and Cabinet members, and university presidents, and writers, and scholars and scientists. Yet did this notable failure have something to do, I mused, with the very timeless beauty of Oxford itself, and its accumulated lassitudes, and how these things exerted themselves on you years afterward? Or had American Rhodes Scholars been too "good," too contained and respectable and self-assured, to fight and flail and expose themselves and their families to the cruel and glad-handed chaos of American Presidential canvasses? Would poor, isolated, plain-spirited Arkansas someday know something that even Oxford University, with its aged wisps and whispers and introspections, did not? This would remain to be seen.

America from afar seemed proud, rich, complacent, mighty, xenophobic, gargantuan. But I passionately cared for it, and I was ready when the time finally came to go home, and felt I must, as Jack Burden had in *All the King's Men,* "go into the convulsion of the world, out of history into history, and the awful responsibility of time." It was to Texas that I returned, just as John Kennedy was about to be elected President. The Sixties awaited me.

The halcyon decade of the Fifties was in remarkable measure rewritten by the almost theatrically contrasting Sixties, just as the

Ronald Reagan Eighties in all their sturdy conventionalism and retrenchment were to recast the Sixties. Or as another of the rebels of that moment, Stephen Gaskin, later suggested of that collision of the generations, Reagan eventually got them back for fornicating in the streets.

It would be understandably difficult for the young American of the 1990s to comprehend the horrendous fears of international Communism in the Fifties, the inexorable Red tide moving aggressively across the globe from Vietnam to Indonesia to the Philippines to Australia and Japan and India, and finally toward, for all one knew, Kansas City, and the satisfying notion that the United States represented the paradigm of virtue against the monolithic evil, as if all history had achieved its happy culmination in the modern American commonweal. It was, as John Foster Dulles popularized it, Christians versus the Anti-Christ: Communism was a heightening menace not merely to the Western hegemony, but to Christianity itself. Everything in our polity seemed related to the Soviets — science, weaponry, culture, economics, sports. Sheer military might buttressed the heathen hordes. Had not the Red Chinese with the Soviets' endorsement sent a million troops into Korea? Onerous, too, to comprehend the terror of nuclear disaster in a time when that prospect was relatively new and human beings had not lived under that horrific cloudbank long enough simply to have gotten used to it. In many parts of the country in the late 1940s there were anti-Bomb exercises for school children, who wore gas masks and dived under desks at the appointed signals; we never had any of these in small-town Mississippi, possibly because even despite the Southland Oil Refinery our authorities considered our neighborhood an unpropitious strategic objective. But that dread of extinction was so pervasive that a great American writer in the first year of that decade felt compelled to address it in his Nobel acceptance: "I decline to accept the end of man. It is easy enough to say that man is immortal simply because he will endure: that when the last ding-dong of doom has clanged and faded from the last worthless rock hanging tideless in the last red and dying evening that even then there will still be one more sound: that of his puny inexhaustible voice, still talking. I refuse to accept this. I believe that man will not merely endure; he will prevail." From the appalling intimations even of an affirmation so striking as this the parents of the 1950s wished to shield their children — to protect them also from what they themselves had experienced in their Depression childhoods and in the trauma of war. The middle-class offspring of these parents, the Baby Boomers, who would take to the streets in the Sixties, grew up with every material comfort and every tender sanction, not least the solicitous injunctions of Dr. Spock. They were a product of the accelerated education which came in somewhat desperate form after Sputnik, and in their varying aspects they were to become involved in one of the swiftest and most sweeping cultural changes the country had ever known. The average existence of American young people was becoming enveloped by elevated notions of license and individuality. The vast majority of them came of age in the burgeoning new suburbias, rich and deracinated vicinities whose privileged priorities glorified the children. Little wonder these children would come to take happiness and fulfillment for granted — would go into the Sixties spoiled in the pursuit of every redemptive expectation deserving of them.

All this may be too simplistic a portrait of the rebellious and embattled youth of the Sixties, but they stirred more unresolved passions than any other young generation in our history, and the one trait they most consummately shared was a rebellion against all authority, the desire to do anything possible to be different from the parents' generation: the idealism, the activism, the tribal identifications, the transcendental omnipotencies, the acts of public theater, the plentiful accompaniments of the Diggers, or the Grateful Dead. In the distance, of course, from the sweepingly reported rich Boomers from the Eastern and Northern and West Coast suburbias were young white kids from marginal middle-class backgrounds in isolated American places and towns that the Scarsdale youth might have somewhat belittled, such as the Hopes of Arkansas, which in this decade would produce young people who for differing reasons, rooted in their own capillary soil and people and history and soul, yet equally responsive to the injustices and contradictions of the time, might prove less fashionable and esoteric and more durable in those years' shifting idealisms. It was still a nation of regions, and the best of the South of this generation was always there, caring in its complexity and rebelliousness for the greater nation.

There was another generation, too. There were scant parallels between the white young of Levittown and the black young of Dixie, who had a different perspective entirely of the real America. The segregated blacks drew on a historical sense of belonging and common oppression to mount a momentous struggle that was to be the most consequential precursor of the Sixties, more significant by far than all the beguiling sideroads which followed.

Some may find it ironic that two Mississippians contributed grandly to the gathering sources of the counter-culture in the last half of the Fifties. Perhaps my impoverished whipped-down Mississippi was at last wreaking its revenge.

Rock and roll as a presage of the 1960s dissidence had always fascinated me. Elvis Presley was a revolutionary from Tupelo. Rock and roll was nothing if not an act of defiance against white suburbia. Could anyone have so much as imagined old hound dogs and blue suede shoes invading the interstices of Westchester? Many thought this a Communist plot. Were there hound dogs in *Das Kapital*? Was Elvis a dupe of Red Square? Had he read his Lenin? He was certainly no Trotskyite. Yet I know for the truth he saw *Rebel Without a Cause* a dozen times and memorized all of James Dean's lines. In Elvis the incipient young white rebels found an early expression more subversive by far than Kerouac, Ginsberg, Corso, and all the Beatniks, not to mention *Catcher in the Rye.* He looked dangerous, he *was* dangerous. He arrived at the right juncture. There is a photograph that gives me an affecting image of him in New York City just before his first fame was to descend with a national television show: alone and playing a piano and singing a hymn to himself. He brought together blues, gospel, white, black, country. He was magic.

They could have done worse. I never met Elvis, and I have since lived to regret it. We were almost precisely the same age; we grew up not many miles apart. Had I not been away from our native

South in those years, I have little doubt we would have become friends, or at least acquaintances; between us there were several mutual friends. I would have allied myself with him against the Yankee suburbs. Then, at the auspicious moment, I would have signed him up to write a monthly column for *Harper's*, and perhaps gotten a pink Cadillac out of it in return. I would have accompanied him to brunch at the Four Seasons, and to dinner at Lutece. I would have shown him around the Century Club, presenting him to John J. McCloy, and perhaps Walter Lippmann and Dr. Kissinger. I would have introduced him to Park Avenue radicals. I would have gotten Alfred A. Knopf to throw him a party.

As for Columbus, Mississippi's, Tennessee Williams, we have the testimony of many, and especially of Todd Gitlin, a young New Yorker at the time who would subsequently become a prominent leader of the New Left and one of its most eloquent historians:

> While northern middle-class parents were deploring the sexual innuendo of rock and loathing the racist white violence they saw on television, without any sense of irony they were trooping to the movies to see a succession of Tennessee Williams movies — five in five years starting in 1955 — about sexual trauma, incest, and the barely suppressed passion and violence lurking in the family living room. Families fascinated by Williams' neurotic passions were the nests of rock and rockers.

Dylan, the Stones, Joan Baez; the Age of Aquarius; Don't Trust Anyone over Thirty; That's My Bag; Make Love, Not War; Whatever Happens, Happens; If It Feels Good, Do It; Flower Power; Acid-Zap; *Hair; Jesus Christ Superstar;* People's Park; Role-Playing; Mind-Blowing; Radicalized. And with this arrival all the very young musicians, in that new and commanding alliance of the music industry and the modern counter-culture, where a great deal of money was going to be made. Nicholas von Hoffman titled a book after an item of graffiti in a coffeehouse in Haight-Ashbury: "We are the people our parents warned us against."

Visible though they were, and colorful to the media, and magnets themselves for small battalions of provocateurs, mountebanks and *fakirs,* their numbers were likely highly exaggerated, and at any rate the hippies, so disquieting to the unsullied middle-class and the culturally conventional working class, were a different breed from the student activists, who as the decade unfolded identified with the oppressed and buttressed the mounting disaffection over the war in Vietnam. I had known the New Left's Tom Hayden in the early days of the decade when he visited Austin for Students for a Democratic Society (SDS). He was attractive and intelligent and, though a shade authoritarian, liked Scholz's Beer Garten, and one would have found it hard to picture him in beads and cape and a soiled cap. Hayden was to marry a friend of mine, a beautiful young woman from Victoria, Texas, named Sandra Cason; "Casey," as we called her, would be deeply involved in the important protests of the decade, in organizing poor whites, and in the beginnings of the women's movement. She was part of the North-South connection in the early SDS, then went South with the Student Nonviolent Coordinating Committee (SNCC) and remained there for many years, even after most of the white workers had been ousted.

Overshadowing all this in the early days, yet oddly in tandem with it, was the Kennedy phenomenon. I was witness to the nearly hysterical adulation of the Kennedys in mass crowds in Texas in the 1960 campaign (even in Dallas, where his motorcade went past Dealy Plaza and the Texas Book Depository), and when he accepted the torch passed to the new American generation there was a sense of high adventure that after the sedative Eisenhower years the nation was truly going to change, that the liberal democracy was going to do something. "He reestablished the republic as the first generation of our leaders saw it," Arthur Schlesinger, Jr., wrote, "young, brave, civilized, reasonable, gay, tough, questing, exultant in the excitement and potentiality of history." Few were more touched by this than the white middle-class young. "I really believed," one of their number said as she looked back on the promise of the Peace Corps, "that I was going to be able to change the world."

An equal catalyst in those vital days was the black Southern protest, the sit-ins and Freedom Riders and bus boycotts, the example of Martin Luther King, Jr.; and the television violence from the South, precursor of the televised war, affected young Americans everywhere. I met King at a small party in the publisher Evan Thomas's apartment in New York. I was introduced to him by my literary agent of the time, Joan Daves, who was King's agent too. "You're from Yazoo?" he asked. We discussed civil rights and my county in Mississippi. He described it as "difficult." He asked about two or three blacks I knew of there. He wanted to know how the young whites there felt.

"I think the letter from the Birmingham jail is a great piece of writing," I said, and quoted two or three of the phrases, such as "tied in a single garment of destiny."

"Thank you," he said. "Of course I had a little time on my hands when I wrote it."

In a sedate city parlor of white intellectuals and admirers and publishing colleagues far removed from the television screen on which he flourished and triumphed, King possessed an almost sweet and attentive languor, soft dark absorbing eyes in repose, a subtle sensitivity to nuance and mood, giving his companion of the moment the largesse of full attention — an aspect not of the big-city preacher but of the comfortable, dutiful small-town professor. His "I Have a Dream" address in Washington, God-like in its breath of hope and freedom, would embody the most resounding words of the 1960s — poignant now in the collapse of that fervor and unity such a short time later — so much so that twenty years afterwards a white Mississippi legislator would visit my dwelling on the Ole Miss campus several midnights in succession to memorize that declaration word-for-word from a tape I had of it, and awaken the neighborhood from my front lawn in unison with the orator with: "Free at last! Free at last!"

Never mind that the Kennedys were late and equivocal on the racial issue, preferring rocketry and appeasing Southern Democrats in the cause against Communism to assuaging the ghettos: John Kennedy later became committed to civil rights, and his brother Bobby, who left the LBJ administration to be elected U.S. Senator from New York in 1965, even more so. First came the improbable telephone conversations they had with the bumpkin but cagey Ross Barnett of Mississippi concerning James Meredith and Ole Miss, recorded on tape for posterity. And there is extraordinary and rarely seen film footage of that time by Robert Drew, who was permitted to run his cameras in the private meetings in the Oval Office when George Wallace had pledged to stand at the schoolhouse door at the University of Alabama to block the admission of two black students. This was June, 1963, many months before the implementation of the Voting Rights Act of 1965. In intimate portrait we see Jack and Bobby Kennedy responding as human beings to the pressures of the moment, for the first time in our history making racial equality a moral issue. They are talking in subdued tones to each other, they are on the telephone with the slithery Governor of Alabama and with their own outnumbered lieutenants on the scene, their brows are furrowed in anxiety and concern, they are baffled by the intransigence, and even by the ambivalence. They are learning.

The assassination was a sundering of the American soul, and not least for the idealistic young. It would embrace much more than the natural grief for a popular young President. It was a dreadful loss of innocence. It would go to the core of our own nurturing hope and promise and possibility: it was the Sixties watershed, an expression of the epic and catastrophic American legend, an event from which this nation would never really fully recover. As with almost every compatriot of my generation and older, I recall with a nearly mythic clarity precisely where I was and what I was doing in the moments I learned of Pearl Harbor, of FDR's death, of Hiroshima, so that later, whenever I passed the hole-in-the-corner restaurant on Thirty-fourth Street where I had lunched alone on November 22, 1963, before returning to the *Harper's* office to be met by the news, I felt ghastly tremors. The assassination reinforced our deepest and darkest strains of paranoia, because we would never truly know who killed him. That night, having to do something, anything, I telephoned Jack Fischer in White Plains to suggest he write a quick "Easy Chair" column for our issue already gone to the press. "Do you feel as badly as I do?" I asked him. "Oh, yes," he said. "You couldn't feel worse." Later, in a tough Irish saloon around the corner from our apartment and next to a tiny brownstone with a historical plaque announcing it as the site where Chester Arthur was sworn in as President on the assassination of James Garfield, I proposed a toast to the new President Johnson, and seconds later was blindsided by a blow from an off-duty cop, so that when I went on national television the following Monday, invited to tell what I knew of LBJ, the makeup artist had to apply undue quantities of talcum around the eye. Even today, years later when I watch the film clips, as the open limousine tortuously turns left off Houston onto Elm in Dallas toward the Texas Book Depository, I pray to myself: maybe it won't happen this time. Metaphorically, perhaps, it was only shortly after Kennedy's death that the Beatles made their first visit to America. I was in a taxi on Fifth Avenue when I saw hundreds of city youngsters rushing traffic barricades on Fifty-ninth Street near the Plaza and the park. I asked the cabdriver what was going on. "Those crazy four kids from Liverpool just got in town," he said.

I vividly remembered Lyndon Johnson from my days in Austin, his big Lincoln thundering around the darkened boulevards at night, usually followed by three or four other vehicles trying desperately to keep up with him, his jabbing away with a finger or forearm at the coat lapels of some politician or reporter in the Driskill lobby or Scholz's Beer Garten or some Mexican cantina. "I can't talk to you now, boy," he said to me one day in the Driskill. "My momma's in the next room and I haven't seen my momma in three months." I remember how big his hands were when he bear-hugged you, or gripped you on the shoulder, bending down with his face right next to yours in extortion or simple salutation. I knew from personal experience how accurate Barry Goldwater was when he said that if LBJ could not persuade you of something by other means, he would lean down and breathe in your mouth to deprive you of oxygen. The scorn for him of many of the liberal intellectuals of New York City of that time was deep and bitter. Even at the summit of his later legislative successes he was profaned in these circles as a crude usurper; the sheer virulence of these criticisms never failed to impress me. No matter how he tried, and he diligently tried, he would never elude the specter of his predecessor. He would be one of our most excoriated Presidents. Yet his congressional programs of 1963 and '64 radically broadened the Kennedy legacy and surpassed the early New Deal: "an end," he said, "to poverty and racial injustice to which we're totally committed in our time." His landslide election in '64 over Goldwater with a coalition of Democrats and moderate Republicans was the most emphatic up to then in American history. (That was the campaign in which Goldwater argued on television that New York City was such an alien grotesquerie that it ought to be carved from the continent and floated out to sea.) By 1966 the accumulation of his accomplishments on anti-poverty, voting rights, civil rights, health care, aid to education, environmental protection, workers' safety, support for the arts, and elsewhere was stunningly impressive.

It was Vietnam, however, that was exacerbating everything, its rampant paradoxes, a war that would reverberate through American life for many, many years. It was gradually becoming a major undeclared war. From the middle of 1965, when twenty-five thousand protestors marched in Washington, to the end of 1966, American troops there multiplied from twenty-five thousand to nearly four hundred thousand. The doves were rapidly vanishing from the Johnson government; every former Kennedy advisor except one urged the escalation. The Gulf of Tonkin Resolution, a political act of considerable cynicism, the principal motive of which was to minimize the appeal of the Goldwater Republicans' exploitation of the international Red menace, was the beginning of this fateful slide: the fear of the Right, of a new McCarthyism capitalizing on timidity in Southeast Asia just as the earlier one had over the disenchantment of the loss of China. "What really matters," LBJ would tell George Ball, the one major dove in the administration, "is the beast of the right-wing." Operation Rolling Thunder, the mass B-52 bombing of North Vietnam, was initiated in early 1965, and by July of that year this country for all purposes was really into a full-scale Asian land war, and with this a mounting suspicion that Johnson was being devious on the true extent of the American commitment and lying about the growing human and economic costs of that war because he still passionately wished his Great Society. As his trust eroded he became more intractable. By

1967 there were nearly half a million American troops in Vietnam, and sixteen thousand dead and one hundred thousand wounded.

As late as 1964 the SNCC students, still committed to nonviolence, were concentrating on black freedom schools and voter registration in the South. They were importing substantial numbers of young white Northerners, especially to Mississippi. Both Michael Schwerner and Andrew Goodman were sons of highly cultured New York Jewish families; Jim Chaney was a poor Mississippi black. Coincidental with their murders in Neshoba County, the nation was approaching a new and volatile period on race. Malcolm X was assassinated in Harlem in early '65, an intense, intriguing, groping figure of intelligence and courage, his final personal and cultural legacy not to be fully secured until a generation after his death.

The standard of the Southern movement was beginning to reach into the black ghettos of the North, where mutinous, embittered young people had grown impatient of nonviolent resistance. Five days after the passage of the Voting Rights Act the Watts sector of Los Angeles erupted; ghetto violence and burnings were beginning to occur in scores of Northern cities. Between 1964 and 1967 there were 164 such uprisings, with dozens killed, more often than not blacks by white police. These constituted the seeds of destruction of the poverty programs of the Great Society.

Americans had before them, but would not heed, for Americans *en masse* are too often tardy in reading, much less responding to, their great poets of the human heart, the abounding truths and harkenings and complexities of Faulkner, the Dilseys and Beauchamps and Christmases, the severance a society inflicts on two seven-year-old boys who are comrades, one white and one black, and that to Roth Edmonds is the "day the old curse of his fathers, the old haughty ancestral pride based not on any value but an accident of geography, stemmed not from courage and honor but from wrong and shame descended to him." Three weeks after the burnings in Newark I went out there, the whole terrain still acrid with smoke and charred rubble, and the lingering adrift presence everywhere of wanton death. The destruction was unbelievable, so that years later, in 1992, watching on television the scenes from modern-day Los Angeles, I was overcome with an eerie, icy remembrance and despair.

The Northern white civil rights workers had returned from the South after the '64 Freedom Summer to other more complex battlegrounds, their own colleges and universities. Their targets would be smug and conventional campus administrations and faculties, complacent about the problems of the enormous coming college generation so skeptical of being mere educated cogs in the corporate society. First would come Berkeley and the Free Speech Movement. Ivory towers across America were becoming foxholes, one academician noted: the campus militants were usually brilliant students in the humanities from prosperous liberal families, more often than not from suburbia, who were strongly committed to a society they wanted to change, and who saw themselves as an oppressed class within it. At the same time countless other students were dropping out of college to devote full time to the service of rebellion; one of its chroniclers would call the events of the many months to come "a cyclone in a wind tunnel." Anti-war protests involving older Americans would likewise increase in numbers and intensity. For one powerful moment in our history the suburbs and the academy were coming together, and all the while the pincers of the Right were hoarding in the shadows. Years later I asked my son David Rae, an elementary school student then, his most graphic memory of those years in the city. "Confusion," he replied. "And cops beating up hippies."

As the decade evolved, so too did I. I tried to stay in touch with the young activists. I had a number of talks with Mario Savio of Berkeley. Some of the more talented college editors, especially Jeff Greenfield of the University of Wisconsin, a brilliant and companionable young man who wished to be a writer, were frequently in the office. So too on a brief trip back to New York came Bob Moses, the young black who had recently been jailed and beaten in Mississippi for his work on behalf of voter registration. They spoke eloquently to me of the wellsprings of the disaffection, of the real depths of the bitterness, keeping me straight on the hopes and fears of their generation. I listened to them. I sensed an America beleaguered and entrapped in its own most facile ideals. I saw the gathering armies poising themselves for the catharsis, the lineaments of which would inevitably re-shape many of the most basic contours of the nation. But how, I wondered, and at what toll? It was just the beginning. "Times, they are a-changing," Bob Dylan sang. "Time for something to happen," the Beatles were predicting.

~ The Nation: 1967

4

WE LIVED ON the Upper West Side. In an archetypical New York irony our telephone number was the same as James Meredith's, who had integrated the University of Mississippi in '62 and was now a student at Columbia, except for the last digit — ours was 8, his was 7. Two Mississippians of disparate backgrounds in the big city kept getting one another's telephone messages.

The Upper West Side in those days before the later advent of the Reaganite Yuppies was a melange of rank and species, of inordinate juxtapositions. It was a grungy and ravaged and down-at-the-heels neighborhood where you could stand on the crowded street corners any night in the welter of tongues and watch people of every race and color drift by. In the not distant past it had been the environ of the Jewish intelligentsia, and of the refugees from Nazism, much of the flavor of this still palpable, and on the benches in the traffic islands of upper Broadway with their invalid patches of vegetation one saw the old Jewish women bundled together with their memories against the chill, little puffs of mist rising from their lips as they chattered in the cold. *Children of Israel.* "I have seen the affliction of my people and heard them cry. Let my people go!" Eli N. Evans, a Jewish friend of my generation from Durham, North Carolina, and Chapel Hill working for one of the philanthropic foundations in the city in our time there, liked to observe to me that our roles as WASP and Jew in New York were now reversed from our days in the South: I was in the decided minority, he the emphatic majority. Later in his book *The Lonely Days Were Sundays:*

Reflections of a Jewish Southerner, he wrote: "I have for years been intrigued with the ways in which Jews and Southerners are alike — stepchildren of an anguished history. From before the Civil War Southerners have used Old Testament analogies to portray themselves as the chosen people, surrounded and outnumbered but destined to survive and triumph against overwhelming odds." One could feel that emotion on the Upper West Side.

The provincial once inured to catfish, fried squirrel, and cornbread soaked in buttermilk took to the enlivening Jewish delis abundant to the neighborhood, the bagels and lox and gefilte fish, the prolific fragrances of them, the twists and modulations of language, the incalculable repartee. Mr. Solomon Platz had a deli on Upper Broadway around the corner from our apartment. He had fled the Nazis from Poland in the Thirties, taken a wife named Marian from Queens, never forgiven the Giants for leaving the Polo Grounds for tinsel land, adored the New York Mets, abhorred the Yankees, and would not take one on his trust that Mississippi was not only a river, but also an actual state of the Union. "You know from nothin', I am telling you, young man. Mississippi only *floats.*" "But it's land too, I'm *telling* you, Mr. Platz." "Aha! Under the water then." We talked of the Mets, of Seaver, Grote, Harrison, Swoboda, Ryan, and Koosman; they brought us across the divide. Koosman might be a Jew, he thought, but not as good as Sandy Koufax. "Sandy will not take to the mound at Yom Kippur." Hank Greenberg had *chutzpa.* "The hitters of circuit clouts drive Cadillacs." One spring evening, the air feathery along the Hudson and the apple trees on the verge of blossom, he said, "Let's go to the park for a *schmoos.*" He left the deli to his wife and walked with my son's black Labrador Ichabod H. Crane and me over to Riverside Park. "I'm not at comfort with your dog, *alevasholem,*" he confessed, and showed me the memorial to the Warsaw Ghetto, where some of his people had perished.

The Holocaust was never very far away on the Upper West Side. There were the old gray Jewish men forlornly wandering the streets of the vicinity, alone or in small groups. Unlike the aged Jewish women and their animated talk, who prattled with the industriousness of sparrows, the men seemed placeless, passive, lost on the fierce polyglot sidewalks of America. I felt sorry for them, much as I did as a child for the old gray-haired Negro men in my hometown, sitting in front of the Negro stores, whittling wood, dozing in the sun, owning nothing but the clothes on their backs. There were moments wandering these thoroughfares when I remembered with terrible clarity the documentaries I had seen of the Warsaw ghetto, of a young woman crazed with hunger holding her infant child and walking up and down, back and forth, before the Nazi cameras, or of the SS apprehending young boys trying to sneak back inside with a few meager potatoes hidden in their pockets. I often sat on the Upper West Side benches and eavesdropped on the elderly Jewish widows in their inexhaustible argot chatter, sometimes exchanging pleasantries with them and hearing out their multifold queries and parlous complaints. They, too, believed Mississippi only floated except when they had heard of "the civil rights." The prices of kosher food were getting out of hand. What about these children with long hair and beads? And kissing in the streets? "Excuse the expression," one quick-witted old lady said. "They're *schlemiels* — no-goodniks they are." The spirit of Yiddish pervaded the city, these park benches, the delis, the most serious salons of the intelligentsia, *Commentary, Partisan Review, Dissent,* where often I found myself the solitary goy, or one of two if one counted Dwight Macdonald. The Anglo-Saxon *émigré* could not wholly survive without a little touch of Yiddish. It might have behooved the Confederacy itself to have had a little Yiddish: All Yankees are *shmegegge.*

The sidewalks of the Upper West Side always intimated real or imagined danger, hovering over it like a veil, but there was laughter too, and the sounds of children at play, and politeness and civility amidst the anomie, for the Upper West Side in the Sixties was at once a war zone and a playground, with fluctuating shades of mayhem and frolic in between.

Years later my son David Rae, then eight years old and riding the Seventh Avenue IRT to school and back every day from Ninety-sixth Street to Fourteenth Street, remembered the pervasive sounds of the garbage trucks and the subways on the Upper West Side, and the smell of the smog in the mornings. "No matter where I go," he says, "I compare whatever city I'm in to New York. I *grew up* in New York." He and his chums devised a city game of throwing a hard rubber Spalding ball purchased across the street from the Thalia Cinema off the front facades of the apartment building and, using Ninety-fourth Street as an asphalt outfield, roaming it with their baseball gloves, and whenever I saw them at this I recalled the spacious, overgrown old ball fields of Mississippi carved out of the raw enveloping earth itself.

The looming apartment buildings lined the main thoroughfares, and on the narrow shady cross-streets were the old townhouses in petulant disarray, home then to junkies and prostitutes and winos and pushers and gray shadowy anonymous creatures who meandered the byways in mute and aimless promenade. Along stretches of Broadway were the vegetable stands with their pungent cheeses and produce, and the bagel places and delis, and the clean swift smells of the Chinese laundries. Not far down from where we lived stood the big, seedy Ansonia Hotel, grand it was said in its *fin-de-siècle* opulence and the early decades of our century, where Caruso once lived, and Dreiser, and Babe Ruth, and one might with little difficulty picture The Babe standing in front waiting for a taxi in the twilights after a game at the Stadium, his nostrils sniffing the possibilities of the night. From our apartment in the evenings you could hear the sounds of rampage at Columbia up the way, of loudspeakers and massed angry voices, and the whining sirens from paddy wagons and squad cars, and along our own streets young people and old carrying placards with truculent words against war, poverty, sexism, and Lyndon Johnson, and signs identifying protesting activists of SANE, or W. E. B. Du Bois Clubs, or Students for a Democratic Society, or Women for Peace, or Inter-University Christian Movement, or Jewish Peace Fellowship.

This was Saul Bellow's territory, the Upper West Side, as much as Hardy's was Dorset or Lawrence's the Midlands or Faulkner's Yoknapatawpha, where, Irving Howe wrote in a later *Harper's*, Bellow saw "the continuities of ordinary living, by no means always a triumph but never to be sneered at, which manage somehow to coexist with the raspy national foolishness our culture casts off like smoke . . . a principle of sorts, a mixture of health and sickness exemplifying our condition."

Within this setting — within a radius of forty blocks or so, roughly Seventy-second to the low hundreds — dwelled a substantial number of America's finest writers, critics, professors, journalists, editors, who grumbled about its muck and strain yet honored its economic and racial diversity and its tradition of cultural liberalism. It was an environ that many small-town and rural Anglo-Saxon Americans would have found nearly impossible to comprehend, much less to be ever remotely comfortable in, such were the disparities in the nation; nothing in their experience could have prepared them for it. To set down a Southern Baptist deacon and his consort at Broadway and Ninety-sixth on a Saturday night of July would have been an act of the most demonic malevolence, but no doubt titillating to observe. The people themselves were an endlessly arresting spectacle, and the unprepossessing Chinese restaurants immensely gratifying, and any neighborhood where one sees *Casablanca* for the very first time will be forever remembered in the emotions, as I saw it in the noble and genteelly shabby New Yorker Cinema on Upper Broadway: the love songs and laughter, the hearts full of passion, the jealousy and hate were resonant for me of what was happening all around.

It would have been difficult for those of us living our daily existences in New York City in 1967 to perceive that year as a critical turning point in the decade, a point of no return, but one sees now in retrospect how much it really was. If the long months from Kennedy's '63 American University speech on peace and disarmament to the Gulf of Tonkin were, as Marcus Raskin had described it, "the We Shall Overcome period of American life" — a fruitful and optimistic juncture when domestic and racial reform seemed possible and there was hope for world concord no matter how tentative — then the events of 1965 and 1966 represented an intensifying disintegration and abandon in the nation. With the escalation in Vietnam and the splintering of the fragile black-white alliance on civil rights, organized militancy grew apace, and nihilistic violence was the ordinary headline; disillusion and bitterness would be inevitable, and even more menacing, strident backlash, eventually to engender bloody confrontations in this country not so widely experienced in a hundred years.

What had occurred in the nation to give rise to such a catastrophic reversal of the earlier idealism? Two among a substantial number of our later *Harper's* writers would address that question for an influential national readership. To Midge Decter, much of the answer could be covered in three words: the Vietnam War. "To put the matter very flatly, the government of the United States has become involved in a military venture which to the vast majority of the educated, enlightened, liberal community of Americans seems at the very best senseless and at the worst evil." To Marshall Frady, travelling to the universities and the cities, the desperations on the campuses and in the ghettos with all their widening amplifications were being sustained, if not occasioned, by "the Tragic Distraction:"

> Certainly, not the least of the crimes of the war is the overwhelming banality of its rationale, the vision necessary for the nation to believe in it and prosecute it — the banality of its presumptions about human hopes and human endurance, about the workings of the human species, about history. We are living with the exalted comic-book cliches which have been imposed, by a process of suffusion, onto the soul of the country. But it is in an even larger sense, that as long as it continues there will continue those potentially mortal crises, that Vietnam could become the war that destroyed the Republic.

For two years Lyndon Johnson had been steadily increasing both the air and ground war. More and more the conflict was assuming disturbing racial overtones. The hideous television images back home contrasted starkly with official Washington's optimism; the TV networks, however, avoided showing the worst bloodshed during the dinner hour. The "credibility gap," a phrase burnished on the Sixties, was peaking fast. More Americans were killed in 1967 than in all the earlier years of the war. There seemed no end to it. By December there were almost half a million American troops there, and the generals were asking for more. Harrison Salisbury's impressive coverage from North Vietnam in the *New York Times* reported the enormous civilian casualties and the damage from bombing and defoliation. Martin Luther King, Jr., was beginning to condemn the war, including the high proportion of black combat soldiers in contrast to the deteriorating ghettos back home.

In March of that year I attended the National Book Award ceremonies at Philharmonic Hall in Lincoln Center where a group of writers protested when Vice-President Humphrey stood to address the New York literati. Even Bob Moses of SNCC, quiet hero of nonviolent reform in the South, joined the swelling anti-war resistance. With the increasing draft calls and sharply diminishing deferments, the movement correspondingly broadened, escalating from protest to resistance to outright violence. Thus was deepening one of the most anguishing human divides of the Sixties, that between the young Americans who defied the war and bore witness against it, and those who chose to serve, a division that would shape the national consciousness for untold years. In one week's time before the march on the Pentagon in October there were mass demonstrations in Madison, Oakland (where the police had used Mace), Chicago, at Brooklyn College and Reed College, and on Boston Common several thousand draft-card burners congregated. Most of the protestors were white college students, and one of the most disquieting social collisions among the many of these times was white blue-collar police with their tear gas and weapons *en masse* against the educated children of white suburbia, and, in the ghettos, their confrontations with the impoverished and rebellious young blacks. The exodus of young men to Canada had grown to the thousands.

Vietnam had not even begun to approach its full fire, nor its farthest calamity. That war, Michael Herr was to write in *Dispatches,* was what he and many of his contemporaries had instead of happy childhoods. "It is necessary that things should pass away into that from which they are born," Anaximander wrote twenty-five hundred years ago. "For things must pay one another the penalty and compensation for their injustice according to the ordinance of time." As Annie Gottlieb recorded in her memoir, *Do You Believe in Magic?*, its impact on the young, as with all wars, would be hard, but this was a war of a kind the nation, idealistic even in its internecine impulses, had not known. For both those who fought in it and those who fought against it, the war "made the Sixties real. It forced our transformation, made it a matter of life and death." Its eventual butcher's bill would prove tragic.

> The Vietnam War was the central event of our generation. Like a massive shock wave, it affected, in widening circles, the 58,022 lost in the war (eight of them women); the 100,000 or more who may have killed themselves since their return; the 153,329 severely wounded, and the 150,375 more lightly wounded; the estimated 250,000 victims of Agent Orange; the half million or more who still suffer from the nightmares and flashbacks of post-traumatic stress; the 3.78 million who saw duty in the war zone; the 11 million who served in the Armed Forces during that time of doubt, drugs, and rebellion; the 27 million men who were threatened by the draft and had to rearrange their lives around it; and all the lovers, wives, friends, brothers, and sisters, as well as the parents, grandparents, and children of those who served, died, vanished, protested, or fled.

The conflagrations that summer in one metropolitan ghetto after another, an accelerating ferment that had begun in '65 in Watts of Los Angeles, where there were twenty deaths and six hundred injuries — the prelude to four "long hot summers" — amounted to a maddening domestic war of its own. Witches were out on the land, and blacks burning blacks, more firepower than all the Klan crosses in history. Amid this turmoil Lyndon Johnson became more and more aloof and withdrawn, more strident in his hostility toward the militants, manifesting the paranoic vein not unsurprising to those of us who had known him from Texas politics. It was as if the very people the benison of his Great Society had befriended were biting the feeding hand. And who among any of us, white and black, really knows? Perhaps they were.

In the spring of 1967 Joan Didion was writing of all this in her indelible words:

> The center was not holding. It was a country of bankruptcy notices and public-auction announcements and commonplace reports of casual killings and misplaced children and abandoned homes and vandals who misspelled even the four-letter words they scrawled. It was a country in which families routinely disappeared, trailing bad checks and repossession papers. Adolescents drifted from city to torn city, sloughing off both the past and the future as snakes shed their skins, children who were never taught and would never now learn the games that had held the society together. People were missing. Children were missing. Parents were missing. Those left behind filed desultory missing-persons reports, then moved on themselves.

So many of these dislocations centered on the Haight-Ashbury section of San Francisco, which was becoming as much a mirror as Berkeley had ever been. The "Hashbury" served as capital of the young drug culture hippies and the activist drop-outs. "The thrust is no longer for 'change' or 'progress' or 'revolution,' " the young Hunter S. Thompson observed there in '67, "but merely to escape, to live on the far perimeter of a world that might have been — perhaps should have been — and strike a bargain for survival on purely personal terms." Pot was selling at ten dollars a lid, five dollars a matchbox, and LSD and all the amphetamines were cheaper than in most places. Psychedelic beggars roamed the streets, especially among the curious tourists on weekends. At the Digger Free Store classes were conducted under the title How to Avoid Gangbangs, VD, Rape, Pregnancy, Beatings, and Starvation. Didion visited the garage of a condemned building which was christened The Warehouse and committed to total theater. "What happened ten minutes ago or what is going to happen a half hour from now tends to fade from mind in the Warehouse. Somebody is usually doing something interesting, like working on a light show, and there are a lot of interesting things around, like an old Chevrolet touring car which is used as a bed and a vast American flag fluttering up in the shadows and an overstuffed chair suspended like a swing from the rafters, the point of that being that it gives you a sensory-deprivation high."

In Haight-Ashbury it would be the "summer of love," and these runaway young became easy prey for the cynical and the practiced and the visionary entrepreneurs. And for long-haired criminals and sadists and even murderers. Haunting Grateful Dead concerts in the Avalon Ballroom that summer, William Manchester remembered, "was a bearded little psychotic who liked to curl up in a fetal position right on the dance floor, and whose secret ambitions were to persuade girls to perform fellatio with dogs and gouge out the eyes of a beautiful actress and smear them on walls. Later he would be well-remembered in Hashbury. His name was Charles Manson."

I was to assume the editorship of *Harper's* in early '67. Some months before that, in an unerring hint of my own ambitions in those days, I had gone to John Fischer: he had come out with a book before *he* became editor, I suggested, and I felt *I* needed to also — to establish one's credentials, in so many words. He readily agreed. I borrowed money from the bank and took a leave of absence; when the money ran out I returned to the magazine. I finished the book, which I called *North Toward Home,* at nights and on weekends.

The Saturday Evening Post, in its final flourishing days with a mass readership, contracted to run a lengthy excerpt before the publication of the book. They wanted to accompany it with a substantial spread of photographs using my own son, David Rae, then seven years old, as the model of my growing up those years before in Yazoo City, Mississippi. At first I was reluctant; a man does not wish to exploit his young offspring, at least not excessively. But David Rae wanted to do it. I was considerably relieved by this precocious magnanimity. The tuition at Bank Street School was unrelenting, and rising all the time.

William A. Emerson, Jr., was the editor-in-chief of *The Saturday Evening Post,* a vivid figure of hyperbolic proportions in the city in those days, six feet three and sizeable. Emerson was a Georgian, a

Harvard graduate, and we met for lunch or in his office four or five times to discuss his project, for he told me he intended to spend a great deal of money on making it right. "Let's be inimitable in our approach," he said. "Let's make them remember our compact with the gods. What are we, men or mice?" Or, leaning across a table toward me with the air of an unregenerate boondocks Machiavelli: "What if we incur the hot wrath of the flatulent money men? We have a larger contract with destiny." One day he quoted to me from Oliver Wendell Holmes, " '. . . a word is not a crystal, transparent and unchanged; it is the skin of a living thought.' " Emerson added: "Words are leading you back home for me in a benign and noble cause." Then he might declare: "I'm sick of men who are scared of their own secretaries. I like people who like to eat and drink and fornicate. If a man's innards are going to give out on him, they ought to give out because of booze, not just venality." He seldom complimented anyone; he would say, "Sir, you have the heart of a Capetown lion!" and instead of calling someone incompetent: "I am surrounded by cretins and miscreants." New Yorkers were not merely sophisticated, but "cool as celery, proud as Spaniards, and solitary as tomcats." He once advocated a national campaign: ADOPT A NEW YORKER. For all this he would later be a complex but sympathetic personage in Otto Friedrich's book *Decline and Fall,* on *The Saturday Evening Post.* "He was always acutely conscious of social distinctions," Friedrich recalled, "and I could not help suspecting that somewhere at the center of that rambunctious, laughing, blustering whirl there was the remnant of a small boy uncertain of his own place in the world — but never mind: if this had ever been a problem, it was one that Emerson had solved to his own satisfaction: 'I never lie,' as he said, 'I just bullshit 'em.' " Much after this, when he wrote a book on Jesus Christ, I sent him a note: "Dear Emerson: I knew sooner or later you'd write your autobiography."

Scant surprise that Bill Emerson and I got along well, a Georgia misdoer and a Mississippi one in the publishing crucible of Manhattan in that particularly sonorous decade. He was partial to the ritual of lunches and deemed New York the greatest city in the world for them, where energy could be felt like "motes in the air" and "the first martini hits the liver like a silver bullet." Among his honored spots were midtown Japanese restaurants. At one such luncheon we tarried until midafternoon, consuming notable quantities of warm saki. Thereupon Benjamin Franklin's latest successor on *The Post* insisted that I escort him to my office at *Harper's.* "You've seen *my* quarters," he said. "I want to ascertain if yours are equally conspicuous, or merely arcane." It was a mistake of egregious dimensions. At *Harper's,* as I hazily recall, he began stalking the secretaries up and down the corridors, shouting "Pussilanimous!" as he may have tried to pinch them. "Have you never encountered a *hero?*" he jocosely asked them. Finally, mercifully exhausted, he departed. "Who was *that?*" one of them asked. "The editor-in-chief of *The Saturday Evening Post,*" I replied, and was glad that John Fischer was not in the office that day. Consistent with such a gargantuan disposition, Emerson was, as he had promised, unniggardly on the projected trip to Mississippi. He retained Hans Namuth, one of America's finest photographers, for the assignment, and he chose his own administrative assistant and two other associates to accompany David Rae and Hans Namuth and me on the trip home.

"The wonderment, perplexity, and curiosity which the very word *Yazoo* used to excite," a Georgia writer recorded in 1852, "I have never been able to forget, its strange exotic sound to the ear. . . . And did it pertain to land or water, or was it amphibious, and akin to both? All was vague, misty, mysterious, perplexed, yet pervaded not doubtfully with the general idea of something that was sinister, abhorrent, and damnable." *Yazoo!* It had followed me in just such spirit wherever I went, when I left it for college and as I grew older: to Texas, to England, to California, and, of course, now to New York, the word itself exerting its own bizarre and inexplicable sorcery, even in the deepest grottos of Sixties Manhattan. Now I had written an autobiographical book, soon to be published, the first one-third of it about my growing up here. Only on this unique return was I suddenly smitten with an irrational trepidation over what I had done, a common emotion to all the American writers I would ever know who had written from their hearts about their small places, but nevertheless I was struck now with a dread incertitude: had I hurt it? Had I dealt with it honestly? Had I been true to it, and to myself?

As the formidable *Saturday Evening Post* descended in all its Yankee profligacy on this poor native ground, there to retain helicopters and tow lifts and tractors and coffins and hearses and firetrucks to illustrate the autobiographical images, my apprehensive spirit was dealt another, more pristine disquiet, having to do with memory and deja vu. As I watched the great Hans Namuth taking his hundreds of pictures of David Rae, in the cemetery, on the main street in a Sabbath hush, in the schoolyard, in the Delta woods with a .22 rifle, on my front lawn with a rental dog hired to resemble my dead fox terrier Old Skip, a crazed misgiving began to germinate in me that time itself had not really passed at all, that David really was *me* at that age, and that I had no more departed to go anywhere than the Confederate soldier on the schoolground had been summarily excavated and transplanted bodily to Darien, Connecticut. In the Methodist Church as my son sat next to my mother in front of the pipe organ while she played "Abide with Me" as we had once done long ago, I said to myself: My God! This is 1942!

This was something I did not want, this warp of old misappropriated time. And yet from this vantage point of home I was able to see my patron city New York in a different and valuable perspective. It was my life now writ large. It had become for me a seething zenith from which to perceive the frustrations and the possibilities of the national society. For all its splendor and seduction, in my early days there the city had intimidated me — the literary parties, for instance, where I had sometimes lurked on the fringes or behind potted plants, overly sensitive to its bias toward anyone with a Southern accent, and the subways, the noise, the punitive discourtesies — so that even in the book I had written I had called the city "The Big Cave" and even fantasized a Faulkner-like bear terrorizing the faubourgs of Manhattan, "epitome and apotheosis of an old dead time." I had been most comfortable, it seemed, not only with people there from my own region, but with Midwesterners and Westerners as well, just as young Joan Didion, a Sacramentan dwelling in the city in the same period, felt most comfortable with Southerners: "They seemed to be in New York as I was, on some indefinitely extended leave from wherever they belonged, disinclined to consider the future, temporary exiles who always knew when the flights left for New Orleans or Memphis or Richmond or, in my case California." It was as if we had subliminally set ourselves against the real New Yorkers. But when the word got out in the New York rumorings that I was to be the editor-in-chief of *Harper's Magazine,* almost overnight, it seemed, I was one of *them:* "they" became "we." And coy as this may seem, the difference was altogether remarkable: I began to feel that the city enveloped me, protected me, required more of me, almost in the way a small town does. I recognized now how much I had really come to love the city, and that I owed it something. From the dwarfed and insular reality of Yazoo, and its common and remembered places, I at last realized how very far away I had gone.

"Looks to me like you're a New Yorker now," a friend on this visit home said, and her swift perception made me pause. I had never thought of it that way. It made me sense for the first time that I felt more convenient and secure in my preeminent adopted place than I did now on my own native ground. Had I finally assumed the city wiliness and tenacity? Its street-smart resilience and resolve? Acknowledged in its true dimensions its grandeur and complexity? I remembered a morning not long before, as I walked with our black Lab Ichabod H. Crane in Riverside Park, how the sunlight in the chilled wind silhouetted the tall birches and oaks. A group of little Jewish kids in school caps and jackets paused in a gregarious semicircle to pet the dog, and as they were beginning to depart a smaller cadre of little Puerto Rican children, about ten years old also, in frayed clothes, from the public school in the corner block on West End Avenue, stopped also before my big dog; for one transitory moment the tiny Jewish boys and Puerto Ricans together whispered to and courted my black dog, glancing at each other uneasily all the while as my Ichabod gently absorbed their prattling ethnic regard. The Jewish and Puerto Rican youngsters were there together for a moment because of the dog, then left me one by one. A pair of middle-aged men in tweed sportscoats, one of them smoking a pipe and carrying a *Partisan Review,* strolled by discussing the Karamazov brothers, the faint outline of the towers of midtown loomed far at the horizon to the south, and to the west at the edge of the Hudson beyond the feverish motion of the West Side Highway I inhaled a little of the salt air and watched the bobbing houseboats etched against the Jersey Palisades and a solitary gull swooping downward to the water, to the echo of a ship's horn far away, and I thought: Well, this is New York, and here I am.

At this critical juncture in my life, it was odd to see one's boyhood soil through the eyes of an eminent photographer who had never been to the South — its white people and black people, its precipitous terrain, its murky serpentine river, its lonesome vistas invested by the snake-infested kudzu, its gnarled cypresses in the streams bent down like wise men which I always thought were trying to tell me something, its crumbling houses out in the countryside darkly recalling the past and the vanished souls who once lived in them — the stirrings of old twilight conversations, of mute possessions and fears and loves in the gone charters of time. Various of the local people followed us everywhere, as if it were a Hollywood movie being shot, or perhaps to ascertain in that cusp between segregation and integration there and the tenacious cruelty of its paradoxes if Namuth and David Rae and the others, and for all I know, *myself,* were outside agitators.

Hans Namuth was in his fifties, a German émigré long noted for his photographs of the Spanish Civil War, of Indians in Latin America, and of the painters of the New York School, especially of the de Koonings, Pollock, Rothko, Frankenthaler. He was a man cosmopolitan in his whims and dispositions. We were staying in the Yazoo Motel adjoining a country restaurant called Stubs, the only real restaurant in town and a long way from the Century Club. After the first day's labors in the broiling heat, the *Saturday Evening Post* group returned to the motel to prepare for dinner. We were having a drink in Namuth's room.

"I've always preferred good Beaujolais at slightly lower than room temperature," he said. "Tonight at dinner I intend to buy us some good, chilled Beaujolais."

"That's fine with me," I said.

When we arrived at the restaurant, he summoned the waitress, who turned out to be a farm girl from Pierce's Crossroads. "Miss, do you serve your Beaujolais slightly chilled, or only at room temperature?"

"What's that you say?"

"Your Beaujolais."

"Bo-*what*?"

"May I see your wine list, please?"

"*Wine* list? We ain't got no wine list."

"Then what *do* you have to drink?"

"We got iced tea, Coca-Cola, Dr Pepper, Nehi-Strawberry, Orange Crush, and ice water."

"No wine, then?"

"*Wine*? You're a *stranger,* ain't you?"

With Emerson's boundless funds the fearless *Saturday Evening Post* decided to stage a mock funeral in the town cemetery, and this became another filament of Hans Namuth's orientation, the purpose being to re-create a scene from my boyhood in which I had played "Taps" on my silver trumpet for the military services of the dead soldiers brought back from the fighting in Korea. The *Post* rented a coffin from the black funeral home and hired two dozen or so citizens to be the mourners, as well as several aging American Legionnaires as the honor guard to fire the ceremonial volleys, and a teen-aged boy with a trumpet. Since Namuth desired the earliest light, arrangements were made to have every detail in place by summoning the entire gathering to an appointed spot in the cemetery near a makeshift grave and the coffin draped in the Stars and Stripes half an hour before dawn. Namuth had his cameras at the ready awaiting the first glimmer of the sun when, all of a sudden from around a bend, came a dilapidated car full of country couples making an accustomed shortcut from the center of town through the cemetery to the highway after what had to have been a long night in a beer joint. When they arrived upon the unlikely spectacle of a funeral in the blackest dark, they stopped momentarily, gazing out at the incredible scene. The garrulous American Legion mercenaries, who themselves had been nipping from a jug of something more brawny than Beaujolais, shouted to the interlopers: "Come on, folks! Get outa that thing! Join the party!" The car remained there for the briefest instant, then with a mad clanking of gears and torrents of dust raced away up the hill and out of sight.

With the coming of the dawn, as the photographer from New York began clicking his shutters, the teen-aged trumpeter broke into "Taps." In the instant, as with David Rae in the church and elsewhere, I felt he was I in that time long ago. As in those vanished moments with my trumpet before I played Echo, I looked down now on the town, spread out like a shimmering diagram on its hills and flat places under the awakening sky, and further out still, the great Delta flatness itself like a timeless sea in the early mist. I felt now, as I had then, that I had everything to myself, the giant sweep of the horizon, the sloping earth, the whole green world. Then the boy's notes, the *real* boy's, dissolved tenderly, reluctantly almost, across the tombstones, into the farthest distance, palpitating into the faraway hush.

Just before the book, *North Toward Home,* was published, I made the fateful blunder of telephoning my mother from New York that I would be on the National Broadcasting Company's *Today* show four mornings hence. This inspiring milestone, my mother informed me two days later, was announced by preachers from several local pulpits, and had appeared too as a prominent item on the front page of the newspaper. I therewith promised myself something: before this national television audience, no matter what, I would say nothing bad about my home. I divined this would be difficult, since the interviewer was a talented and dedicated young woman who was already establishing a reputation, even in those early morning hours, for aggressive questioning. All the more reason for reconfirming my gimlet-eyed resolve. In front of the kleig lights in the studio in Rockefeller Center I awaited the questions of the handsome young woman, named Barbara Walters; then came the fourth or fifth one. On page seventy-seven of this book, she suggested, you describe hiding in the shrubbery in front of your house when you were twelve years old, and for no reason at all jumping out and slapping and kicking a helpless three-year-old Negro child. What does this suggest about the society in which you grew up?

I had indeed performed that despicable act back then, but my brain whirled with how to answer. "It wasn't so much that he was Negro," I heard myself replying, "as that he was so little."

This demurrer notwithstanding, my book, as such things always do in our country, profoundly disturbed the town. Many people there thought I had damaged and condemned it. One person wrote me that I had besmirched the memory of my father. My mother received a few threatening calls and anonymous letters. I got pointed warnings of what would happen if I ever came back. Since the town did not have a bookstore, the publishers had placed a substantial number of copies in a pharmacy on the main street. A friend called me long distance in New York to report that the book was the biggest event to hit the town since the Civil War. People were standing in line at the library to get it. "I think half the people in town kind of like it," he said, "and may be a little proud of it. The other half of the town is extremely agitated." He went on to say he had the impression that the half which was so agitated consisted mainly of the people who were not in the book. The most gratifying letter of all came from my old childhood comrade and classmate Henjie Henick, who now ran his father's auto parts store on the lower end of the main street: "I don't know why they're so upset. You told the truth. You told it like it was. And that's what I'm telling *them.*" The *Yazoo Herald* published an open letter to me on its front page from a contemporary accusing me of having brought "undue hurt and embarrassment to my school, church, and friends." All this was beginning to assume the aspect of Wolfe's *You Can't Go Home Again,* and I could not help but reply to the *Herald*: "I feel confident that after the momentary passion, and after the passing of time, you and others there will see my book for what it is, an evocation of a place and a period that will endure in the hearts of others far removed from Yazoo, and hence an act of love." The very title itself came under scrutiny in those home precincts: a renegade traitor, selling out as Faulkner had for the "Yankee dollar," the most efficacious of pejoratives of that period, a judgment that neglected the irony of the words, which the man who wrote the book intended to connote, in the American sense, not repose, but movement. The roguish Philip Roth may have understood this. We had been corresponding about his contributing to *Harper's.* "I liked your book *Up from Slavery,*" he chided.

All this was acutely irrelevant, perhaps, to the lordly challenge at hand. Or was it? In New York City, for me at least, there would be no repose for a very long time.

John Fischer gave a small dinner for Celia and me shortly before I took over the magazine's editorship. One of the guests was Alfred A. Knopf, that towering and crusty presence in New York publishing, and an infamous curmudgeon. Fischer drew the two of us aside and told Knopf that he was retiring and I was shortly to become editor. The old man looked me up and down, then made a growling noise in his throat. "It will take more than one man to ruin *Harper's,*" he said. That was something I did not need.

I remember my excitement and gratification. Yet there was an enormous heritage to assume. And there were corrosive omens and stalemates and misadventures enveloping one's beloved America that required much thought and responsibility. Was I up to the task at hand? I do not think I was afraid, nothing quite that mordant, but as in those moments just before football kickoffs I was for the first time growing a little nervous. The football coaches called it "butterflies".

In an "Easy Chair" column in 1967, Fischer announced the editorial transition.

> These additions and changes will give *Harper's* the best-balanced, and youngest, editorial staff in its 117 years. The new people are joining a group of editors which already is remarkably able and conscientious — at least to my possibly biased eye — and which is supported by a strong and youthful management, under John Cowles, Jr., president of the firm, and Daniel J. Brooks, publisher. I step down from the editorship in good conscience, knowing that the enterprise (in which I have a considerable emotional investment) is in good hands.

Norman Podhoretz, for seven years the editor of *Commentary,* telephoned his good wishes. "They all love you now," he said. "Just wait."

~ Declarations of Independence

5

THE *HARPER'S* CIRCULATION was 276,638, the most recent annual deficit having been about $150,000. My overwhelming priority, however, was to improve the pay for writing, which was notoriously low even for those times. In almost all cases the magazine had not provided expenses of any kind on assignments, and fees for full-length contributions ranged from about $300 to $600. What writer could even begin to make a living on that?

To understand the subsequent few years of *Harper's,* it is necessary to perceive just how modest our whole operation was, in terms both of the size of the editorial staff and of the total budget. The contrast, for instance, with a magazine such as *The New Yorker* with its extensive staff and scores of contract writers, was seismic. There were never more than six editors and our annual editorial budget did not approach $250,000, which was less than what the Cronkites, Brinkleys, and Chancellors of American television earned individually in a year. To offset this, the best writers had to be pursued relentlessly, and that meant constant contact with agents, editors, and of course the writers themselves. As an individual editor I had the conviction that writers would give their best efforts to subjects they personally thought interesting or important. Much of this would be a matter of matching the right writer with the right subject, and of approaching the great writers when they were between books and willing to take magazine assignments that truly fascinated them. I abolished weekly editorial meetings for the sake of what might be called a "crisis mentality," going back to my inherent newspaper background, and there would be more than enough crises to testify to that, but somehow the issues came together. Colleagues, too, were encouraged never to reject a submission on the former grounds that it was "not for us," a restrictive and self-serving judgment tending to easy formula; anything could be "for us," I reasoned, if it were good enough.

In addition to the older editors who remained, we assembled a small staff and an equally modest stable of contributors on retainer who would have done honor, I believe, to any publication. As our lives converged in this mutual undertaking, each of us with his own personality and temperament, we would become a close group, singular as a family.

My choice to succeed Russell Lynes as managing editor was Robert Kotlowitz, the senior among us at forty-two, who had joined the staff some two years before; his monthly column on the performing arts had attracted respectful attention in the worlds of music, ballet, theater, and the cinema. After this time working together, and as Upper West Side neighbors, we knew each other well. There had been many pleasant dinners with him and his wife, Billie, and their young sons. If I were the impetuous one of the tandem, Bob Kotlowitz was the accomplished, gentle professional. He was ten years older than I, and because of that it was awkward for me to approach him about taking the managing editorship, but I respected him enormously. He thought about it for two or three days, and accepted. He was a native of Baltimore, member of a deeply cultured family; his father was cantor in a synagogue. The library in the home of his childhood, he remembered, contained all the classic novels and histories, and biographies of esoteric figures like Napoleon's chief-of-police, Fouché. "My mother, sister, and I had never heard of Fouché," he said. "Who had, in Baltimore? It was a library that mainly spoke with a Central European accent." Music, too, was an essential element of his upbringing. A baby grand arrived at the Kotlowitz household during the Depression long before his parents found the money for a car. For years he studied the piano with a succession of private teachers, "most of them sweet, virginal young women," as he recalled them, "without imagination or dreams." Eventually he enrolled in the Peabody

Conservatory prep school, and graduated from Johns Hopkins. Before Johns Hopkins, as an eighteen-year-old infantryman, he was shipped to France, too late for D-Day, and went into combat in Alsace. "I was scared to death the whole time," he once told me, and subsequently wrote in our pages of how his platoon was ambushed "in one of those wasteful engagements that litter the landscape of war and benefit no one but the enemy." He was one of the few survivors. In a decade of certain "macho" American men, men who exulted in violence and the memory and evocation of violence and the efficacies and possibilities of violence, it was the truly gentle men like Bob who had really known first-hand serious annihilating violence and almost never talked of it.

As with a number of fine editors, Kotlowitz was also a talented writer. In the 1920s, I reminded him, H. L. Mencken, also from Baltimore, wrote in *The Smart Set,* that recklessly knavish New York journal, of his managing editor George Jean Nathan:

> He dislikes women over twenty-one, actors, cold weather, mayonnaise dressing, people who are always happy, hard chairs, invitations to dinner, invitations to serve on committees however worthy the cause, railroad trips, public restaurants, rye whiskey, chicken, daylight, men who do not wear waistcoats, the sight of a woman eating, the sound of a woman singing, small napkins, Maeterlinck, Verhauren, Tagore, Dickens, Bataille, fried oysters, German soubrettes. . . ."

Kotlowitz always admitted to disliking some of these things, especially talking over a telephone and rye whiskey, as well as verbose writers of questionable ability, and dictatorial owners of magazines, but I remember how much he liked good writing, good movies, good concerts, the Upper West Side after the garbage was collected, dry martinis in our other headquarters the Empire Chinese Restaurant, *Hair,* his friend George Ballanchine, Igor Stravinsky, and the piano. I never knew a man who so relished hate mail; I had long since, from the Texas days, formed the habit of leaving the hate letters unread, perhaps on the supposition that the writer might materialize at any moment and shoot you through the head, especially in the Sixties, but Bob Kotlowitz never failed to show me his latest, and to do so with a kind of philosophic pride, so that he began reading mine too, one of the most emphatic ones having come from Kay Kaiser, the old band leader of my boyhood. Kotlowitz advised me to answer hate letters by saying, "Dear Mr. John Smith: A man named John Smith is writing demented messages and using your name. I feel you should be apprised of this." In all such as this, in those contentious and gratifying years, he was a fount of fun and civility and resourcefulness. He knew the business. I once remarked to him after some particular crisis, "As Ashley said to Scarlett, Bob, 'You carry the load for all of us.' " He represented *civilization* to me. "*Harper's* came out of our deepest sensibility," he would recall to me years later, "and we both understood that without wasting words. You know how rare that is. I remember the difficulties in cutting the ties with our predecessors. That severing was absolutely essential. Nothing would have happened without it."

The first four contributing editors, a euphemism for staff writers, were robust and experienced people who knew America, its temper and its rhythms. In background they provided a salubrious reflection of the American regions.

At thirty-three David Halberstam was already an inspiring figure in our journalism. His father was a surgeon, and the family moved from Army post to post across the country, including his favorite, Fort Bliss in El Paso, riding horses and watching polo, the dying days of that vanished kind of empire. Ralph Nader was an elementary school friend in Winsted, Connecticut. Unlike many of the bright young Ivy League writers of the Fifties, Halberstam had deliberately avoided the pull of the cultural capital; when he left the *Harvard Crimson,* where he was managing editor, he went to work as an apprentice on the smallest daily in Mississippi. "I learned as a cub reporter in West Point, Mississippi," he said, "that the lies they tell you in city hall are the same lies you'll be told later on by senators or generals or diplomats." Writing for *The Reporter* magazine in those perilous days on the murder trial of a white man in the Mississippi Delta who had killed a Negro with no provocation, Halberstam placed the white people of Mississippi into two groups:

the good people and the peckerwoods. The good ones, he surmised, would not participate in racial violence but would not take a stand to discourage it. Somebody had hung several dead crows on a barbed-wire fence on an interracial farm as an act of intimidation. In what would become a classic line Halberstam wrote: "It is the peckerwoods who kill Negroes and the good people who acquit the peckerwoods; it is the peckerwoods who hang dead crows from the trees of a small town, and the good people who do not cut them down." Later he joined the *Nashville Tennessean.* "Mississippi is different now," he would remember for me, "it's going through its own amazing revolution, but then it had a special darkness. For a variety of reasons it lacked freedom of speech. As such it was probably the only state in the Union with a genuine set of exiles, young, talented men who could no longer stand it and were driven out, going to New York, Atlanta, or Washington and keeping in touch with the homefolks almost by underground. The contrast between that particularly suffocating atmosphere and Tennessee was startling."

On the *Tennessean* Halberstam claimed to have hit .365 his first year with 127 runs-batted-in, and .382 his second with 155 RBI, and was discovered by the perspicacious *New York Times* scout James "Scotty" Reston and dispatched to the major leagues under the wizened manager long around the league, Turner Catledge. In '62 he received a Newspaper Guild award for his coverage of the troubles in the Congo, where he had to take his copy for cabling on dangerous shuttle flights in small aircraft, was nicked by shrapnel and fired on by Katangese militiamen. His reporting from Vietnam for the *Times* won him the Pulitzer in '64. The generals had not liked him very much over there, nor was he especially beloved by Madame Nhu ("I didn't like her very much either," he said.) The Pentagon secretly tried to monitor his contacts and whereabouts, and even John Kennedy had once attempted to persuade Arthur Ochs Sulzberger to transfer him. He covered the whole developing disaster: the infantry ambushes, the rising strength of the Vietcong, the growing isolation of the Diem regime, the Buddhist crisis. He was one of the earliest and most eloquent critics of our engagement and not long after the American combat commitment in '65 became convinced the war could not be won. Later, as the *Times*'s man in Warsaw, he met and, after considerable aggravations with the Communist bureaucracy who had expelled him for writing "slanderous articles," married the country's leading film actress, Elzbieta Tchizevska, and returned to the States. We hired him, and soon after that John Corry, also from the *Times*. We lured Halberstam because he believed in the possibility of *Harper's*, and as a writer wanted more freedom: freedom in instinct, and in words, length, mood, assignment. One did not take people from the *Times* in those days, and some of its editors, as I recall, did not speak to me for two years.

We got Halberstam for $16,000 a year, which was about $4,000 more than a copy boy made on the *Times*. CBS was interested in making a rather large offer to him at that moment which would have been two or three times higher. What he wanted was professional freedom, he recalled for me years later. "Not only was it a time when everything in American society was being reconsidered and reevaluated, but for those of us like myself who had worked in city rooms for twelve years, and chafed all those years at the form — who, what, why, when, where, and the space limitations [eight hundred words] and the lack of time — everything reported and written in five or six hours, the freedom *Harper's* offered was precious. The real tyranny of journalism has always been the lack of time and lack of space to break away from the pack. And then suddenly we were working for *Harper's* and we had six weeks on a piece! Six thousand words if need be! And emancipation from all those dopey rules which inhibit real reporting. I remember going out and doing a big piece on Dick Daley for our magazine, and working from morning to night, doing three and four major interviews a day, going out at night when I was exhausted, because I knew if I got good stuff it would make the magazine. I had worked hard for the *Times*, but I had *never* worked like this before."

From the beginning Dave Halberstam proved to be more consistently right on the inflamed issue of Vietnam than almost any of our contemporaries; if, as many would subsequently judge, the *Harper's* of that time was the first major established institution in the country to take an adamant stand against the Vietnam quagmire, then he was a principal reason. Months before he came full-time to *Harper's,* while he was still in Vietnam, he filed an important story that was at variance with a background piece the *Times* had on hand on the same subject based on Washington sources. I happened to be that night in the apartment of Homer Bigart, the famous *Times* reporter, previously of the *Herald-Tribune,* who had served a tenure in Vietnam and was now on assignment in New York. When Bigart learned of the conflicting stories he telephoned the *Times* foreign desk. "Go with our man in the field," I heard him say. "And our man is *Halberstam.*" The *Times* ran both stories juxtaposed on page one; the man in the field proved to be right.

Halberstam's profession, he liked to say, was "reporter," and he was happy to be called one; one of the crucial moments in interviews, he always said, was "when to bring out the notebook." David Halberstam was a very tough man, as tough a man as I ever knew on the things he cared about. He was not really a fighter, though he could have been, and would have been hard to deal with physically, like Larry L. King, but *words* were his real weapons. He was a lanky, good-looking young man, an athlete, curly black hair prematurely graying, who knew just about everyone in America, and he had more solitary variegated sources of information on matters then taking place than a good portion of the *Times* national news desk. In one instant he would be jolly and prankish, and in the next almost gravely serious, and in these times he would offer some bit of counsel in his deep, growling voice, reinforced by a colorful yet impeccable idiom. He was a person of intense moral concerns, for truth and morality mattered to him. In moments in which I was impatient or ill-tempered about something that had occurred, he would say: "Save your powder!" meaning in his philosophy of the calling that one should husband one's most efficacious wrath for the times that counted. Had he chosen, he probably could have made a million on the nightly news of the monolith, television, but he was a printed-word man, proud and quirky, zealously independent and intense, brilliant and irrefragable, a maverick. His combative personality coexisted with a charming generosity and kindness. I had never known a man, and never would, with such a blend of belligerence and sweetness, nor one who so loved the possibilities of America.

Often in those early days of our collaboration Halberstam and I left our offices after work and walked the thirty or so blocks up Park or Lexington to his apartment on East Sixty-first. Along the way he was perpetually running into people he knew, and would stand there on the sidewalk in spirited dialogue about mutual acquaintances, or about what was happening in various locales around the country, or in Vietnam, so that the journey always took considerably longer than one would have expected. He would suddenly pause on the midtown pavements with their scents of streetcorner bagels and good perfume and turn to me and say, "I've got an idea," pronounced *idear,* the way the Kennedys managed to say it, and launch into an exposition on such and such an article we needed quickly. "King!" he said. "Martin King. He's a crucial figure. We have to get him." Or: "That young preacher in Chicago — Jesse Jackson. We've got to tell about him." He loved the city: "It's *my* city," he would say, "a very great city, the *international* city." One late afternoon up around Park Avenue and the Fifties he suddenly stopped short, grabbed me by the arm, and motioned sweepingly: "Look at 'em, Morris! Just look." "Look at what?" I asked. "Look at these women. The most beautiful women in the world, right here in this city. And the wonderful way they dress. Even the secretaries could be royalty. What a town this is!"

His and his wife's rambling household swarmed with travelling journalists, a number of whom were fresh back from Vietnam for rest and recreation, ball players, down-on-their-luck editors, and European émigrés, especially Poles, a volatile and hotly endearing cadre which included Roman Polanski and Jerzy Kosinski, who had lived through the big war and the Stalinist occupation and had not long before come out with *The Painted Bird.*

For a man with such a dismal view of civilization, Jerzy Kosinski was a dynamo. He was only a year or so older than I, six feet tall and about 125 pounds, with a great shock of black hair, a gyrating scarecrow, swift, intense, with prominent nose, glittering eye, speech rushed, excited, sardonic. *The Painted Bird* was his autobiographical recollection of a solitary six-year-old boy who in the wartime year of 1939 wanders through Nazi-occupied Eastern Europe like a hunted beast. When I met him he was working on a second novel, *Steps,* set in modern totalitarian Europe. Polish was his native language and English his adopted one, and there were strong shades of Conrad in his writing, prompting Irving Howe to write later in my magazine: "Simply as a stylist, Kosinski has few equals among American novelists born to the language. And I have also become convinced, after reading *Steps,* that he is one of the most gifted new figures to appear in our literature for some years."

At the Halberstams' apartment, Jerzy at the merest suggestion would deliver the opening lecture he gave at Yale to launch his seminar on "Death and the American Imagination," when hundreds of students turned out and he wanted only a few, so he told them the class would study death itself first-hand by visits to morgues and mortuaries. "Regrettably, in order for the experiences to be complete," he said, flourishing his skinny arm, "it will be necessary for one member of the seminar to die. I ended with a very small seminar." He reserved a special, cantankerous venom for the excesses of the Sixties and its faddish youth culture. And he retained a wry affection for his countrymen. Once he got a dinner invitation from an old college professor from Poland, who was on his first trip to America and was temporarily borrowing someone else's apartment in the city. "I arrived at the apartment," Jerzy said at the Halbertstams one night. "My professor was opening cans to make a stew. In Poland when a red heart is on a can, it means good meat. It was really Red Heart Dog Food, but how could I have the rudeness to complain, especially to someone I so vastly admired? I said nothing. And the stew turned out to be pretty damned good. Believe me, *Weelie,* I've had to eat much worse."

Halberstam's wife, Elzbieta, was beautiful and sexy and volatile too, hence it was easy to see why she was known as the Marilyn Monroe of the Warsaw film; she spoke English with a Polish accent uncannily similar to the one Meryl Streep would use as Sophie Biegánski in *Sophie's Choice.* The telephone rang for Halberstam so often that at first I half-suspected he might be running a booking enterprise on the sly. Halberstam's best friend, close as any brother, was Gay Talese, who lived right down the street, one of the best-known practitioners of what came to be known in those years as the "New Journalism," expanding the mold of the nonfiction form; the two of them were constantly engaged in the New York joust and parry, about political personages or writers or members of the Mob they knew, so that someone unaware of their comradeship might in moments have mistaken them for the most mortal of adversaries. These were warm, gay evenings with considerable food and wine, and there was always a ball game of one or another kind on the television, the Knicks or Jets or Yankees, and lightning volleys of discourse and persiflage all round on various American considerations. Halberstam himself had a sensitive temper in debate, which meant he blended in perfectly with Kosinski and the other Poles.

Our second staff writer, Larry L. King, was thirty-eight, a burly, bearded Texan with a hardy and questing eye, the only dropout I ever knew from Texas Technological University, where he was on a football scholarship his freshman year until one of the coaches discovered him drinking beer under the end zone bleachers during a lull in practice. He had grown up poor on a West Texas farm during the Depression, product of a violent, isolated, impoverished heartland of America — a land of jangling country tunes and limitless spaces, of fierce personal politics and racial oppression, of blood-letting fundamentalism and secret poetry. In King's lifetime this West Texas country would superimpose upon itself a savage new wealth that gave the region an oddly disjointed and unpredictable character: the land of his youth was a reluctant civilization, and to escape it was to come a very long way. As a teenager he got in a fistfight with his father and left home to become a migrant worker in the wheatfields of Kansas. He returned to dig postholes in the hard rock earth, and on the night he was to have graduated from high school, missed the school bus and went squirrel-hunting instead. He claimed he was dismissed from his job as a mailman for killing, along his delivery route, two mean dogs and a cat.

I had gotten to know King in Washington three years before, where he was an administrative assistant on the Hill; he once carried suitcases for Lyndon Johnson on the campaign trail and had learned in the backrooms and at the crossroads and statehouses the hard ironies and realities of American politics. He had been writing wonderfully uproarious and poignant pieces for *Harper's,* blends of Mencken and Twain and his fellow Texan, one Brann the Iconoclast, eccentric reforming editor of the nineteenth century who was murdered in a journalistic rivalry. Brann's freewheeling prose touched a whole generation of aspiring writers from the Southwest; in a provincial context this prose may have seemed old-fashioned, but in the hands of an adept writer attuned to contemporary American existence it was a good instrument for expressing something of the nihilistic fragmentations of the age. When I first met King on the Hill his net assets were approximately twenty-five cents (subsequently, by the year 1991, his *The Best Little Whorehouse in Texas* would have earned about $200 million) and, when he entered the "free-lance" arena at his own hazard, enjoyed quoting an item from Malcolm Cowley, which he claimed formed his own most insidious autobiography, that writers "as a class have distinguished themselves as barroom brawlers, drawing-room wolves, breakers of engagements, defaulters of debts, crying drunks, and suicidal maniacs." Later during his years with our magazine, King would have his brush with higher education when awarded a Nieman Fellowship at Harvard, only the second magazine writer to receive that award. Rumors proliferated among his many friends and foes that he would major in astrology and Christian Science. "In the matter of *King versus Harvard,*" one of them said, "I will take King and fifty-two pints." I was with him his first day there when he drove his car into a service station near Harvard Square and asked the attendant, "Which way is the schoolhouse?" As the Nieman Fellows were stiffly posing for their official class photograph on the steps of Widener Library, the passing undergraduates demanded to know who they were. "The New Canaan Chamber of Commerce Committee to Eradicate Potato Bugs!" King shouted. Early in his stay at Harvard, since he had never gotten a college degree, he took me up on a dare to try out for the Harvard football team. He telephoned the athletic department and got an assistant coach on the line, introducing himself as a football player who had just received an academic scholarship.

"Fine, Larry," the coach said. "I just need a little information. Did you play in high school?"

"Yessir. I was all-district in Texas."

"At what position?"

"Tackle."

"Have you ever played in college?"

"I played a little at Texas Tech, but I didn't like the academic climate there."

The coach was quite interested now. "How big are you, Larry?"

"I'm six feet and weigh two hundred and thirty pounds."

"That sounds good. We report for practice Thursday afternoon."

"I'll be there, Coach."

"One more thing," the coach said. "How old are you?"

"Forty-one."

"I beg your pardon?"

"I'm forty-one."

There was a long pause. "Say, what *is* this?" the coach finally asked. That was always an apt question with King.

In his *Harper's* stories it would be the unforgettable and slightly inane incident which often stood out: a Honda ride up Park Avenue with a conservative political icon; a minor-league pro football team pushing a stalled bus up the Gulf Freeway; a flamboyant county judge getting a "three-minute lesson in integrity" from a future President of the United States; a black cabdriver expounding the wonders of America's space program; a fundamentalist's dialogue on education; a jazz musician's demonstrations on how to cure all the diseases known to man. But what King would contribute to our undertaking was more than a feeling for the irrational and unpredictable. Even at his most cutting, his writing would be characterized by a commitment to authentic American values — almost to an older and vanished America whose expressed ideals of democratic justice and humility touched somehow the unsophisticated young men in its provinces and shaped them into maturity. In the mood of that decade, he understood the underdog, the dispossessed, the wayward tramp. He was also a *talker,* and talked very much the way he wrote, spontaneously and inexorably and with no prodding whatever, especially after dips into the corn gourd, and in some of the foulest and most graphic language known to the species. Many was the evening I would see him surrounded by incredulous New Yorkers, struck dumb by his plethora of words and tales, by his baroque and flaming japes, wondering, I was sure, from what aberrant derivations sprang this most unaccountable figure. He relished his frequent forays to New York. "What a town!" he would exclaim. "How many people do you think are doin' it *at this very moment?*" Once in these years, at the first annual writers' conference sponsored by some institution or another in one of the substantial hotels, King and a poet from Dixie sat in a bar praising each other's work. The mutual endorsement proved insufficiently profuse, however, and King and the poet got in a fight, which alternately lapsed and erupted anew at various parties and seminars all weekend, and was so intrusive to the proceedings that the first annual conference was likewise the last. One night at my farmhouse in Putnam County he offered me several drags of some marijuana, as with the ill-fated writers' conference to be my first and last. "How did you like the grass?" he asked me the next morning at breakfast. It did nothing to me whatsoever, I replied. "Then why were you on the roof of the house at midnight," he said, "shouting *Hee-Haw, Sani-Flush?*" Later at *Harper's,* he was regally courted by book publishers. At one time he had been hiding for several weeks from Tom Guinzburg, director of the Viking Press, because he owed him $140,000 for two unwritten books. Guinzburg saw King in Elaine's Restaurant and invited him and his consort, a young Texas woman of candid persuasion named Kathy, to his table for dinner. Everything went fine in this trying situation until the check arrived. As Guinzburg and King argued over it, Kathy said: "What the hell, let him pay! What's another hundred bucks on top of what you owe him now?"

John Corry was a New Yorker, attuned as anyone to its pitfalls, its pleasures, its wise-guy smarts. He was born a Protestant in a lower-middle-class neighborhood of Brooklyn, a place he grew to hate. He escaped it by attending a small Dutch Reformed College, Hope, in Michigan, and in the Army he was, of all the things one would never have thought, a military policeman, probably the most unlikely one in the long and honorable annals of the American militia. He had had a Nieman to Harvard and was then with the *New York Times,* where his abilities, I felt, were not being adequately turned to account. He was a consummate stylist, with a sparse prose that was clean, flexible, and incisive, this accompanied by uncompromising reportorial instincts, which brooked no official deceits. "Although he did not inspire confidence," Gay Talese would write affectionately of him in his book *The Kingdom and the Power* about the *Times,* "he did not discourage it, and . . . he was entirely reliable, solid, possessing keen powers of observation balanced by good judgment — Corry was not the sort who, wishing to call attention to himself, would overdramatize a story or distort it with clever or conspicuous phrases." He was mainly apolitical, his eye always cocked for the irony, the inconsistency, the pomp; his *Harper's* pieces on a spectrum of subjects, people and places, would be honest, and not the least, unpredictable. He was intrigued, he said, by the America of the 1960s, "its fascination with glamour and trivia, its vulgar commercialism, its hypocrisy." Once I showed him a clipping from my hometown paper about a mad rapist attacking elderly ladies in Yazoo City, Mississippi. "Send me down there," he said. "I want to write about somebody who's hit the bottom of the barrel." His endless sources included established figures as well as ambivalent ones, and some others who were immersed in the obscure shadows. One day when he was out of town I heard the telephone in his office and answered it. The caller's fervid whispers and idiom bore a supernatural resemblance to Meyer Wolfsheim's in *The Great Gatsby,* the man who fixed the 1919 World Series. Corry pursued his craft with a theatrical flair, as when, en route as I knew to Cuba, he telephoned one day and said, "Hey, right now I'm in Prague, Czechoslovakia — it's the only way I can get to Havana!" On that assignment he also thought he got married in the airport in Mexico City, although he was not sure.

Corry had a nervous stomach, and suffered over his writing more than any person I had ever worked with, a convulsive and nearly infectious agony. He would roam about our offices trance-like in his laborious throes, muttering often to himself that the task could not be done. Often he would stay up two or three nights in a row, sipping whiskey and smoking cigarettes, taking quick naps on the sofa in my office in the languishing hours. We had a ritual. He would turn in his story on the appointed day of a deadline at the maiden stroke of noon, not a moment sooner or later, walking in tentatively and with the deep stillness and suffering of the mendicant, after which I would read his piece and we would retire to a long and celebrative lunch at the Empire Chinese up the way. He would hand me the manuscript and say, "It's no damned good." He always looked awful. The story would be pristine, however, requiring not so much as the slash of a pencil. On one such day the two of us were walking up Madison Avenue toward the Empire Chinese. I turned to say something, but he was not there. I sighted him at the far corner of Madison and Thirty-fourth, where he was quietly throwing up on the sidewalk.

The fourth of those early staff writers, Marshall Frady, who lived in Atlanta, was twenty-eight years old. He had one of the most pronounced Southern drawls even I had ever heard, and I had heard many; he was darkly handsome, and looked and walked like a Hollywood Indian. In our times together Frady would disappear frequently, for he was by deepest disposition nomadic, but he never failed to come up for the count. His father was a Baptist preacher, and he grew up through transient pastorates in an inauspicious succession of faded little towns, mostly in South Carolina and Georgia. After reading a short item in *Time* about a swashbuckling band of guerrillas in Cuba's Sierra Maestra, he left high school for a year and unsuccessfully tried three times to make his way down there. "That's when I decided," he told me later, "that the next time I wanted to go somewhere dangerous and write about what was going on, I'd have the right *credentials* at least to get *in*." He eventually got a degree from Furman, and had a Woodrow Wilson at the Iowa Writers' Workshop. I had been following his work with *Newsweek* and *The Saturday Evening Post,* which he had joined as a staffwriter, and was familiar with his classic study of George Wallace, a sensitive, funny book nearly Faulknerian in its depiction of Wallace as eerily similar to Flem Snopes, that and an almost breathing articulation into flesh of Willie Stark in *All the King's Men.* His precocious work derived from the violent and paradoxical lineaments of that generation of Southern politics, his prose from its complex inflections. "I wanted to write kind of journalistic novels," he said, "employing all the stagework, style, and large vision of the novelist." When *The Saturday Evening Post,* as he described it, "submerged like the last floundering mastodon in a tar pit," I asked him to come with us. We could not offer him much money and he was hesitant at first, for Frady was perpetually broke back then, but he remembered making his decision on a lyric May afternoon "in a sudden blaze of epiphany on the sidewalk right outside Rich's Department Store in Atlanta: 'What the hell am I hesitating about? *This is Harper's.*' "

He recalled himself as "a right raw and simple young provincial" when he joined *Harper's.* Sometimes he called me "Sire," at others "Boss." In those years of the mod style David Halberstam was all the time trying to give him fashion counsel ("Not a little droll," Frady complained to me in his usual Biblical lilt, "coming from such a source resembling a junior Lincoln in attire tending toward Carnaby Street.") Halberstam told him, "Frady, you look like an FBI agent in those wing-tip shoes, for God's sake."

Frady was a genius of the language — his teacher at the University of Iowa, R. V. Cassill, had advised him, "Frady, you just a writin' fool" — and although he demanded considerable editing at first, mainly the deletion of adjectives and adverbs, which he loved with an equal and impartial passion, I then thought him destined to be one of our great novelists, and his high journalism at its best was an expression of both skilled reportage and lyrical inspiration. He would become banefully lonely on the road, and early on I learned he feared loneliness much more than the omniscient physical danger implicit in some of these assignments, and he would telephone at all hours of the day or night. "Get me outa here!" he once called me from Gary, Indiana. "It smells bad." In those days even sardonic New Yorkers had a sensitive ear for the complexities of the Southern-American experience; editors who later complained during the Jimmy Carter years of having been conned by Southern writers and intellectuals were paying close attention to the Marshall Fradys. Frady himself had a thoughtful perspective on such matters. "I'm still not too sure it's benign," he said, "for a writer to spend any great length of time in the company of New York's estate of assessors, appraisers, traffickers in reactions and responses, because you start, after a while, writing from those secondary vibrations, instead of the primary pulses and voltages that you can't afford to lose. I think maybe writers ought to be scattered out over the land, one here and another one way over there, isolated from each other and more or less lost in the whole life of the country." One night, after we had been out dining with several politicians, including Senators William Fulbright and Fred Harris and the future Senator Bill Bradley, then with the New York Knicks, and Congressmen Paul Sarbanes and Morris Udall, I asked Frady, at the moment working on a story on Congressman Wilbur Mills of Arkansas, how he was getting along with Mills. "Willie, ah luv 'em all when ah'm with 'em," Frady replied in his gelatinous drawl. "It's when ah sit down to the typewriter that ah make mah judgments."

It was with these four staff writers that we started, and they were not an extravagance; they labored for less money than they got for comparable work on other magazines. In a year, for instance, in which he wrote five long articles, one lengthy Washington column, and several book reviews, Larry L. King's salary was $14,000, and that was in the range of the others, likely as much as the television network anchormen spent annually on shirts and ties. Halberstam examined many of the important issues and personalities of the day. He wrote about the experience of having been expelled as a Western correspondent from an Iron Curtain country, the deepening involvement in Vietnam to which he returned for us for three months, and substantial political profiles of McGeorge Bundy and Robert McNamara and other of the Kennedy-Johnson intellectuals: "the architects of Vietnam," he wrote, "which I and many others thought the worst tragedy to befall this country since the Civil War," exploring for the first time the actual decision-making that had led the country into its military commitments in Southeast Asia, subsequently to be part of his *The Best and the Brightest.* He contributed pieces on Martin Luther King, Jr., John Kenneth Galbraith, Eugene McCarthy and the American Left, Claude Kirk of Florida, Albert Gore of Tennessee, Mayor Daley of Chicago, and

Allard Lowenstein. King, Corry, and Frady wrote, too, about the political figures of the day, the sexual mores, the "flower children," the racial politics, the small towns and industrial cities, sports, and ordinary people. They were not sitting in sequestered parlors writing demolishing or detached essays about the nation, but going into real, often dangerous places investigating real people, real events, interpolating their real feelings. They were reporters in the best American lineage who knew their country. "They're heating up the atmosphere just right," Bob Kotlowitz remarked to me. "They're like a washing machine going full blast. It's a new way, and it makes a lot of good noise." Bill Moyers came in one day to discuss some writing. "The *Harper's* offices," he remembered, "were like going into the Coliseum where everyone was a lion and there were no Christians. The atmosphere was carnivorous, creative, and chaotic." Marshall Frady recalled that his periodic flights to the city on magazine business from "Atlanta's outer suburban barrens became like coming in from the remote cold into an ongoing, roistering, Breughelian literary journalistic fair."

"Frady, with all your regard for the Bible, how'd you like to do something on Israel?" I remember asking him in a dingy restaurant on East Thirty-third called the Black Bass. He went to Israel and also to Egypt and did his three-part series on the Middle East. Through the door of an adjoining office he overheard Midge Decter come into mine with her copy of the manuscript and say, "This could be another *Homage to Catalonia.*" "However far short of that it fell," he remembered, "at best those were the excitements, the possibilities shimmering in the air of the place."

Every sound investment, however, had its risks, and the older people on the staff who had been there for years through the staider times, tolerant and courteous though they were, never I think grew accustomed to the sight that often greeted them on arriving at the office in the mornings after the staff writers had been there all night working to make their deadlines: ashtrays overflowing with cigarette butts, empty pint bottles under desks, shreds of pizza crusts, carpets strewn with Styrofoam cups and balled-up copy paper, one or more of the writers themselves barefooted and fast asleep on a sofa or an easy chair, the whole setting pungent with the stale accumulated odor of coffee and cigarettes and whiskey and unwashed socks and nocturnal masculine sweat. In such moments I could see the older women gathered secretly in some neutral office whispering agitatedly among themselves. Many was the time under the last guillotine edge of deadline I would have to sneak up from behind on one or other of the writers in their little pantries of offices and make off with thirty or so pages of draft and lock my office door with them. "What's he doing in there, anyway?" from beyond the door I heard Frady ask Kotlowitz. "Just seeing what you've got," Kotlowitz said. After his retirement Jack Fischer, on returning from abroad, spent time in the office writing a piece and observed these scenes. Halberstam was a couple of days behind deadline on a fifteen-thousand-word piece and was laboring in his cluttered cubbyhole. Jack shook his head at me and smirkingly said, "He hasn't made it on time yet, has he?" God bless them. We were not easy.

There was a reason, I see now, for our hothouse atmosphere, and for the pressures. What some called "the New Journalism," which really reflected in the profession a new freedom for reporters to delve beneath surfaces and write without restrictions what they saw and knew, had been inculcated earlier in the decade most prominently by *Esquire*. But this was mainly a social-cultural voice. Our emphasis at *Harper's* would also be social and cultural, but at the same time far more *political,* hence more heated and controversial, and the challenge and the responsibility were exceedingly daring and risky. As Halberstam observed in a gathering after work one day, "Boys, the price of poker is going up."

He recalled those days:

> The profession of journalism was exploding with new techniques and rules, and the larger society was at fever pitch because of Vietnam. Which meant that all of us in some way or another were wired by events around us. There was an electricity to everything that happened and the passions even more than twenty years later seem greater and more kinetic than at any other time in my life.
>
> It was also in many ways an anti-hierarchical time. That chal-

> lenge to the hierarchy was taking place in all aspects of society — pushed by affluence and technology and very specifically driven by Vietnam where the hierarchy of the country had gone down the wrong path and was losing its credibility. And our magazine with its intelligent, concerned readers was at the center of the events. They were bothered by what was happening to the country.

One of the accomplished women of the city had also joined us and eventually became executive editor. Midge Decter, forty-one, was the wife of Norman Podhoretz, the editor-in-chief of *Commentary*. She had studied at the University of Minnesota and the American Jewish Theological Seminary. "You'd be a fool not to hire her," Podhoretz confided to me in those days of our friendship. "She's a better editor than I am." She grew up in St. Paul, daughter of a sporting goods merchant, and came east at age nineteen. "Although many people are surprised by the fact now," she once wrote, "when I first arrived a yearning young immigrant to New York City, no one had the least difficulty in recognizing me as an immigrant from the deep Middle West." She was the mother of four children and had long become established in the city as a reputable book and magazine editor with broad and serviceable contacts in the Jewish intellectual community, the city and nation. Many was the late afternoon we would meet in some midtown bar and discuss *Harper's* and its possibilities. We offered her the job, and she took it. "Being an unreconstructed amateur sociologist," she would write for us, "which is to say, a twentieth century American given to a certain degree of self-awareness, I find at the least stimulus of the new that my mind is filled with minute questions of power, of hierarchy, of relation, of history." Like Bob Kotlowitz, she was an imperturbable professional, cool under pressure, and an excellent writer. Her *Harper's* pieces would be significantly rooted in the Sixties and addressed to many of its excesses and severities, including "Sex, My Daughters, and Me"; returning to contemporary Minnesota; and "Anti-Americanism in America," in which, although herself a left-of-center intellectual, she would assail many of that number for contemporary fashion-mongering and self-destructive postures.

Our final addition on *Harper's* staff in those days was Herman Gollob, who was thirty-seven years old and came on from Atheneum publishers as editor-in-chief of Harper's Magazine Press, a hard-cover book publishing enterprise which we established in the spirit of mutual projects. He had been a book editor, a literary agent, and a story editor for the movies, and he soon became an essential part of the magazine itself. Harper's Magazine Press was a one-man operation, which befitted Gollob's origins as a graduate of Texas A & M, the stringent military institution on the Brazos amply loathed by Texas Longhorns such as myself and scantly noted for its literary alumni. Of our New York group he was the only consistent commuter, journeying by bus, tube, or train twice a day between Manhattan and Montclair. Several times I went out there with him, Gollob carrying his manuscripts in a Texas Aggie knapsack and reading all the while. He adored his father, Abe Gollob, an aging lawyer in Houston, and one sweet snowy Manhattan Sabbath Mr. Abe, Herman, and our two young sons David and Jared attended on Times Square the large-screen movie *Tora! Tora! Tora!* and all of us emerged cursing that day of infamy.

Herman and I and our two sons once journeyed to West Point to see Army play Texas A & M; Army had the ball on the Aggie nine-yard line directly in front of our seats in the end zone. The crowd was suddenly quiet as Gollob stood and shouted in a voice that could have been heard to the farthest bend of the Hudson: *"Hold 'em, ol' Aggies!"* In all our work together it was the only time he ever embarrassed me. One day Gollob and I were having lunch in the Four Seasons with Bill Moyers, a University of Texas Longhorn and former Baptist preacher, about a writing project. Moyers looked at Gollob's glass and said, "I didn't know Aggies drank wine." Gollob replied, "It was water until you got here, Reverend."

Herman was seldom maladroit, and often adventurous, particularly when we were toiling together on mutual magazine and book enterprises, which excited us both as young men in the city in those days, and how much we saw in the possibilities of the experiment we were launching. One day he came into my office and said, "Let's go have drinks with Orson Welles." Why indeed not? — magazine business once more. Gollob had recently signed Welles to collaborate with the young director Peter Bogdanovich on a book. On the way, between Forty-second and Fiftieth Streets on this oppressively hot day, the subway broke down for a while, and we arrived perspiring at Welles's suite in the Plaza. Orson Welles did not seem to notice. He was lounging in an easy chair drinking champagne with Bogdanovich and talking at considerable length about himself. He was mid-fiftyish and imperially fat, so fat that I did not think the chair in which he was sitting stood much of a chance, and he reminded me in that moment less of Charles Foster Kane in *Citizen Kane* than of the corrupt detective in *Touch of Evil*. It was his voice which enthralled me, the magnificent velvety voice which I had once tried with scant success to mimic in a high school skit. I longed to tell him about the panic he had caused in my town with his "War of the Worlds" when I was four years old, my father later reminding me that I had accompanied him that Halloween night to Buddy Reeves's grocery down the street where the old men were drowning themselves in corn whiskey, one of them saying, "The sons-uv-bitches gonna get us anyhow, so we just as well sit here and get good and drunk" — but could I discern no fortuitous way to interrupt Mr. Welles. He was an ingratiating host, bounteous with the champagne, and he began reading to us from his book of memories of Charlie Chaplin, very evocative and funny, and then of John Barrymore. I absorbed the resounding words of this master, the precocious genius from Kenosha, who gestured with appropriate flourishes as he read. As he did so, the clamor of Manhattan traffic rising from far below, I remembered him as Harry Lime in *The Third Man* when I fell in love with his Austrian girlfriend, Valli, and the precise moment Harry Lime delivered his line, because just then in the Dixie Theater in Yazoo Henjie Henick dropped his box of popcorn and crawled on the floor looking for it: "In Italy for thirty years under the Borgias they had warfare, terror, murder, bloodshed — they produced Michaelangelo, Leonardo Da Vinci and the Renaissance.

In Switzerland they had brotherly love, five hundred years of democracy and peace, and what did that produce . . . ? The cuckoo clock."

When Orson Welles finished reading in the Plaza that day, there was desultory talk, about the deadline on the book, about excerpts in *Harper's*, about the new Hollywood which he deplored, and then about women, for he had been a husband of several wives. I was in the presence of a man who had once been married to Rita Hayworth! "Never trust a woman," I remember his saying, and when Herman Gollob and I finally departed and were descending on the Plaza elevator, one of us said to the other, I cannot now recall which, "*I'd* trust Rita Hayworth."

I have dwelled on these half-dozen or so resourceful souls at *Harper's* because given the sparseness of our editorial number devoted to what was really a national enterprise, and in increasingly strident times, we became a band of allies, with a warmth and camaraderie I have never known professionally before or since. I can close my eyes now and hear the echoes of our laughter. Sometimes late in the day we would gather in my office under the *Joan of Arc* posters for drinks and New York gossip and discuss what needed to be done and the affairs of the nation. Some contributor or other might be with us: William Styron, perhaps, or James Dickey, or Norman Mailer, or Gay Talese, or Sara Davidson, or the sportswriters Dan Jenkins and Bud Shrake and Pete Axthelm, or George Plimpton, or Ralph Ellison, or Joan Didion and John Gregory Dunne, or Ronnie Dugger, or Ed Yoder, or any of a number of our friends and would-be writers who had just drifted in from the provinces. More often than not we would adjourn after dark to our magnetic grotto at Madison and Thirty-fourth, the Empire Chinese. With the exception of Halberstam and Decter we were enthusiastic drinkers. We have it from Mary McCarthy's intellectual memoir of New York in the 1930s that the radicals and bohemians of that time were likewise immersed, in their case in a stunning array of martinis, Singapore slings, double Manhattans, Tom Collins, B and B, and "dago red" wine. Too, in the stunning Sixties drug culture just about every writer I knew then in New

York was a drinker, and so were most of the book and magazine and newspaper editors — "for literary people it went with the territory," Podhoretz remembered — and so especially the Southerners, for there were a great number of these fellow brethren in the city then and they drank like Russians, and were in auspicious positions of some power, and a few of them sharpers and rogues and blackguards on the run, and we seemed to know them one and all. "There's a lot of nourishment in an acre of corn," Faulkner had said, and we assented to that, as we would have, too, to Walker Percy's aesthetic of bourbon "to warm the heart, to reduce the anomie of the late twentieth century, to cut the cold phlegm of Wednesday afternoons. . . . The little explosion of Kentucky U.S.A. sunshine in the cavity of the nasopharynx and the hot bosky bite of Tennessee summertime." But we also drank dry martinis, and brandy, and beer, scotch being deemed appropriate only for college professors, establishmentarians, stockbrokers, headshrinkers, university vice-chancellors, and pests.

Frady, fresh in from California, or Alabama, or Israel, eyes aglitter with sourmash and his latest adventures, wrote and in such moments *sounded* like the Old Testament, not unbefitting a Carolina Baptist pastor's progeny, and he might be talking about those primary pulses and voltages that a writer cannot afford to lose, saying to "beware of New York City." "Aw, Frady, horseshit!" Corry would say. "Why horseshit?" "Because this ain't a barnyard, its the foremost town in the world." There was a sense around us of excitement and of unlimited opportunity, of a piece also with that decade. "We shined with all that energy," Larry L. King would later remember of those times. "Flying into New York from Washington I would be so revved up about seeing my buddies and meeting new people, of drinking and talking, writing, and spinning yarns, I could hardly contain myself. And on the road, being so *in tune* as an observer, wanting to see and feel and capture and record everything about America." In our own way we would be in the eye of the 1960s zeitgeist, and although cliques were a mode of survival in the city of the Sixties, I believe we moved about too much to be an authentic one, for my own theory is that to be cliquish above all else you have to be stationary. The spirit of comradeship included our families as well, and our children, and I became a devotee of *bar mitzvahs*.

Over these months we succeeded in bringing to the magazine, most of them for the first time, a roster that included James Dickey, Jules Feiffer, Irving Howe, C. Vann Woodward, Robert Penn Warren, Justin Kaplan, Sara Davidson, Walker Percy, Frank Conroy, Jack Richardson, Elizabeth Hardwick, Norman Podhoretz, Arthur Miller, J. Anthony Lukas, Louis Simpson, Pauline Kael, George Plimpton, Bud Shrake, Robert Coles, Michael Arlen, Joe McGinniss, Jerzy Kosinski, Otto Friedrich, Alfred Kazin, John Updike, Ralph Ellison, Bernard Malamud, Peter Schrag, Richard Hofstadter, Joe Goulden, Richard Schickel, Isaac Bashevis Singer, Edwin M. Yoder, Jr., Jeremy Larner, Neil Sheehan, Ward Just, Truman Capote, Herbert Gold, Tom Wicker, Gay Talese, Larry McMurtry, Nancy Milford, Jorge Luis Borges, W. H. Auden, Joan Didion, Philip Roth, John Fowles, Igor Stravinsky, Peter De Vries, William Styron, and Irwin Shaw. (We got Shaw, one of the country's highest-paid writers, to cover the Cannes Film Festival for $500. "Aren't you missing a digit?" he asked.)

Bob Kotlowitz, Midge Decter, and I worked hard — I have an honest recollection of our sitting down at some point and making a master roster of whom we really wanted — to make this list of good writers and artists grow: courting agents, cornering writers, martini lunches, letters, phone calls. The telephone was both a weapon and an adversary. Never an admirer of that invention, I used it relentlessly, being so audacious as to telephone writers I had yet to meet at their homes, and more often than not they were friendly and helpful. Editors of book publishing companies such as Robert Loomis and Jason Epstein and Joseph Fox of Random House or Robert Gottlieb of Knopf or Robert Gutwillig of New American Library or Dorothy de Santillana of Houghton-Mifflin or young Andre Schiffrin of Pantheon among the many were unfailingly supportive with ideas and suggestions and books in progress, as if they wished to share in the new adventure. The seasoned in-house editors at Harper & Row, especially Cass Canfield and Evan Thomas, son of Norman Thomas and editor of John Kennedy and Martin Luther King, Jr., were constantly in touch. Once Evan Thomas brought in a fellow who claimed he was going to dive into the depths of the Atlantic to find the *Titanic*. If the man wrote something about it, Thomas wanted to know, would the magazine be interested? Yes, indeed, we replied, if he found what he was looking for. The best of the literary agents were sources of counsel and writing lore. Younger agents just getting their starts in the city with established firms, such as Lynn Nesbit or Candida Donadio, were helpful on how best to approach various writers. Early on I established a close alliance with one of the city's most influential agents, Sterling Lord, a friendship that was to last a lifetime. Lord was an Iowan, a former nationally ranked tennis star and veteran of the magazine trade who represented a wider range of writers in the disparate fields of fiction, politics, sports, commerce, and journalism than any other agent in town. Once one of his writers had a book he had dedicated to Lord translated into Portuguese. The dedication line read, not "to Sterling Lord," but "to Almighty God."

"Have you ever had a party for all your writers?" I once asked him.

"All my clients in one room talking?" he replied. "Oh no, it wouldn't work."

"I'd strike now while you've got everyone's goodwill," Sterling Lord said one day at a midtown lunch. He often spoke in a very low voice, as if he were a fellow conspirator, wary of eavesdroppers. "It's your era of good feeling."

"Will this magazine ever make any money?" I asked.

"I don't know. That's what you have to find out," he said, and proceeded to give me crafty tips, such as the number of the saloon in Queens where Jimmy Breslin conducted his telephone business.

Our collaborator Halberstam with his uncanny network of allies in newspapering and magazines introduced me to many of the most intrepid reporters and commentators in domestic and foreign affairs, including his Vietnam comrades Peter Arnett, Charlie Mohr, and Neil Sheehan. Often were the lunches we had with men or women briefly in town from assignments around the country or the world. One day we were meeting the legendary Tom Wicker of the *New York Times* in the restaurant of the Algonquin. We arrived a little early and took a table in a corner. The place was packed. "Do you think Wicker will be able to find us?" I asked. "He'll find us," Halberstam replied. "Tom Wicker's been in a lot tougher situations than this."

The crowded restaurants of midtown at lunchtime were striking spectacles in themselves, particularly the handful of svelte French and Italian ones in the Forties and Fifties which drew on the affluent "literary" trade. I often arrived at an appointment a little early to sit alone at my table with a martini, and with a magpie's relish absorb the fine ethnic odors of garlic or pasta or vinaigrette and the opulent, roseate aura of luxury and power, as the *grands maîtres,* themselves Manhattan eminences of high order in those heightened milieux, flourishingly escorted their familiar clients to their favorite spots. Three or four tables over might be Edmund Wilson dining with a *New Yorker* editor. Was the substantial lady in hat and furs with her two dapper elderly gentlemen really Pearl Buck? Jacqueline Susann and her bald-headed husband might sweep through the sophisticated chatter of the room with their own palpable mien of large and imminent profit. Everywhere deals were being talked and negotiated between editors and writers, agents and writers, editors and editors, agents and agents in the high metallic broad-daylight tinkle of Manhattan commerce, so wonderfully *soigné* and nefarious. And I suppose they are doing it still.

The first notable declaration involved William Styron, and it was a purposeful one, as much as anything symbolic, a breaking of ground. We passionately wished to re-establish the connection between the magazine and many of the finest imaginative writers of the country for fiction, essays, and even reportage. Styron himself as one of America's two or three foremost novelists was an appropriate choice. Through our friendship I knew he was not far from finishing *The Confessions of Nat Turner.* The Turner insurrection had taken place in southern Virginia in 1831; the book was, as the author said of it, "less an historical novel in conventional terms than a meditation on history." Several nights at his place called "Styron's Acres" in Connecticut, not far from our country farmhouse across the line in New York, Styron had read me portions of the book on Nat Turner's early life and of the white world in which he lived. To me it was an extraordinary, controversial work, an expression of a courageous writer at his prime. The magazine got forty-five thousand words of it, comprising the central portion of the narrative — a long reverie that takes place in Nat Turner's mind as he lingers in jail through the cold autumnal days before his execution — and gave it the cover for September, 1967. I recall the afternoon Styron came to the office at deadline to write a thousand-word introduction to this book-length excerpt. He asked for a yellow legal pad and a #2 pencil and sat down at a coffee table nearby and straightforwardly wrote it without crossing out a single word. This impervious *tour de force* convinced me that Styron was a man to be reckoned with, and we forthwith took him to the Empire Chinese for a little explosion of Kentucky U.S.A. sunshine in the cavity of the nasopharynx. Styron was important, and his willingness to let us have *Nat Turner* was important too for the future of our journal.

When I first met Bill through C. Vann Woodward in New Haven in '65, he was in his early forties. He was central to my *Harper's* days, and it was the beginning of a comradeship that would span many miles, literally and figuratively, on the American landscape. It was a friendship that would last the longest among those of us still living.

Bill was tall, slender, with graying brown hair and a leonine head, impeccable when he wished to be, but as his friend Robert Penn Warren observed, sometimes known to go unshaven. He did a number of pieces for our magazine in those days, including an essay on masturbation which shocked old subscribers, and he often dropped into our office for the chatter, part of the *Harper's* group. As an editor I learned from him that with an exception or two the very best writers, in their rigorous professionalism and thoughtful regard for their words, were the easiest to work with.

Styron was anything but detached from the 1960s scene, even having contributed some words to LBJ's famous civil rights speech of '64, and having the framed original manuscript of that speech, given him by the speechwriter, Richard Goodwin, on a wall of his house, but Styron soon became an impassioned opponent of Johnson's Vietnam policy, to the point of being a delegate from Connecticut, along with his neighbor Arthur Miller, for Eugene McCarthy at the turbulent '68 Chicago Democratic Convention. He later testified in behalf of Abbie Hoffman in the trial of the Chicago Seven. He and I often talked of the events of the Sixties, and how best *Harper's* could deal with them. When Richard Nixon, shortly after he was elected President in '68, announced that he was soliciting nominations for important federal positions in the new administration and the White House widely circulated long and intricate nominating forms, Bill Styron nominated me for the post of Warden of the Women's Federal Reformatory in Alderson, West Virginia, and mailed the form to Washington. It must have taken him the better part of two days to fill out the document, but I never did hear from Nixon about that job.

Bill was a native of the Tidewater section of Virginia, where his father was an engineer in the Newport News shipyards, and I can remember the precise moment and setting in which I began reading his *Lie Down in Darkness* down there in Austin, the opening journey of the hearse through the Tidewater terrain. When I later moved to New York I could literally feel the descriptive passages of the city in the sooty summer heat that the doomed Peyton Loftis knew and felt in that book. As with Norman Mailer, Bernard Malamud, Robert Penn Warren, Walker Percy, Philip Roth, and others, my early young man's reading of his work made me promise myself that if I ever became editor I would purposefully seek him out for the magazine's pages.

Bill Styron had strong connections with Mississippi, which I once got a historian friend down there to research. I did not know until then that he and I had close family associations there. His great-great uncle William Clark of Mississippi, after whom Bill Styron and his father were named, was a comrade and political ally of my great-great uncle Henry Stuart Foote. Running on a Unionist ticket in the canvass of 1851 Foote defeated Jefferson Davis for Governor and William Clark was elected State Treasurer. Did that tandem help postpone the big, terrible war for ten years, I wonder?

Bill's indwelling memory and obsession with our mutual South had a great effect on me as an editor and man in those days and caused me to see how much we had in common. He would write:

> If you were born and reared in the South it is certain you will remain a Southerner as long as you live, no matter how far you've travelled or wherever you've made your home. You may consider yourself alienated from your native soil. You may think your early life in the South a disposable integument, something to be shed like a snake sheds its skin, but you would be mistaken.
>
> Throughout your days you will be seized by memories, memories desperate and sweet enough to make you lose your breath, and they will entwine themselves into an umbilicus firmly linking you once again to the violent, tender, inexplicable land of your beginning.

There were good times in those years at Rose and Bill's place in Roxbury, Connecticut — always music, Baroque or early Romantic, and Kentucky Gentleman, and French vintage wine, and guests from the neighborhood like Alexander Calder and Arthur Miller and Richard Widmark and Philip Roth and Jean Stein and their consorts, and as at Elaine's or George Plimpton's or Jean Stein's in the city one was able to conduct his magazine solicitations there; you never knew whom you would meet next in that domicile, and it was an editor's paradise. Rose Styron, a Baltimore beauty, poet and author of children's stories, was a caring woman, and one of the most steadfast wives of writers I ever knew. In an adjacent house on the premises James Baldwin had sojourned while writing *Another Country*. Bill was laboring then to finish *Nat Turner*, on which with its complex narrative and risky first-person approach he had reached many dead ends. One late night he talked out to me the last long section of that work.

Celia's and my farmhouse was not many miles over in New York state, and our own occasional Saturday night dinners in those years were later described by my colleague Larry L. King, whose words I choose to present because of his neutral yet vivid eye:

> One . . . could monitor, in front of the old stone fireplace and over an astonishing variety of drinks, the yarn-spinning qualities of Robert Penn Warren, Ralph Ellison, William Styron, Tom Wicker, C. Vann Woodward, Marshall Frady, and a half-dozen others. There were black-eyed peas, ham, grits, biscuits, watermelons, and other Dixie delicacies; the longer the night and the more prominent the fumes, the deeper became boondock accents. Late in the evening bogus literary prizes were distributed, the presenters making exaggerated oratorial declamations full of southern rococo and rhythms quoting, likely as not, from Huey Long's "Evangeline Tree" speech, Faulkner, the Old Testament, and the combined works of those assembled. Styron, winning the Bull Connor Award for the best dog story or some other imaginary honor, once was presented with a pair of Boss Walloper work gloves, a tin of Harvest snuff, a Mexican pornography book. . . . On Sunday mornings, as the weekend seeking new fun and old roots came to a close, survivors gulped bloody marys and sang their favorite fundamentalist hymns. The closing number was invariably "Jesus on the Five-Yard Line."

All that was a very long time ago. The old farmhouse has been gone from me these many years, as if it were ours in brief trust only, but I still see it in my memories and dreams, and its woods and hills and hollows, and the crisp, dreamy sweep of autumn in the Hudson Valley, and I hope whoever dwells in it now can hear the vanished voices.

There were also summer visits to the Styron household on Martha's Vineyard. The house was on an inlet of the Atlantic where the big ferries came by and docked from Nantucket and Woods Hole. Once, unobserved by her owners, one of Styron's female black Labs walked onto the ferry and ended up on the mainland twenty miles away, where a friend recognized her and brought her back on the next ferry to the Vineyard. Down a small street from the Styron house in the summers were the dwellings of Lillian Hellman next door, then John Hersey, Philip Roth, and Philip Rahv. I remembered the batting order of the indefatigable 1927 Yankees, and named this street Murderer's Row. Lillian Hellman prepared small pot-luck dinners for us where her talk often was of her years with Dashiell Hammett — always "Dash."

One morning at about ten the phone rang in my office at *Harper's* and it was Bill saying he had just finished, after the seven years of work, *The Confessions of Nat Turner.* He had not been able to sleep and had stayed up all night listening to Mozart and then roused his family at dawn to celebrate. "I don't know whether to be the happiest man in Connecticut or to throw myself in my pond," he said. Come on into town, I suggested, and drop off the manuscript with Bob Loomis at Random House, and meet me in the little bar of the St. Regis at four — we would discuss the *Harper's* excerpt and celebrate too. At four o'clock we did indeed convene in that tiny, well-bred bar which laid claim to having invented the Bloody Mary years before. It was very much a New York scene. Since I was not unfamiliar with the strange, complicated feelings writers have on finally finishing a big book, I sought to divert my companion. There were only six or eight barstools, and at the farthest one sitting alone was an elderly white-haired gentleman in bucolic tweeds. I began a conversation with this elegant figure, who turned out to be English, and had in fact been correspondent for one of the larger London dailies in Germany and France in the 1930s. Did he ever meet Hitler? I asked. "I most certainly did," the stranger said. "I had tea with Hitler." Now even the drowsy-eyed Styron in his inward postpartum reverie was interested. Tea with *Hitler*? "Yes," the gentleman said. "He offered me some cookies. How can you refuse a dictator? They were in fact delicious." And what was he like — what was Hitler really like? "Well, actually," the old man replied, "I found him rather charming."

When *The Confessions of Nat Turner* was eventually published, I went down to the all-night newsstand at Broadway and Ninety-fourth at one A.M. to pick up the early edition of the *New York Times,* as I usually did, and saw that Eliot Fremont-Smith had given it a rave review, admiring it to the extent that he would continue his review in the next day's paper. Since Styron was a nocturnal creature like myself, I telephoned him in Connecticut to inform him of the *Times*'s eloquent treatment. He suggested I read him a little of it. I did so, but after several glowing paragraphs I tossed in a couple of counterfeit sentences. "One of Mr. Styron's faults is that he does not know the meaning of many of the big words he uses."

"What?" came the voice on the other end. "*What* words?"

"His main weakness is that he cannot describe landscape and weather."

"Come off it! Really?"

I do not believe Styron foresaw on that afternoon with the Führer's interviewer that this superlative novel would elicit such inflammatory controversy and backlash among certain whites and blacks, especially black intellectuals. Only James Baldwin among that latter number publicly defended it. Perhaps, given the times, 1967 and beyond, in an American society so fraught with racial bitterness, the reaction was inevitable, a repercussion that might never have occurred only a few years before.

There were family involvements. Bill's own father, Bill Sr., made me remember my own dead father. Bill and I were only sons, with loyal fathers we loved. To my knowledge there has never been such a fruitful and mutually supportive relationship in American letters between a male writer and a father as theirs. The later portrait of Stingo's father in *Sophie's Choice* would be a faithful portrayal of the real-life elder Styron. The senior Bill, who was eighty years old, and I struck up our own friendship. He wrote me many letters over the years about articles *Harper's* should publish, and about his son's upbringing, once even dispatching me a copy of one of his son's baby pictures; and one time he sent the clipping of an angry letter he had written to a Virginia editor who had attacked, as Southern renegades, both his son and me. When he came to New York from Virginia we went out on the town. Late one afternoon he came to my office to fetch me. "You won't believe who my driver is," he said on the elevator down. Rose Styron had retained a limousine for him, and when we got into it as it waited there at Park and Thirty-third the elder Styron introduced me to his coincidental companion. "This fellow is from Beaufort County, North Carolina, my *own* home county! Can you beat that?" The driver was about my own companion's age, thin and wiry, with short-cropped hair and a vintage sunburned nose, and spare as hardtack. I knew from my own inheritance he would have been one of those with Stonewall when he outflanked Hooker at Chancellorsville, the only contradiction now being that he wore a liveried uniform and immaculate white gloves. "Mind if I take off these damned gloves?" he asked. "They make my hands feel like ham hocks," and as we drove north on clamorous Park Avenue the two of them talked of Beaufort County people they had known long-since dead, and crops, and weather. "I'll be damned," Bill Sr. kept saying, and when we finally got to Elaine's, he told the movie girls and the writers and composers of the fellow he had found by happenstance that very day out of all the Manhattan manswarm.

When the younger Bill Styron went to get his father from a nursing home in Goldsboro, North Carolina, to bring him to a similar establishment near Roxbury so he could be close to him, he asked me to accompany him in a small private aircraft. The plane was a Cessna, and the pilot bore a striking, uncanny resemblance to Truman Capote, and as we flew over Manhattan circling south, the lowest I had ever flown over that island, the stunning intimate vistas of skyscrapers and thoroughfares and great arching bridges rose before me like phantom sentinels and caused me to catch my breath at its wonderment — *my* hometown now, *my* workplace, and I looked hard for my office building at the inchoate juncture of Park and Thirty-third. "A lot of mischief's taken place down there," Bill said, and pointed out to me Riker's Island, where he had once been stationed as a Marine, and Hart's Island with the city's lugubrious Potters Field which he had explored in those days and which formed the genesis for the passage set there in *Lie Down in Darkness,* poor Peyton Loftis having been buried there:

> The towers of Manhattan are faint and blue in the distance, rising like minarets or monoliths; near by on summer days yachtsmen sail their boats out of City Island, and the patterns their white sails make on the water are as pretty as kites blown about against a blue March sky. Here in the field weeds and brown, unsightly vegetations grow in thick clusters, tangled together over the numbered concrete markers. There are no proper gravestones in the meadow. Rusted strands of barbed

> wire traverse the field, serving no purpose, preventing no intrusion, for few people ever visit there. It's an ugly place, full of rats and spiders, and crisscrossed, because of its prominence above the water, by raw, shifting winds.

Later that day, when we went into the room of the nursing home to get the elder Styron, the expression on his face when he saw his son and his son's friend come to get him was one of such transparent and unmitigated joy that it has warmed me forever.

From the beginning my friendship with Bill Styron suggested something to me of the importance of mutual trust in the relationship of an editor to a writer. And more than that: the deep dedication of the serious writer's calling, the hazards inherent in it, the long stretches of loneliness, that a writer literally cannot *live* without his words. All this was long before the near-fatal depression into which he fell and his eventual coming back from it, as chronicled in his book *Darkness Visible.* I only perceived brief hints of that encroaching despair then, and could not have predicted the full of it, although I see now it was ineluctably enveloped in the calling.

On the wall of his workroom Styron had a motto from Flaubert: "Be regular and orderly in your life, like a good bourgeois, so that you may be violent and original in your work." Bill was a sufferer, but unless one knew him well, and his emotional connection with his words, and his incredible sense of memory, you would have been hard put to see this beneath the entertaining and easygoing Old Dominion surface. Always he was very sad, and always very much fun, and I learned from that too.

Words! I was lucky to have grown up in an American place obsessed with words, even in ordinary conversation — their rhythms, sounds, nuances, words in the churches, in the baseball bleachers, on the front porches: the older people giving us as children a great gift, which we did not know then, giving us a way to see. In Dennis Potter's classic BBC drama *The Singing Detective* the writer-protagonist finally regains control of his crippled hands. In his hospital bed a writing pen is taped to adhesive on his hands. He painfully begins to write. He says to the nurse:

> For the first time in my life I'm going to have to think about the value of each and every word. Now that's dangerous, isn't it? . . . *Words* . . . Words make me hold my breath. . . . Who knows what you're gonna say? Who knows what they've been. . . . Words, little devils, *words*.

Those long-ago first issues of our magazine included good pieces on a broad range of social and literary and artistic topics by writers of all ages and regions. Larry L. King, for instance, who had travelled the country with Louis Armstrong, drinking bourbon and trading stories till dawn, contributed an affectionate portrait of the Satchmo (later to be reprinted in the program distributed at Armstrong's funeral) concluding:

> We paused at the end of the pier jutting into the Atlantic; Pops lit a cigarette and leaned on a restraining fence to smoke. For long moments he looked up at the full moon, and watched the surf come and go. The glow from his cigarette faintly illuminated the dark old face in repose and I thought of some ancient tribal chieftain musing by his campfire, majestic and mystical. There was only the rush of water, gently roaring and boasting at the shore. "Listen to it, Pops," he said in his low, chesty rumble. "Whole world's turned on. Don't you dig its pretty sounds?"

And John Corry on Francis Cardinal Spellman and New York politics:

> It is almost certain that Cardinal Spellman, along with the system he represents, is an anachronism. And there is something sad about this, because the Cardinal represents an orderly world that no longer exists and because his virtues, the small generosities and random kindnesses for which he is famous, are virtues of the New York Irish. And they, I think, are declining, too.

David Halberstam wrote two prophetic pieces. One was domestic: Martin Luther King, Jr.'s new involvement in the anti-war movement and in the Northern black ghettos:

> In the year 1967, the vital issue of the time was not civil rights, but Vietnam. And in civil rights we were slowly learning some of the terrible truths about the ghettos of the North. Standing on the platform at the UN Plaza, he was not taking on George Wallace, or Bull Connor, or Jim Clark, he was taking on the President of the United States, challenging what is deemed national security, linking by his very presence much of the civil rights movement with the peace movement. Before the war would be ended, before the President and King spoke as one on the American ghettos — if they ever would — his new radicalism might take him very far.

The other was "foreign," but the two enmeshed. Halberstam had spent three months in Vietnam and returned to write a twenty-thousand-word cover story for December. Using evidence gathered on the battlefield, in the villages and the towns, and with great compassion for the land and the people, he told why this war would not be won. He concluded with this paragraph, which I quote in its entirety:

> I do not think we are winning, and the reasons seem to me to be so basic that while I would like to believe my friends that there is a last chance opening up again in Vietnam, it seems to me a frail hope indeed. I do not think we are winning in any true sense, nor do I see any signs we are about to win. That is why this is such a sad story to write, for I share that special affection for the Vietnamese, and I would like to write that though the price is heavy, it is worth it. I do not think our Vietnamese can win their half of the war, nor do I think we can win it for them. I think we will finally end up lowering our sights, encouraging our Vietnamese to talk to their Vietnamese, hoping somehow they can settle what we cannot. That is what this country longs for right now, and *it may well be that even if we stay here another five years, it is all we will end up with anyway.* [italics mine]

In those felicitous days Celia and I liked to give parties in our apartment on the Upper West Side: "big, crowded cocktail parties," Gay Talese recalled them later, "wall to wall with books and writers and cigarette smoke (ah, those days when people could smoke and not offend anyone!)." In early New York days much of the literary cocktail party scene offended and even embarrassed me, and now here I was *giving* them, but the range of participants was diverse and at least reasonably congenial. They might include some of the group who had drifted uptown from the Empire Chinese, and book and magazine editors from around the town, and *Harper's* contributors briefly in the city, and national and foreign reporters brought over by Halberstam, and sports people like Muhammad Ali's trainer Bundini Brown and a player or two from the New York Jets, and over the effusive babble would waft the latest Beatles' record put on the stereo by my son David Rae. Once when I sighted Marshall Frady in a corner taking notes on what someone was saying, I asked if he intended to turn the fellow in. "I'm cloaked in the sanctitude of the First Amendment," he said. And then with the neighborhood group we would walk the one block over to Broadway for garrulous dinners at one of the thrifty little Chinese places. One evening several of the number, including Jules Feiffer, who also dwelled in the vicinity, adjourned to a nearby movie house to see *Gone with the Wind.* In the tense moment when the Federal deserter on his mission of individual pillage sneakily enters the ruined hulk of Tara in the moments before Scarlett shoots him down with a Rebel revolver, Larry L. King shouted in a voice that reverberated throughout the cinema: "There's Jules Feiffer!"

We had recently bought the run-down old farmhouse mentioned earlier, seventy miles north of the city not far from Brewster, with the largest and most beautiful dogwood in the front lawn I had ever seen. Eighteen thousand five hundred dollars! — likely the last authentic bargain in Putnam County, New York; because of the relentless exodus from New York City the county would double in population within the next decade. On one of our first weekends out there, a Saturday evening in the fall of intermittent rain, with makeshift furniture and the house still in great need of work, we had Eleanor Clark and Robert Penn Warren, and the Warrens' weekend guest, Robert Lowell, to dinner. We had drinks around the fireplace inside, and then I went out back to call in our black Labrador, Ichabod H. Crane. I was sitting at a picnic table under a maple waiting for Ichabod to descend the grassy slope from the woods beyond when Lowell came out the kitchen door and sat down with me. That evening was the first time I had met "Cal" Lowell, the most distinguished poet in America in his durable tenure; it also happened to be the week that his picture was on the cover of *Time* magazine. We sat there drinking and talking as we looked out at the June dusk, the Hudson Valley hills and the ancient stone walls and the hickories and maples and apples outlined in the rainy and fading horizon. Suddenly Ichabod H. Crane appeared from nowhere and lay breathlessly at our feet.

"How does it feel to be on the cover of *Time?*" I asked.

Lowell faintly shrugged, then briefly bent down to pet our dog. "It doesn't feel anything, really. It doesn't amount to anything either."

He was fifty years old then, with slightly graying hair, an attractive and easy person, shy and quiet, with slumping shoulders and an awkward boyish sort of quality, this tortured and conscience-stricken and consummate Boston Brahmin genius, with the subtlest trace of a Southern accent which he must have first acquired as a young man when he lived in a tent on Allen Tate's lawn in Sewanee, Tennessee: "his features at once virile and patrician," as Norman Mailer would one day describe him in our pages, "and his characteristic manner turned up facets of the grim, the gallant, the tender, and the solicitous as if he were the nicest Boston banker one had ever hoped to meet." This descendant of the great literary clan, who once said his family admired his great-great uncle James Russell Lowell more for his tenure as Ambassador to the Court of St. James's than for his literature, had not too long before created a national stir by refusing to attend the White House Festival of the Arts to protest Lyndon Johnson's Vietnam policy and in writing a public statement signed by many prominent intellectuals. In his own unsparing verse he was reflecting all the terrible anxieties of that American age.

Pity the planet, all joy gone
from this sweet volcanic cone;
peace to our children when they fall

in small war on the heels of small
war — until the end of time
to police the earth, a ghost
orbiting forever lost
in our monotonous sublime.

He said he had been reading our magazine and that he liked it, and also some of the poems in it. He wanted to know our plans for it.

Emboldened by my perquisites as host, I told him. I may even have paraphrased the scribbled declaration to my colleagues in all its avid lyricism the week we had taken over.

He was silent for the moment. "It's admirable," he finally said, "but forgive me for saying it will never work. You won't be able to have the kind of magazine you really want for this country. You can't sustain it."

Why not? I asked.

"Because your people won't allow it."

"What people?"

"The people who own your magazine. I know a great deal about people like that. Maybe for a while, who knows? I'm sorry to say it, but in the end they'll never allow it. How on earth could they?"

~ The Proprietors

6

JOHN COWLES, JR., was thirty-eight years old and scion of an immense publishing fortune, one of the most extensive in America. His wife Sage, née Fuller, was the stepdaughter of Cass Canfield, Sr., aristocratic New Englander, Groton and Harvard, for many years president and chairman of the board of Harper & Brothers Publishers, later Harper & Row. Less than two years before I assumed the editorship, Cowles Jr., as heir apparent to the Minneapolis Star-Tribune Company, had bought *Harper's Magazine* from the book publishing firm, formed a new corporation, and become the magazine's president. For the first time in its long and eminent history *Harper's* was the property of interests other than the book publishers, whose progenitors had been the venerable and resourceful Harper brothers. Although few perceived it at the time, it was a sharp break, part and parcel of a new kind of America.

This meant that the magazine, in essence, had become one minuscule facet of a Midwest-based empire basically of moneyed absentees extending from the Atlantic to the Pacific; this hegemony was exerted through a labyrinthine network of family interests and finances. Cowles's father, John Cowles, Sr., and his uncle, Gardner "Mike" Cowles, had the monopoly newspapers in Minneapolis and Des Moines, with flourishing publishing interests in Florida, Puerto Rico, Wisconsin, the Dakotas, California, and New York. Uncle Mike also owned *Family Circle* as well as *Look* magazine, the mass circulation weekly, in that day when *Life* and *The Saturday Evening Post* also still existed. Their Midwestern dailies alone, the

Minneapolis *Star* and *Tribune* and the Des Moines *Register*, were doing many millions in business a year, and in both cities they owned all or part of local radio and television stations. After 1941, by which time they were the newspaper monopoly in Minneapolis, they had easily managed to crush every attempt to start opposition papers.

That example had been established much earlier by their patriarch, Gardner Cowles, Sr., a small-town Iowa banker and son of a Methodist elder who had helped organize the Republican Party in Iowa. Gardner Cowles, Sr., had purchased the Des Moines *Register* in 1903 and succeeded over the years in eliminating all other competitors. One of the few adversities of this adamant and God-fearing cornfields entrepreneur must have been the defection of his eldest son, Russell, brother of John Sr. and Gardner, soon disowned, who did not take to the publishing business and chose as a young man to become a painter, declaring years later to a home-state writer that he had sprung from a "dysfunctional" family, a family of rich and thrusting heartland autocrats. "How many paintings did you sell today, Russell?" the father often chided this unilateral offspring in the presence of others of the clan. Under the younger two sons both the Des Moines and Minneapolis papers had worthy qualities; they were internationally minded and enlightened on the race issue, and they ran a blend of the best columnists.

There were pronounced personality differences, as I would later see, between John Cowles, Sr., and Uncle Mike. The former had come up on the business side, Gardner on the editorial. John Sr. was once-married and lived in Minneapolis. Mike had been married four times, and relished the life of the playboy on Park Avenue in New York, where he concocted the mass media pablum of *Look* magazine.

John Cowles, Sr., was once deemed by Richard Rovere the Midwest's principal member of the American Establishment, having been a trustee of the Ford Foundation, overseer of Harvard, and consultant to the National Security Council, not to mention a directorship in the First National Bank of Minneapolis. He was on close terms with many of the commanding middle-aged and elderly WASPS of that national axis — publishers, editors, politicians, corporation executives, bankers, statesmen, the military, the Cold War warriors. In an illuminating article that ran, interestingly, in *Harper's* under John Fischer's editorship in 1963, under the rather typical *Harper's* title "The Midwest's Nice Monopolists," William Barry Furlong characterized John Cowles, Sr., as "a Republican the way that de Gaulle is a Frenchman — by birth, instinct, tradition, and resolve." The Cowles empire consistently endorsed the Republican candidates for President, with the exception of 1920, when for whatever arcane reason it supported neither Harding nor Cox. A loyal employee confessed to the *Harper's* writer that the Cowles papers were "not of the very first rank," with a candor that the employee himself might not have immediately perceived, "but certainly high in the second rank." When John Cowles, Jr., bought into *Harper's* he was the editor of the Minneapolis papers and inheritor presumptive of the family suzerainty.

Jack Fischer had first introduced me to John Jr. in 1965. He was a dark, slim, attractive young man of bland expression and severe demeanor, in tortoiseshell glasses, thin-lipped, with slightly balding, glassy-smooth dark hair like the most astringent periwig. In retrospect he was sometimes not at all dissimilar in comportment to the Emperor Joseph II of the court of old Vienna in the Hollywood movie *Amadeus*. His mirth was infrequent, but he had a good smile, and he moved about at an invigorating patrician pace from one task to another, as if there might have been interior tensions he himself could not, or would not, address. And he could be *serious:* a somber ascetic glint would brush his eye, a cheerless purse of his parsimonious lips, and in such moments he could be gray and spare as an Alabama parson. As his father and uncle had done, he went to Exeter and Harvard. One of his contemporaries subsequently told me of him that as a substitute quarterback for Exeter he was conducting the offense during practice when the coach sounded his whistle. "Cowles!" he shouted. "You're giving away the signals!" Cowles replied: "*Habitually?*" Several of the more sardonic reporters on his papers privately called him, a bit unjustly I thought at first, "John-John," or the more cryptic "Junior," and one of their number advised me he had never really forgiven him for fortuitously coming across a murdered corpse in someone or other's dwelling and telephoning, not the city desk, but the cops. "Yeah," the reporter said. "Newspaperman! He was more concerned about the lines of authority than a good scoop." Jack Fischer had him attend an editorial meeting of the magazine one day to introduce him to the staff and to have him present ideas for articles. He suggested one on the finer points of bridge. When he departed Bob Kotlowitz came into my office a little grim and unnerved. The new publisher reminded him of a rich owner he had had on another magazine who was always making asinine proposals. "We're in for trouble," Kotlowitz said.

"What kind of trouble?" I asked.

"Troubles of a rich and dim-witted nature," he said.

That, of course, was not all, and in the original impulses I am being a little unfair. It was odd, beginning a relationship of importance with a figure one did not know, and an eminently wealthy and powerful one at that, a relationship that would have something to do with language, and literature, and the things one thought mattered to our society. I had had one similar association with a rich person, the owner of the *Texas Observer,* the Eleanor Roosevelt of Texas, Mrs. Frankie Randolph of Houston. I had known her well and truly loved her. "Some rich old women collect antiques," she once said to me. "I want to make my state a better place to live." She rather resembled Ethel Barrymore, Bogart's newspaper owner in *Deadline USA,* but was considerably tougher and more earthy. She was a strong and funny woman of blunt and graphic tongue who drink for drink could outlast a chamberful of young men, and we agreed about most matters, yet even she and I had our fiery disagreements. Only near the end of my tenure there had she invited me to her plantation house in East Texas, for she owned a good part of the county, and a ragged timber town which was the apex of the county, and when I came upon the dusty forlorn facades of that proximity, and the poor whites and poor blacks shambling along the rutted lanes, and the desolate boondocks poverty, I asked myself: has *this* been subsidizing our reforming little journal all along?

When I first got to know John Cowles, Jr., he seemed to enjoy his trips to New York from the heartland to look into the business of his recent acquisition. *Harper's,* after all, had a more star-touched past than the Minneapolis *Star* and *Tribune,* and even, one might venture, than the Des Moines *Register.* Did this have something to do with getting away from Minneapolis, out from under the scrutinizing eye of a strong-willed and workaholic and exceptionally successful father? And delving into the aspects of an enterprise that, though existing under emphatic deficit, was something of his own, something he alone could stand by and help augment and preserve? He relished too, I sensed, meeting well-known writers eccentric or unusual to Midwestern city-rooms, such as the brilliant and candid populist Larry L. King, who remembered in meeting Cowles "a man whose clothes and bearing screamed *rich boy, right schools, right clubs, tennis!* I had always been ill-at-ease in the company of such people; perhaps by way of compensation I would sometimes rudely ask were they getting any or had they ever roughnecked in the oilfields. Willie Morris flashed me one of his don't-you-dare looks, however." Even the wary King was taken with Cowles's talk about how *Harper's* had grown arid and needed new vigor and rejuvenation.

John Jr. could take a few drinks, and those early conversations in the Empire Chinese and the Sign of the Dove and the Century and the Four Seasons were not unrelaxing, and at times even he seemed genuinely enthusiastic about the possibilities of *Harper's.* I was touched one evening by something he said to me, and the memory of it after all that subsequently happened moves me even more in later years, that he had longed to be a writer like Fitzgerald, but then recognizing that this could never happen, aspired to become at least a medium and agent for publishing others who might have such promise. Hence *Harper's.* Often we were joined in these sessions by one of his ranking financial lieutenants from the Minneapolis headquarters, Philip von Blon, a cultured Amherst man, to whom I took an instant trust and liking. In such moments of rapport a histrionic ripple of the brain would seize me: "*Achtung!* Cowles and I are going to change America!" There were the first happy indications. Cowles agreed with me that we had to increase payments for writers. We were to pay William Styron $7,500 for the forty-five-thousand-word excerpt from *The Confessions of Nat Turner*. "Pay him ten thousand," Cowles said. "It will sound better when word gets around in the trade." We exchanged felicitous letters and telephone calls, mutual communications full of hope and assurance. One evening when we were departing the Empire Chinese he abruptly turned on his heels and asked:

"Are you in *Who's Who?*"

"Who's Who?"

"You know, *Who's Who in America.*"

Of course not, I recall saying.

"Well, you should be. We'll see about it." It is aching to ponder now, after all the years. Should I have asked: what does *Who's Who* have to do with running a magazine? I did not do so. I was named to *Who's Who* with such alacrity that even my own Mississippi mother, who thought I should have been in there since junior high school, was duly affected.

With time's clarity, I see now, Cowles was a little unsure of himself in that circumstance: inheritor of power with an empire soon to be thrust upon him. Often in those days I felt an empathy for him, for the pressures that empire must have exerted on him. As the years progressed, should I have been more of a friend? Deferred to him more? Encouraged his confidences? Would it at all have mattered? I doubt it. But whatever happened to his original enthusiasm, to the hopes he seemed to share?

Certain things became disturbing. There was often something wooden about him, stolid and impervious, an absence of emotional feeling, yet with this a curious compulsive quality about ideas and commitments and values. A classmate recalled his nickname at Harvard had been "The Funlover," since his approach to everything was mainly the opposite. And there were other things, innocuous on the surface. Or were they innocuous? I discovered early on, for instance, that John Jr. and his corps of assistants thrived on meetings, meetings on anything for any purpose, and they had the "Cowles Media Gulfstream I" to take them anywhere they wished to meet. In October, 1967, the Red Sox and the Cardinals were in a dramatic World Series. If the Red Sox won the sixth game, the

Series would go to the deciding seventh. My book publishers at Houghton-Mifflin in Boston had two tickets for me to the seventh game, and a room in a Boston hotel. My son David Rae was eight years old; I had promised him that if the Red Sox won Game Six we were on our way to Boston. This excited him. I myself had never witnessed a World Series game; at age eight, down there in darkest Dixie, the chance to have seen not only a Series game, but the *concluding* one, would have been a largesse of the Deity. On the afternoon of the sixth game I brought a portable radio into my office and listened. It was close, but the Red Sox pulled it off. I telephoned David at home; he had been listening too. "Get packed," I said. "We're off from La Guardia tonight."

A few minutes later the telephone rang. It was John Cowles, Jr., from Minneapolis. He had arranged a spur-of-the-moment meeting for the next day at the Century Club. I told him I could not come. I was taking my son to the last game of the Series.

"You have to. It's important."

"As important as the seventh game of a World Series?"

"Yes."

"Are you sure?"

"I'm sure."

I tried to get George Plimpton to take the tickets and escort David to Boston. He was unable to. I tried Jules Feiffer, then Bob Kotlowitz, and I think perhaps even the literary critics Irving Howe and Alfred Kazin. In the end David's mother, Celia, who could not have distinguished a suicide squeeze from the infield fly rule, had to accompany him. As for the meeting in the Century, it was an opaque and somnolent affair, about marketing research, and to this day I cannot quote a single noteworthy consonant uttered there — it was an exercise in simple nothingness. But I remember the seventh game of that Series. My beloved Cardinals won the championship of the world. David remembers something of it too — the hippies on Boston Common the night before the game, the big green left-field wall of Fenway, and Bob Gibson's stately three-hitter.

Shortly after that, John Jr. invited Celia and me to Minneapolis as his guests for a couple of days, the first of numerous trips I would make out there in the line of business. It took one only an instant to determine who called the tunes in *that* town, and knew it. Minneapolis was a white, clean, prosperous town, as white and clean and prosperous as Upper Midwest Protestants can make a town, and dazzling with and dazzled by its burgeoning culture, an affluent culture of theaters and galleries and museums amply garnished and buttressed by a well-satisfied establishment. I always loved it most in the snow, when it was its cleanest and whitest, and there was always something fine about its brisk, towering facades and its immaculate frozen lakes and the great sprawling metropolitan university with its agreeable and expansive mall. In the chilled forenoons of a January it seemed the most of a piece with itself, of a piece too with the fertile and limitless prairieland and the tidy and infinite little Nordic settlements which encompassed it. At a party our first evening there, the buzz of talk among its prominent denizens concerned some racial problem that had arisen in the city, and having long before become accustomed to such talk in the Mississippi Delta, I politely asked a lady what percentage of the population of this city was black, and she with equal civility replied that she would have to ask her husband. She returned to me and reported, "About five percent." There was considerable chatter, too, of the Sixties having sprung full-blown on the West Bank: hippies, free love, pot, lewd and angry placards, deafening guitars, all the appurtenances of narcissism, and, on the Twin Cities, narcissism's extracting revenge.

John Cowles, Jr., and his wife, Sage, lived in a splendid modernistic mansion which Ed Barnes had designed for them out in a gladed and spacious countryside. And it *was* magnificent, with great sweeping rooms and alcoves and patios and fine paintings and tapestries and brick walkways leading to detached guest quarters with superlative vistas of a pristine pond and of the copious wooded terrain beyond. I had not, in truth, been overnight voyager in many grand and tasteful dwellings — perhaps a millionaire's or two in the River Oaks stretches of Houston with all the *nouveau* accoutrements, once even a small domestic castle with a moat in upper Yorkshire in my overseas student days — but this one exuded incomparable wealth and security and comfort and power and an almost dauntless assurance. One could have fit the whole country club of Yazoo City, Mississippi, into it and still have had a great deal left over. The Cowleses were generous hosts. Sage was as lovely and poised as anyone could ever be. There was a faultless and cheerful dinner party with bankers and newspaper executives and businessmen and financiers and John's fellow members of the boards of directors of the Guthrie and the Walker, and the senior United States Senator Walter Mondale, who would later be Vice-President and in '84 a direly unsuccessful candidate for President — a charming and intelligent man though highly deferential to the Cowleses — with brandy in huge Tiffany snifters at the end, and over it all the faint hovering aura of organized containment. I try hard to retrieve what my honest emotions were in the moment: not beholden nor intimidated, I think, but might there have been a swift, stabbing recognition that with sly resilience one could be of this world? Yet at such animating crossroads the Dixie Jeffersonian and the Mississippi hothead always seemed to lurk coevally inside, whispering as my great-grandfather the Whig and Major, vanquished originally by secessionist Southerners and then by rapacious Federals, always had appeared to me as a boy to be whispering from his portrait in my grandparents' parlor in Jackson: "Beware of the rascals." Did I sense on this night, or did the comprehension come later, that it was all too easy for them, that they could really get away with anything, that they were *dabbling*?

John Cowles, Jr.'s wife was four years older than he. She was born in Paris in 1925, where her father was studying architecture at the Sorbonne, and she grew into an upper-class childhood in Westchester County. If her husband were phlegmatic and somber, she was contrastingly warm and effusive, a beautiful woman, graciously gay, presiding over the evening's party and its palatial elegance with a lithe and nimble panache. Soon, as with her Eastern contemporaries, I was affectionately calling her "Sagie," and now and again her talk as I knew her in the days to come would border ever so precipitously on the saucy, the racy, and sometimes even the importune. I liked Sagie. One of her finest hours came for me at a later evening in New York, at a small elegant restaurant dinner after a magazine publishing party for Norman Mailer, when

Mailer's wife of that particular time drunkenly tried to taunt and embarrass Sage in vivid idiom for her well-bred manner, and she held her own. "Who the fuck do you think you are?" the writer's wife said, and talked about her clothes and demeanor and her way of talking with people. "I am who I am, and I don't apologize," Sagie replied, "and who gives a damn anyway?" Her accent and intonations magnetized me; up to then I had never quite heard such a voice in a woman, though there would someday be others like it in my adopted city, and it bewitched and mystified me with its beguiling lilt and parse, and I wanted somehow to *identify* it, to *classify* it in my vast glossary of American tongues, but try as I might I could not do so. A long time after that evening, and those years, in a university town in Mississippi, I was re-reading passages of my favorite Fitzgerald, and these words made me pause.

> Gatsby turned to me rigidly:
> "I can't say anything in his house, old sport."
> "She's got an indiscreet voice," I remarked.
> "It's full of —" I hesitated.
> "Her voice is full of money," he said suddenly.
> That was it. I'd never understood before. It was full of money — that was the inexhaustible charm that rose and fell in it, the jingle of it, the cymbals' song of it. . . . High in a white palace the king's daughter, the golden girl. . . .

I said to myself: That was Sagie all along.

On one of those early trips John Jr. took me to meet his father. John Cowles, Sr., was sixty-nine, and clearly the more serious and sedate of the two elder siblings. In subsequent months I would attend a gala Saturday night party at his younger brother Mike's estate in Westchester: "Call me Mike," he said at the doorway. The celebration was for Nelson Rockefeller and his recent wife, Happy, and the princely assemblage included other Rockefellers and Cowleses and show business and Wall Street and publishing grandees, and there was a mischievous, nearly elfin quality about the natty, ebullient Uncle Mike, as if he were telling the world he could be rich *and* fun-loving and take four wives and run *Look* magazine as a sporting dalliance and still have the Rockefellers *en ensemble* come to call of a Westchester Saturday.

His brother John Sr. in contrast was plain, almost old-shoe. Unlike John Jr. in his manse out in the capacious Aryan threshold of Twin Cities suburbia, John Sr. lived in a well-worn old dwelling in the middle of a settled, sedate Minneapolis neighborhood. There was a fire going in his fireplace that evening, and a stinging wind coming down from the Canadian tundra, and in his parlor a cozy nudge of belonging and ease; I do not remember if there was a big Midwestern dog curled in front of the fire, but there should have been. Unlike his son, John Sr. did not at first glance *look* rich, but any dolt from the outback could have perceived in him, in his strenuous questionings and perseverance for detail, an elemental self-assurance, a legacied mindfulness of wealth and power: that he expected to get his way and was fully accustomed to doing so, that given the cynosures of authority any challenge to him was in the nature of it expected to be the most circumspect and diffident, that he might brook a little mitigating nonsense now and again, but not too much of it, and not at all persistently. It was well known that even the novice reporters would often get from the high eminence of his offices pieces of copy marked in querulous pencil. I should have taken more to mind the observation of a Cowles acquaintance: "John is more likely to get emotional in conservative causes than Mike will in liberal causes." Had the Jeffersonian miscreant a troy ounce then of the Machiavelli, or even of the nimble and dodgeful courtier, he should have discerned in the instant and written in pen-quill on his heart that this gruff, down-to-earth, likeable man had in him strains of the pitiless, his own history having shown it. He also had a languid kind of arrogance all the more royal for its comfortable languor. Despite his son's — the president of *Harper's Magazine's* — private intimations of independence and aspirations of autonomous achievement over strong spirits in the dining rooms of great Manhattan, the youthful editor should have divined, thunderous as any epiphany, *this* was really his man, and always would be, this man who held the privy purse, and that the Yankee poet-aristocrat Lowell that evening in the orange and rainy Hudson Valley dusk had not been far from the truth of the matter. But the hothead was young, full of his own lofty assurance, and not about to court anyone no matter who he was or what and how much he owned, and this was very far removed from the moment when he finally comprehended that the true antagonist in the tale would not be self-righteous WASP Midwestern gluttony itself, but something more, and that was gluttony's aridity.

"Our attention, all our concentration," the gentle and percipient Bob Kotlowitz, our managing editor, would judge in remembrance years later, "was on the heart of the magazine, as it should have been. And our publishers and owners didn't have a clue. The magazine scared the shit out of them, and you can quote me."

But all that was in the future, and there were more vibrant adventures yet to come.

~ The Place

7

I HAD FIRST SEEN New York City when I was twenty-one years old, pausing a few days there before boarding a transatlantic liner to England for school. I remember taking my first subway ride on that maiden visit out to Ebbets Field — *Brooklyn!* — for a game between the Dodgers and the Pittsburgh Pirates. How I loved Ebbets Field! — its cozy, weathered, intimate confines, its haphazard touch of the past. I saw Snider and Furillo that day, and Campanella, and "The Barber," Sal Maglie, and Jackie Robinson, and recalled the words of a fireman in my hometown boyhood, listening with my father and me to a Dodgers game in Firehouse Number 2 in Robinson's rookie season: "You can say what you want to about that nigger, but he's got guts." There were not many people at Ebbets Field that afternoon, and after a decent time I ambled out to the Pirates bullpen, leaning down toward it from a banister in the empty outfield seats to say hello to a boy several years my elder nicknamed Baby from a dusty hamlet in my own home county. A couple of other Pirates relief pitchers were lazily warming up, but the home county boy was relaxing on a bench with his spikes off when he saw me.

"What are *you* doin' here?" he inquired.

"On my way to England," I said.

"How do you like *this* town?" he asked.

"I like it just fine," I replied.

I never lost my awe of the city. One's judgment of a city is nothing, of course, if not a reflection of one's own most inner self — New York remained for me an unambiguous fact of the sensations, and I wanted to experience it all. Perhaps one must be a stranger to it to solicit emotionally, and to be absorbed by, its dazzling and painful images. "The sudden vision of success that the city gives provincials, rustics, outsiders who come to it from afar," Alfred Kazin would write in *Harper's* in 1968, "is a vision that the city usually destroys; but not before it has summoned up, perhaps uniquely in modern industrial civilization, the romantic vision." It was common for me to describe to New Yorkers interminable aspects of the city which struck me as remarkable or titillating, and which they considered merely mundane or gratuitous. Yet my whole existence there was an unceasing progression of first impressions: I came to the city as a stranger, and although I became a New Yorker, I left it finally as a stranger, too.

To me, more than Whitman, or Crane, or Dreiser, or Fitzgerald, or Roth, or Malamud, or Bellow, it was the shade of Thomas Wolfe that was to continue to haunt me in the city, because his florid and torrential portraits had so passionately ensnared me as a boy. Once I actually sat at dinner in a Park Avenue salon next to a blood relative of Aline Bernstein, flesh-and-blood prototype of the fictional Esther Jack in *The Web and the Rock.* I later asked Irwin Shaw, who had known the city his many years, if he had ever met Thomas Wolfe, and Shaw said he ran into him on a corner of Fifth Avenue one day with Maxwell Perkins, who introduced them, and Wolfe was a gangling giant with a head so small it did not seem to go with his body, and he only said one thing to Shaw.

"What did he say?" I asked.

"He said, 'I'm horny, and I'm gonna get laid tonight.' "

True for me, these Wolfean words:

> The peculiar power and property of spring for evoking the whole sense of man's unity with all the elusive and passionate enigmas of life came, Monk felt, from the effect of the color green upon his memory and his sense of time. The first green of the year, and particularly the first green in the city, had a power not only of drawing all the swarming chaos and confusion of the city into one great lyrical harmony of life, it had also such a magical

> power over all his memories that the life that moved and passed around him became an instant part of all the moments of his life. So, too, the past became as real as the present, and he lived in the events of twenty years ago with as much intensity and as great a sense of actuality as if they had just occurred.

Or his divination of the desolation of the city's young, born of violence and the barren stone, as real to me in the 1960s as it was to Wolfe in the 1920s, for one saw them everywhere; many feared them, but I too felt sorry for them:

> . . . those straggling bands of boys of sixteen or eighteen that one can always see at night or on a holiday, going along a street, filling the air with raucous jargon and senseless cries, each trying to outdo the others with joyless catcalls and mirthless quips and jokes which are so feeble, so stupidly inane, that one hears them with strong mixed feelings of pity and of shame? Where here, among these lads, is all the merriment, high spirits, and spontaneous gaiety of youth? These creatures, millions of them, seem to have been born but half made up, without innocence, born old and stale, and dull and empty.

Fortunate perhaps for poor Thomas Wolfe not to have lived in the later drug madness of the city, when he would have conducted his nocturnal prowls at his peril. An easy mark he would have made with the gangling body and undersized head, though it likely would have taken a dozen concerted junkies to bring him down.

"Left-wing, Communist, Jewish, homosexual pornographers," Woody Allen warned Annie Hall of the stereotypical provincial assessment of New Yorkers. For the younger Tom Wolfe, and to others, such as the first astronauts in *The Right Stuff* just arrived for their ticker-tape parade down Broadway, New York was an alien universe populated by an odd breed of "curiously tiny malformed gray people." It was really in its prodigal excess and differentness like "a free port, a stateless city, an international protectorate. Danzig in the Polish corridor, Beirut the crossroads of the Middle East, Trieste, Zurich, Macao, Hong Kong." Unlike Paris, or London, or Madrid, or any of a number of other comparable foreign cultural capitals which were reasonably steadfast reflections of their national societies, New York stood proudly removed from, or more accurately in its own dogged reasoning, *above,* the greater America's will for homogeneity. Someone from elsewhere, Alabama as I recall, with a perspective not unlike that of the astronauts, once interrogated me on certain facets of New York. How do your children trick or treat on Halloween? Do you *have* Halloween? How do people shop for groceries? Do you have turkey at Thanksgiving? Do you *have* Thanksgiving? How long does it take to buy a pair of socks? Do you have to stand in line to buy toothpaste? How do you know exactly where to go on the subways? How do children get to school? How do high school students date? Where do you have high school football games? How do you keep the trees alive? — and this was nothing if not reminiscent for me of Quentin Compson's Harvard roommate's questionings of him in *Absalom, Absalom!:* " 'Tell about the South. What's it like there. What do they do there. Why do they live there. Why do they live at all.' "

I had lived in the city now for more than five years, had shared its ceaseless quests and extravagances, and I had grown to feel that it was in truth both our city state *and* America done large, that far from being an aberration from the national life the city was if anything the crux and apogee of our contemporary existence, because it somehow brought together, however tenuously, the whole range and spectrum, manifestation and extreme, of the American breed and temper. In the Sixties, as in the broader settlements of Scott Fitzgerald's "vast obscurity beyond the city, where the dark fields of the republic rolled on under the night," the disposition of the great city was inordinate and almost breathlessly intoxicating, but it also seemed to be waiting for something.

It was fortunate for all of us that they laid out Manhattan in the grid, following the example of the Christian cross, as the Mormons themselves would later do when plotting Salt Lake City, or Tom Jefferson when he designed Jackson, Mississippi, without having seen it and before anything much was there. It was Jefferson himself, despite his trepidation of big cities as being hazardous to the nascent democracy, who suggested that New York be planned in checkerboards, squares of buildings juxtaposed with squares of open greens. To the British writer Jan Morris, sojourning there as I was in the 1960s, New York City still felt consciously created, unlike the great European capitals "which seem merely to have grown, like old trees of the forests." New York seemed "deliberately unloaded there upon the foreshore, and stalked about, and added to, and restarted, and given calculated infusion of fresh concrete, and started again." An exception was the Village, with its quaint but irrational tangle of streets and byways, turning in and out of themselves, which I would remember forever from the day of John F. Kennedy's funeral as my wife and son and I wandered them: how empty they were, and hushed, and from the interiors of the dwellings the blighted mournful throb of drums from the televisions. Though the hippies were moving in on the Village, to the chagrin of the old settled Italian families and even not a few of the veteran bohemians, yet it was still more quiet and muted and sedate than the rest of the island could ever be.

So yes, New York was easy to get around in, in the way of knowing where you were, but by New York I mean here Manhattan, not the glum forbidding outposts of the mighty city, not the old ragged seed of Brooklyn's Bensonhurst with the thundering elevated trains and garbage gutters, not the borough of Queens — "the most rancid broken-down industrial terrain you have ever seen," Tom Wolfe wrote of it, "a decaying landscape that seemed to belong to another century" — nor Staten Island except when taking a pleasure ride on the ferry, or even the Bronx except to see the Yankees play — though sometimes Hoboken for the clam chowder and oysters and beer at the old saloon over there and conversations with the salts who had known Frank Sinatra's mother and father — for rightly or wrongly these were not really of the New York days, paradox and ancillary as they were to me, unfathomable and vast and indistinguishable and not only in another century but another country as well. I'll take Manhattan.

Sometimes I showed people from down home a little of the town, as with young Bill Clinton of Hot Springs, Arkansas, an affable, baby-faced twenty-one-year-old who turned up at my office the day before he was to embark on a transatlantic liner to England on a Rhodes Scholarship. I had gotten a phone call from Senator Fulbright's office that the young man, who had worked in Fulbright's most recent re-election campaign, had read the book I had written and followed our magazine and wanted to pay his respects. He was intelligent and inquisitive and funny and warm and wanted to go into politics someday, he said, and his hero was John F. Kennedy, whom he had once shaken hands with during a Boys' Nation ceremony in the White House. As we later cruised around midtown in a taxi and I pointed out some of the sights, the conversation was of the great adventure before him, and of Oxford University, what it was really like and what to look for in it as a young American, inevitably turning to the South and including the specific topics of watermelons and boll weevils, and growing up in American places like his birthplace, Hope, and my Yazoo; against the glittering Manhattan backdrop we talked of how poor Arkansas and Mississippi were, and how much he loved and felt for his native ground. We spoke of history books and family, and dogs and cats, and the feel of belonging in this nation. I think we talked about women and love. The youngster had grit. At Elaine's Restaurant it did not take our companions at the table too long to ascertain that Hope was the watermelon capital of Arkansas. "What good is a watermelon, Bill?" one of them asked.

"What good is a *watermelon?*" he replied. "It's good for everything. For one thing it tastes good."

"But isn't it a parasite?"

"A *parasite?* Of course not. It grows on its own. And Arkansas's a poor state. It's good for the economy."

The New York days! I remember the long taxi rides at night, sitting in the back seats as I did as brazen as a glowworm, the rides swift and furious and bumpy like ships riding the hardest waves, the dim facades of the nocturnal diners with shadowy figures out of Hopper, the interminable traffic lights switching in metronomic cadence up the broad avenues as far as the eye could see — going God knows where, only up and down Manhattan. As they sometimes said in the city then: Go know.

It was the cabdrivers themselves, in multifarious authority, who ruled the town. Despite the myth that likened them to the Venetian gondoliers, many of them were among the meanest, sorriest creatures I had ever encountered, meaner than the worst Mississippi misanthrope, yet how could it not be so as they fought and scratched and snarled through the city's teeming entrails? Three or four times when I got one of these, growling on with his racist soliloquies, I would say, just to divert him from his acrimonious spleen, "I think I'm being followed. Can you get away from him?" "Goddamned right!" he would respond, taking it as a mission of honor, and silently rip through the cross streets and avenues and alleyways with the risk and responsibility of a bloodstone warrior. The number of drivers who did not speak English was increasing. One such was a recent arrival from Lebanon. "La Guardia Airport," I said. "Where's that?" he replied. But some of them too were the kindest and most generous of souls, beatific in their good-humored helpfulness, and prominent among these the elderly black men long up from the South. One in particular, named Andrew from Mississippi, usually tried to take his last fare after his nocturnal toils in the mornings around Broadway and the Nineties, and sometimes he would look for me when I was waiting on a corner for a cab, and drive me downtown to work, talking all the while of home.

One snowy night Marshall Frady, James Dickey, and I were riding in a cab with one of the newly adapted bullet-proof partitions between the front and back seats and with an aperture at the bottom so one could talk to the driver and put in the taxi fare. Overhearing our Southern accents and assuming he was among receptive company, the driver, whose name from the identification tag was O'Ryan, launched into a racist diatribe about all "the Spades" swarming up here to New York, the likes of which for vitriol I had never heard even in the Mississippi Delta. When he had finished, Frady leaned to the aperture and said, in his deep-gullied Georgia drawl: "Mr. O'Ryan, if there's anything I can't stand it's an amateur bigot." A block passed in silence. Then Frady told Mr. O'Ryan the South had the best fighting men in the field in history, and only our machines failed us. All the South had was one ball-bearings factory, and it was so low on bullets it had to substitute a few ball-bearings for them. "Twenty-five dead O'Ryans,"

Frady declared. "Then what are you doing here now?" O'Ryan asked. It was Dickey's turn at the aperture. "We came up to buy a ball-bearings factory."

Those were the days of the new glass towers of midtown, blocking off the older vistas, magnets to the thousands who worked enclosed in each of them all the livelong day, and sometimes they seemed to be saying to me, "Leave us alone! You'll never know what we do in here!" in the neighborhoods of which I would have my business lunches with a spectrum of manifold and diverse human people, listening in on the dialogues of commerce at neighboring tables (noons being given over in this city of both ceremonial and acquisitive lunches, as E. B. White reported, to "individual stomach disorders and private gain"), then later emerging into the brassy glare and tumult of the Manhattan afternoon perhaps never again to see the person I had lunched with. There were other kinds of business lunches too, in the executive suites of the skyscrapers with men such as the editor of *Time,* or the Mississippian who was the president of ABC Television, or the presidents of the big philanthropic foundations, lunches in plush private dining rooms with mahogany panelling, waiters in white jackets hovering about with drinks and the day's cuisine on silver platters, rooms alive with the buzz and accoutrements of power. At one such rendezvous with John W. Gardner, president of the Carnegie Foundation, who wished to discuss a magazine piece he was writing, lanky and aristocratic with the eyebrows under a copious forehead that moved up and down as he conversed, he told me he had just been telephoned by President Johnson and was flying to Washington the next morning to meet with him. "Then take to mind the saying we had in Texas, Mr. Gardner," I said. "Ask not what you've done for Lyndon Johnson. Ask what you've done for him *lately.*" My *confrere* must have listened to me, because later in the week Johnson appointed Mr. Gardner to the Cabinet, though he would eventually resign over the injurious effect of Vietnam on domestic problems.

Meanwhile, over around Times Square was the jungle, with junkies like grains of sand in the wind, black beggars, vacant-eyed runaways, placards emblazoned with embittered slogans: *No Vietnamese Ever Called Me a Nigger* — and beaded hippies, and hippies with bongo drums, and hippies in tropical bush jackets carrying duffel bags, hippies in soiled white smocks or flowing multicolored capes or Buddhist robes or Viking masks with horns like antlers, hippies garbed in black wearing gunbelts and chains, hippies in buckskin like Old West gunmen or benign and happy minotaurs, or dressed like Batman or Superman or Wonder Woman or the Lone Ranger or Zorro: murky down-in-the-heels Babylon, a tangle and glut of modern urban humanity so mutinous and heterogenous and unaccountable as to make other sections of midtown nearly Iowa Rotarian in contrast, the first big portable transistor radios playing at highest decibel, the newly arrived pornographic bookstores and pornographic equipment shops and X-rated films.

"What are *you* doing all dressed up in a business suit?" a young lad got up like Batman's Robin accosted me.

"Well, this is what I wear to work, I'm afraid."

"Then I feel sorry for you."

Or another young chap in a flowing green cape: "Can I have fifty cents for a cup of coffee?"

"Fifty cents? Coffee's only a quarter."

"Yes, but won't you join me?"

And then there was Grand Central, the vast cavernous echoing lobby reminding one of the old war movies when lonesome GI's from the outbacks waited under the prodigious clock for their loving young New York girls. And Central Park itself, where in 1967 Mayor Lindsay conducted a mass wedding — an impressive stretch of urban earth where elegant, sartorial figures sat on benches or strolled the sidewalks and pathways and where long blonde women in furs walked their long blonde dogs.

And then, way uptown, Harlem. Ralph Ellison's *Invisible Man* begins in a basement there, this striking allegory of provincial innocence which the city eventually ensnares and destroys, and the scenes of it vibrate with his fiery and glowing images of Harlem, so it must have been fated that my visits there were in the company of Ellison himself, and his friend Albert Murray, a fellow black Southern émigré. The drugs were beginning to descend on 125th

Street then in an incalculable way. Could I have been the last white man of the Sixties to have the pork chops, sweet potatoes, and biscuits in the Red Rooster on Lenox Avenue?

And Battery Park, where in *Moby Dick* the city people came to look out on the sea, when there was a sea to look out on, before it was encroached upon by concrete, where somewhere out there during World War II the German U-Boats roamed unmolested, and what in the world did the scuttle-chinned Nazi submariners gazing through their periscopes make of the blazing and riotous Manhattan skyline? And the Bowery and McSorley's Old Alehouse and the memories of North Carolinian Joseph Mitchell's vivid stories of the city between the wars, the old riverfront hotels and flophouses and the raffish characters such as the bearded lady who noted, "If truth was known, we're all freaks together," and Mitchell's enduring descriptions: "From the streets, there is a panoramic view of the river and the Manhattan skyline. It is a changeable view, and it is often spectacular. Every now and then — at daybreak, at sunset, during storms, on starry summer nights, on hazy Indian-summer afternoons, on blue, clear-cut, stereoscopic winter afternoon — it is astonishing." And the whole incredible finger of the Lower East Side. The crowded sidewalks of Chinatown, so vivid and alive, with their panoply of alien foodstuffs and animated people. And Little Italy, calling there for the great blending olfactory sensations of Mulberry Street, pastry and espresso and garlic and olive oil and baking loaves of bread and spicy sauces, Italians and Chinese in querulous juxtaposition, almond eyes and slanted ones, the old tenement railroad flats with their fire escapes all along that boisterous artery, and high shrill laughter, and the pungent little *trattorias* and restaurants touched with frolic and an odd premonition of vaporous floating violence: Mediterranean kith at a long neighboring table, napkins stuffed in collars, children sipping watered-down Chianti, and likely as not at the next a modest young cadre of the Mob, dark-suited and loud in their exaggerated gestures and their farrago of banter, oddly less menacing in their moment of play than mischievous.

And yet, and yet. . . . The glittering intoxication of the New York days, all their playfulness and gratification and drama, existed in moments for me in emotional counterpoise with other vestigial aspects of it. Some natives say the seeds of the future decline of the giant metropolis were being implanted even then in the Sixties.

Once, on the last day of a sojourn in Shanghai, Paul Theroux tried to decide what it was he did not admire about big cities. It was not just the noise and filth and constant movement and traffic and ill temper, nor the sense of squeezed-in claustrophobia. "It was also the creepy intimation of so many people having come and gone, worked and died; and now other people were living where those had died. My impression of wilderness was associated with innocence, but it was impossible for me to be in a city like this and not feel I was in the presence of ghosts."

In mystical or dispirited moods, New York City to me was a place of ghosts. Even in times of happiness I never outgrew this uncanny sensation. Surely much of this pertained to having come up in a small, settled, isolated town, where death was associated with familiar and accepted landmarks, and with remembered progeny, but there must have been something more for me: the anomie of human beings *en masse* and anonymous, the insignificance of death, the banality of it, where people would not be missed. In such moments the crowded city shimmered for me with death. Often, walking along its swarming sidewalks and stony gray rubble, I would have a spooky vision of the scene before me thirty or forty years hence, the same people in the march of the dead. I would be crossing a large block in midtown and obsessively begin to ponder just how many people who lived or labored in this very vicinity had died in the last twenty years, and what they had left behind, and where the remembrances of them might be, and where on earth they were buried — only fossils for the forensic anthropologists? There were no working cemeteries on Manhattan. Once I had accompanied a friend who wished to put flowers on the grave of his long-dead father on some kind of anniversary; the man was buried in one of those grim behemoth cemeteries in Queens which one always saw coming in on a plane to La Guardia, dozens upon dozens of acres with what appears to be a million tombstones pressed tightly together, and search as he might my friend literally could not find his father! This sense of omniscient and everlasting death also had something to do for me with the jackhammers and drills and demolition and construction where little tangible seemed to last very long, nothing under the sun was permanent, and if buildings could not last, then why should people? Even the rampant graffiti on the temporary construction barriers and the vacant storefronts and the subways seemed to proclaim to me: *I wrote this. I am not dead yet.*

I could count the deaths I saw on the streets, people run down by cars, derelicts expiring in the doorways of stores, ambulances at the entrances of skyscrapers or office buildings bringing out the naturally dead or dying, but even these palpable reminders had little to do with my feeling of the propinquity of mortality in the city, but rather from the daily experience of mingling with the relentless flow of flesh itself, or the premonitions of griefless death, the horrific flood of humanity going eternally from nowhere to nowhere in nearly rank and churlish resolve. Against the glass and concrete ramparts of infinity, these visions were sometimes of such frightening clarity to me that I would never escape them. I had never forgotten the scene which greeted me twice a day, each morning and each afternoon, from the old *Harper's* office directly across Thirty-third Street on the sixth floor of another building, clerks holding their own personal coffee mugs in a long winding line for coffee, waiting there wordlessly, uncomplainingly, like specters at the same precise hour two times a day, and my secret view of them, my voyeur's greedy intrusion of them, never failed to fill me with a nameless horror, this ritual daily queue of death. In such moments I knew it was time to go to the Oak Room of the Plaza and admire the beautiful women in furs.

As with Henry Adams and the London of the 1850s, I sometimes liked the city best when I deplored it.

As early as the 1920s Dorothy Parker claimed that her dog had contracted a social disease from using a New York City public lamppost. "It is impossible to live in New York" was becoming a conversational litany. With all its grandiose magic, was it overreaching itself?

A friend from Michigan who lived in my Upper West Side neighborhood described to me a chilling scene that occurred one afternoon in 1962. His young daughter was waiting on a corner for a bus. For no reason at all some anonymous passing figure shoved her into the street where she narrowly missed being hit by a car. In a 1968 *Harper's,* Alfred Kazin would write of the "intolerable weight of guilt we all bear in the city, how uneasy we are with ourselves."

> For there is so much humanity packed up in these streets, so much friction, so much hatred, that we are haunted by the screams we hear in the night — the screams against which we close our windows, our ears, our minds. Too much we say, it is all too much: why should *we* have to confront all the injustice of our time just because we live in a big city? But the hatred of the anti-Semite for the Jew, of the white man for the Negro, of the *nouveaux riches* for the poor, does pose in the city the fascinating excessiveness of human nature. In a great modern city everything is excessive; human nature seems more irritable, more demanding, more naturally unsatisfiable, more bent on violence. How is the writer to do justice to this extraordinary rage in human beings, to this endless clamor in the human heart especially when the city arouses us with the same forces by which it defeats us?

The black and Hispanic influx to the city was continuing with little interruption. It was a decade in which the white population fell by more than a million while the nonwhite increased by more than sixty percent. Within the city itself there was ceaseless movement. The Brownsville area of Brooklyn, which had once had more Jews than any section except the Lower East Side, was becoming completely black. Here, as in other wretched hells like Bedford-Stuyvesant and Harlem, the mailmen who delivered the welfare checks twice a month were escorted by armed guards. With the mass advent of the Puerto Ricans, the Italians of East Harlem retreated to the Bronx. As early as the 1930s successful blacks in Harlem were migrating to Jersey or Queens or New Rochelle. The exodus of whites to the suburbs, to the insulated constituencies of

Connecticut, New Jersey, Long Island, Westchester and Putnam counties, was at its zenith in the 1960s, and with them the city's tax base dramatically diminished. The city, and especially Manhattan, consisted more and more of small white upper- and middle-class enclaves surrounded by an impoverished and estranged and irreconcilable tide of nonwhites. Substantial stretches of the city had taken on the countenance of embattled war zones. Violent antagonism hovered in the very atmosphere. The wary New York sidewalk look, the subway glaze, were actualities of daily existence. People were beginning to be afraid. The burnings in Harlem of these years, the destruction of the property of *neighbors,* could have had only one explanation, and that was simple rage, if rage itself is ever simple.

Fitzgerald's enchanted Manhattan twilights contrasted with some of the real images of the Sixties, described in *Harper's* by another immigrant in the city, the journalist Bill Moyers, who as chief of staff at the Lyndon Johnson White House had been a principal architect of the Great Society programs, as he boarded a bus in New York to begin a journey of thirteen thousand miles for our magazine.

> The bus cut across the ebbing heart of Manhattan's life, through clogged streets (seven minutes to move one block between Dyer and Tenth Avenue on West 41st), past the rotting buildings and the vacant lots filled with refuse, along Tenth Avenue where children play baseball in the streets, past boarded up stores and junkies on the make; and suddenly, in one of those startling contrasts of New York City, Lincoln Center rising like some Parthenon from a junkyard. A few blocks from its splendor I saw a child, nine or ten years old, who had cut his foot and was washing the wound in the filthy gray water cascading down the gutter.
>
> The city is tolerable if you can leave it occasionally. These people cannot. For them the air is always trapped, the inversion permanent. And as the Greyhound inches through the traffic, the rhetoric of the Sixties — the slogans about quality of life, a livable society, qualitative liberalism — seemed to be choking in its fumes. A language far less grandiloquent was emerging. At St.

> Nicholas and 162nd a store conspicuously boasts: "Police Locks, Door Locks, Window Gates Installed." The sign is painted red, white, and blue.

This yawning contradiction between the old alluring divinations of the city and certain of its dawning realities could not help but engender a stabbing schizophrenia of the emotions for those of us who had come here, and this, I am afraid, would only deepen with time.

On the workaday dimension in the Sixties there was a sharpening feeling of vulnerability among all classes. The middle-class catalogue of muggings, sometimes called "head-knockings," was standard fare. These confrontations were spreading to safe neighborhoods, and occurring in broad daylight. On his subway rides to school if my nine-year-old son was carrying any dollar bills, he put them in his shoe. A *New Yorker* cartoon of the era showed the assailant using a rolled-up Sunday *New York Times* as a billy club. In all my years there, I myself was never once mugged, although many people I knew had been. The closest to it for me happened at Lexington and Forty-ninth where I stood waiting for the light to change. Suddenly a tall, skinny woman emerged from the crowd on the sidewalk and began hitting me on the shoulders and head with her umbrella. "You beast!" she shouted. "You almost let me get hit by that taxicab." "Madame," I wished to say, "I didn't see it either," but the blows continued to descend, and I retreated into the doorway of a Nedick's, watching as my antagonist mercifully disappeared.

One evening David Halberstam, my son David, and I paid our money to watch a closed-circuit television broadcast of an Ali-Frazier fight in the Hunter College auditorium. The electrical power went off halfway through round one. People began to curse and shout, to push and shove, waving their fists in the air, and gathering in concentric clusters searching for who might be culpable, and then chairs started to fly. The crowd calmed down on being told the money would be refunded, more serious mayhem was avoided, and we listened to the last fourteen rounds on the audio.

For years I kept an old Plymouth station wagon in a garage off Broadway and Ninety-sixth. Two or three times each week I would see the young parking attendants, and despite my occasional attempts to make polite conversation, or the tips and the gratuities at Christmas, I cannot recall one single instance of pleasantry, or banter, or courtesy, or even the smallest human salutation — only the hard unseeing eyes, the surliness and disdain, the clipped alien oaths and expletives, the loud grinding of gears and screeching of brakes, and I learned from them what a thousand sociological theses could never have told me: of the glinty fury inside them, the swelling hot wrath and bitterness, pent up in that dark, murky compost of their daily labor.

Incivility varies in proportion to how big the city is, so it was only fitting that the country's most populated city in the Sixties was at times the rudest. Calvin Trillin, the Kansas exile in New York City, perceived correctly that this had to do not merely with the gathering daily tensions of the city, but, of course, with plain anonymity. "In a small town," Trillin surmised, "what you shout at someone who makes a sudden turn in front of you without a signal is limited in nastiness by the realization that you might find yourself sitting beside that person the next day at the Kiwanis lunch or the PTA meeting. If the town is small enough, the chance that you'll never see the offending party again is nonexistent. That puts a sort of governor on your behavior. In New York, the odds are almost the opposite; you are almost certainly not going to see that person again. Knowing that, you might do a lot worse than 'Ya jerky bastard, ya.' "

And the daily grievances *did* intensify, not least during the various strikes. During the sanitation workers' strike of '68, the city was so laden from days of uncollected garbage that even the Upper East Side reeked of a thousand Yazoo civic garbage dumps. The subway strikes made the town an invalid and ensnarled bedlam. On the first morning of one such calamity I collected the four or five of our *Harper's* secretaries who lived on the Upper West Side and headed south toward our office in the Thirties. The journey took more than three hours and, not able to find a space in the parking garages, I deposited the young women and returned home after another two hours of driving, in subsequent days taking a hotel room in the vicinity of the magazine and spending the nights there. The gravediggers struck for six weeks. During that noteworthy predicament the wife of someone I knew died. The family held a funeral service at the Frank E. Campbell mortuary, a chocolate-colored edifice on the Upper East Side well known to affluent New Yorkers and somber as a frozen Hershey's candy bar, but the poor woman was left floating around nude in some decompressed vat with dry ice, or perhaps formaldehyde, in a back vault until the diggers made their peace with a new contract. Before that covenant was reached, scabs were smitten on the head with shovels. In this attenuated setting the fine and uncomplicated ditties of the city inscribed on the hearts of two generations of strangers — *Autumn in New York,* or *Manhattan,* or *Lullaby of Broadway* — assumed a certain impertinence. What could Gershwin, or even Cole Porter, do with a gravediggers' strike?

One windswept autumn afternoon, in my wandering city spirit, the air suddenly chilled and a few lonesome crimson leaves sweeping the pavements, I found myself in the East Fifties, a block or so from the river, when I suddenly spotted Garbo. I *knew* it was Garbo. I had seen her only a week before at the Bleeker Street Cinema in *Grand Hotel.* Two or three others of my acquaintance had sighted her on her lonesome strolls, this magnificent recluse in her exile, why indeed not I? There she was, a solitary presence on First Avenue in a tan trench coat and floppy wide-brimmed hat and carrying a big canvas purse, walking leisurely on the city pavement, wraith-like and imperial and alone. No one was paying the slightest attention to her, but I began to follow her, feeling somewhat like Gene Hackman trailing the Gallic drug czar on many of these same streets in *The French Connection I.* First she stopped at a deli. I glimpsed her inside at the counter as she ordered a sandwich to go, and I watched as she chatted momentarily with the proprietor, then put the wrapped sandwich in her canvas purse. On leaving she strolled farther up the block, pausing at a vegetable stand, where she bought a half dozen tomatoes, then at a tobacconist's, where she came out with a magazine. I secretly observed her as she tarried at First Avenue and Fifty-fourth for the light, tall and lithe with that vague patrician slope of shoulder, and as the light turned green I was tempted to proceed in the impervious wake of her, *gliding* it seemed among the unrecognizing citizens, but something dissuaded me from doing it: a flatulent tug of guilt, perhaps, for spying on her — a supple nip of acknowledgment that fame had not been enough for her, and that she had paid her dues? I gazed affectionately from afar as she disappeared into the avenue throng, one of my city ghosts.

But always, over all of it for me, was the Upper West Side, Saul Bellow's Yoknapatawpha. It was here one day, on Upper Broadway as I was walking home, that a partial eclipse of the sun fell on the North American earth; I had read of its imminence in the papers but had forgotten. Suddenly, with no warning whatever, the edifices of the neighborhood were bathed in an eerie noontime darkness, enigmatic particles seemed to float in the air, and the human creatures scurrying along the pavements faded to lifeless specters in the descending obscurity, looking briefly toward the confusing heavens as the druids must have done at such catastrophic transgressions of the universe, as in dread and supplication: the hippies, the junkies, the old Jews, the whores, the pickpockets, the gabbling hecklers from Columbia with their howling placards, the children, the shopkeepers and bartenders and butchers in their bloodied aprons. Fate itself seemed to hang there in the passing, and forms loomed like apparitions in the quick enveloping gloom. A dog howled on a housewife's leash, and the traffic lights burned like incandescent orbs, and over the whole *ensemble* a crazy lurking vulnerability seemed to seize the city heart, the neighborhood and its phantoms caught in a second's frieze of funny mystery and mortality. Then, as quickly as it had come, the dark began to dissolve again into the metropolitan glare. As the light of day arrived once more on the Upper West Side, a band of Puerto Rican youths began to laugh and prattle, and the old Jewish widows on the benches of the traffic islands laughed too. A cockamamy eclipse! *Eclipse shmeclipse!* It was not really such a big deal, was it?

* * *

In all such as this, it was the city itself that was one's own personal competitor, *mano a mano* in glory and aggrandizement and faithlessness and mishap: you versus the city, the city versus you — the city sometimes ally, sometimes antagonist, but never for a moment neutral.

~ City Lights

8 "I BEGAN TO LIKE NEW YORK," Fitzgerald wrote of it, "the racy, adventurous feel of it at night, and the satisfaction that the constant flicker of men and women and machines gives to the restless eye." To Fitzgerald from St. Paul it was the epitome of the American dream, and he the poet of "the enchanted metropolitan twilight," of the glamour of its money and gratification, of its high romance and adventure.

> Again at eight o'clock, when the dark lanes of the Forties were five deep with throbbing taxicabs bound for the theater district, I felt a sinking in my heart. Forms leaned together in the taxis as they waited, and voices sang, and there was laughter from unheard jokes, and lighted cigarettes outlined unintelligible gestures inside. Imagining that I, too, was hurrying toward gaiety and sharing their intimate excitement, I wished them well.

I too loved the Plaza, the string music in its Palm Court, its Oak Room bar, its wordly throngs who seemed so to know the whole planet and its rapturous mysteries. The Plaza in my day was not New York, merely an exciting landmark anomaly. Yet it was Fitzgerald's romantic evocations of all such as this from the Twenties, before his later disenchantment, that often remained for Americans from elsewhere, the city's sharp and gleaming textures, its hidden promise and expectation.

At night the heart comes out, the Welsh poet destined to expire in this very town affirmed, like a cat on the tiles. I drank too much, ate too much, talked too much, energy incandescent and atilt, skittering across its luminous tiles. In the Twenties Hart Crane wrote of Paris, and except for a detail or two it could have been my Sixties New York: "Dinners, soirees, erratic millionaires, painters, translations, lobsters, absinthe, music, promenades, oysters, sapphic heiresses, editors, books . . . And *how!*"

There were the Christmas parties in the highest floors of one of the magazine weeklies, the holiday lights down on Sixth Avenue shimmering in a winter's veil, the inebriated editors and executives talking festively, or bumping into each other around the opulent hors d'oeuvres, conversing to the accompaniment of the celebrative squeals and laughter of the secretaries and researchers.

"I like your magazine," one would say. "I wish I could get away from here and do something like that."

"Why don't you?"

"I've been here twenty years. I've got all the equity. I'm hooked on the expense accounts. That's why. But we're watching you. We're with you."

There were big parties of other sorts, in the lavish flats of the Dakota perhaps, or the fine buildings along Central Park West, or the solid imposing old townhouses dotting the cross streets of the Upper East Side. More likely than not I would have been invited there by the hostess, perhaps a wealthy reader of *Harper's* who had sent a gracious note, or someone I had met at an earlier literary gathering or one with a proclivity for entertaining up-and-coming young novitiates in the city. *"Hello, dahling, how good of you to come."* Once in a commanding, well-appointed chamber of vivid prisms and dancing sparkles of light I glanced across the room and saw Lauren Bacall, dashingly glamorous in a sequin pants-suit, cigarette holder arched high, laughing and chatting with a theatrical producer in the rich throaty voice I had all but memorized years before in the boyhood shadows of the Dixie Theater. Something deep inside me compelled me to make my way through the milling throng in her direction, perhaps even to be introduced to her! — but before I could get there she was irretrievably gone, gone from me, out the enormous door into the New York night.

And the women at these parties! They were beautiful and sexy in their sleeveless Bloomingdale's sheaths, or their short Saks Fifth Avenue skirts laced on the side, with their perfect coiffures and knowing city faces, their unprim laughter high and boisterous, and culture on their tongues, amid the lilting truant riches only of this city. And on all sides of the outlander, the great wafting scent of New York perfume, mingling as a tint and memory, and like the city itself, subtle and seductive and efficacious.

One such ravishing creature, late thirtyish, balanced a glass of champagne in a perfect hand crowned by long tapering aquiline fingernails, a filtered Benson & Hedges held languidly in the other, soft gray eyes touched with delicate shadow: "You're the young editor, aren't you?"

"Yes, I am" (almost saying "Yes, ma'am").

"Do you know our city very well?"

"I'm certainly trying to."

"Then beware. It may seduce you."

"I hope it does!"

A murmuring laugh, head thrown high, a brush of finger, and then she drifts away, to a fluid little semi-circle of others not unlike her, and soon I see her across the room, gyrating to the Twist.

I had gotten a Truman Capote story, gotten it for $250, and his publisher at Random House, Bennett Cerf, telephoned and said he had an invitation for me, but first he wished to make an introduction on the phone: "Mr. Morris, meet Mr. Capote." The indescribable voice came on in a tiny lisp, "You pay just enough for a case of champagne. You must come for *quiche*" — and then Bennett Cerf again, a dinner at his house, the formal invitation would arrive tomorrow. And in the townhouse parlor a city galaxy, each presented to the other in formal succession, black tie and evening dress: the theater, the dance, publishing, the movies. In a corner Capote converses with a U.S. Senator and his consort, and John Cheever is drinking in sturdy swallows at the side of Albert Erskine, and the elegant Mayor Lindsay gestures in some mild disagreement with Mr. and Mrs. Fredric March, and can that really be Irving Berlin, who once long ago had been Izzy Baline the singing waiter from Cherry Street on the Lower East Side? And poised ever so delicately in an easy chair, frail and demure, sits Claudette Colbert, my boyhood heroine as Army nurse, tortured and defiled by her Japanese captors on my everlasting Dixie Theater screen. "Did they really hurt you, Miss Colbert?" I wished to say. "I wanted to rescue you."

"Helen, this is Mr. Morris. Mr. Morris, may I introduce you to Helen Hayes?" Her family had subscribed to my magazine, she said. She remembered reading it as a child.

Standing alone in a lush little alcove, examining an Impressionist painting on a cream-colored wall, is Leonard Bernstein. Gathering my wits, I walk over and introduce myself, for it is indeed a companionable gathering.

"I've always admired your work," I say. "I saw *West Side Story* four times."

He is an easy, effusive presence, in company with the night: shorter than he seemed from the conductor's podium, craggy of feature and boyish. "Four times? Then I must have done something right."

"I like what you've done for the movies, too. *On the Waterfront.*"

"I can see you're of versatile bent."

"I hope you'll write something for my magazine one of these days."

"*Harper's?* I probably should, you know. I'm in a low mood about politics. I wonder if we're not falling apart."

That was the moment I reached in my pocket and gave him the fountain pen, the one with *"I'm a Yellow Dog Democrat"* inscribed on it.

Such evenings come back now in widening montage, touched by old, dim, fugitive time. Inevitably, it seems, there is a Gershwin tune being played on a baby grand, perhaps by a guest now in a Broadway musical, and the notes rise in light resonance to the gay commingling of city voices.

I'll take Manhattan,
The Bronx and Staten Island too.
It's lovely going to the zoo . . .

"Gershwin played on that piano," someone passing by says to me. "That *very* piano?" I ask. "That very one." In these moments, in those early New York days, recalling a little boy in a little town so far away, I could not fully convince myself I was there. Could *you*?

In Walker Percy's *The Moviegoer* Binx Bolling spots William Holden on a torpid afternoon in the French Quarter in New Orleans. "Holden has turned down Toulouse shedding light as he goes. An aura of heightened reality moves with him and all who fall within it. Now everyone is aware of him. He creates a regular eddy among the tourists and barkeeps and B-girls who come running to the doors of the joints."

In New York this would never be. The city of the Sixties in all its heightened irreverence was too raucous, cunning-wise, and street-smart for that, far too accustomed to the glittering and glamorous, for this was part of everyday life, and for the average New Yorker to show such opiate respects would to them be nothing less than bane and betrayal of their own hard-earned workaday imperviousness. That is what it was: *imperviousness.* Let the tourists from Wisconsin or Tennessee gawk and swoon, but never the real natives, who considered the celebrities themselves the lucky ones to be there and among them. The casual recognitions were expressions of this, the loud insouciance, the most chemical blend of practiced cynicism and good-natured amusement. Once I was in a taxi waiting for a light at Fifth Avenue in midtown. The actor Jack Lemmon was crossing the street in front of us. All through our ride the driver had been morose and silent. Now he erupted. "Hi, Jacko, babe, how ya doin', Jacko! Give 'em hell, Jacko!" he suddenly exclaimed, and Lemon, who had been laboring along in sweet anonymity paused in his tracks, removed his hat, and made a deep exaggerated bow. In another cab one day, mired in the gridlocked traffic on Madison Avenue, I was half-asleep in the backseat when the driver abruptly awakened me. "Donny, sweetheart! Back in town where you belong, aincha, Donny? Sock it to 'em, babe!" I looked out the window at Don Ameche strolling down the sidewalk, stopping now as Lemmon had done, grinning widely and giving the cabbie a brisk military salute. One afternoon I was walking up Third Avenue when a bevy of construction workers began shouting and whistling, a swift jagged little ignition on this mid-Manhattan day. "Katie, baby, there's my Katie!" And another: "Oh, Katie, babe, ain't you swell!" and others joining in the metropolitan chorus, and there coming my way in all her lofty and storied dignity, carrying a shopping bag on her arm, was Katharine Hepburn, who nodded her head, smiled a patrician smile, and said, "Hi, guys." I was witness to the rotund and stately and beak-nosed actor Robert Morley, surely not the most recognizable of stars, halting quickly and swinging about with a sharp air of surprise and chagrin, as a construction foreman on Second Avenue in a hardhat yelled, "Bobby Morley! My wife's favorite Limey! Hang in there, Bob-o!" In bohemian environs such as the Village the salutations would have an added timbre of finesse, such as the day I sighted the actor Ralph Bellamy, who had played Franklin D. Roosevelt in *Sunrise at Campobello,* walking a few feet ahead of me, and a man in a tweed jacket approaching from the opposite direction casually doffed his hat and said, "Good morning, Mr. President."

There was a down-at-the heels hotel just off Park Avenue three blocks or so from the *Harper's* offices with a neon bar-and-lounge sign in front, and I dropped in there late one afternoon and sat at a table and ordered a beer. The place was musty and nearly deserted, and the woman who took my order seemed obliquely familiar. She looked in her fifties, with long blonde graying hair, and lines in her face testifying to hard wear, not unlike the attractive yet wanly worn women one saw waiting tables in diners and truck stops in the small-town South and Southwest. "Haven't I met you somewhere before?" I asked. "I'm sure you have," she replied, in a curious throaty voice that evoked something in my past, and then walked away to other customers. I had an image of an alluring beauty with her hair always obscuring one of her eyes, the way she tossed her hair every now and again, and suddenly I divined who she was. Veronica Lake! I was tempted in that moment to tell her I had seen her for the first time when I was eight years old in *This Gun for Hire* with Alan Ladd, but something gave me pause, something so forlorn and sad in her, a countenance of suffering and decline. *The Blue Dahlia. The Sainted Sisters.* Later I would see the aging Ingrid Bergman in Elaine's and was overcome then too with transience and loss in this city of cities, for the celestial stars flamed, and then burned out, and who would believe it? I came in two or three more times just to look at Miss Lake in her rounds, and to summon something fragile and indefinable in my own childhood. A little while after that one of the tabloids ran a piece about her as the barmaid there, about her meteoric Hollywood career, her many marriages, her boyfriends such as Howard Hughes and Aristotle Onassis, her fall into alcoholism. It was merely another New York conundrum, these careless encounters, for they do not happen quite this way in other American places, as with the late night I was having coffee at the counter of the downstairs quick-order restaurant of the Waldorf, and Broderick Crawford swept in and sat down at the adjoining stool. He was quite drunk and turned to me and said, "How're you, friend?" "Just fine, Governor Stark," I replied, and we had a jovial little chat about Huey Long and the novel *All the King's Men,* which he said he liked and also appreciated, since it eventually led him to his Oscar.

There were certain things New Yorkers did not do, but that visitors often did. I was having dinner in a small Mexican restaurant on Second Avenue with two companions from Texas times, one of them a gregarious and convivial state senator. Two or three tables across the room, dining with companions, was Anthony Quinn. "Good God!" the senator exclaimed, "look who *that is!*" He stared at Anthony Quinn a long time, then said, "I'm gonna go talk to him." I tried to dissuade him, explaining that people in this town were faithful to a policy of leaving the stars alone when they were having their dinners. My Fort Worth friend, ignoring this counsel, rose and bounded vivaciously to the other table where I heard him introducing himself. "I'm a great fan of yours," he said. Quinn stood and shook hands and they talked for a while. The next thing I knew my Texas companion was not only sitting at the actor's table, he was eating a plate of tamales with him, their heads close together in weighty talk. In a few minutes he returned. "Wait till I tell 'em back home," he said. "Just you wait."

* * *

It is the most candid of acknowledgments, shared by almost all my contemporaries from similar backgrounds no matter how successful they became in the city, to confess that, having grown up in a small, isolated American town in the pre-television age (and the Hollywood heyday), I never once grew accustomed to being around the movie stars. The main reason for this was memory itself: the memory after all the years of being a lonely little boy in the darkened air-cooled movie theater of home with its gritty floor and popcorn smells on a hot afternoon and seeing on the screen before me the magic images of those people from the exotic faraway world, especially New York City: how they smiled and talked and danced and kissed and sipped their drinks, the things they said and did, the clothes they wore, how they hailed down taxicabs, the way the men always ordered for the beautiful women in the fancy restaurants, how long it took to dial a call on a New York telephone (our own telephone central being oral and in the three digits), all of this fired by them in my imagination and fantasy by those vital beings who seemed to hold the keys to some of life's unexperienced mysteries — and then, when it was over, suddenly back again on the broiling little main street of summer's reality.

It was a long way from the Dixie Theater to Manhattan, yet after a time there, with all the casual and fortuitous accesses of the world I inhabited, it was not unusual to be seated at dinner or on the sofa at a party in conversation with someone like Deborah Kerr who would chat about the filming of *From Here to Eternity,* or Jane Russell talking about *The Outlaw,* or Lena Horne recalling growing up in Georgia, or Richard Widmark who could discuss baseball and his son-in-law Sandy Koufax, or Alexis Smith to whom I quoted the precise line she had spoken to a leading man on the Dixie Theater screen, which had sent me into the bright roil of the afternoon with the pulsing mystery and promise of the world: "We have our whole life before us." On the evening of a shining event at the Waldorf, given by one of the national book clubs, I was introduced by Irwin Shaw to Evelyn Keyes, the Atlanta girl who had played Scarlett O'Hara's younger sister years before, and as we conversed about city topics I told her of the day my mother and grandmother had literally pushed me alone into the Dixie at age ten against my will to see that movie, and that when I came out four hours later something in my life had somehow changed, having I think to do with history and its sweep, and I asked my grandmother how many times she had seen it and she said sixteen, the sixteenth just to look at the furniture. Once, at a dinner the very night after I had seen *Pride of the Yankees* on late television, I was seated next to Teresa Wright, a shy and lovely creature, and we talked about Lou Gehrig and what the Triple Crown was in baseball.

"I'm sorry you had to die in *Mrs. Miniver,*" I said.

"But I had to, you see. Wasn't it a fine plot?"

How they affected me, my celluloid images: Shirley MacLaine, a pixie-like figure in our circles on scattered nights in the city of the Sixties, an activist on civil rights and Vietnam (all this long before her subsequent reincarnations), and Lauren Bacall, her tawny cat's eyes, her smile knowing and spontaneous and curled a little at the corners of the lips — Betty, we all called her. I could never quite believe I was with Bacall, the Bacall who taunted Bogart in *The Big Sleep* and cast loathsome glances at Edward G. Robinson in *Key Largo* in that dark lingering sorcery of the tenacious Dixie.

My young *Harper's* colleague Marshall Frady had a long-standing urge to do a piece for *Harper's* on the aging, Viennese-born (Hedwig Eva Maria Kiesler) pop-goddess Hedy Lamarr, a darkly ravishing Hollywood beauty in her day, so much so that she had actually been the first choice to play Ilsa in *Casablanca,* but MGM would not release her, the role going instead to Ingrid Bergman. Frady had been bewitched by Hedy Lamarr since he saw her in *Samson and Delilah* when he was nine years old in Georgia, a bewitchment, he confessed to me, which had propelled him over the years into a number of romantic misadventures in pursuit of her memory, including possibly even one marriage. Frady had recently seen her on the Dick Cavett television show not long after she had been detained in some shopping mall for appropriating various items from a counter. Because of Frady's obsessive, nearly stricken fascination with her that had endured through time, I encouraged him to do the piece, but warned him he might have trouble enlisting her cooperation because of a recent review by our Larry L. King in *The New Republic* of her putative memoir, *Ecstasy and Me,* in which he had written, "If there is a sexual experience Miss Lamarr has not partaken of, it belongs to the future tense." Frady persisted. She was living in the Blackstone Hotel in New York and when he telephoned her, she was wary, but agreed to discuss the matter at dinner. Frady asked me to go along. Why not? I replied. Wasn't it magazine business? "Ah, hah, Boss!" Frady said. "I figured! Can't resist dining with Delilah too." The spot she chose was not the Four Seasons or Lutèce or even Elaine's but a somber and modest eatery near the Blackstone. Moreover, she arrived in the protective company of one of Dick Cavett's associates, a long, weedy fellow who informed us he had come along to represent Miss Lamarr at her request.

We sat there at the table across from Hedy Lamarr. The cling of boyhood recall is incredible — I actually remembered she had two "r's" in her name, remembered her vividly too, not so much in *Samson and Delilah* but in *Algiers,* in which Charles Boyer had said to her, "Come with me to the Casbah." She was in her late fifties and obviously had undergone a succession of face-lifts, and her hands were mottled and wrinkled, yet her famous features with her enigmatic gray eyes still had a ghost and more of her sorceress's mocking sexuality. I felt a strong emotion for her in that moment, and so of course did the unflagging Frady. It was plain from the start that she did not trust the whole affair. She wanted to know how much money we had in mind. She also told us that her book of reminiscences had been totally invented by her ghost-writer. "He made *up* all doze zings. I am suing him, yez." Suddenly, apropos of absolutely nothing, she said to Frady, "You have very nize teeth, if you would only" — and leaned toward him across the table and delicately tapped the nail of her forefinger on his two front teeth — "if you would only get doze straightened a little." Though it was some years after this small bauble of guidance, Frady did so.

The evening ended inconclusively, and we all rose and went to the cash register. As I was taking care of the check, Frady and I exchanged a startled glance. Hedy Lamarr was methodically yet hurriedly scrabbling mints and candies and gum and lighters and other incidentals from the counter into her purse and pockets. The man behind the register was observing this transaction with a certain growing apprehension until I asked him to add the items to the bill. Miss Lamarr herself said nothing about this and we left her on the sidewalk outside, as she clicked away on her stiletto heels back to the Blackstone. Several days later Frady heard from Cavett's man, "She doesn't feel she can do it unless there can be some sort of remuneration, you understand." Many years later Marshall Frady remembered the evening: "There's some sort of tragedy of beauty in all this, you know — a woman who was once like Ishtar among the mortals, left now with only some bottomless furious avidity for whatever trivial trinkets of tribute she can scavenge from the world and that city in which, once a goddess, she's long been a forgotten discard."

New York City had so many rich people, the Midwestern immigrant Calvin Trillin concluded, that other people were sending it the rich ones they wanted to get rid of. ("Listen, if Frank down at the bank doesn't quit talking about how much his Jaguar costs, we're just going to have to put him in the next shipment to New York City.") The chic parties of the Upper Park Avenue *bourgeoisie* or the rich old Anglo-Saxon widows of the day were notable for importing pale young aesthetes and pederast poets and inflammable young logicians of the Marcuse school from the Village or the colleges or elsewhere. These were sometimes pretheater dinners, before the guests were to be bussed *en masse* to some fashionable Broadway play. At these Park Avenue evenings there would be Ben Shawn drawings on the walls and Andy Warhol paintings and, more often than not Bob Dylan or the Beatles on a secret stereo. I was once introduced to a pop-art painter who had just completed a canvas, I had been told by the hostess, by haltingly driving a car up and down it two or three dozen times and calling it "Nocturnal Brakes." I was standing next to him, a solemn young man in a nondescript suit and tie with long hair dangling in a ponytail held intact by several rubber bands, and I could not think of a single word to say.

"Congratulations on finishing your work," I finally said.

He looked at me so intently that I feared I had committed some *faux pas* so egregious that only the most faithless philistinism could have accounted for it. "I hate these parties!" he hissed at me in a hard little whisper. "I hate these parties!" he repeated.

"Then why do you come?" I found myself whispering too.

"Public relations," he said.

I stood in a corner as I often did, absorbing the strains of Sergeant Pepper's Lonely Hearts Club band, my young son's favorite album, and diligently observed Andy Warhol, pale and small like a blue-eyed boy fearful of any undue scrutiny, standing in a remote corner observing *us*. Then I absorbed a quick punitive exchange between a pair of Marcuseans.

"Lyndon Johnson should be impeached."

"Better drawn and quartered, don't you think?"

"He's a cracker liar! He killed Kennedy — now he's killing a whole generation."

A Black Panther or two might be there, with Field Marshall ranking. "This is the first time I ever met a Panther!" a young lady was overheard to say. Such were the radical chic evenings.

William James spoke of New York City's "permanent earthquake condition." The "intellectual" life of the city of my day was sometimes nervous, raw, edgy, competitive, internecine, exhausting, once more a reflection of the era, and the parties where much of the intelligentsia gathered were often that way too. I was at first thoroughly intimidated by the aloofness and even rudeness to the newcomer. At the intense parties of "the Old Left," more often than not in roomy apartments on the Upper West Side, the spirit of the Thirties was evident still: the Moscow trials, the Stalinist liquidations, the Spanish Civil War, the Popular Front, the Trotsky-Stalin split, the lingering antagonisms of that far time. Had Lillian Hellman *really* tried to stage a walkout at Kenneth Fearing's funeral? Book reviews, too, offered a mode of personal retribution. I once overheard: "I waited fifteen years to get him back."

The adjective Henry Adams used to describe certain aspects of London society in the 1860s was *crazy*, an applicable word for portions of New York society a century later. One facet of this was the flirtation of some of the romantic intellectual Left with the fashionable revolutionism and disorder. Arthur Schlesinger, Jr., had strong words in the pages of *Harper's* for this phenomenon. "Little is more dismaying," he wrote, "than the way in which some, a few, in the intellectual community have rejected the life of reason, have succumbed to the national susceptibility for hatred and violence, have, indeed, begun themselves to exalt hatred and violence as if primitivism in emotion constituted a higher morality."

The impact of Harold Robbins on the young editor who then was I came from only an afternoon's duration, yet to this day it is oddly imperishable, a part of the New York tableau right along with literary lunches, rampant taxi rides, and holiday doubleheaders at Yankee Stadium. The author Clancy Sigal and I had been discussing his writing a magazine piece about the enigmatic figure Robbins, who wrote the glitzy blockbuster novels about power, violence, and sex and netted millions every time he came out with one. Up to that time Robbins's books had sold about seventy million copies, with total earnings including movies estimated at between $20 million and $40 million. Sigal, a Midwesterner whose novel *Going Away* had won the Houghton-Mifflin Literary Fellowship, came by the office one day considerably excited. Harold Robbins was in town, and he had traced him to the Regency Hotel on Park Avenue, where that very afternoon he and an assorted group of entrepreneurs were trying to settle a multiple contract involving television, movies, and paperback rights for a novel yet to be written called *The Inheritors*. Robbins himself had said he would see Sigal, who had talked with him a little and was adamant that I go back with him. "I mainly need moral support," he said. "I'm a little nervous." It did not require much persuasion, since I too was curious to meet Robbins.

The atmosphere in his suite in the Regency was singularly animated. In addition to Robbins there was his lawyer, a secretary, some TV and movie people, a couple of editors, and an unidentified hanger-on who in such entourages, I had intermittently observed in the city, fit the dual role of gofer and bodyguard. Various mini-conferences involving these individuals took place in other rooms and in corners of the main parlor, dissolving like musical chairs and then conjoining again, certain individuals brandishing legal-size pieces of paper as they alternately whispered and shouted. In the midst of this tiny maelstrom, calm and pleasant as the most respectable Kiwanian, sat the author himself, on a sofa where I soon joined him. Robbins, I had been advised by Clancy Sigal, lived an epicurean life in a *château* near Cannes, and also had a place in Beverly Hills, and an eighty-foot yacht, and was known to drop many thousands on the Monte Carlo tables, and hob-nobbed with the "jet set," an appellation that came into vogue in the Sixties, but one would scarcely have guessed this from his appearance: he was a small man with a small paunch, nearly bald but with hair grown in sideburns on the fringes, and wearing glasses with heavy frames. One would have thought he might be wary of a couple of *Harper's* men on his premises — Clancy himself at this very minute was talking with others of the gathering as they assessed the *gelt* — but this was far from the case. He was easy and unpretentious, his conversation friendly and straightforward, and I think he relished that Clancy and I were there. They said that Hitler, after finally settling on his grandiose strategy that became the Battle of the Bulge, was so pleased with himself that he sat calm and bemused while his generals all around querulously agitated over specifics, and the Regency suite had something of this lineament.

"I grew up not too far from here," he was saying. "Hell's Kitchen. You can't tell, of course, from what it is now. They superimposed Lincoln Center over it, which is probably just as well." He was an orphan who had lived in foster houses and soon learned the hard-bitten streets, a street urchin who became one smart hombre, and as he was describing all this a man came over and showed him something on a piece of paper, and he nodded briskly: "Sure, sure." Truman Capote said of Jacqueline Susann, "She doesn't write, she types," and many said this too of Harold Robbins, but it never seemed to bother him. I had bought a paperback off the Carr's Drug Store rack in high school of *A Stone for Danny Fisher,* the tale of a poor New York boy who became a prizefighter and was drawn into the city underworld, and I had really liked it, for the book had a power and candor that affected me at that young age, and I told him so. It was his third book, he said, in his "social and economic period," published by Alfred A. Knopf as had the previous two, well-received by the critics, and Elvis Presley had played his protagonist in the movie, which was called *King Creole,* "but Elvis didn't remind me too much of my guy."

The telephone kept jangling, and the activities surrounding us continued undiminished (my companion on the sofa would eventually get one million dollars for the movie rights to the work just then under bargain) and what I really wanted to know from him was what happened after *A Stone for Danny Fisher.* Did he consciously turn to the money-making pulp style? — and I was trying to put this into a civil context, beginning with something on the order of, "You're a phenomenon, but . . ." when he knowingly interrupted. "Oh, shit," he said, clipping his words, "I don't write for the critics. I write for myself, and I write for my readers. Readers are more important than critics. Look, I've been at this damned business nearly twenty years, and the average writer lasts about eight." I was not aware of these arcane statistics, but he was so absorbed with them that he repeated them, not once but twice. "I'm a people writer," he said. "That's why people like me. That's why I like Steinbeck." What was his favorite Steinbeck? I was about to ask, but he said, "What kind of people read your magazine? Who are your people? That's something you should look into," and suddenly an assistant came to him and escorted him into another room. "Excuse me," he said politely, and then Clancy Sigal came over and whispered, "Let's get out of here." I wanted to stay—perhaps to get an audition for the movie as one of the tycoon supermen?—but Sigal gave me a look, and we departed as inconspicuously as we could. What did this bizarre afternoon with Mr. Robbins teach me? Without wishing to seem righteous in my own eyes, the Regency scene made me in the worst way want to go to Milledgeville, Georgia, and visit Flannery O'Connor in her loneliness and solitude, or have a sourmash in Memphis with Shelby Foote laboring in seclusion on his monumental trilogy, or afternoon tea with Isaac Bashevis Singer, or a sedate twilight mint julep way down home on a front porch, as I had years before at age seventeen, with the droll and beloved Eudora. Clancy never did get that piece.

It was a town for sports, and also a halcyon time for them, with the Knicks winning, and the Jets, and the Mets at long last beginning to. James Jones and his family were home for the summer from Paris. Jones's young son Jamie had never lived in the United States; his father asked me to teach him about baseball. I took the bilingual youngster to a Mets-Giants game at Shea Stadium where we were as guests of their play-by-play man Lindsey Nelson. We were in the hospitality room even before batting practice, and a crowd of all ages was encircling a black figure in civilian clothes. "Who's that?" Jamie Jones said. "That's Willie Mays," I replied. "Who's Willie Mays?" he asked. I said, "There's a lot I have to teach you about baseball."

The Yankees were in decline then, but I loved going to the hallowed Yankee Stadium with its pervading ghosts of Ruth and Gehrig to admire Mantle settling under a towering fly to deep dead center, or on the same day hitting one home run batting left, and another the next time up from the right. I could conjure for myself the great heavyweight bouts that had taken place there over the years, in the brightly lit ring beyond the infield, surrounded in the smoky Bronx darkness by the agitated thousands, the great bouts I had heard on the radio as a boy brought to us by the Gillette people.

Back in that time when souls of all callings liked to mingle, among the most neighborly of all spots in the city of the Sixties were indeed the sporting establishments. Sportswriters were poets of the night, too inured to the deceits of men to be portentous, and I enjoyed their company. Dan Jenkins and Bud Shrake, up from Texas, were with *Sports Illustrated,* and as fellow cats on the tiles were invigorating to meet at the end of a day with companions such as Jimmy Cannon and Blackie Sherrod and Pete Axthelm and Gary "Jap" Cartwright and CBS's Jack Whitaker. In its simplicity Jenkins's sports prose was among the best then being written.

Shrake was a big, gruff man of poetic disposition who once had accidentally won a Chili Eating Competition while serving as the contest referee. Cartwright one evening after too many cocktails had thrown up all over the Michigan State University football coach, named Duffy Dougherty, while sitting next to him on the sofa of a hotel suite. Cartwright enjoyed telling disbelieving New Yorkers of his hoaxes on the *Dallas Times-Herald,* including the continuing saga of the Corbet Comets, a small-town high school football power in Texas whose accomplishments were reported in sober-faced sports stories under fourteen-point headlines in the Saturday editions. The Comets kept winning on the talents of their twin halfbacks, Dickie Don and Rickie Ron Yewbet, their surname deriving from the TCU football coach Abe Martin's speech pattern: "We gonna play some footbuhl, yewbet we are!" Corbet did not lose a game in two years, during which time Rickie Ron contracted the mumps and died. Cartwright suggested a story to the editor of the society page when E. D. (Shug) Kempleman, the Corbet Ford dealer, donated the world's largest tuba to the Fighting Corbet Band in memory of Rickie Ron Yewbet. Whenever "Jap" Cartwright recounted these freakish tales, even chattering New Yorkers lapsed to attention.

The locales of these men of sports were as various as they were democratic: the mungy, the ambiguous, the unstinting. One such was "21" at 21 West Fifty-second, its origins having been as a speakeasy where the cellar was a catacomb of wine bins and storage caches with a bar which could be lowered out of sight in an instant, booze and all, with the secret push of a button. "Bugs" Baer and Damon Runyon and Rube Goldberg and Gene Tunney had been patrons, and Ernest Hemingway too for the sports hearsay, and where on a given evening one might encounter Casey Stengel or Mickey Mantle or Yogi Berra or Jack Dempsey or Rocky Graziano standing at the bar, for New Yorkers thought nothing of standing four- or five-deep at a bar for hours on end, and I believe preferred it to sitting, as if sitting might amplify their assailability. Jake Gibbs of Grenada, Mississippi, was a catcher with the Yankees in those years, and it was Mississippi legend that early as a rookie fresh from the Triple A farm club in Richmond he was brought here for dinner by Mantle, Billy Martin, and Whitey Ford, and when the time came for dessert Jake Gibbs told the waitress, "Honey, I want some of that apple pie a la mode, and put a little ice cream on it too."

Another such establishment was P. J. Clarke's at Third Avenue and Fifty-fifth, an Irish saloon of historic flair with its memories of the old Third Avenue "El" outside and of Ray Milland getting unhinged in the movie *The Lost Weekend,* with its big juicy hamburgers with many onions and pickles, and its hearty mix of the bilious racing-form set, actors, professional athletes, and writers, and with the best jukebox in town for the old songs, and whose Italian proprietor once named his winning racehorse Charles Conerly. It was here that I became acquainted with a distinctive nucleus, four or five heavy-drinking homicide detectives from Queens and the Bronx. I liked those tough, foul cops and their raw, florid idiom, their cynical yet irrepressible brio, their sports gossip and racy badinage. They pronounced words like *tawk, towuh, whatsoevuh, ting,* Sixty-*foist* street. One of their number, named Charlie, had not long before been shopping in B. Altman's on Fifth Avenue for Christmas presents when he noticed a streetcorner Santa Claus slyly drifting among the counters slipping wristwatches and rings and perfume and other items into his big pack. Charlie approached him, and when the Santa Claus saw him, he raced toward the nearest escalator, initiating a primitive chase scene which ended when Charlie finally cornered and apprehended the culprit in the toy department on the top floor and applied the cuffs.

"Come with me on my rounds one day, Mr. Editor," another of them, named Clarence, but with the nickname Cherokee, said. "I'll show you some *tings* you never saw down in Dixie."

"Like what, Cherokee?"

"Like big-town crooks and dead corpses."

"I'm not so sure I want to do that," I said.

"You run a rag, doncha? You gotta know things, doncha? Ever see a *exit* wound? I took my brothuh around one night and he nearly puked." But I am afraid I never went. "Whatta ya hear? Whatta ya say?" another might intone. "If ya gotta minute or two, Mississippi, I gotta bridge over in Flatbush I can sell ya."

A third sporting link was Toots Shor's, recently transplanted from the Madison Square Garden neighborhood to the West Fifties and sadly in its decline, but whose notable round bar still brought in the sardonic old Hearst men like Don Whitehead and Bob Considine, who had been a few times around the league. Toots Shor had travelled the league, too, and was an unsparing host with his omnipresent brandy, as eager in his own home precinct to talk about American literature as to demonstrate how much he knew of the nuances and complexities of baseball. Until now I had never seen a prize fight from ringside seats, but had just witnessed a light-heavyweight bout from that perspective in the Garden.

"I never imagined the power of the blows," I observed to Toots Shor. "They're frightening. You could hear them a mile."

"So what's new?" Toots said. "Where ya been all your life?"

Once he introduced my son David Rae to the irascible Leo Durocher, and in a chance interlude of another evening presented me first to Hemingway's widow, then cheerily escorted me to an obscured back table, where Joe DiMaggio dined alone. He was very gray, and looked up with a wan smile. We briefly exchanged a pleasantry, then I left him to his own hard-earned solitude.

This big city, or certainly its airwaves, would have been diminished without the acrimonious and commanding presence of that notable curmudgeon Howard Cosell, the most famous sports commentator of the day, whom I met when I was a guest several times on his national radio show often devoted to matters of the culture, and whom I got to know around the town. "I was right for those times," Cosell later said of himself, meaning the Sixties, and this was true, for he was as hyperbolic as the age, and equally contentious. He was in many ways, as he also called himself, "the conscience of sports," strong on civil rights and against the greed and hypocrisy of much of professional athletics, and unequivocating in his outrage over the deposition of Muhammad Ali as heavyweight champion for refusing to be inducted into the Army in the Vietnam period on grounds of conscientious objection. "Nobody says a damn word about the professional football players who dodged the draft," he said. "But Muhammad was different, he was black and he was boastful." For this and other reasons Cosell rapidly became one of the most hated men in the United States.

I liked Cosell, admired his feistiness and flair, was amused by his undisguised and unflappable ego. He was very tall, slouching and angular even in repose, with a lengthy nose that widened greatly at its base, and a hairpiece as ersatz in appearance as a patch of synthetic black twill. He talked on radio and TV in unravelling rhetorical rhythms, a spiked Brooklyn nasal at once abrasive and magisterial, long labyrinthine soliloquies of perfect syntax and booming alliteration honed by gruff histrionic pauses. He spoke much this way in private too, which had to have taken a gargantuan energy, not to mention a volcanic concentration.

Before I went on the air with him one of those days in the CBS Building, called "Black Rock," on Sixth Avenue, he greeted me at the reception desk in polysyllabic salutation, then as we ranged through the corridors, wisecracked with the clerks and flirted with the secretaries in the same torrid riposte, and in his cubbyhole of an office pointed to the stacks of unopened letters, what looked to be thousands of them. "All hate letters," he proclaimed, "for I am without the slightest or most unequivocal doubt the most abhorred and ignominious personage in the lambent sweep of the fifty commonwealths. Half of them, I punctiliously surmise, will say 'nigger-loving Jew'." He even took a crank call while we were there, from some anonymous dissenter whose rasping metronome filled the room with its brisk staccato as Howard Cosell rolled his eyes toward the ceiling and made a rejoinder as brisk as any vaunted criminal attorney ever made to a jury of peers. During the radio show itself, about American magazines as I remember, he deigned not to use a script or a single note, and later in the week I began getting a few hate letters myself, from listeners who roundly berated me for having anything to do with the likes of the interviewer.

After one such radio show, Cosell wanted me to stroll with him several blocks over to a restaurant for a party and press conference for Dandy Don Meredith, who was joining "Monday Night Football." Walking with Cosell on the sidewalks of midtown, I got a sense of what it must be like to pursue a tornado through a Kansas cornfield. As with my earlier sightings of various movie people on these Manhattan streets, the cabdrivers and hard-hats made their irreverent recognitions, but this time more torrentially, and certainly more abusively. "Hey, Howie honey, when you gonna get a new *tou*-pee?" "Hi, Howie, you're full of *shit!*" "Say, Howie, how soon before you just *shut up?*" On and on this city chorus, to which the recipient responded with uncharacteristically terse and earthy rejoinders. We were nearing our destination when one last worker yelled down to us from a third-floor girder: "Say, Howie, don't listen to 'em, baby. You got class!" Cosell turned to me. "Indubitably a gentleman of dimension," he said.

By any measure one of the most impressive people I got to know in those days was Bill Bradley. From the time I met him, when he was twenty-six years old and playing pro basketball for the New York Knickerbockers, I never wavered in my intuition that he might someday be President or Secretary of State. I first met him at a small party in the city. The host and hostess had arranged a dinner so the two of us could meet. I had known much about him from a distance. As I have suggested, it was not difficult in those days to get to know other young people involved in interesting pursuits that seemed to matter in New York City. Bradley was no cloistered athlete, and we had a number of mutual friends in publishing, teaching, journalism, and politics. I had read John McPhee's book on Bradley and was taken by the source of its title, *A Sense of Where You Are.* Bradley, practicing basketball alone one afternoon in the Princeton gym, sank several hook shots in a row while not even looking at the basket. McPhee asked him how in the world he could do that, Bradley responding that you must have a feel, mystical almost, for the dimensions of a basketball court to have at all times a sense of where you are.

At the dinner in New York that night he exuded this especial sense, but in the shyest way imaginable. He was tall, about six feet five, with an uncanny likeness to the young Gregory Peck, and wore a floppy gray woolen sweater that could have been the Ivy style of the decade or two previous. I had not expected this shy unspokenness, but I recognized that he was a listener, a rare trait in the Manhattan of those times. That evening was his first date with the young woman he later married, Ernestine Schlant, a scholar in comparative literature, and I remember his asking us questions about Joseph Conrad, whom he was then reading, Texas politics, Oxford University in the 1950s, and the exigencies of the magazine business. He was a close reader of our magazine and brought up some of the recent articles in it. He began talking about life in two dozen American cities, the constant moving about as an athlete from one place to the next so frenetic that there were mornings when he woke up in some hotel room and had to look at the telephone book to ascertain where he was. "You must write a book about all that," I said, and he replied, "Maybe someday I will."

Other evenings followed in the city, dinners where one might see Bill in conversation with an art historian, or a museum director, or with Norman Mailer or Bill Moyers or William Styron. Always there was the informed intelligence, the desire to know about people from diverse backgrounds. And with it a sly humor. He was in the marching band in Crystal City High School, he said, and was the tallest French-horn player in history. On a Boy Scout trip to Memphis they went to Elvis Presley's house, Graceland, and he climbed a fence and plucked a leaf from a tree there and carried it in his wallet for years. In the 1964 Olympics, where he was captain of the United States basketball team, he got to know some of the Soviet players and felt so sorry for them for having to do nothing but play basketball all their livelong days that when they eventually came on the court to play his own team he tried to pretend they were Yale.

There were the times my son David and I went to the Knicks games as his guests. After one of them Bill, David, and I came out of the Garden to be surrounded by a dozen or two black kids who had been waiting for him there. They accused him of having lost the game for the Knicks on a bad play. He bantered with them for a while, then whispered to us, *"Come on!"* and we sprinted fifty yards or so to a taxicab stand, the black boys in hurrying pursuit, and we bounded into a cab, and suddenly the diligent and vivacious regiment who had been taunting him broke into applause as the taxi drove away up Seventh Avenue. "That's our man," they shouted. "That's Dollar Bill!"

Although Bradley had a number of years before his retirement from basketball, I was aware of his interest in getting into politics and arranged to go with him one day to Washington to introduce him to a few people I knew there. On that long-ago forenoon of spring, we met with several Congressmen and lunched with Senator William Fulbright. Fulbright, then in his mid-sixties, was a lithe and self-effacing man, yet considerably more ribald than his reputation. I remembered that John Kennedy had wanted him for his Secretary of State, but did not make that appointment because of the Arkansan Fulbright's purposeful and dissatisfying conservatism on race, and as we talked with this amiable, worldly man I considered this unfortunate; the course of the Vietnam commitment might have been different if he had been Secretary rather than the silent acquiescent hawk Dean Rusk, especially under LBJ. The three of us remained in his private dining room far into the afternoon, two hours or more, long after the dishes had been cleared and everyone else had departed, and when Bradley and I left the office building the early shadows were already lengthening on the Hill. "An impressive man," Bill said. "We forget he had to fight for reelection time and again in Arkansas." Our last stop that day was at the office of Bob Eckhardt, an old friend who was the Congressman from Houston. We sat in the dying sunlight and talked for a long time about Congress and the people in it, and about the nation. Soon Eckhardt's wife, Nadine, came in and sat down with us. "Bill, what do you do for a living?"

"I'm a basketball player," he said.

"Aren't you a little old for that?" she asked.

"I tape my ankles before every game," Bill Bradley replied.

The Sixties in New York City were antipodal: acute and high-strung as they were, they were also exciting and idealistic and fun. One of the principal foci was George Plimpton, one of the most striking and uncommon of the contemporary American breed. Plimpton knew something about the conflicting American regions and their disparate callings and believed in bringing people together in concordant exuberance, and in a time when they needed to be.

I had gotten to know Plimpton not long after I arrived in New York, when he came to our apartment every now and again to work on a couple of articles he had done for *Harper's,* one of them on Muhammad Ali, the other on taking Marianne Moore and Robert Lowell to a World Series game at Yankee Stadium. His prose was invariably witty and engaging and true. My son David Rae was enthralled by Plimpton, his tales and banter and incorrigible mischief. Once I was teaching David the likenesses on the American currency. "Who's on the penny?" "Lincoln." "Who's on the nickel?" "Jefferson." "Who's on the dime?" "Roosevelt." "Who's on the dollar?" "Give me a hint," he asked. "George . . ." and David squealed, *"Plimpton!"* Plimpton told us of the day he had pitched against a National League all-star team in a post-season exhibition at the Stadium. "I got Willie Mays to pop up behind third base," he reported, "but then my arm got flaccid and I walked ten in a row." Then he described the time Hemingway, in the middle of lunch in his house in Cuba, suddenly wanted to find out how good a fighter the visitor was, and got him with a solid left hook. To avoid further calamity, Plimpton said, "How did you do that?" and Hemingway proceeded to give him a little lecture on the art of the counterpunch.

George Ames Plimpton was tall and slender and dashing, athletic and clever and rich, a Harvard and Kings College, Cambridge, man of immaculate WASP New England inheritance. At Harvard he had edited the *Lampoon.* He resembled Ray Milland in, let us say, *Dial M for Murder,* except that he was taller than Milland and knew more of the double steal and the shovel pass. He and I had something in common. His great-grandfather General Adelbert Ames, who had won the Congressional Medal of Honor at First Manassas, was the Radical Reconstructionist Governor of Mississippi after the Civil War. My own great-grandfather Major Harper, as a wise luminary of the Mississippi legislature, was instrumental in bringing impeachment papers against Plimpton's great-grandfather Ames, who I had been instructed in junior high history was the reincarnate Lucifer. It was an unusual yet authoritative connection. Plimpton had told us he once was chatting with President Kennedy at a White House dinner and Kennedy said, "When are you going to get your grandmother off my back?" Plimpton explained to me, "Kennedy had written something disparaging of Adelbert Ames in *Profiles in Courage,* you see, and my grandmother had been sending him letters to rectify the blasphemy."

In the early Fifties Plimpton and an assortment of other young Americans, mostly graduates of the Ivy League, had descended on the Left Bank of Paris. Irwin Shaw called them "The Tall Young Men," but their most durable cognomen would be "the *Paris Review* Crowd," after the literary quarterly they soon founded in the sidewalk cafés and bistros along the boulevard St.-Michel. In this varied assemblage of young *litterateurs* were, among others, Terry Southern, Peter Matthiessen, John Phillips Marquand, William Styron, Robert B. Silvers, John P. C. Train, Donald Hall, Thomas Guinzburg, Harold L. (Doc) Humes, and Sadruddin Aga Khan. Plimpton was appointed the editor-in-chief, and was forthwith observed strolling the *arrondissments* of the Left Bank in a long black evening cape, reminding some of Toulouse-Lautrec's well-known lithograph of Aristide Bruant. He took to walking Montparnasse at night stalking the spirit of Hemingway, and of Jake Barnes and Lady Brett Ashley. Plimpton had arrived in Paris, Gay Talese had written of those days, with a wardrobe that included the tails his grandfather had sported in the Twenties, and which he himself had worn in 1951 at a London ball as one of the escorts to the future Queen of England:

> He moved immediately into a tool shed behind a house owned by Gertrude Stein's nephew. Since the door of the shed was jammed, Plimpton, to enter it, had to hoist himself, his books, and his grandfather's tails through the window. His bed was a long, thin cot flanked by a lawn mower and garden hose, and was covered by an electric blanket that Plimpton could never remember to turn off — so that, when he returned to the shed at night and plopped into the cot, he was usually greeted

by the angry howls of several stray cats reluctant to leave the warmth that his forgetfulness had provided.

Much of the early policy of the *Review* was shaped in an all-night *boîte* in Montparnasse called Le Chaplain. The secretaries were a diverse group of young American college women who were collectively referred to as "Miss Apthecker," since none of them had work permits and they were more or less fugitives from French justice. The *Review* attracted both promising young American writers and a roster of outstanding international contributors, and its "writers-at-work" interviews would soon be distinguished fixtures in the literary world.

In '56 *The Paris Review*, and its crowd, came back home, to New York City, where it would be edited from Plimpton's bachelor quarters on East Seventy-second Street high above the East River, its walls lined with photographs of Plimpton fighting bulls with Hemingway in Spain, or playing tennis for King's College, or trying his curveball on Willie Mays in the exhibition game, or sparring with Archie Moore in Stillman's Gym. This was the setting for Plimpton's parties of the Sixties.

More often than not they were spur-of-the moment frolics. Plimpton would telephone me at the office. "Come on over. We're having a get-together for John Marquand and Phil Roth, I think."

"What's the occasion?"

"Hell, I don't know. John's just back from Europe. Roth's just finished a book. That's good enough."

As I glanced around the crowded room at its array of writers and hangers-on, I recalled my first days in the city, and the lonely weekend in my office when I gazed at the drawing of all the congenial people here in *Esquire*, and wanted someday to be among them. It may be hard to believe, but one conducted a certain amount of magazine business at these *soirees*, as later at the restaurant named Elaine's, for the Plimpton atmospherics also had the excitement and stimulation of a club, and the long-vanished chatter comes back to me in funny waves of memory.

"Was your character in *The Disenchanted* really Scott Fitzgerald?" I asked Budd Schulberg.

Schulberg leaned down conspiratorially, a great shock of silvery hair on his forehead. "It was Scott, all right. I wanted to do something to help him, but I couldn't keep up with him."

"Did you like him personally?"

"He was so fragile in those days you couldn't help it. He was half maniac, half angel. Say, who do you like in the Sugar Bowl, Arkansas or Georgia?"

One such evening I eavesdropped on a conversation between a civil rights preacher from South Carolina and James Baldwin. Baldwin was talking about Richard Wright. "Dick should've come home, you know," Baldwin was saying, appraising me as he spoke with big, liquid eyes, ancient sad eyes with puffy shadows around them. "Don't you agree?" I realized he was talking to me.

"I spent an evening with him once," I said.

"You did? Where?"

"In Paris in 1957." I had gotten his number on the Left Bank from the *Paris Trib,* I explained to James Baldwin, and telephoned him and said I was a student in England and was reading his books. He was aloof until I told him I was from Mississippi, then he said to come on over. As Baldwin and I conversed about Richard Wright, Plimpton across the way was introducing someone from Queens to a football coach from Groton, or it could have been a retired cymbalist from Brooklyn to a returned Vietnam veteran from Long Island. Then momentarily he presented Baldwin and me to Alex Karras of the Detroit Lions.

"Are you a writer like George?" Alex Karras asked me.

"I'm just an editor," I said. "He's a writer." I pointed to Baldwin.

"What do *you* do?" Baldwin asked him.

"I butt heads for a living. I spend half my time on my ass."

It was a feast of an evening, a vivid pastiche, inciting my adrenaline. Unexpectedly, yet with the ease of a Mozart minuet, I found myself tête-à-tête with Lillian Hellman, who was lighting a new cigarette from the glowing stub of a previous one.

"I know you're from New Orleans," I said.

"And you?"

When I told her, her eyes gleamed, then she spoke in her hoarse, rasping voice. "I spent the night there once. When I was a little girl. My father was a travelling salesman."

"Where did you stay?"

"I've never forgotten. The Lamar Hotel."

"It's still there, but they don't use it anymore."

"Too bad," Miss Hellman said, as if they had just closed down the Parthenon.

One night the function was for the running back Jim Brown of the Cleveland Browns, who was raising money for black colleges. Plimpton gave a speech, then passed the hat. The cause was a worthy one, and I put in a check. Plimpton later described the scene as he and the great Jim Brown counted the money.

"Somebody gave us a check for a hundred dollars," Brown said.

Plimpton examined it. "He's a white man from Mississippi."

"No kidding?" Brown said. "From *Mississippi?* You've got to be putting me on."

When Bud Shrake, the writer from Texas, came out with a novel, *Strange Peaches,* Plimpton organized a party in his honor. Shrake and his wife and I arrived at the Plimpton flat an hour early. By happenstance, however, we were preceded by the novelist Terry Southern, who was carrying an armload of posters for a book of *his* just being published, named *Red Dirt Marijuana;* he began to circulate through Plimpton's apartment putting his posters on the walls, so that when the guests arrived they thought it was a book party for Southern. More bemused than resentful, Shrake later asked Southern, another Texas émigré from Alvaredo, how he had the presumption to steal the evening with his own posters. "In the writing racket," Terry Southern said, "you've got to promote yourself." It could have been a motto of the Sixties.

I later became accustomed to such Manhattan gatherings, and youngsters from other places even wanted to meet *me,* but those first evenings at George Plimpton's are still a song in the heart.

The people. The places. The neighborhoods. Anything could happen in the city, bizarre juxtapositions, prodigal confrontations. Late one afternoon I met my editor at Houghton-Mifflin, Dorothy de Santillana, down from Boston, for drinks in the lobby of the Algonquin. She wanted to introduce me to another of her authors, Margaret Walker, the black novelist from Mississippi, an old friend of Mississippi's Richard Wright. We sat there talking about things we knew in common, watching all the while the flow of publishing people arriving for their after-work replenishments, including the *New Yorker* cadre from their quarters down the street: the ebullient salutations, the hugs and kisses, the cool *bon mots* and cooler assessments, drifting across us in warm little rivulets from the foyer and walkway and lounge.

"I think he's absolutely *carnivorous,* you know."

"But he has style, can't you see? And felicity."

"Not an ounce of felicity. All uptown *bon ton.*"

"You know he writes well. I do suspect you're a little jealous."

Or: "I never saw anyone so naive. He came to us from the swamps of Kansas."

"But Kansas has no swamps, does it? Only wheatfields — and tornados. Remember *The Wizard of Oz?*"

"No swamps then. But you do get my gist."

Across the way was the same Round Table where the Algonquin Group once had their wet and parlous repasts, reproving just about everyone but themselves, "showing off," William Faulkner in subversive observation said of them, all largely dead and most of them forgotten now. As my companions and I chatted pleasantly who should drift by but Eudora Welty, up on a Manhattan visit from Jackson, Mississippi, and she tarried at our table for a moment: soft hair and radiant eye and a whimsical and diffident smile. "It's refreshing to come to the city every once in a while," she said. A couple of minutes later Turner Catledge of Philadelphia, Mississippi, editor of the *New York Times,* stepped out of the elevator to greet us, and he dallied too for a refreshment. Seconds after that who would show up but Chunkin' Charlie Conerly, the dexterous former quarterback of the New York Giants, from Clarksdale, Mississippi, and he paused with us there for a moment also.

"Old home week at the Algonquin," Turner Catledge said.

~ 1968: Annus Mirabilis

9

IT WAS THE *ANNUS MIRABILIS*: with the exception of the Civil War years, surely the most tragic and cataclysmic in our history, transfigured by war, assassination, mayhem. Cruelty, excess, fury, fed upon themselves in the life of the nation, generating an atmosphere of flagrant recklessness and chaotic stimulation and polarization of the spirit that in moments seemed to sever the very textures of a troubled society. It will not be easy to convey, as one profoundly involved in those days, the heart's abyss, the nullifying mood, the mind's despair, elegiac almost in their intense fire, of doom and sorrow and omen and death. And in Marshall McLuhan's global village, everyone was watching everything, as if in the burning images of electronics, not even the imagination was left to its own devices.

It was Paul Simon's tune of that year, of course, which caught the rueful mood: *Where have you gone, Joe DiMaggio? A nation turns its lonely eyes to you.* Even Elvis wrote and sang his own words of the moment about a country "trapped in pain": *If I can dream of a better land/Where my brothers walk hand in hand.* The reality of the time came to us in wrenching filaments of the emotions. After the passage of the years the sparest chronology of '68 does meager justice to the essences upon the land, to the *feel* of things, to the everyday doubt and fear: the Tet offensive; My Lai; the abdication of Lyndon Johnson; the assassination of Martin Luther King, Jr.; the uprisings in Memphis, Brooklyn, Harlem, Washington, Detroit, Newark, Boston, Chicago, and 150 other towns and cities, numerous dead and wounded, federal troops surrounding the White

House; Mayor Daley's "shoot-to-kill" order; the takeover at Columbia; the assassination of Bobby Kennedy; the sentencings of Spock, Goodman, Ferber, and Coffin; the upraised clinched fists of the black American athletes at the Mexico City Olympics; the bloodshed at the Democratic Convention; the early protests of women's liberation; the police shootouts with the Black Panthers; the election of Nixon. And finally, into the following year and of a character with the prodigal Aquarius, and inseparable, the first human creatures on the moon.

Our magazine was inextricably a part of this, "Establishment" in heritage though anything but that now in temper, a vanguard I trust now to think in mirroring and interpreting and shaping the configurations of the nation, its free voices addressing themselves time and again, in Alfred Kazin's words on its pages in that year, to "this extraordinary rage in human beings, this endless clamor in the human heart." As much as any other American writer it was Norman Mailer who discerned and seized these days, and brilliantly penetrated them. "The disease was beneath the skin," he wrote in *Harper's,* "the century was malignant with an illness so intricate that the Yippies, the Muslims, and the rednecks of George Wallace were all in attack upon it. They might eat each other first, but that was merely another facet of the plague — cannibalism was still the best cure for cancer." Among segments of the intellectuals and the young, to Irving Howe in *Harper's,* "there keeps growing a quasi-religious hunger for total system, total solution, total apocalypse; and soon enough idealogues appear with doctrines to match":

> In the 1960s the United States has become, with the possible exception of Communist China, the most tumultuous country in the world: the most self-critical, self-lacerating, self-destructive. With Kennedy there was a moment of healing; with the early Johnson some legislative benefits. But then, for reasons everyone can point to but no one fully grasp, the country started to come apart.
>
> It isn't mere foolishness, these days, to wonder whether the United States will survive as a democracy — though it is worse

> than foolishness when certain sorts of academics predict the death of democracy with a suicidal glee. For the first time since the Depression, one keeps encountering the fear that our social problems may turn out to be intractable, or, what is perhaps even worse, that solving them might not be an adequate solution to the malaise creeping into our bones.

The nation, Richard Hofstadter reflected in *Harper's* pages, "seems to slouch onward into its uncertain future like some huge inarticulate beast, too much attainted by wounds and ailments to be robust, but too strong and resourceful to succumb."

In early evening of the day King was shot in Memphis, I sat before the television in our apartment mesmerized by the images of the blood on the motel balcony, the grief and bafflement and rage. Outside, on the pavements of the Upper West Side, bands of young blacks were roaming the streets in aimless wrath; I had seen them earlier as I emerged from the subway, and I will never forget the look in their eyes, a glazed expression of utter desperate fury. Many whites were getting home quickly. My son David would remember knocking a big wooden salad bowl off the top of the refrigerator in our apartment, and he thought that was why his mother was crying. As I watched the television, the telephone rang: it was my literary agent, Joan Daves, a German *émigré* whose father had died at Auschwitz, calling from down in the Village. She was King's literary agent also, and had introduced me to him that night we talked about my hometown in Mississippi. She had been on the telephone with him several times that day from Memphis, discussing a book contract. "You'll be doing me the greatest favor if I can come up and be with you," she said. I offered to come get her. She said she would take a taxi. She and I and David sat on the floor watching the television. "What's wrong with our country?" she asked in her anguish. "What's wrong with it?" It was a question we would often hear in the months to come.

That night armed troops guarded the White House for the first time since the Civil War. David Halberstam, who had travelled around the country with King and gotten to know him well, wrote for *Harper's* a eulogy entitled "Notes from the Bottom of the Mountain":

> The terrible thing about this country today is that when the murder came it was impossible to be surprised; if it was not exactly expected, it was not unexpected. There is a quality of hate in this country which is quite terrible; the country seethes with it. I leave it to the psychologists to determine exactly why a country so rich should be so unstable, but it seemed to me in his final years King was a recipient of an extraordinary amount of that hate, ironically I think a good deal more than Stokely Carmichael or Rap Brown. . . . Many of the young men and women who marched on Washington in 1963 and went to Mississippi in 1964, frustrated now, have left King's movement, have joined and hailed the new apostles of violence. The climate and the hopes which gave birth to Martin Luther King are gone; so this week in Atlanta if we weep, it is not for him but for ourselves. For him it is over, he knew the end; he had always ended each speech with the words from an old slave song which applies more to him now than it does to us: *Free at last, free at last; Thank God Almighty, I'm free at last.*

More than ever Vietnam was engulfing everything. By the month of King's assassination, American troops had reached 550,000, combat deaths 22,951. In May alone 2,000 Americans were killed. The war was dividing families, friends, the nation, and after the stunning success of the Tet offensive was soon to ignite massive rebellion. "Taps" echoed across the land. Young white activists were spitting on returning veterans and calling them baby-killers. On Saturday, March 16, 1968, in a village in Quang Ngai province called My Lai, an American platoon under the command of a lieutenant named Calley systematically massacred 567 old men, women, and children. The word of this American Lidice, as it came to be known, would not begin to filter to the domestic public for a long time. Eventually the most graphic and authoritative account of that event would be published in *Harper's,* and would elicit the most heartfelt response among readers that I ever encountered in my life as an editor.

Among the magazine's extensive treatment of Vietnam in that year were articles by Jeremy Larner on an Air Force officer in a small town in New Mexico receiving dismissal and a year's hard labor for opposing the war on reasons of conscience, Ward S. Just's combat reportage, Stephen Minot's on the anguish of draft counselling in a Connecticut college, and Halberstam's "Voices of the Vietcong," based on his interviews with Vietcong and North Vietnamese. Halberstam also contributed substantial pieces on the frailties and strengths of the Eugene McCarthy campaign and the divisions among liberals caused by Vietnam, as well as "The Man Who Ran Against Lyndon Johnson" on Allard Lowenstein and his "System" coalition of anti-war activists. In answer to those who claimed Vietnam was needed as a prop to the national economy, Walter W. Heller cited the war's injurious economic effects. The desired end of the war should "show beyond a doubt that we also know how to do it the best way—by rehabilitating our cities, by helping our poor, by cleansing our air and water and land, and by increasing the range of private pleasures and comforts—in short, by converting our rising productivity into a rising standard and quality of life." And Robert Heilbruner, in the September number, on "Making a Rational Foreign Policy Now," gave expression to the better instincts of the embattled nation:

> The great lesson of the Vietnam war is now clear. It is that the mightiest nation in the world has not been able to defeat the forces of revolutionary nationalism in one of the smallest nations in the world. . . . What exists in most of the world beyond our borders is a condition of human indignity and degradation that verges on the unspeakable. . . . Now the question is whether America will take its ultimate stand on the side of fear, open-mindedness or dogma. The challenge goes to the very core of this nation—its structure of power and economic interest, its capacity for reasoned discussion, its ultimate inarticulate values. It is not alone the life and death of anonymous multitudes that is weighed in the balance, but that of American conscience, as well.

As the war worsened, there had developed an enormous change between the young people of the early and the late Sixties. In the course of '68 came the succession of campus bombings and acts of arson. The dynamitings were directed mainly at ROTC buildings and university government centers. Demonstrations multiplied, taking place on more than one hundred campuses alone in the first half of the year; someone in our office defined "moderate revolutionaries" as makers of middle-sized firebombs. The Columbia University uprising, following the assassination of Martin Luther King, Jr., by less than three weeks, was the most serious since Berkeley of '64. The Columbia crisis was synonymous with the real and visible emergence of Students for a Democratic Society, committed now to active militance against "oppression, racism, and imperialism" which they claimed had compromised institutions like Columbia with their landholdings and investments, racial politics, and administrative complacencies. From our neighborhood in the West Nineties on those April evenings we could see the police vans roaring down West End Avenue from Morningside Heights and the Columbia campus. The infamous confrontation between the Yippies and the police at Grand Central Station also occurred that spring, when six thousand souls converged on that massive conduit of the working world and unfurled their banners, exploding cherry bombs and ripping off the hands of the big clocks. In the subsequent melee the police charged the crowd with nightsticks and Abbie Hoffman himself was clubbed unconscious. It was merely a mild portent of what would ensue in Chicago four months hence.

At the heart of my existence, in the midst of these stormy events of 1968, was the magazine. Even in the moments of play, which were considerable, it was what mattered, for a magazine if you love it enough will consume you, and takes on a life of its own, and, like a person one loves, is to be nurtured, cajoled, pampered, vindicated, even in moments feared. I was discovering that many of the nation's best writers wanted to appear on its pages. They were truly interested in what we were trying to do. Not a few of them were coming to *us*. Could it come together? Was it beginning to?

Far away from that life, I am perusing now its volumes for 1968, strangely reminiscent for me of those unhurried afternoons in the library in Palo Alto when I had so immersed myself in its past. In a random sampling, there is fiction by John Updike, Bernard Malamud, Isaac Bashevis Singer, George P. Elliott, major poems by Robert Penn Warren and James Dickey, literary essays by Irving Howe on James Baldwin, W. E. B. Du Bois, the Russian novelists, hippie novels, and the 1960s.

Not unlike a cherished diary, each page of these old volumes brings back memories for me. Bernard Malamud sent his wonderful story, "An Exorcism," not long after a telephone call I had made to him asking if he would give *Harper's* something of his that he cared about. Shortly after, I called him to see if he would have lunch with me. I had long admired his work, his compassionate treatment of everyday lives, his rich landscape of shops and tenements and New York streets, and was a little intimidated to meet him tête-à-tête, fearing he would be remote and forbidding, wishing I had brought Bob Kotlowitz or Midge Decter along with me. He was already at the restaurant when I arrived, a man in his fifties of medium height and sober mien in a dark suit and tie, a modest fringe of graying brown hair, a mustache, for all appearances more like a successful Upper West Side Jewish merchant than a writer of moving tales of dispossession and distress. We talked about literature, especially about some of the parallels between Jewish and Southern writing, and about the mood of the students on campuses like Bennington and Harvard where he had been teaching. The conversation turned to poker, and then to baseball. I believe I even asked him to do a nonfiction baseball piece for us — perhaps go to spring training? Or write about the old Polo Grounds and Ebbets Field? "It was an honor to meet you, Mr. Malamud," I said as we parted. "Call me Bernie," he replied.

The telephone introduced me also to Robert Penn Warren, whom I called one day to ask for a poem or two, and we ended up chatting for a long time about dogs, and about the politics of the South. Robert Penn Warren was the only American who had won the Pulitzer Prize for both fiction and verse — late in life he would be the first official poet laureate of the United States — and he began sending our magazine some of his poems. He too was of the South, from the hill country of Kentucky and the town of Guthrie, and both his grandfathers had fought for the Confederacy. At Oxford University his old rooms were not far from the ones I later occupied in New College, and I enjoyed telling that to visitors in those days, long before I imagined geting to know him.

We called him "Red." He was then in his late sixties, rusty hair turning gray, a craggy face with stony cheekbones, a voice not at all consistent with these harsh, imposing features: warm, witty, and rapid, but hanging long onto certain words, in the older Southern way. He taught at Yale. One evening I was being inducted as an honorary fellow of Silliman College, one of my first responsibilities being that I join Warren in after-dinner questions and answers with three or four dozen students in the master's lodgings. All the questions were sharp and civil except the last one, which was addressed to me, and right out of those whirlwind times: "I've been listening closely to you gentlemen. I have only one query. How can such seemingly civilized men have come out of such a barbaric region as the American South?" I diligently thought for a moment. On a matter of such import, I finally suggested, one must defer to his distinguished senior, Robert Penn Warren. Red Warren had the dregs of a bourbon in his glass. "I'm sick and tired" (pronounced "*tied,*" and much drawn out) "of hearing that question from Yankees," he whispered almost inaudibly to me, then shook the ice a little in his glass and turned to the quizzical party. "My answer is," he said, "it must have had something to do with inoculation against hookworm."

He was married to the writer Eleanor Clark, and they too lived across the Connecticut line from our weekend farmhouse in New York and would come on Saturday nights for dinner, when it was not uncommon to hear Red Warren quoting Yeats, or the Elizabethans, or to join him in the old Protestant hymns. In the city we sometimes had lunch in the Century where, tongues loosened by the famous martinis in that staid, imperious institution, we talked of the imposing twelfth-century wall with its turrets and apertures for arrows that ran through our Oxford college, and the ghostly silences of the fortressed midnights there. I loved his stories of the old Fugitive poets, of the South of two generations ago, of Huey Long and Louisiana. It was more than a pleasure sitting at a corner table of the Century dining room peopled by the frosty and contained avatars of the American Establishment with Red Warren of Guthrie, Kentucky, and telling him about my grandparents and great-aunts, and describing my excitement on first reading the opening words of *All the King's Men,* the shimmering heat mirages in the far distance on the lonesome highways. And that inevitably led to a somber discussion of the assassinations, and the violence afoot in the land.

A native New York City intellectual observed to me of Warren in those years, "The trouble with him is he's too *kind*. I can't take him seriously." That said more about the city of the Sixties than it did about Warren. I was always very affected by his generosity of spirit and of the link he showed me between the generations in their passing. A young editor and writer in the turbulent metropolis could have learned worse. Further, his vivid descriptions of his days helping to edit the old *Southern Review* and *Sewanee Review* were valuable to me in the perspective of my own magazine in different times, and he gave quiet yet nearly lyrical counsel that a national journal should be essential to the creative literature of its day, suggesting that one must strive for that even when failure came, that a magazine could be measured by the strength of its efforts. I was impressed with how Warren and others of his stature, such as Arthur Miller and Malamud, made themselves accessible to what the magazine was trying to do.

For years, in their reconverted barn in Fairfield, the Warrens had had a resplendent black-tie dinner a few nights before each Christmas, about fifty friends in all. Red Warren telephoned me at my office one day. "Whenever some one of our number dies," he said, "we add new young people to the party. We have two vacancies for you and Celia." I have seldom in my life felt more blissful and serene than on these Christmas evenings each year at the Warrens, for there was something wonderfully merry and sustaining about them: the snow on the pines, the tall spruce near the open fire, the yuletide music, the lambent holiday talk, the cheerful countenances of others in the room, the Cheevers and Ellisons and Styrons and

Millers and Woodwards, the conversations with Walker Evans about what got him started in photography, or Max Shulman about humor, or Lillian Hellman about New Orleans, the uproarious toasts by all at the long dinner table in the basement. Every one of those Christmases I would visit the Warrens' son Gabriel in his room and admire his toy trains, which got more complicated each year just as Gabriel himself grew taller. At the end of one of those evenings Celia and I discovered that we did not have enough gas in our car for the return to Putnam County. No problem, Red Warren said. He pulled his car next to mine and brought out a hose, and then the author of *All the King's Men* and *The Ballad of Billie Potts* proceeded in his tuxedo to siphon the gasoline with his mouth into our tank, then spit out the residue into the New England snow. "That should do it," Robert Penn Warren said.

Among those who dwelled right there on safe, sane Manhattan Island, Midge Decter's husband, Norman Podhoretz, was indeed for a while my best friend, very much a part of the magazine scene and of my own life. He had been the editor-in-chief of *Commentary* since 1960. He was irreverent, amusing, bawdy, and courageous. Months before I became editor of *Harper's* he had talked with me at considerable length about New York, about the magazine business, about the Jewish intellectual community: its particular strengths, its infighting, how brilliant and complicated it was.

At first I called him Norman, but then it became "Pod," or when not in his presence, "The Pod." Pod was short, not much more than five and a half feet, and stocky, with very blue eyes, boyish and balding, in his late thirties then, and he wore very fine suits. There is an adage that Jews cannot drink: Pod was the proof of that lie. The *Commentary* offices were on East Fifty-sixth just off Third Avenue, with a comfortable bar and restaurant in intimate proximity named Le Moal, which the noble Murray Kempton called "the *Commentary* commissary," and many was the late afternoon I would meet Pod there after work for magazine conversation and gossip. He would usually hurry in a few minutes late and sit down and order a drink and start talking, for there was a breathless quality about him, a not unattractive air of rush, a sense of movement and accomplishment and briskness trailed in his wake, and he was never for a moment banal or boring. The talk would be of what his editorial day had been like, and mine. I once told him I had to go home for an hour sometimes and think over the day's events in my office. "Then you're a writer," he said. "You may be in the wrong end of the business." Here we were in Le Moal, the young Dixie WASP and the young Brooklyn Jew, joined by literature and America and mutual friends and liberal politics and magazines. And when his wife joined *Harper's* as an editor, we had even more in common. Or did we ever really have much in common at all? Perhaps this, too, is an American question.

He was born and raised in the ravaged Brownsville neighborhood, where his father, an immigrant from Eastern Europe, was a milkman who sent him not only to the public schools but to the Hebrew high school. He graduated first in his class at age fifteen, and progressed from one success to another: at Columbia he came under the tutelage of Lionel Trilling and F. W. Dupee, and as a Fulbright later at Cambridge University of F. R. Leavis. Back home he established a growing reputation as a controversial, iconoclastic book reviewer and critic. When he took over *Commentary* he enlivened it and moved it to the left politically. He admired Jack Kennedy: "He was a man," he wrote, "who was post-Freud, post-Marx, post-Einstein." In my esteem for Pod I enjoyed the life that swirled around *Commentary* in the mid-Sixties and later, including the intellectual parties at his and Midge's huge apartment on West End Avenue which brought together what Podhoretz himself called "The Family," the mostly Jewish, leftward New York intellectuals, including Trilling, Irving Howe, Hannah Arendt, David Bazelon, Paul Goodman, Leslie Fiedler, Dwight Macdonald, Alfred Kazin, and others, parties so removed in tone and mood from the ones, say, at George Plimpton's flat on the East River with their athletes and *Playboy* bunnies and disarranged writers of fiction and spiffy songs on the piano as to seem a different American setting altogether. In this stimulating *melange,* so foreign to my own upbringing, I had contributed occasionally in my junior editor days to *Commentary* — the outlandish goy boy met at the Wailing Wall? Once Pod phoned me and said he desperately needed a lead piece for an issue approaching deadline: he would be my friend for life if I put everything aside and came up with something, and I wrote a memoir of my confrontations with the Radical Right in Texas. Later they even invited me to give one of the main tributes at a banquet on the occasion of an anniversary of *Commentary*.

Podhoretz did not mind telling stories on himself. He reported that once at a party he introduced himself to Lauren Bacall, who said, "Butt out, Buster, I'm talking to my peers now," an event that so made the rounds of the town that it even came back to Bacall, who said regretfully, "Well *I* didn't know who he was." Nor did others mind telling stories on him. John Phillips Marquand told me he was disconcerted when, on taking Pod on a snowy day to the family burial plot of his mother's aristocratic New England forebears in Stockbridge, Massachusetts, and showing him the grave of his cousin Kate, Pod started dancing about near the grave and said, "See me shimmy like your cousin Kate." Alfred A. Knopf at a Manhattan dinner claimed he had to step over Pod, naked and passed out, on the balcony of a hotel during a conference; before this paradigm of New York publishing I found myself defending my fellow editor and pal, nude or otherwise. The Pod was becoming an enlivening and spirited presence in the city. His confessional memoir *Making It,* in which he said ambition was the "dirty little secret" of the American day, including the New York literary one, and described how the aspiration for fame, power, and money were central to his own life, was to be bludgeoned and reviled in many circles, including and perhaps particularly "The Family," and this would embitter him.

On the telephone, in a New Delhi lilt: "Mr. Podhoretz, this is Sastha Bratha."

"Who?"

"Sastha Bratha. I wonder if I may come to your office and pay my respects?"

"Your *respects?* After that piece of filth you wrote about my book in England?"

"I'm so sorry. I've changed my mind."

"It wasn't Bratha, Norman," I heard Midge Decter later say into the phone from the office adjoining. "It was Morris."

Shortly before I became editor I was to return to my hometown to address the students first at the white high school, then the black, during National Library Week. Pod asked me to take him along: he had never been to the Deep South, he said, and suspected it was not all that *different* from the rest of the country, as his Southern writer friends had said it was. It was the height of the fantastic Mississippi springtime, its lush odors of perfumed air and growing things, when we dismounted the airplane in Jackson. "What's that I smell?" Pod asked. "A chocolate factory?" He wanted to see cotton growing. We went to a plantation and he began talking to an old black sharecropper. The poor old fellow was straight out of Markham's "The Man with the Hoe." Podhoretz and the old man could have been talking different tongues, for each barely comprehended a word the other said. In this brief trip home friends, including Larry L. King, descended from numerous directions of the country, and Pod regaled them with some of the stories he had already told me, as of his recently having been invited by Jacqueline Kennedy to visit her in her apartment in New York. He noticed that the servants had been dismissed, he said, and was tortured by the idea that she was soliciting an advance. "I didn't know what to do," he told us. "You know if anything happened you could never *tell* anyone." Of the people he was meeting in the South, he asked us, "Have you seen the expression of hatred they get in their eyes when you look at their women?"

In our New York days Pod edified me about the jousting intellectual life of the town, the rivalries and grudges, the jeopardies of driven ambition there even when one admitted to it. He demonstrated to me the importance of wide "contacts" in keeping a magazine in the middle of significant thoughts and events. In the early pieces I had written for him I learned much about deft and serious manuscript editing and the importance of faith to broad context and theme. He was a marvelous editor.

He and I remained comrades in the city, and his wife, Midge, was as invaluable and professional a collaborator as anyone could ever hope for, trustworthy confidante and friend. Only with time did he move to the Far Right, taking *Commentary* on that side with him, and drop his old friends for reasons of politics. For a time I was intrigued yet bewildered by why he would journey so far and so quickly to those distant ramparts from what had seemed genuinely shared feelings about the nation in those days. I cannot help but speculate, however, that the genesis of this drastic shift lay in the timbre of the 1960s themselves, and in his autobiography that the literati and intellegentsia disparaged, so that his split with this community over Vietnam and social issues began here — and that things became personal rather than political with him. Who knows? From his new perspective he wrote that he had been misinformed and misled — perhaps even *corrupted?* — by the Southerners in New York in the 1960s, myself among the foremost, and he also attacked me in personal terms. I granted him his politics — "It's a free country, ain't it?" as even the most fustian of the backcountry troglodytes were wont to say in my Texas legislature days — but was nonetheless strangely saddened. I loved the guy, and still in old memory do, and choose to recall those youthful early evenings in Le Moal with the world alight and all its rewards and risks and circuities before us. As Oscar Levant said of Doris Day, "I knew her before she was a virgin."

We were also running in these months the previously unpublished letters of e. e. cummings, John Fowles on the writing of a novel, James Joyce's pages on an unpublished study of love, William Styron on the ghost of Thomas Wolfe, conversations with Konrad Lorenz, the World War I years from Bertrand Russell's autobiography, Robert Kotlowitz's pieces on the performing arts, portraits of Joseph Alsop by Merle Miller, of Charles Evers by Robert Canzoneri, of Mayor John Lindsay by Larry L. King, and of Mayor Richard Daley by Halberstam, the latter appearing shortly before the disastrous Democratic Convention in Chicago, and prophetic:

> It was his city to an extraordinary degree, and now his party was coming to his city to choose a President. The more contested the nomination would be, the more the poor blacks and the long-haired white kids worked in the primaries to offset the Democratic party establishment, why, yes, the more powerful

> Richard J. Daley would be in August; and he was aware of this, aware that in his own way he could dominate the convention. . . . But there was also a suspicion that part of the problem was Daley, that his machine had been too smart for itself, and that finally perhaps Daley was not equipped to understand the complexity and the intense pressures of new times.

Presumptuous as this may seem, I wished for each finished issue somehow to be durable rather than merely transient, so that if readers of the next century chanced to read it, they would find in it something which interested them and which was true to our own times and said something to them about theirs. Essays appeared by two of the great emerging American writers. In "Take My Saddle from the Wall," Larry McMurtry writes of the last of the old Texas cowboys:

> Texas is rich in unredeemed dreams, and now that the dust of its herds is settling the writers will be out on their pencils, looking for them in the suburbs and along the mythical Pecos. And except to paper riders, the Pecos is a lonely and bitter stream.
>
> I have that from men who rode it and who knew that country round — such as it was, such as it can never be again.

And Walker Percy's "New Orleans Mon Amour":

> If the American city does not go to hell in the next few years, it will not be the likes of Dallas or Grosse Pointe which will work its deliverance, or Berkeley or New Haven, or Santa Fe or La Jolla. But New Orleans might. Just as New Orleans hit upon jazz, the only unique American contribution to art, and hit upon it almost by accident and despite itself, it could also hit upon the way out of the hell that has overtaken the American city.

In a time characterized by the polarization of syntax, not to mention the ideological appetites, humor was sometimes the first thing to go, but we tried to encourage it, in pieces such as those by Larry L. King on the Grand Ole Opry, J. Anthony Lukas on life on a minor-league baseball team, and Gary "Jap" Cartwright on "Confessions of a Washed-Up Sportswriter":

> Influenced in part by men like Blackie Sherrod, Dan Jenkins, and Bud Shrake, almost all sportswriters were experimenting with words in the name of literature by 1960. It is impossible to overestimate the damage this has done to subsequent sportswriters, as this lead, selected at random from the October 22, 1967, Dallas *Morning News,* suggests:
>
> *Houston — There was mutiny of SMU's Good Ship Destiny here Saturday night and the Rice Owls found themselves marooned all alone on the Southwest Conference's unbeaten Isle of Desire.*

And, as always, there were my comrades and colleagues on our magazine, fellow-writers all, and the fun and nonsense which often enveloped us were workaday buffers to the national despair.

What was the Old Guard to make of the continuing unstaunched flow of esoteric visitors who came to our magazine offices? There was Bundini Brown, the deposed manager of Muhammad Ali, who wrote the Ali adage "Float like a butterfly, sting like a bee," a large black man who arrived at Plimpton's recommendation to sell me a carpet for my apartment; George Sauer, Jr., a tight end for the New York Jets, who was writing poetry; the actor Rod Steiger, who was also writing verse; three or four of the homicide detectives I had met at P. J. Clarke's; an elderly black man from my hometown come to discuss a shoe factory he was seeking to establish there to provide jobs for poor blacks, submitting during his visit an article refuting Professor Galbraith on Keynesian economics, and who eventually killed himself by jumping off the Yazoo River Bridge; old homeless Thirties radicals; bearded Village playwrights; small-town readers of *Harper's* from Dixie on their first sojourns North. Over the years the roster would be endless. One young gentleman wanted to search out J. D. Salinger at his anonymous farm in New England and blow his cover. When I rejected this invitation on the grounds that Salinger should be permitted his privacy, he proposed another exposé, this one of General MacArthur's only son, who had taken up the piano and changed his name and chosen to vanish into obscurity. If Larry L. King were in my office while some especially self-important out-of-town writer vainly waxed, he would say, "We're sure glad you dropped by. I just read in Leonard Lyons's column that you'd be in town." Leonard Lyons was a gossip columnist for one of the city's tabloids, and often the visitor would accept the casual intelligence without challenge, asking only to know the date of the mention, which King with a straight face would promise to supply soon.

One day several dozen homosexuals arrived *en masse* to occupy the offices. They came to demand redress for a paragraph in an article by Joseph Epstein which they considered unsympathetic to homosexuality. Herman Gollob was working on a manuscript at the desk in his office when a young man suddenly burst inside, followed by a television cameraman and a lighting technician. "Hi, I'm Hal, I'm a homosexual," the young man said. Taken by surprise, the kindly Gollob replied, "Gee, I'm sorry," to which the demonstrator shouted, "I don't want your pity!" and stormed away in a rage. The protestors had brought sandwiches and hot dogs and proceeded to sit on the floor to eat them. It was at this unpropitious moment that a Mexico-Texas border rat of my past acquaintance who taught school in El Paso came into the main entrance to the offices looking for me. He examined the scene which greeted him. "I always knew your editor believed in diversity," he whispered to the distraught receptionist.

As William Faulkner conceded of himself, I too was the world's oldest living sixth-grader. Sadly perhaps, nothing of New York would alter that. In my home country I was the product of an inherited tradition, no doubt having to do with the boredom of long and heavy afternoons and rich slow evenings when the frogs scratched their legs and made music, of elaborate plots, hoaxes, and practical jokes, reinforced by God's gift of many voices in disguise. Even as a grown man and magazine editor one could not satisfactorily purge any of this from his vainglorious blood and lineage. In the heady, boisterous, yet hard-working atmosphere of *Harper's*, ideal victims abounded. Larry L. King was likewise an inveterate prankster, having sprung from parallel traditions in the barren steppelands of West Texas, but it had not taken me long to discover that the sharpened poniard could be turned against him too, and to satisfactory effect. Surely this was all of a piece with our distinctive enterprise, and helped oil the axles of our wrought-up pixilation, but still, in the dogeared cliché of the trade, I suppose it was one hell of a way to run a magazine, and perhaps I should subscribe to Babe Ruth's confession about his 1948 autobiography when he said maybe he should have written two books, one for kids, one for adults.

I was well aware, for instance, that our managing editor Kotlowitz was an enthusiastic admirer of Leonard Bernstein, whom he had treated generously in his performing arts columns. In the Manhattan telephone directory Larry L. King and I discovered a dentist named Leonard Bernstein. When Kotlowitz returned from lunch one day, he found a note on his desk to call Leonard Bernstein at a certain number. With the cooperation of the secretaries we monitored the telephone from an extension in an adjacent alcove. Kotlowitz got a young woman on the line.

"Hello, this is Robert Kotlowitz at *Harper's*."

"Yes? What can I do for you?"

"I believe Mr. Bernstein called me."

"He called *you*?"

"Yes."

"Well, do you want to see him?"

"Sure. Yes, that would be fine."

"Well, he's tied up through tomorrow unless you're in great pain."

"I beg your pardon?"

"Are you in any pain?"

"Well, no more than usual."

"Then I'm afraid he can't see you immediately. He only takes emergency patients on short notice. Is it a bicuspid problem?"

"No," Kotlowitz said, a light having begun to dawn. "I think the pain's in a much lower region."

Once we hid a fake tarantula from the novelty store on West Thirty-third in a pile of copy paper on John Corry's desk while he was taking a nap before pushing ahead on a deadline. A few minutes later we heard a shriek down the corridor, and then sighted Corry, ashen as a specter. "Don't you ever, under any circumstances, do that again! The piece ain't worth a damn anyway." During his intermittent sleeping between high bursts of labor we enjoyed giving him the hot-foot; once while he was asleep we deposited counterfeit dog droppings on his carpet. A little later he had me accompany him to his office. "Did *I* do that?" he asked. Marshall Frady also provided rich possibilities, especially when he was grouchy and debilitated under deadline pressure on his long, complex pieces. King and I were to meet Frady for dinner one evening in the Empire Chinese. We arrived before Frady with a long needle and some fortunes typed in pica on thin colored slivers of paper. Mr. Suey Han, the maître d', permitted us to withdraw the fortunes from a pair of fortune cookies and insert the substitutes. At the conclusion of dinner Frady cracked open his fortune cookie. "I've never seen anything like this in my life," he said, and handed us his fortune. It said: *We know what you're up to, Bubba. You're out for the Yankee dollar.* We advised him, then, to try another. This one said: *When was the last time you washed your feet?* "As a matter of fact," he said, "if it's any Chinaman's damned business, I washed my feet yesterday."

Or:

"Mr. Gollob, this is Orson Welles."

"Goddamit, Willie, I ain't in the mood for practical jokes. I got a lot of shit to clean off my desk."

"Beg pardon, this is *Orson Welles*."

"Oh, yeah, really?"

"But it *is!*"

Because of his pride and intensity, Halberstam was always a suitable target. As Corry, Frady, King, and I moved about the country on assignments or scouting trips, Halberstam began receiving letters and notes from fans all over America. One came to him from an eight-year-old farm boy in Ohio, which Halberstam showed me as an example of one of the most unusual letters he ever got. "Dere Mr. Halbinsterm: I like your riting. I like it because it is so simple. In fact my mommy and daddy says you are the simplest riter they know. Love, Bruce." A missive from Washington declared: "If you have written seven good lines I have missed at least six of them," and recommended he take up veterinary medicine, plumbing, or the civil service. A young North Carolina woman, Alma Faye Frumpkin, wrote Halberstam a number of letters alternating between lewd propositions and requests to use his influence to publish her exotic verse. One such poem was titled "Kites and Wind."

Look! In the sky!
Kites.
Red. Orange. Blue. Green. And then,
I run, freely,
The string in my hand.
Breaking wind.

While King was doing a piece on Governor Nelson Rockefeller, he took Halberstam with him one night and introduced him to Rockefeller in Rockefeller's Manhattan quarters as "Frank Halpenstorm." "Good to see you, Frank!" King later reported Rockefeller's amiable response. "Frank, this is my wife, Happy. And this is my brother Laurance. Now, Frank, say hello to my brother David. Would you like a drink, Frank?" Halberstam was silently incensed: one's byline, he always said, was a writer's currency. He later demanded that King apologize. King profusely sought forgiveness, which Halberstam accepted. As he was leaving King said, "See you around the office, Frank."

Poetic retribution would intervene in King's instance. Soon he received in Washington a lengthy telephone call supposedly from an editor of *Time* informing him of that journal's intentions to publish a substantial feature about him pertaining to his latest book and asking if he could receive a staffwriter on the following Thursday. King asked the editor to hold on while he consulted his secretary, who we knew did not exist, then agreed to the appointment. The book editor began interviewing him about his approach to writing, his literary influences, his thoughts on symbolism and onomatopoeia, and where he got his ideas. For twenty minutes or so King prattled on. Someone of our number on one of the office extensions could not help stifling a chortle, and then a laugh. "Why you goddamned horses' asses!" King shouted.

After King's article on Nelson Rockefeller had appeared in the magazine, Rockefeller's press secretary, a gentleman named Les Slote, told him Rockefeller had privately decided to run for the Republican Presidential nomination to prevent Richard Nixon from getting it and they wanted to hire him as a speechwriter at an impressive salary. When King asked my advice I told him I thought he would be making a mistake; since he wrote frequently on politics, I suggested, it would not help him to be known as anyone's man. Shortly after that King got a phone call. A silken-voiced young woman asked him to hold the line for Governor Rockefeller. This time King was ready. "Governor Rockefeller" came on the wire, and began to talk about how much he needed him in the campaign, how much America needed him, how they would reach for the stars together. He would refuse to take no for an answer and expected to see him at three o'clock the next day in his offices in Manhattan.

"Sure you will," King said. "Then right after that you can go piss up a stump."

"I beg your pardon?"

"Come off it, you bastards."

"Who *is* this?" the voice said. "Who have I got on this line?"

In the moment's passing the hapless King realized it was indeed the authentic Rockefeller.

Soon to come was the relationship with one Max Ascoli, suggestive of much about the magazine business of that era. If what ensues in the next few pages were a piece of short fiction, its title would be "The Subscription List"; I learned something from it.

Nearly forty years divided Max Ascoli and me, and sever us they did — a schism not just of age, but of personality, money, the language, people, the very madness and reality of America itself. Ascoli was seventy years old when our lives converged, a tall man of swarthy visage wearing heavy eyeglasses. He was born in Ferrara, Italy, the only child of a wealthy coal-and-lumber man. He acquired a Ph.D. at the University of Rome and taught in several other universities before eventually fleeing the Mussolini regime in the early 1930s, carrying with him a Gauguin and a Tintoretto and a substantial part of his considerable fortune. In the United States he taught at the New School in New York City and took American citizenship. After his marriage to the Italian poetess Anna Maria Maddalene Paolina Giacinta Cochetti dissolved, he married the heiress of one of the nation's largest fortunes: Marion Rosenwald was a daughter of Julius Rosenwald, philanthropist and executive of Sears, Roebuck. In 1949 he founded, with the help of his wife's money, *The Reporter,* a liberal fortnightly of facts and ideas dealing with national and international issues, and he was its editor and publisher. I had read *The Reporter* in college and admired it, often quoting it in our editorials in the *Daily Texan,* for it published Bill Mauldin, Meg Greenfield, Theodore H. White, Arthur Schlesinger, Jr., Douglas Cader, David Halberstam, and many other honorable contributors. I had found it laborious, however, to read Max Ascoli's columns, which were among the most turgid exertions in the mother tongue in the Western Christendom of that time; one could call them assiduous. In the Sixties *The Reporter* itself, I thought, was becoming increasingly somnolent and aloof.

By 1968 *The Reporter,* after nineteen years of publication and a substantial yearly deficit, was about to fold. To avoid having to satisfy *The Reporter's* unfulfilled subscriptions, the Ascolis approached the Cowleses with the proposition that with a mutually suitable payment from *Harper's,* the paid-up *Reporter* subscribers would be added to the *Harper's* list and receive *Harper's* in lieu of *The Reporter*. Part of the agreement was that Max Ascoli would join *Harper's* as consulting editor, his articles and columns to appear regularly in its pages, with some of *The Reporter's* editorial features to be incorporated into those pages too. Before this arrangement could be consummated, however, Max Ascoli must get to know, and approve of, the editor of *Harper's.* Thus began my irascible and unfortunate covenant with Max Ascoli on behalf of the Cowles publishing kingdom.

Max Ascoli was infamous in New York for his tyrannies and impetuosities. He had left in his wake over the years a trail of shattered relationships, professional and personal, nearly transcontinental in its smoky breadth and sweep. He was at the outset of our unlikely association a paradigm of charm, of solicitude, of warm and intimate camaraderie. A man I knew on the fading *Reporter,* a high editor there for years, nearly collapsed in his restaurant chair in a paroxysm of mirthful dementia when I told him this. I thought one of his escargots had gone down the wrong tributary: "*Charming?* Well, yeah, right, at first. Then touch him the wrong way and he has all the charm of his compatriot Mussolini." This, on the face of it, was not salutary.

Ascoli would pick me up in his chauffeured limousine at the corner of Park and Thirty-third and take me to our interminable private lunches in the most sumptuous and expensive Italian restaurants of Manhattan. As the waiters floated obsequiously about his presence awaiting his every metronomic command, he ordered from the menus for me, lecturing me avuncularly on the cuisine and wine. He would lean across the table and talk to me conspiratorially about American politics and foreign policy, his friendships with Presidents and diplomats and European ministers of state. We were indeed *conspirators!* One of my special hindrances, however, was that I could not fully understand him, particularly when he whispered, which was often, for his Italian accent was as ponderous as the Tuscany sauce, and amid his monumental soliloquies and disquisitions, I found myself nodding my head asininely and smiling a moronic down-home smile at remarks as comprehensible to me as the chorus of an Afghan anthem. His expressions would oddly contort as he talked, reminding me of what Dorothy Parker said of Basil Rathbone, that his face was like two profiles taped together. To pass the time in these esoteric monologues I turned my thoughts to other things: imagining, for instance, my boyhood chums and fellow ballplayers from Yazoo entering this most well-bred of restaurants and swooping upon our table and slapping my companion on the back and shouting, "Gettin' much, ol' Maxie? Ever seen a ball game in that smelly ol' gym in Satartia, Maxie?," or remembering the oleaginous Italian joints in Austin which would not have known calamari salad from souse, or recalling the good, simple Italian people of the Delta. During his fustian ramblings at these best Mediterranean houses in New York — as my grandmother had said of certain people, "He talks a lot with his mouth" — I heard my own silent plea: "Please God, allow this to be over fast." But it never was. Always, when he at last was finished, he would spread out his big hands on the table and say, strangely, "Any-*whoo* . . ." and I was for that moment reprieved.

"He'll love you for two months," counselled my Deep Throat at *The Reporter,* "and then he'll turn on you so bad you won't know what's happening. Believe me, your arrangement won't work. Take the damned subscriptions and run."

Then why was I doing this? Was I dissembling with the wordy fellow? Outlasting him? Sometimes he would telephone me in the middle of the day to come to his house for a talk, a grand mansion on Gramercy Park filled with books, paintings, classical records, electronics gadgetry. He would dispatch his liveried chauffeur to my office for me, a ruddy Irishman from the Bronx who, despite his employer's expertise on foreign affairs, did not know the NATO Alliance from the Green Bay Packers. While Puccini resonated on the stereo in his house, Max Ascoli would tell me he had been studying the recent issues of my magazine, and what was wrong with it, and what needed to be done about it — use *The Reporter* as an example, he said, and *The Economist* — and he looked forward to being my partner and consultant, and to counselling me on a day-by-day basis. *Oh, shit!* I was in trouble. Beaten down, I would return to my office three hours later. "Where have you been?" Bob Kotlowitz would ask. "With Max Ascoli." "What do you *talk* about all that time?" "I'd have to make a list for you to believe it." Or if the sessions lasted longer than that, I would telephone my wife Celia to say I would not be home for dinner. "Why not *this* time?" "I'm with Max Ascoli."

I telephoned my owner, John Cowles, Jr., in Minneapolis. "I've got to get off this assignment. I can't do this and put out a magazine."

"It's important," he said, just as he had when I missed a World Series.

"How important?"

"*Important.* We need those subscriptions."

"You don't have to be around him all the time. It's killing me."

"Hang in there. It's worth it."

"I don't like to lie."

"Don't lie. Just hang in."

Ascoli was a spoiled, embittered old man, bitingly righteous with his injunctions, an anomaly from the vanished epochs. I see now that his brackishness surely had to have been rooted in his dark Mediterranean intuition that the Great Republic had never adequately appreciated him, that his fellow publishers no longer truly respected him, and that the salons of the intellectual and the powerful had long since more or less turned away from him. Complicating this dismal aspect was his wife, the Marion of the Rosenwalds, who had Southern antecedents and was quite wonderful; she served his countless whims, which were not especially uxorious, and I secretly suspected sympathized with my gathering internal misery, glancing solicitously at me from time to time. The sunless and fanatical side of him had harsh words for everyone, nearly without exception, including his own past and valued contributors. Schlesinger? Had nothing to say. Galbraith? Greedy ideologue. Teddy White? Believed his own clippings. On and on went the list, a veritable Mount Rushmore of crimson invective, and more and more trenchant concerning one's own magazine, its contents, make-up, contributors. Larry L. King: crude and provincial. Halberstam: untrustworthy and impetuous. Alfred Kazin: too Jewish. Irving Howe: dully predictable. Richard Hofstadter: too soft. William Styron: too melodramatic. Bob Kotlowitz: too facile. Midge Decter: too angry. On and on went these verbal scimitars. He took to telephoning more and more frequently at my office, outlining his writing plans in a detail that would have shamed the general staff of the Wehrmacht in the Advance on Paris, venting his Gulliverian vituperations, so that whenever he called, my secretary would buzz on the other line: "It's *him*. Want to go to the men's room?" I would listen for a while as he pursued another oracular spoor, then put the telephone on the desk and go about other tasks while the voice staccatoed on Mr. Bell's invention: a mounting crescendo and compendium, and at the apex of it Norman Mailer, so detested by him he could scarcely mention the name, but spit it out in expletive, like a brothy gurgle.

Yet there were moments I felt sympathy for him. Would I myself, after all a magazine editor too, be so bitter someday? Turn so to calumny for survival? Shortly after Lyndon Johnson announced he would not run again, Ascoli got an appointment and flew to Washington to see Johnson, and to commiserate with him. He waited in the White House all afternoon, he told me, and was finally summoned into the Oval Office at the end of the day. Johnson gave him two minutes. "He looked so tired," he said. "I didn't want to bother him."

The time arrived for John Cowles, Jr., and his associates to come east from Minnesota to seal the contract. I was happy to see them, my reinforcements from Olympus, getting there just as the flanks were failing. They wanted to be sure they pronounced the name right. I wrote for them on a napkin: *a sko le*. They practiced it two or three times. They closed the deal at Max Ascoli's house, conferring privately two or three times in another room before getting the price just right. Outside, in the cool night air of regal Gramercy, we slapped hands like cornerbacks after an opportune interception and ventured out into the city to celebrate. I felt just fine, and as close to them in that moment as I ever would, and I wish it had lasted.

The break with Ascoli came a little after that. His first *Harper's* article was to be on violence in present-day America. I had heard Arthur M. Schlesinger, Jr.'s address at a university commencement on much the same subject and asked Schlesinger to recast it for our magazine. When Max Ascoli noticed this item on our future editorial list he telephoned me, calling me, as I remember it now, a back-stabbing pretender plotting to strip him of his dignity. He cursed me in three languages, then demanded an urgent meeting with the owners and myself. I got them to New York. In Ascoli's empty *Reporter* offices on East Fifty-seventh he declared he would have nothing more to do with our enterprise. The subscription list contract had already been signed and delivered, he said, and he could do nothing about that, but he himself was to have no part of it. Pointing to me, he said: "This man is not a gentleman." As we were leaving he shook hands with John Cowles, Jr., and his advisors. I offered my hand. He turned away.

The Midwestern financial empire had prevailed, as it would and must. As we departed into the corridor of the desolate chambers of *The Reporter,* John Cowles, Jr., and the others smiled and smirked. "You did it!" one of them whispered to me. "You won't have to worry with the old bastard anymore." I shared in this quick, private exuberance, for I would never indeed have to see Max Ascoli again, never suffer again his somber and everlasting acrimonies. But in the very act of leaving I glanced back into his office and saw the old embattled anti-Fascist exile there for the last time in my life. He had already long since lost his magazine, and that could not be easy, as I myself would someday learn. He was standing tall there beside his deserted desk, the waning sunlight of the city catching his hefty eyeglasses, proud, tormented, arrogant, and alone, a very long way from Ferrara, the only man in my whole life who had ever refused to shake hands with me. And in the glimmer a premonition passed my hotheaded spirit, not in paranoia but in an ineffable sadness, darkly as time as the Cowleses grinned: *Ask not for whom the bell tolls. . . .*

Not too long after this, John Cowles, Jr., brought in a man named William S. Blair to be president of the magazine, the Cowleses' high-salaried overseer on the premises. Blair was a dapper figure of fifty-one with a gently modulated voice, sartorially impeccable with an eye both for himself and the ladies, married to a rich wife, with a house on Gramercy Park not far from Max Ascoli's. He was a product of advertising, having previously served for some time as president of the Madison Avenue firm which handled advertising jointly for *Harper's* and *The Atlantic Monthly.* When John Cowles, Jr., had solicited my thoughts on appointing Blair to the position, I had witlessly said it sounded okay to me, for my relationship with him as the advertising executive had withal been pleasant and harmless enough. It was a mistake. The first act of his tenure was to redecorate at considerable cost the office down the corridor he had just moved into. With its robust decor, its plush sofa and zestful carpet, its nearly analgesic neatness, it was a good exemplar of post–Madison Avenue Gothic, considerably in contrast with the quarters of most of the editors, especially mine, with their air of breezy neglect, manuscripts stacked in corners, books in haphazard array, not to mention the inchoate cubbyholes used by the staffwriters Halberstam, King, Corry, and Frady, to which only the U.S. Army Corps of Engineers could have lent coherence.

Blair's habit was to wander about our office sniffing things out, gleaning and gathering like a squirrel. In all our time together I could never quite ascertain what precisely he did to earn his keep. One afternoon when I was about to promote Midge Decter to executive editor, he came in for a word. He had soft eyes, my wife once describing them as the most beautiful she ever saw on a man, and the oblique dash of an English accent, and he smiled frequently without opening his lips very much, as if benignity without mirth were a virtue of the programmed enigmatic.

"I imagine you're aware that if you go through with this," he said, "we'll have a Jewish managing editor and a Jewish executive editor."

I told him I was aware of it, and also that the editor-in-chief was from the boondocks of Mississippi.

"Okay, okay. Just so you're aware."

Blair, as my grandmother also would have said, was a "pesterance," but I rather liked him after he had had two or three drinks with our group of brothers in the Empire Chinese bar and sat there with his tender child-like smile nodding at our rampant badinage. "During the day Twining was a man of fairly wide interests," Wilfrid Sheed described his New York magazine personage in *Office Politics,* "but over the martinis he tended to narrow sharply." He still seemed harmless enough. I merely did not want him to get too much in the way.

This, in 1968, was some moment removed from the ownership's becoming more studiedly impersonal, mute, detached, retinued, corporate, precursors of rootless publishing takeovers someday to sweep the land. We were having fun, even as our offices were fallen upon by arcane corporate interlopers, odd harbingers, strange fellows of neutral aspect who for all we knew might have risen from the honeycombs of the subterranean CIA vaults of Langley, Virginia. There were reader surveys quizzing the subscribers on what they read, which article first, what article last, how much of this article did they read, did they read this poem, did they like poetry, should the language be simpler, what time of day did they pick up this issue? These unflagging chaps would mount the monthly issues onto charts with percentage points, computer tabulations, reasoned conclusions accompanied by gritty graphs and diagrams. On and on went these resolute tallies. Do you have a sense of humor? What do you wish to read in this magazine? Should this magazine run poetry? Should it run fiction? Do you like sports? What are your hobbies? Will you recommend this issue to your friends? *Any* of the articles to your friends? And then, in the midst of these remote barometrics, the "psychological" assayers drifted about the quarters querying the editors on *their* internal topography — their mandate, I believe I recall, to match the interests of the editors with the interests of the readers, overlap itself being desirable. Do you have nightmares? Do you have specific ideals? Do you have a favorite hour of the day? What do you think of graffiti? Ghettos are burning, and napalm is on the jungles, and young men dying unexplained, and kids kidnapping college deans, and blacks in berets wanting mutiny, and children aciding out everywhere, and assassinations, and these adenoidal corporate squatters schlepping around, and it's about *graffiti* they want to know? As I had concerning poor Max Ascoli, I eventually telephoned John Cowles in the towers of the Twin Cities. This was frivolous and wasteful, I argued, and spurious. Oh, no, he said: merely routine. If I had suggested, as had his football coach at Exeter, "You're giving away the signals, Cowles," would he have replied: "Habitually?"

It was 1968, all right. And with it came Mailer.

~ Mailer, LBJ, RFK, the U.S. from Afar

10 OCTOBER, 1967, had contributed another important event of the Sixties, crystallizing the country's discords. With the mass March on the Pentagon of that month, in the judgment of the SDS's Tom Hayden, "resistance became the official watchword of the anti-war movement." Yet it was by no means a decisive or climactic moment, and would be remembered in history only because Norman Mailer was there and wrote about it, which surely says something about the act of literature.

Mailer was an intriguing figure for me, a mythic and elusive man who, whatever one thought of him, and almost everyone I knew had vehement opinions of him, had been in the epicenter of matters in America, its monumental travails and hopes, ever since the publication of *The Naked and the Dead* in '48. "For a writer to inspire the controversy and divisions that routinely orbit Mailer's life and career," the *New York Times* would write, "is perhaps unprecedented in American literary history." Mark Twain might have been more popular, and Hemingway more influential, "but neither of these writers, whose books conquered both the academy and the marketplace, ever had so many thousands of people at their feet — and at their throats." Dan Wakefield, in his *New York in the Fifties,* saw Mailer in those years at *Village Voice* parties and other social events. As long as Wakefield was speaking with him one-on-one, Mailer was gracious and pleasant, "but as soon as a group of people gathered around to listen, his voice tended to rise, and his manner and opinions became more brash and pugnacious."

Mailer was, in his own later words in *Harper's*, "a warrior, presumptive general, ex–political candidate, embattled aging *enfant terrible* of the literary world, wise father of six children, radical intellectual, existential philosopher, hard-working author, champion of obscenity, husband of four battling sweet wives, admirable bar drinker, and much exaggerated street fighter, party giver, hostess insulter." He, too, was inherent to the 1960s, a decade so unusual in relation to other decades, he himself confessed, that he had begun it by stabbing his second wife, and ended it by running for Mayor of New York City. Despite the flaws and excesses, I thought him in many ways a literary genius; never fearful of using his own complex and extravagant persona, he had possessed the grit to take the big risks against the house odds, to confront complex themes, and to do so in a prose that in its vibrant energy was out at the contemporary edge, and burned with fierce and funny and incandescent brilliance. His words were to be among the best and most enduring by any American of the Sixties.

I had little notion when I first met him, in Austin in '61, that we would someday be, in the broadest sense, collaborators. The novelist Barbara Probst and her husband Harold Solomon, New York intellectual exiles at the University of Texas, gave a party for him after a lecture, and he ended at Celia's and my house for nightcaps. I saw little in that initial encounter of his reputation as a veritable Coriolanus of the city pavements. Quite the contrary. He was gracious, witty, well-mannered, and for one who had grown up among Jewish Southern boys with their sunny and expansive countenances, and deep abiding drawls, a rather nice Jewish boy from Brooklyn: short, blue-eyed, with outsized ears and an abundant crown of wiry hair. Beyond the hair and ears he had a strong, almost suffering, Jewish face, Old Testament somehow to me in its lines and contours in repose. Was it not true that he built model airplanes all through high school? After arriving in New York and expressing my regard for his work, not a few people were scornful to me of his demanding personality, his combativeness and megalomania, his obsession with crime and violence and suicide and psychosis, his incessant feuds and sharp-elbowed machoism. ("The trouble with being gentle is that one has no defense against shame," he wrote.) He often moved about the city with a small entourage, not unlike his hero Hemingway, or like prizefighters; indeed, one of his closest companions was the former light-heavyweight champion José Torres. In parties I attended all over town he was constantly getting into fights. At one such evening in the Village I saw him across the room in aggressively intense conversation, his voice as heated as the July night in its rise and crackle, and less than a minute later I noticed him standing there with a bloodied lip. A friend visiting me from El Paso approached him at a party and told him how much he had admired *From Here to Eternity*. "Tell Jim Jones," Mailer replied, "he wrote it," and turned angrily away. At the famous Truman Capote costume party at the Plaza in '66, Mailer had confronted McGeorge Bundy about Vietnam. Vietnam was too complicated to talk about, Bundy replied. "I paid you too much respect," Mailer countered, and suggested that Bundy take off his glasses and step outside. "Mr. Mailer," Bundy said, "I admire your talent very much and it grieves me to see you behave this way. You and I have better things to do than fight." David Halberstam would note of this in *Harper's*: "Judges gave the first round to Bundy though there is a feeling in the long run that Mailer may come out of the decade somewhat better than Bundy." Lillian Hellman bore down on Mailer for the confrontation she had witnessed, and was all for Bundy, and Mailer did not speak to Hellman for a year.

As the junior editor, in the occasional meeting I asked him to send something to *Harper's*. He could not afford to, he rejoined, because he was aware of the magazine's rates, and he asked $200,000 for each piece because that was what he owed each year, he said, in alimony and child support. Obviously he was putting me on. Also, he added, it would be a waste of good time because *Harper's* was so arid it would not take anything of his anyway. Once he relented, however, and sent me a small section from his forthcoming *Cannibals and Christians*. I defended it on the grounds that *Harper's* should start publishing Mailer because he was attuned to

America and people paid attention to him even when they disagreed with him, but my colleagues voted it down unanimously, John Fischer merely shrugging his shoulders when he returned it to me with the hostile assessments attached. It was a hard phone call. "Didn't I tell you?" Mailer said. "That's the last thing you'll get from *me.*" The fellow had plainly been testing me.

As I grew to know Mailer in the years ahead, I seldom saw in a person a larger variance between the public image and the real man. Almost without exception I found him to be a kind and considerate human being, and as a writer one of the most genuine professionals I would ever know, and one of the most arduous workers, one of those writers who was always writing even when not actually putting down the words, a Jew from the Eastern Parkway precincts of Brooklyn intensely American in his interests, concerns, and idioms, zealous about even the most demanding deadlines, loyal and straightforward to the editors he trusted. Surely it was an unlikely alliance in those demanding years of the late 1960s, the writer and the editor, the volatile urban Jew and the village Dixie WASP, involving the things I so fervently wished to do with *Harper's* in taking the language to its limits in a popular and established national journal, in revealing the American truths behind the American shams, in opposing the Establishment's glutinous war and its fatal domestic effects, in exploring the ironies of the new man-and-woman relationships, in confronting the true nature and dimension of power in America, and in other aspects as well — but as I look back on it now, perhaps the alliance was not really that unlikely a one at all.

The morning after Houghton-Mifflin's publication party for my book *North Toward Home,* I arrived a little hung over at my office to be greeted by a telephone call from Cass Canfield, Sr., the head man at Harper & Row. He had heard a rumor around town that Mailer was planning to write a magazine article on his participation in the anti-war demonstration in Washington of three or four days before.

I had read the accounts in the papers over the weekend of Mailer's having deliberately gotten himself arrested at the Pentagon and of his time in a Virginia jail. All the editor's instincts I had assiduously acquired on the Yazoo *High Flashlight,* not to mention the *Daily Texan* and the *Texas Observer,* told me this would be an exceedingly important piece, one that would strike to the taproots of all that was happening at that moment in the nation. I tried most of the morning to reach Mailer all over the city on the telephone; he was in hiding. Then I began talking off and on all day with his agent, a mysterious figure I had heard much about but never met named Scott Meredith, a "big-money" agent, as he was known around New York, who would introduce the practice of the book auction to publishing. Mailer wanted to do the piece quickly, the agent said, and then to have it subsequently published as a pamphlet-length book. Much as I tried, the agent Meredith would not disclose to me where his writer was. He himself would relay my messages. To the credit of the owners in Minneapolis, we were able by the end of the workday to get the price to $10,000. The agent and I reached a verbal agreement: the writer would get the article to the magazine under deadline; the magazine would prepare the article for publication and provide the finished manuscript to a book publisher for publication the month after it appeared in *Harper's.* He left it with us to find a publishing company that would pay an additional $25,000. I saw no problem there. We would start in on that the next morning. "We've got it!" I told my colleagues, and I recall someone cheered.

It was a good day's work, and I left the office late to meet someone for drinks at the Algonquin, imbibed with that special euphoria which only Manhattan gives you when you have done something rewarding and glad, when the very stone canyons of the town seem soft and inviting and the citizenry well disposed, and the first lights of evening thrilling and merry.

I met the person at the Algonquin, an elderly columnist for the *Memphis Commercial-Appeal* who was gracious enough at first but after a couple of sourmashes told me I had sold out the South, and half an hour or so later was mulling over this indictment while walking among the crowds in a sepia sunset up Seventh Avenue toward the nearest subway.

One has to have resided in New York City a sufficient time to appreciate as an indigenous congruity that at the corner of Seventh and Forty-fourth whom should I run into but Mailer. I nearly stumbled into him as he strolled in the opposite direction. He was in company of the boxer José Torres. "We just closed the deal," I said. "I know, I know," he replied. Then, bent into a boxer's stance, he began shadow-boxing at nothing in particular, until a gratuitous left jab grazed across my jaw. Sidewalk New Yorkers parted about us and proceeded in their eternal journeyings without paying any undue attention. The writer continued jabbing the empty air in his prizefight crouch. He was going up to Provincetown the next day to write the ten thousand words. "This one could be kind of good," he said. "I'll be in touch," and disappeared into the human tide as abruptly as he had come.

The next day, Midge Decter, a good friend of Mailer's, and I met with three book publishers of different houses, each of whom turned down the joint offer. "Not worth it," one said. "Too big a gamble," judged another, "for something so short." It turned out that within two days the agent Meredith made a deal with the editor Robert Gutwillig at New American Library for publication of the little pamphlet after *Harper's*. As promised on the streetcorner Mailer retreated to his place on the Cape in Provincetown. We scheduled his article for our February 1968 number. Two weeks later the writer called from Provincetown. His piece was growing beyond ten thousand words; he needed an additional month to five weeks. We rescheduled it for March, with a final printer's deadline of January 10.

With the deadline pressingly imminent, Midge Decter and I flew in a small plane out of Butler Aviation in Queens to the Cape shortly after New Year's for several days' work. We had not seen a word of the manuscript. Mailer's house was on the water, Cape Cod Bay, with the mournful sound all round of the sea and wind, the buoys and gulls. It was a red-brick three-story house two miles from the end of the great final curve of the Cape. It was cold, with a light skein of powdery snow. His wife, the actress Beverly Bentley, was there. She was a very beautiful woman, and there was obviously a strong bond between them, although the New York City literary prattle said Mailer changed wives after every big book.

One of her brothers had served in Vietnam. The writer had only recently written of her in the manuscript nearing completion there:

> Mailer finally came to decide that his love for his wife while not at all equal or congruent to his love for America was damnably parallel. It was not inconceivable to him that if he finally came to believe his wife was not nearly so magical as he would make her, but was in fact petty, stingy, small-minded, and evilly stubborn (which is what he told her in many a quarrel) why then he would finally lose some part of his love affair with America, he would have to, because there were too many times when thinking of his country and some new one of the unspeakable barbarities it invented with every corporation day, he would decide that no it could not be an altogether awful country because otherwise how would his wife, a Southerner and an Army brat, have come out so subtle, so supple, so mysterious, so fine-skinned, so tender and wise.

Also there was a large black twelve-year-old poodle named Tibo with halitosis, and Mailer's typist Sandy Charlebois, a young activist who along with Jerry Rubin and Abbie Hoffman would come up with the name "Yippies." There was a bundle of manuscript. Mailer wrote in long-hand with pencil, with considerable crossing out, and spidery inserts, and petulant excisions, and sentences running completely off the pages and across the top and back, which he would pass along in installments to Sandy Charlebois, who was still typing from the handwritten pages. He had been working twelve or fourteen hours a day, and considering the speed of the work, the typescript too was messy. I would read fifteen or twenty pages, then give them to Midge Decter in another room. Mailer was nearing the end and was still working on an epilogue elsewhere in the house. It was not at all unlike the newsroom of a paper, the taut pace of which I more or less had missed in the monthly magazine business. I recall reading one-third or so of the typescript pages and telling Midge we had something extraordinary. It was "an event," she later said, "an editor's dream come true." Mailer came down several times a day to go over the typing with an emery board. Midge, who was a resilient editor in every facet of the trade, had no difficulty with the handwriting. She was erasing many of his interpolations and reprinting them legibly so that certain pages would not need to be retyped. From time to time she and Mailer would sit down and do minimal editing, then he would retire upstairs again to finish.

"Let's see how many words we've got, Midge." We went through the pages, then glanced at each other. We had more than ninety thousand. We called up for the author and had a fleeting discussion about breaking the ninety thousand words into installments, and concluded absolutely not. Our office in New York was impatiently waiting; the entire March issue was suspended and on the line. I had promised our managing editor Bob Kotlowitz that I would telephone him in New York City the moment we knew what we had.

"How is it?" Kotlowitz asked.

"It's marvelous."

"That's great. How many words?"

"Ninety thousand."

A brief silence at the Manhattan end.

"*Ninety thousand?*"

"About that."

"You think we should run it in installments — two, three?"

"I think we should run all of it at once."

"All of it?"

"I really do."

"Well, why the hell not?"

I did not remotely know how the man wrote these words in little more than six weeks, and still do not, but he had done so (and, indeed, had just that day completed in the room at the top of the house the additional twenty-thousand-word epilogue, which I told him we would not publish in *Harper's*), and since Midge and the typist Sandy and I were taking the small plane back to the city early the next morning with the manuscript, surely it was an occasion to celebrate, which we did that evening with a great deal of wine and spirits and good food. Mailer had not had a drink since he began the writing, and I had brought up from the city a full quart of Wild Turkey bourbon, and he and I set about doing amends, soon to be joined to a remarkable degree by his consort Beverly Bentley, and in modest and ceremonial measure by the more abstemious Midge Decter. All the while Beverly and Mailer were chopping a small mountain of ingredients for, as I remember, mushrooms stuffed with *duxelles,* and the writer dashed about the kitchen explaining the culinary process.

"Come on, Morris," Mailer said after dinner, "I'll show you where the Pilgrims landed." We took the Wild Turkey to his jeep. It was snowing harder now, and the jeep lurched and jumped madly across the sand dunes while the driver told me Hemingway was a better boxer than most people gave him credit for. On one especially precarious dune the vehicle stalled momentarily in the sand, and we had to get out to push it. Mobile again, as we took turns with draws on the bottle, he began talking in the redneck Texas accent he said he had acquired from back-country Texans in the Army. He rolled out in prefaces to sentences a lot of twangy "little ol's" while gesturing sharply with his arms. He said he liked Southerners. "Why did you say I had frizzy hair in that book you wrote?" he asked. "Well," I replied, "because you do." The motor of our conveyance began to buzz and hum a little, and the driver put his wary ear to the dashboard and said, "I think this thing has tuberculosis." Somewhere up in the frosty dark of the Eastern littoral must have been the granite tower to the Pilgrims, but with the snow and the bouncing jeep, which reminded me of a certain ride at the Yazoo County fairs of my childhood called "Bump-O-Bile," I could not readily testify that we saw it.

He was now talking in the tones of an Irish cop about why he liked winters on the Cape. "I'll buy you a drink at the VFW," he said, sounding much like Barry Fitzgerald in the movie *Naked City,* or Victor McLaughlin in *The Informer.* The VFW hut was by his testimony the only bar open on a snowy January night in Provincetown. On this evening of the gathering elements he and I and the jovial bartender were the only creatures there. I toasted to what he had just finished writing. "Look," he said, "I wish you'd stop praising it. It makes me edgy." We ordered another drink. He was describing the running style of Southern Cal's O. J. Simpson. "Why won't you publish my epilogue?" he demanded. I argued that we were already running ninety thousand words and that the epilogue would be fine for a book but only an afterthought to the drama of a magazine treatment. "You're dead wrong," he said. "Let's go." Back again at his house, Midge Decter was watching Mailer's wife Beverly as she crawled on the floor looking for something. "You're evil," she said in slurred words when she saw her husband, who more or less ignored her. She had been listening to records on an old stereo and the phonograph needle had fallen out, and that was what she was now searching for. "You're evil, Norman," she repeated. "You hate this record player. You worked voodoo on it."

"There's always in Norman a rational, Jewish son who has his wits about him," Irving Howe once said. As I was about to leave the next morning I said goodbye to Mailer in the kitchen. "What will my father think?" he said, a reference I took to the four-letter words and scatology in his manuscript, but he was being more jocular than serious. "What will my *mother* think?" I myself said, explaining that she had taken out a number of subscriptions to *Harper's* and donated them to libraries in small Mississippi towns such as Belzoni, Durant, and Flora. "Guess we can't worry," he said.

We had a brand-new copy editor, who had come highly recommended from a journal of commerce. Her tirades against the language were wrathful and indignant. The woman was enraged, even onomatophobic. She said: "I wonder what he writes like when he's sober?" She was gone within the week.

"The Steps of the Pentagon," in the March, 1968, issue of *Harper's*, was the longest magazine article ever published (John Hersey's "Hiroshima" in *The New Yorker* having previously had that distinction) and was one of the signal and most controversial events in the long history of American magazines: its impact on the country and the times on a variety of levels was stunning and instantaneous. It opened radical new ground in subject matter and in the uses of the language in popular national journals. Subsequently in book form under the title *The Armies of the Night*, it won the Pulitzer Prize and the National Book Award, as well as the

George Polk Memorial Award for magazine journalism from Columbia University, which called it "an American epic." The *New York Times* recalled Walt Whitman: "I am the man. I suffer'd. I was there," and said: "Whitman staked his work on finding the personal connection between salvation as an artist and the salvation of his country," judging Mailer's as brilliant as Whitman's towering personal testimonials.

The magazine preface read: "We believe that Mr. Mailer's account of himself and some of his fellow Americans in a peculiarly representative moment of crisis carries hints and reverberations that will make themselves felt in American life and politics for many years." Using the third-person persona, "History as a Novel," the author as part observer, part protagonist, indeed as self-mocking comic hero in all his fault and tumult, it moved from the rich panorama of the demonstration itself to a consideration of the moral, social, and political temper of the nation, doing so with a crackling energy and high humor and gusto for the graphic detail: portraits of individual people — Robert Lowell, Dwight Macdonald, Paul Goodman, William Sloane Coffin — of federal marshals ("they emitted a collective spirit which, to his mind, spoke of little which was good, for their eyes were blank and dull, that familiar small-town cast of eye which speaks of apathy rising to fanaticism only to subside in apathy again"), of liberal academics, Black Panthers, old Snick warriors, harassed young soldiers, Jewish lawyers, anti-war college chaplains, clean liberals and New Leftists and women's activists, and professional radicals and hippies and Yippies — a roster itself of the decade. And lusty digressions:

> HAWKS 95 DOVES 6
> *NFL Footballers Approve Vietnam War*
>
> Doubtless. All the healthy Marines, state troopers, professional athletes, movie stars, rednecks, sensuous life-loving Mafia, cops, mill workers, city officials, nice healthy-looking easy-grafting politicians full of the light (from marijuana?) in their eye of a life they enjoy — yes, they would be for the war in Vietnam. Arrayed against them as hard-core troops: an elite! the Freud-ridden embers of Marxism, good old American anxi-

ety strata — the urban middle class with their proliferated monumental adenoidal resentments, their secret slavish love for the oncoming hegemony of the computer and the suburb, yes, they and their children, by the sheer ironies, the sheer ineptitude, the *kinks* of history, were now being compressed into more and more militant stands, their resistance to the war some hopeless melange, somehow firmed, of Pacifism and closet Communism. And their children — on a freak-out from the suburbs to a love-in on the Pentagon wall.

Armies of the Night, née "Steps of the Pentagon," embodied a nearly excruciating kind of personal honesty, Mailer as champion *schmuck*: urinating in the darkened bathroom of a theater, delivering of himself a drunken speech embarrassing even to his drunken comrades, darting about in a three-piece suit trying to get arrested, fervently wishing to get out of jail in time to return to New York for a Saturday night party, the uproariously blemished and human context of collective instabilities and public acts. The lengthy description of the protagonist in a police van with a Nazi ("*Dirty Jew*" . . . "*Kraut Pig*") was to me one of the strongest and most unexpungeable in contemporary American writing. And the concluding paragraph in the magazine:

> Then he began his history of the Pentagon. It insisted on becoming a history of himself over four days. He labored in the aesthetic novelties of the problem for weeks, discovering that his dimensions as a character in a novel were simple: Blessed had been the novelist, for his protagonist was a simple of a hero and a marvel of a fool, with more than average gifts of objectivity — might his critics have as much! — this verdict disclosed by the unprotective haste with which he was obliged to write, for he wrote of necessity at a rate faster than he had ever written before, as if the accelerating history of the country forbid deliberation. Yet in writing his personal history of those four days, he also delivered a discovery to himself of what the March on the Pentagon had finally meant, and what had been won, and what had been lost in that quintessentially American and most contemporary event — the scheduled happening which begins with

the given and ends on the road to that mystery where courage, death, and the dream of love give promise of sleep.

"The Steps of the Pentagon" drew more letters-to-the-editor to that point than any piece in the 119-year history of *Harper's:* an outpouring vast and electric. Hundreds of them were hostile; the sizeable subscription cancellations, most of them, had to do not with the anti-war substance of the piece, but with the uses of the language. Most of the letters were long and thoughtful and deeply felt and pertained to the American civilization of that day. Mailer wanted to come to the offices to read them. It took a few hours, but he looked over every one, and finally came bleary-eyed into my office and said: "All these people sitting all over America writing these letters. They're carrying on a conversation with a magazine as if a magazine itself were a human being."

"The Steps of the Pentagon" was in every aspect an affirmation of my dreams for *Harper's,* bringing together as it did the artistic sensibility with the trustworthy eye for detail and event in a palpable moment passionate and important for the civilization. It seemed to have been read and discussed by everyone who mattered in America, and it provided one with great confidence and hope for the future. The people at Columbia responsible for the Polk Award had their annual banquet in the ballroom of the Roosevelt. Would I introduce Mailer? More important, they asked, since he had told them he would not attend, could I get Mailer *there?* I telephoned him about it. He did not care for big Establishment events like that, he said, and prizes frightened him, as if he might be taken over by people he neither knew nor trusted. "If I come," he said, "it will be for you and Midge." When the day came, however, he was reluctantly there. I gazed out on the enormous ballroom, filled to capacity with all the luminaries of American television, journalism, and publishing, and on Mailer himself, miserable and embarrassed at the center table.

Lyndon Johnson's in many ways tragic story was equally innate to the times. Could one imagine it having happened in the Fifties? He had succeeded in his most fervid domestic ambitions and was at the pinnacle, having gathered together the powers of government more than any other of our Presidents, but was to be destroyed politically by a land war ten thousand miles away. Vietnam would coincide with the disintegration of his sweeping coalition against the Right in '64 (he got *ninety-four percent* of the black vote in that election), the deterioration of the civil rights movement into riot and looting and burning, and the crumbling of his admirable and far-reaching social vision. He knew the human costs of Vietnam, and they literally broke him. He had gambled that he could wage that war and still succeed in all the worthy facets of the Great Society in that moment in history, and he had lost. One of the mysteries of this decade was that a man so skilled and intelligent grew captive to the extreme military mind he himself had more or less distrusted for years.

Given my own time in Texas, as writer and editor, I always had mixed, even confused feelings about him, as did most who knew him then. "I was determined to be the greatest President of them all," he had said, "the whole bunch of 'em." He had known poverty and racism first-hand, considerably more so than all the Kennedys multiplied. His speeches as President on the American poor were heartfelt and powerful. He never really forgot his origins. His "We Shall Overcome" address had already entered history as one of the most forceful and stirring by any President. Years later Bill Moyers remembered observing the members of Congress in the joint session in the instant Johnson uttered those words; he saw the hands of the white Southern segregationists suspended in mid-air as the rest of the chamber cheered and applauded, then they too began clapping, tentatively at first, then with vigor. Liberated from his Texas constituency which I myself had known well, a greedy and grasping society when his nearly Snopesian ambitions were on the rise and where he had committed more than a few hard and unsavory and pitiless acts, the ruthless acts of a bully, he was able to give expression to the populism of his forebears. His disdain for and envy of the well-bred, the rich and successful was legend; he believed they had turned their backs on the average people. "The way to end urban pollution," he told his aide Joseph A. Califano, Jr., "is to make the auto company executives and their wives ride around Detroit in non-airconditioned cars during the summer. Then, they'll damn well solve the problem." Once, when Joe Califano handed him a report that Stokely Carmichael was organizing a black power group at Fourteenth and U streets to march on Georgetown and burn it down, Johnson read it and said, "Goddamn! I've waited thirty-five years for this day." He was hardscrabble and paranoic, but in his inward, complex composition lay strong and noble instincts, among the deepest of any of our Presidents'.

In the three years or so after John Kennedy's death he was magnificent. He was responsible for more domestic legislation than any President in our history, amounting almost to a social revolution, much of it having to do with the have-nots, the disfranchised, the homeless, the minorities. He received more hate mail on his civil rights stands than he did on Vietnam. When he was signing the Civil Rights Act of 1964 he turned to Bill Moyers and said: "I think we delivered the South to the Republican Party for your lifetime." Southern Republican elective power was to spread quickly from the country clubs to the emerging shopping malls, from the white Baptist churches to the feed-and-seed stores, from the courthouse squares to the advancing Dixie suburbias, from the quiet settled boulevards to the makeshift trailer parks, this burgeoning Southern party of Thaddeus Stephens, Charles Sumner, Abraham Lincoln, William Tecumseh Sherman, and Ulysses S. Grant. Nor was it fortuitous that he would be our last Democratic President who won with a majority of the white vote in America, for there was a hard price to be exacted for his Civil Rights Acts from his own political party.

His Vietnam advisors, principally John Kennedy men, foremost Robert McNamara and McGeorge Bundy and Dean Rusk, served to shore up his most uncompromising Cold War instincts, the domino theory, the ultimate menace of the Soviets and Red Chinese. He trusted them. He had listened from the outset to the old policy-of-containment men, the same men who sooner or later would desert him, but he was not sure. After a White House meeting on the war on November 1, 1967, George Ball, a lone voice of dissent in the high private counsels, turned angrily to Dean Acheson, John

Cowles, Sr., and others who had been arguing hawkishly on Vietnam and said: "I've been watching across the table. You're like a flock of buzzards sitting on a fence sending the young men off to be killed. You ought to be ashamed of yourselves." When Vietnam had begun to threaten his Presidency, on his social programs Johnson became, as C. Vann Woodward described him, "like a man pursued by a time bomb"; after his further achievements in the 1966 Congress, it was "down hill all the way." Guns *and* butter simply could not work.

Into this vacuum in early '68 stepped Eugene McCarthy and his young "Clean for Gene" liberals. McCarthy, the wry and reluctant crusader, tapped a pervasive need. At a benefit "celebrity" softball game on Long Island later in that year, with McCarthy and me teammates, he collided head-on with the opponent's catcher at home plate to score a run; blood streaming from his nose, this rueful and ironic intellectual got up and, brushing off the dirt, remarked to me in the on-deck circle, "And they say I'm not tough enough." He was a very good ballplayer too. (Four years after this, when he was considering running for the party nomination again, I was having lunch with him and Kevin McCarthy, the actor, in a house on Long Island. The playful yet Jesuitical Gene McCarthy said Kevin McCarthy would be his running mate; I would be Secretary of Commerce. The telephone rang. I answered it and could not help saying: "McCarthy headquarters. Two Jesuits for the price of one.") His impressive vote in the New Hampshire primary signified the end for Johnson, who could no longer control his own party, much less an anarchic nation, a capitulation so complete that on the advice of the Secret Service he would not even attend the Democratic Convention in Chicago that summer.

The 1960s were such that, as time passes, I remember with a sharpened clarity where I was at the precise moment the big events of those years occurred, one following another, it seems now, in singular progression. One such moment was LBJ's abdication. I had given a talk at a girls' boarding school in New England that Sunday, March 31, having done so as a favor for George Plimpton, who was supposed to appear there and could not, and returned to the motel and switched on the television just in time to hear

Johnson's concluding statement. "I shall not seek — and *will* not accept . . ." Even considering the stern logic of this withdrawal, I could not fully believe it. I telephoned my wife in New York — she, too, a product of the Texas Johnsonian era, and equally incredulous. Vietnam would last another seven years.

The war pursued Bobby Kennedy. He could hardly avoid it. At first he had been hesitant to stand unqualifiedly against the war itself, then to challenge Johnson for the Democratic nomination. The Tet Offensive had roused him to an adamant anti-war position. Then came the Johnson withdrawal. To the embittered accusations of opportunism from the Eugene McCarthy campaign, he got into the race.

I admired Bobby Kennedy just as I had his brother, who had been one of my heroes; for a number of reasons I believed Bobby would have been a much finer President than Jack. In the last several months of his life Bobby was beginning to come to terms, personally and politically, with the terrible complexities of the country; he was catching this need, this vibrancy for a true national leadership in a moment when there was no one beyond the Right to do it, and doing so with verve and passion. To me, in 1968, he was the most fascinating figure in American politics, not only because he was a Kennedy, nor because he had changed so much, educated himself to the failures of the nation while directly in the public eye, committed himself fully to civil rights and the cause of the poor, but also because, as Halberstam noted in a *Harper's* cover piece that came out the same week as his death, "at a time of great flux and enormous change in American life and politics, Robert Kennedy was a transitional figure, exactly at the halfway mark between the old and the new." He had grown. His trips to places like the Mississippi Delta, where he saw starving black children in dilapidated shacks, had deeply stirred him. He had learned from the sufferings of the country, and of his family: "tough now of mind and spirit," a Stevensonian who had once distrusted him said of him, "and not just tough of mouth." Yet he had also mellowed from the ruthless younger sibling, and before that from the arrogant, rich Ivy League fledgling who had labored in the cause of Senator

Joe McCarthy. In his final weeks, campaigning against Gene McCarthy in the Midwest and the Pacific Northwest and California, I sensed in his expression, even in abrupt feeling and vehemence, a Lincolnesque quality of nearly resigned sadness and withdrawal — surely he had a premonition.

I first met him in New York City in 1967. He had been the junior Senator from New York for two years; I had recently become the editor of my magazine. Jean Stein, a good friend of his, and I were having a drink at the Empire Chinese, and she asked if I wanted to meet him. She traced him to Le Côte Basque on East Fifty-fifth Street. When we entered it was the after-dinner hour, and the restaurant all but deserted; he and an assistant were sitting at a table in a corner drinking coffee. Jean Stein introduced us. "You're the editor of *Harper's?*" he asked. "And they tell me you're thirty-two? You must be smart."

He said it, not cleverly nor challengingly, as some in Manhattan often did in those days, but almost in a Boston whisper, with the *smaaht* at the end, even diffidently it seemed, and I was surprised to see how shy he actually was, with a private half-disguised vulnerability, I thought, before a newcomer, whom he welcomed with whimsical questions about the magazine trade, about what would be in the next issue, and about the state of Mississippi. He wanted to know what was going on in Mississippi, and did I know Ross Barnett, whom he said he had talked with on the telephone quite a few times five or six years before, and that after the Meredith crisis the University of Mississippi had invited him to give the commencement address, and that they were quite nice to him — "a very interesting state," he said, and chuckled to himself. He was younger than he appeared on television, and smaller, a hard wisp of a man, boyish and wry, laughing a lot, and he alternately played reticently with his empty coffee cup and then gazed at the stranger as the stranger talked with the most translucently blue eyes I had ever seen, and then playfully chatted with Jean Stein and his assistant. Why, I thought, this man is a mischievous boy, but I knew better than that, for I sensed a hidden pain and sorrow in his eyes a world removed from the casual and friendly talk.

The next time I saw him was at a cocktail party at Jean Stein's.

Jean was the daughter of Jules Stein, chairman of the board of the Music Corporation of America. She was a wealthy and stunningly beautiful and generous-hearted young woman my age who at nineteen as a script girl for Elia Kazan's movie *Baby Doll* being filmed in Benoit, Mississippi, had met William Faulkner, and they had had a serious affair. Faulkner often came to see her in New York. It was she who had persuaded Faulkner to consent to his widely read *Paris Review* question-and-answer interview. In answer to questions about his work in the past he usually told interviewers he was a dirt farmer, and not a writer, but he responded to her questions seriously, except for the occasional irresistible twist: Q. "Do you mean the writer should be completely ruthless?" Faulkner: "The writer's only responsibility is to his art. . . . If a writer has to rob his mother, he will not hesitate; the 'Ode on a Grecian Urn' is worth any number of old ladies." Jean elicited from the great Mississippian a rare and revealing candor about himself and his work, and he went over the script with her to make sure it was right. One evening she gave a small dinner at her place for Faulkner and overheard him and Terry Southern talking intimately at the table. "Mr. Bill," Southern whispered, "why are you and I already drinking brandy and everyone else is still drinking wine?" "Terry," Faulkner replied, "there was a saying in currency in the court of the Emperor Napoleon at the beginning of the last century: 'Claret is for the ladies, and port for men but brandy is for the heroes.' "

Jean had a large apartment in one of the established buildings with their ornate front columns and opulent towers along Central Park West, and she had a "salon" there which brought people together. At one of these evenings at Jean Stein's, I met for the first time James Jones, the honoree, soon to become one of the best friends I ever had. It was high summer and Jones and his wife, Gloria, were on a visit from Paris, and he and I were talking about mutual friends and about southern Illinois, where he was from and which he called "copperhead country," and the Mississippi Delta and the war in Vietnam. It was a savagely hot Manhattan night. The air-conditioning was not functioning properly, and Jim Jones took off his coat and rolled up his sleeves and suggested I do the same.

He went away for a moment and I was standing near the bar alone in my shirtsleeves. Suddenly Senator Ted Kennedy came up. Mistaking me for the bartender, he said: "Another scotch and soda, please." I was so taken aback that I mixed the drink and handed it to him. I glanced toward the corner of the chamber and saw Jones laughing so hard he had to prop a hand against the wall. Later I heard the author of *From Here to Eternity* tell Ted Kennedy, "That's not the bartender, that's the damned editor-in-chief of *Harper's Magazine*."

It was an equally sizeable gathering that later evening at Jean Stein's when Bobby Kennedy and I were there. Bobby and I were sitting on a sofa talking, his knees drawn up beneath him like a college student in a desultory dormitory bull-session of the 1950s. We were discussing Texas politics, and I told him a story or two about the colorful Maverick family. "Yeah, I've heard about them," he said. "They're tough." Who should enter the room but James Meredith himself, then a student at Columbia and whom I had never met, although as I have reported our Manhattan phone numbers were one digit apart, who made his way in our direction accompanied by his brother, a top sergeant in the Air Force. Bobby stood to shake hands with Meredith and introduced us, then said, in irreverent countenance, "Integrated any schools lately, Jim?"

Now, in the spring of 1968, he was on a whistle-stop campaign, addressing whites and blacks, though rarely together, speaking with passion of Vietnam and poverty, the rat-infested ghettos, the shabby and dangerous schools, "the almost impassable barriers between the poor and the rest of the country," the alienation of the young, the need to bring an end to the divisiveness and mayhem, and people were listening. In the Indiana primary in particular he was demonstrating that it was politically possible to bring together poor blacks and working-class whites in mutual interest; the United States would not see this again in national politics for many years. "He had finally the look of a man who intended to rock the boat," *Harper's* described him, "and rock it indeed he probably would. He sensed the country needed a little rocking." This had to have been hard on Lyndon Johnson in the lame-duck days of his Presidency. It was no secret that he and Bobby Kennedy genuinely loathed one another, the result of antagonistic political memories and the simple personal chemistry of each of them. The most cutting hurt must have come, as his advisor Joe Califano would in hindsight judge, "as blacks, Mexican-Americans, and the poor began to adulate Kennedy, for it was Johnson, not Robert or even John Kennedy who had put muscle and flesh on the dusty skeleton of the Emancipation Proclamation, and hammered into law the progressive Democratic legislative agenda that had accumulated for a generation."

On the day Martin Luther King, Jr., was murdered, Bobby broke the word to a black crowd on an Indianapolis street corner:

> . . . we can make an effort, as Martin Luther King did, to understand and to comprehend, and to replace that violence, that strain of bloodshed that has spread across our land, with an effort to understand with compassion and love. . . . I had a member of my family killed, but he was killed by a white man. But we have to make an effort in the United States, we have to make an effort to understand. . . . What we need . . . is not division; what we need . . . is not hatred; what we need . . . is not violence or lawlessness, but love and wisdom, and compassion toward one another, and a feeling of justice towards those who still suffer within our country, whether they be white or they be black.

I mentioned that he must in those days have had a portent of his own death. Considering his own personality and his political commitments, the new and real American "radicalism" of a Kennedy, and all that had gone before, how could he not? "He set me ablaze," young Bill Bradley, later to be U.S. Senator from New Jersey, remembered, "— his strength, his candor, his pain." In the complicated, hazardous society of the time he moved deep and dangerous emotions. "He thought of the fear Bobby Kennedy must have known," Norman Mailer, who admired him as much as I, would write in our magazine: "It gave eyes to the darkness of his own fear — that fear which came from knowing some of *them* were implacable, *them!* All the bad cops, U.S. Marshals, generals, corporation executives, high government bureaucrats, rednecks, insane Black militants, half-crazy provocateurs, Right-wing faggots, Right-wing high-strung geniuses, J. Edgar Hoover, and the worst of the rich surrounding every seat of Establishment in America." The sight of him on the television lying in the pool of blood on the floor of the hotel pantry in Los Angeles, a busboy kneeling by him while Bobby's friends George Plimpton and Roosevelt Grier are subduing Sirhan, was almost too much to bear. As he lay dying in the hospital the next morning with his shattered brain, like his brother Jack's, I wandered the streets of the Upper West Side, remembering the silent pavements of the Village on the day of his brother's funeral, the smoke spiralling from Harlem on the night of King's death; I never felt more sorrow for my country. The Jewish widows spoke in small whispers from their benches, people walked along Upper Broadway with their heavy faces, the patrons in Mr. Solomon Platz's deli sat hunched over their coffee like specters of gray — the hush of death and the early Sabbath pierced every now and again by the squeal of a junkie, the supplication of a panhandler, the dirgeful echo of a boat's horn from down on the river.

That afternoon, a Sunday, my wife Celia was receiving her Ph.D. in the first graduating class of the new City University of New York. The site was Bryant Park behind the New York Public Library. Robed graduates and professors, loiterers, bums, passing businessmen and merchants, and parents and mothers with small children composed the audience. From everywhere came the reckless sounds of the city.

My mother was up from Mississippi, and she and Celia and young David Rae and I were sitting on the front row. After the reports from Los Angeles I had not slept much the night before, and I sat there drowsily with my family, feeling miserable and helpless before my own sorrow and anger, and watched a jetliner descending high above toward one of the airports with neat puffs of smoke in its wake, and lethargically absorbed the odors of the flowering trees and foliage of that early summer's day. The commencement speaker was Arthur Schlesinger, Jr., Schweitzer Professor of City University, close friend and advisor to Bobby Kennedy, as he had once been to his brother Jack; I knew him from my days in the city. He looked red-eyed and exhausted in his gown and mortarboard, and when he rose to address the assembly it was with effort that he controlled his voice, and there were several lengthy pauses in his talk. That day the world was asking a terrible question, he said, a question which every citizen of the Republic should be posing to itself: what sort of people are we Americans?

> We are a frightened people because for three years we have been devastating a small country on the other side of the world in a war which bears no rational relationship to our national security or our national interest.
>
> We are a frightening people because we have already in this decade murdered the two of our citizens who stood preeminently before the world as embodiments of American idealism — and because last night we tried to murder a third. . . .
>
> We cannot take the easy course and blame everyone but ourselves for the things we do. We cannot blame the epidemic of murder at home on deranged and solitary individuals separate from the rest of us. For these individuals are plainly weak and suggestible men, stamped by our society with a birthright of hatred and a compulsion toward violence.

In unsteady tones he went on to assail those aspects of the society, including that substantial number of American intellectuals who had themselves begun to exalt hatred and absolutism and destruction as if primitivism in emotion constituted a higher authority. And he concluded with Bobby Kennedy's words to the black audience in Indianapolis on the day of Martin Luther King's assassination, and Kennedy's own conclusion, from Aeschylus: "In our sleep, pain which cannot forget falls drop by drop upon the heart until, in our own despair, against our will, comes wisdom through the awful grace of God."

When Schlesinger had finished, rather than returning to his place on the rostrum he abruptly gathered his notes and hastened away toward the office building which quartered the university graduate school offices directly across Forty-second Street from Bryant Park. His words, and his own barely concealed emotions of that moment, had affected me. I remember thinking: you have to do *something*. I turned to my family, apologized for having to miss the degree ceremony. I needed to talk with Arthur Schlesinger — needed, too, to get his words for my magazine. I followed at a distance as he disappeared into the university building. When I went into his office, a secretary challenged me in the anteroom. Mr. Schlesinger was unavailable, she said. "Who is it?" came a voice from the shadows inside. I identified myself. "Please come in, Willie." He was standing alone at the window, a glass in his hand, gazing wordlessly at the tableau in the park below: the begowned graduates filing by for the diplomas, the string ensemble playing the Tannhauser march, the children gamboling on the fringes of the crowd, all of it very miniature and evanescent and sad, an oddly transient enclave in the Manhattan abyss. His polka-dotted bow tie was askew, and I think he had been crying. "Have a drink or two with me." There was a fifth of bourbon on the table; anything would have served on this wretched hour of June. "What's wrong with our country?" he asked, just as Joan Daves had in front of my television the night of King's death. "God, what's wrong with us?" He had seen him the day before yesterday, he said; he was filled with hope and enthusiasm. We sat there for a long time in the gathering darkness as he talked between silences, the fading sunlight reflecting on his eyeglasses, until half the bourbon was gone, and I departed into the early lights of the city. We subsequently got the article from him.

Later that week I walked from my office up Fifth Avenue to watch the long lines of people inching their way into the Gothic eminence of St. Patrick's to file past the closed coffin. It was an incredible scene, the poorest of the city's poor: "poor Negro men and women," Mailer later described the scene for us in *Harper's*, "Puerto Ricans, Irish washerwomen, old Jewish ladies who looked like they ran grubby little newsstands, children, adolescents, families, men with hands thick and lined and horny as oyster shells, callouses like barnacles . . . a river of working class people came down to march past Kennedy's coffin, and this endless line of people had really loved him, loved Bobby Kennedy like no political figure in years had been loved."

Tom Hayden called King's murder "the decapitation of liberalism." With the assassinations of both King and Bobby Kennedy, the young radical activist Annie Gottlieb remembered, "We lost our last hope of combating racism or ending the war through the System, and the System lost our consent. Some simply gave up. But many more of us took to the streets. After 1968, the anti-war demonstration was the standard adolescent rite of passage." With all that had come before, and Bobby's murder, John Updike then observed, God might have withdrawn His blessing from America.

I felt *Harper's* should have the best and most distinctive treatment of the 1968 political conventions, Mencken's "nine-ring circuses of American democracy," of any publication, one of the most detailed and insightful looks at the national political processes ever. We assigned Mailer. His account of the Republicans in Miami and the Democrats in Chicago of '68, running nearly one hundred magazine pages, and Jules Feiffer's sketches and shorter pieces by Halberstam and King were classics of the genre.

The GOP convention in Miami, which nominated Nixon, was a flavorless exercise in contrast with what would ensue later in the summer in Daley's Chicago.

> Miami was materialism baking in the sun, then stepping back to air-conditioned caverns where ice could nestle in the fur. It was the first of a hundred curiosities — that in a year when the Republic hovered on the edge of revolution, nihilism, and lines of police on file to the horizon, visions of future Vietnams in our own cities upon us, the party of conservatism and principle, of corporate wealth and personal frugality, the party of cleanliness, hygiene, and balanced budget, should have set itself down on a sultan's strip.

And on the nominee himself:

> . . . his posture on the stage, hands to his side or clasped before him, gave him the attentive guarded look of an old ball player — like Rabbit Maranville, let us say, or even an old con

> up before Parole Board. There was something in his carefully shaven face — the dark jowls already showing the first overtones of their gloomy blue at this early hour — some worry which gave promise of never leaving him, some hint of inner debate about his value before eternity which spoke of precisely the sort of improvement that comes upon a man when he shifts in appearance from looking like an undertaker's assistant to looking like an old con seriously determined to go respectable.

It was the Democrats' siege in Chicago which marshalled the Mailer skills. Everything which had been seething in the nation in that decade, the recklessness and commitment, the vengefulness and anarchy, converged in that battleground:

> The police cut through the crowd one way, then cut through them another. They chased people into the park, ran them down, beat them up; they cut through the intersection at Michigan and Balbo like a razor cutting a channel through a head of hair, and then drove columns of new police into the channel who in turn pushed out, clubs flailing, on each side, to cut new channels, and new ones again. As demonstrators ran, they reformed in new groups only to be chased by the police again. The action went on for ten minutes, fifteen minutes, with the absolute ferocity of a tropical storm, and watching it from a window on the nineteenth floor, there was something of the detachment of studying a storm at evening through a glass, the light was a lovely gray-blue, the police had uniforms of sky-blue, even the ferocity had an abstract elemental play of forces of nature at battle with other forces, as if sheets of tropical rain were driving across the street in patterns, in curving patterns which curved upon each other again. Police cars rolled up, prisoners were beaten, shoved into wagons, driven away. The rain of police, maddened by the uncoiling of their own storm, pushed against their own barricades of tourists pressed on the street against the Hilton Hotel.

The writer's description of Chicago itself as "the last of the great American cities," of its stockyards ("tens of thousands of frantic beasts, cattle, sheep, and pigs, animals in an orgy of gorging and dropping and waiting and smelling blood"), of the acrid smell of tear gas upon the Hilton convention center and Michigan Avenue and the parks and "the sour vomit odor of the Mace," of the vengeful Chicago cops ("chaotic, improvisational, undisciplined, and finally — sufficiently aroused — uncontrollable"), of New Leftists and hippies and Yippies and aging beatnik poets, of Mayor Daley ("looking suspiciously like a fat and aged version of tough Truman Capote on ugly pills"), of Humphrey and McGovern and Gene McCarthy and Abe Ribicoff (as the latter denounces the "gestapo tactics" of the police, one lip-reads Daley in the Illinois delegation right there on television: "Fuck you, you Jew son of a bitch"), and Tom Hayden and Allen Ginsberg and Lester Maddox ("the face of a three-month-old infant who is mean and bald and wears eyeglasses"), and John Connally ("a handsome man, mean, mean right down to the gum, has wavy silver hair, is cocky as a dude, sports a sharp nose, a thin-lipped Texas grin, a confident grin — it spoke of teeth which knew how far they could bite into every bone, pie, nipple, or tit"), of black revolutionaries and Southern WASPS and immaculate young reformers — all these merged into a montage of the single most embattled spectacle *en masse* of the 1960s.

My wife and son and I had gone to England those days before and during Chicago for the London publication of my book. As it always had for me, England offered a detached perspective of America from afar, and on my own life. Everywhere there were people anxious to know what was happening in the United States. The student revolt of the American kind had touched Europe, especially France, where it crystallized not around race and war but on an outmoded educational system under a centralized government authority, much more so than England, although one saw an occasional demonstration in London with incendiary placards not dissimilar to the ones in New York and on the campuses. One day, as I was waiting in the studios of the BBC in London to be interviewed, the word arrived by Reuter's of the early moments of the uprising in Prague, and of the Soviet tanks rolling into Wenceslas Square.

"How ungenerously in later life we disclaim the virtuous mood of our youth, living in retrospect long summer days of unreflecting dissipation, Dresden figures of pastoral gaiety! Our wisdom, we prefer to think, is all of our own gathering, while, if the truth be told, it is, most of it, the last coin of a legacy that dwindles with time." I remembered these words from Evelyn Waugh's *Brideshead Revisited* when I returned to Oxford for the first time since my earlier years there in the 1950s. Wandering about the old town of lost causes, I found in its cloistered aspect and grand imperviousness to time much to ponder about my own country.

The moist gray chill of Oxford enveloped me and evoked in supple evocation the memories of those days, and of the people who shared them with me in that time of youth and suspended ambition. And, of course, there was the Oxford rain — a teased, beguiling little drizzle more often than not, punctuated by fleet downpours, and then a charitable summer's sun would escape the cloudbanks and bathe the spires and domes in a gloaming. That was always Oxford for me, its shifting interludes, all shadow and act, as far removed in time and spirit from the Times Square of the 1960s, or the Upper West Side, or Tompkins Square, as any place on earth. The silent gray of the stone silhouettes amid the flowering bushes and shrubs, the lush green leaves and gardens greener beyond measure than the most opulent Aprils of the American South, brought a timelessness to the familiar hush. It was as if I were in a declivity of old time itself as I wandered the town, for I recognized no one, and no one me, an anonymous wisp resurrected to explore the medieval lanes and byways and cul-de-sacs I once knew in my heart. The "Yanks Go Home" slogans on the walls, I noticed, were no longer in such abundance. In the Regency elegance of Beaumont Street, where Richard the Lion-Hearted was born, with its row upon row of dentists' offices, I remembered Johnny D'Arms of Princeton inviting me to his flat here and gravely soliciting my counsel, as he withdrew clothes from a battered wardrobe, on which Ivy League suit to wear to Evelyn Waugh's country estate the next day to ask his daughter's hand in marriage. Whatever the suit we chose, a Princeton seersucker as I recall, it served the purpose. All about me in the city were the tucked-away Dickensian shops, a little forlorn at first sight, yet oddly ancillary to the business at hand of a distinguished university: antiquarian booksellers and numismatists and Indian art dealers and tiny tailoring establishments, and at the foot of the Broad the inviting exterior of Blackwell's, the greatest bookstore in the world, whose forbearing proprietors had once allowed me three years to satisfy my considerable arrears when I went home at last to America.

The bells were beginning to ring now as I walked about, resonating in the precocious gloom. South of the High, only a few minutes' walk from its noisome clamor, the view of Christ Church and Merton from Broad Walk with its protective elms, then Dead Man's Walk with the Old City Wall standing gaunt and forbidding before me, was always to me the most imposing in Oxford, revealing the city and the colleges in their true origin: medieval, fortressed, embattled. In the diaphanous fog and rain I had this alluvial terrain all to myself: In the distance the miniature, childlike Thames, called Isis in this neighborhood, in its diffident twistings and turnings, and at the skyline the looming shape of tower and cupola. Often was the day I walked alone along these water paths, a little histrionically perhaps with a Matthew Arnold in hand, or a Lewis Carroll, who first told his Alice stories to the children on a boat somewhere along this stretch of river. And it may have been on this bench under this elm in a morning of June on the somnolent meadows that I read aloud to myself:

In a Wonderland they lie,
Dreaming as the days go by
Dreaming as the summers die:
Ever drifting down the stream —
Lingering in the golden gleam —
Life, what is it but a dream?

In Oxford, you belong to your college by right forever. This was not the visiting hour at New College, and a stern front-lodge porter challenged me just inside the gateway. "I'm a member of the college." He was all charm in a twinkling. "Welcome back, sir."

And suddenly, there it was, the fine sweep of the Great Quad in its fourteenth-century grandeur, its oval lawn as manicured as a golf green, its stringent staircases and passageways, precisely as I had departed it, catching the day's rain and declining sun now all tawny gray and gold. Had I ever really left it at all?

My last stop, I knew, would be the college cloisters, a damp hidden quarter with an enormous oak in a corner, as I remembered it, planted there, we were told, by the druids. All about me, on the floors and walls, were the memorials to the dead, and on the bell tower above the mad carvings of the gargoyles. In the cloistral quiet I indulgently reflected on all that had happened with one in the years he had been away from this place. Only eight years ago I had been a student here, heavy with history and time's thrall, and now I was a New York editor, deeply involved in my own catastrophic civilization. It all seemed to have happened so quickly. And as for this, my college, circa 1379, how much had *it* changed? Many generations had passed through here. What were eight years, the first eight years indeed of the 1960s, to six hundred? And would the American Sixties be merely a microscopic footnote one day hence to the great sweep of history which so touched these gray stones of Oxford?

We went down to Winchester on the downs of the Itchen, capital of the old Wessex nation of the Saxons: King Alfred and Thomas Hardy country, where the resourceful Dane, Canute, had ousted Ethelred the Unready, neither of whom had so much as heard of Richard Nixon, Flower Power, SDS, Columbia University, LSD, the Black Panthers, or Ho Chi Minh. We booked into a hotel in proximity to the Winchester Cathedral, one of the great mother churches, my favorite in England, where in early evening in the magnificent shadows of its interior I placed a rose on the crypt of Jane Austen. I returned to the hotel room and turned on the BBC. Suddenly, leaping out before me with no warning, were the bloody images of the Chicago Convention: the advancing phalanxes of the marauding police with billy-clubs and guns firing in the air, the huge rumbling trucks spraying their curtains of tear gas, the young people throwing rocks and stones, the blaring police cars with their angry blue lights, the students sprawled and beaten in the streets and parks. As with the other flickering replicas of those years I sat hypnotized before the television screen as all this unfolded, only this time I was in a foreign land, watching America in its self-effigy from far away. As in those moments after Bobby Kennedy was shot, I felt helpless and angry, and guilty that I was not at home where I belonged. "What, do tell me, is happening in your *Chicago*?" a sympathetic publican later asked me. Cutting Mother England short, we flew home the next day.

I promised myself never to be so far away again from my office there in Manhattan, vortex and epitome to me then, clearing house and command post, for all that I saw, for better or worse, that was sweeping the land. I would not return to my beloved Oxford again, or England, for more than twenty years.

Nixon would be elected President over Humphrey by a margin of seven-tenths of one percent, pledging the traditional virtues and to bring America together again. But as the Sixties progressed, virtue and togetherness would remain elusive, with worse times still ahead.

~ Fame, Family, Failure

11

IT IS A SHRILL and misty Manhattan dusk. A sliver of dying sunlight catches the windows of the skyscrapers. I am standing furtively at a street corner of the Upper East Side. Soon my wife emerges from a door across the way. No — my ex-wife. We have been divorced a fortnight, though I have yet to acknowledge the reality. I have been waiting here for her; I know she is the psychiatrist's last client of the afternoon, and that he himself will sooner or later come out, too. I watch as she drifts away into the New York crowds, receding from me like a pebble in a pond, my college sweetheart. My heart literally palpitates with rage and fear and chagrin, all of it so horrendously vainglorious, yet it is the man I have come to see, as if merely knowing what he *looks* like might ease some grievous wrong.

For weeks I have harbored the vindictive incubus that he and he alone has razed my marriage. That even had she been an axe murderess he would have counseled her, as surely they all did in that taut and debilitating American era: "Do what you must to be happy. If it feels good, do it." Psychoanalysis is in highest flower in the city now: get it out in the open, don't internalize it. The *presumption* of him: He is my faceless *bête noire,* incognito as the great city night, and he has unleashed my most ferocious Confederate tantrums. Frequently have I been tempted to compose for him epistles of nearly Herzogian compass, have even seriously contemplated what I imposed upon cruelhearted adults in my small-town childhood: gift-wrapped fresh cow manure or dead rats or possums deposited on their front porches in the yuletide.

The mist has turned now into a grim, unhurried rain. Then, suddenly, he emerges from the same doorway. In stark intuition I know it is he. My heart begins beating fast, and secretly I hasten across the raucous thoroughfare for a closer view. All of this is not unlike the day I trailed Garbo; it is the motives that are more obsessive and despondent.

I am nearing him now as he pauses at a newsstand in the Manhattan ritual of buying the afternoon's *Post,* then the *Village Voice.* I slip into an aperture near a Chock Full O'Nuts and observe him. He is of medium height and wears a gray overcoat. He is young! He looks innocent! He has red hair! This is my final subjugation. I really want him to look like Bernard Malamud. As he walks away I consider moving in on him at the flank, in the manner of Stonewall at Chancellorsville, confronting him nostril to nostril, demanding what arcane knowledge he has appropriated of our joys and sufferings and the things we shared together: the fragrant spring twilights at our university those years ago, the gallant Longhorns whipping the loathsome Aggies, the catfish and beer in the Balcones Hills, the midnight chimes at Oxford, the birth of our child, the old love and promise and hope. Then helplessly I watch as he descends into the steely entrails of the asphalt earth as New Yorkers do, down deep to the rattling IRT.

During my tenure in the East nearly three marriages in four were ending in divorce. One summer forenoon in the Hamptons, at a lawn party off a blue and sparkling inlet, I gazed across at the celebrants, some fifty couples I more or less knew from the city: With only two or three exceptions, I was drawn in the moment to note, everyone there had been divorced at least once. Among my contemporaries in those days there seemed a profound desperation about abiding relationships. I searched my friends who had dwelled in the crucible of them for answers, but I found that they knew nothing I did not know. So, as with me, since self-righteousness is surely the mightiest mode of survival, the blame fell on the partner. Everyone was too highly keyed, seething with fickle introspection and aggrandizement. People were always talking about themselves, their lives, their troubles, everybody killing everybody through neurotic love, or the lack of love: the city neurosis, the "unearned unhappiness" poor doomed Sophie saw later in the Freud-driven narcissistic city dwellers in *Sophie's Choice*. Nothing lasted. It all seemed in character with the American Sixties.

She and I were very young when we married, and a very long way too from the East. The Almighty has always been Southern in that regard: Get on early with the pristine charter of procreation. One of the clichés of the day held that young marriage was especially desirable; you would "grow up together," the irony being that growing up can also mean growing apart.

Nonetheless, it survived eleven years, across many terrains, American and otherwise, in good times and bad, and the denouement was terrible, and more than one would ever have bargained for, and the trauma of the ultimate break lasted longer than its duration. The anger, bafflement, jealousy, and sting threatened never to go away, and their scar tissue is probably on my heart forever. Yet whose *fault* was it? I ask myself now, hundreds of miles and a whole generation removed. And what did it say about ourselves? And what on earth did it mean?

She came from a raw and sprawling metropolis on the rise, I from the flatland and canebrakes of deepest Dixie. I remember as yesterday the first time I ever saw her. I was playing in a fraternity intramural football game, and I saw her on the sidelines talking with some friends, a singularly beautiful, dark-complexioned brunette, and she was caught for me in a frieze of mirthful laughter, and to this day I could show you the precise spot near the university where we first kissed. The two of us were important on the campus in those languid Eisenhower years. I was editor of the student daily; she was a Phi Beta Kappa and was even elected "Sweetheart of the University"; five thousand students sang "The Eyes of Texas" to her in the school gymnasium. Her favorite popular song of the era was Nat (King) Cole's, the one with the words, "When I fall in love, it will be forever." On my twenty-first birthday she gave me a book of English verse, and she wrote in it the inscription:

Grow old with me,
The best is yet to be,
The last for which the first is made.

We were married in an Episcopal chapel in her city, Houston, not far from the house where she grew up. Our families were different, mine Old South, hers Southwest *nouveau*. My best man was my oldest friend from home, and both our families participated, except for my father, who was very ill. He died while we were on our honeymoon, and I remember the passion and grief.

Not many American marriages begin in that Home of Lost Causes, that City of Dreaming Spires — Oxford. Arm in arm we strolled through the gardens and hidden places of the magical town, reveling in its bleak gray treasures. A wing of an old house was ours, surrounded by lush gardens, the Isis twisting upon itself in the emerald distance. The bachelor Yanks were eternally there, all of them a little in love with her. On a cold and frosty Christmas Eve, the two of us sat at the high mass in the cathedral of King's College, Cambridge. There was a thin skein of snow on the magnificent sweeping quadrangle outside, and the wonderful stained glass and the elaborate flickering candlelight and the resounding organ and the grand processional in Henry VI's vaulted chamber, the little English boys in their red ceremonial robes coming ever so slowly down the aisles with their flags and maces, their voices rising, and this was one of the most beautiful things we would ever see in our lives, and we were happy. And then a term break in Paris, and I am walking up rue Gît-le-Coeur, which abuts the Seine, and with the ineffable sights and sounds I conjure Gershwin, and soon there she is, leaning indolently against the upper balcony of our pension, five months pregnant and in a red dress, looking mischievously upon me as I approach, and her sunny words come down through time: "My distinguished husband."

After that, our heady New York days were touched with happiness, and then slowly advancing pain. Did the city itself implant the seeds of our own growing recklessness?

The fields of fame and ambition grew heavy with pitfall, though I doubt either of us would have acknowledged that then. Imperceptibly at first, our lives became tense and theatrical — all of celebrity's appurtenances. I was editor of the national magazine, she a young scholar, and our lives converged portentously with the great writers, the critics, the publishers, the millionairesses, the Hollywood heroines, the avatars of the moment's culture. At a book-and-author luncheon in the Grand Ballroom of the Waldorf-Astoria, sitting at the head table next to a television celebrity and our ambassador to Japan, I glanced into the balcony and saw dozens of Westchester County ladies in hats looking down on us with binoculars! And there were the casual lunches in the Century with the men of the Establishment: what act, pray tell, could follow steak tartare and a fried egg on top with *Ralph Bunche?*

In our provincial years our friends thought our marriage would last forever because we were so similar, mainly, I suspect, because we liked books, yet almost against our mutual will we were seeming to become so *different* — had we always been, I wonder, but lacked the experience to see it? How to explain such things, or even to remember them and be honest about them, for memory itself subsumes and expurgates and diffuses. It was not as fun as it had been.

We bought the farmhouse in the country, even acquired the black Lab puppy named Ichabod H. Crane to shore up the marriage, and the small-town boy actually did join that anonymous phalanx of Harlem River Line commuters in the summer, but the real trouble was just beginning. Doubt is inherent in any reality. She had begun to doubt — the life, the love, the man, the marriage — and doubt is a contagious hazard, yet the arguments, the insecurities, the melancholies, the insomnias, the inconstancies had to be symptomatic of something deeper, more elusive and mysterious.

All these merged in a daily tangle of hostility and distrust, punctuated by chilly, apprehensive silences. Silence speaks for itself, of course, and there were nights when I did not come home; our precocious love mocked us now, those threads of faded affection seemed frivolous and meaningless, and before our very eyes we had become rivals and antagonists.

What responsibility did *I* bear for the deterioration of our marriage? I ask myself these years later. Where does the blame lie for the evisceration of a love? At the time the question was, who was more right and who was more wrong? It was the genesis of an appalling obsession. "Fear stirs," Norman Mailer, who knew more than most about divorce, would write of this dominating fixation, "precisely the fear of spiritual consequence. It is then that the ego — its hand on the throttle that will keep us moving forward — discharges funds of nuance. One must keep up the certainty that one is right even when one does not know, and somewhere, off to the side, one wonders if one's will is being corroded." The inner assurance, the elemental justification that I was really in the right would linger for a very long time, and so too the corrosion.

With the long passage of time, however, certain horrid memories, exegeses, *ex post facto* incriminations begin to stir inside you, mocking the self-protective righteousness borne of that long-ago pain. Even now, a generation — a lifetime — removed, these honest memories are not easy, especially to write about, but they reaffirm anew for me the incredibly intense feelings, mine and hers, about that love, for it was not a coupling that died of boredom.

There were certain things about the destruction of our marriage that were peculiar to New York City, and to circumstances there, and to that moment there, but time has taught me they were probably more universal at their base, and the tale fits a not unclassic pattern. My interpretation of one of the costs of my own youthful success was that she and I had almost unwittingly, even against our own separate wills, set ourselves in competition. We had each become drastically concerned about our own *ventures:* hers in getting a Ph.D. in English and becoming a teacher and scholar, mine in creating what I hoped to be the greatest magazine in the country. When we arrived in the city, I believe I tried to participate in her world, and she in mine. Then I commenced to believe my own demanding yet animating life in the fulcrum of American letters and journalism should be sufficiently stimulating for her: the panoply of the city, the glitter of its nights, meeting and getting to know fine writers, dinners at our place in town or in the country with the Arthur Millers, the William Styrons, the Norman Podhoretzes, the Robert Penn Warrens, the C. Vann Woodwards. This was not enough for her, and I could not understand why.

I disliked the fact that she felt on the fringes of my fortune and friends, that she less preferred the colorful and individualistic writers than the scholars and analysts and interpreters. "She doesn't want to be Mrs. Harper," one of those friends said to me. When I was a child I overheard one of my parents' incessant quarrels. My father's comrade A. J. "Buddy" Reeves's wife, Ruth, always went fishing with Buddy, my father confronted my mother. "You *never* go fishin' with me." I wanted my own wife to go "fishing" with me. She chose more and more to envelop herself in her own work; I am afraid that many academics bored me, just as I probably bored them. One New York day, after she had had difficulties with her graduate panel over her Ph.D. dissertation, she took the telephone off the hook and locked herself in our apartment, so that our son and I could not get in for hours.

Soon my acrimony began to settle upon nothing less than psychoanalysis itself, its rituals and commitments and cosmic divinations, all the dire self-righteousness of the analysand. Our arguments about analysis grew tireless. I called it a counterfeit religion, even tossed up Chesterton to her: "Confession without absolution." I warned that people in constant psychoanalysis lost their hearts. I likened all the dream interpreters on Fifth and Park between Fifty-ninth and Ninetieth streets to fundamentalist Baptist pastors, but worse, and I may even have described the nether aura in that neighborhood somewhat as Dan Wakefield later would: "I imagined the dreams then drifted into the air above those buildings and bumped into all the other dreams emanating from the analysts' offices as thick as factory smoke until they were crowded off into space and finally disappeared because the earth's atmosphere over the Upper East Side of Manhattan simply could hold no more dreams." Often I dreaded to think what her *mood* would be every day at 6:30 P.M. when she came home from the headshrink's couch. So I started coming home later and later myself.

There was a great deal, however, to dislike in me. She did not like those late hours at my magazine office, and less the partying and drinking with my writing and editing cronies. She distrusted certain of the established writers and celebrities. She did not take to the glamorous, zany New York women I talked with at the evenings we attended. I believe she found hidden treacheries in our city. Were her doubts justified? If so, why did I still do it?

Anger is a fearful thing, yet surely illuminates the force and intensity and hazard of a precocious and despoiling love. The frequent moments of unbridled rage gave signal to the sharpening of our mutual distress. I had saved all her youthful love letters to me, kept them in a leather satchel in a closet. I discovered them missing one day. Where were they? She had destroyed them, she said. Why had she? "They're out of date and embarrassing," she replied. On a holiday visit to intellectual friends at Harvard from our Oxford time, as I sat in a room with them reading the sports section of the *Boston Globe,* she ripped the paper from my hands and shouted: "Talk!" This is an arduous admission, but one evening during an argument I slipped the wedding ring off her finger and tossed it out the apartment window. Then later, in hang-dog remorse, I trudged downstairs with a flashlight and with the wits of the scavenger lifted it out of the garbage bin into which it had symbolically fallen, and brought it back to her, returning it to her finger with words of guilt and love. One evening up around Morningside Heights I left her at an academic *soiree* and came home, locking the door from the inside and expiring into a heavy inebriated slumber. This time on returning she could not get in for a long time, and kept ringing the doorbell until finally rousing our son. I do not think I did this in deliberate retribution, but it could have been Freudian.

Was my career more important than my marriage? Why did she want divorce, and not I? Would I have done those New York days differently to save my marriage? Home every night at 6:30 P.M., more balance about my job, more human perspective? Was I too ambitious, too driven? That was a long time ago, yet try as I honestly may, I cannot answer these questions. They remain as mysterious to me as youth and aspiration and love, as the smoky unrestraints of the city itself. In the end we had become different human beings from those we had once mutually known and trusted: one of us introspective, academic, and disciplined, the other inchoate, nocturnal, uncompromisingly headstrong; one of us unable to "relax," the other finding it in the midst even of hard work too easy to do so; one of us contained and sophisticated and formulated, the other, as at whatever hazard I have no choice but to say it, just an old complicated Southern boy.

Shortly before our last Christmas together, she made a request. Her analyst had suggested, she said, that she tell me to surprise her with some special gift at Christmas, something individual to her, inherent to her, as a suitable test of how much I understood her. I settled on finding something in the Village, and I perused the shops there for two or three afternoons. Christmas came, and I presented her a beautiful fragile gold necklace. She found it inappropriate, and so one assumes did the dream doctor. "That's something you would give to Susie Tuckett," she said, a demurely lovely sorority girl we had known those years ago at the University of Texas. Do all defeats, just as victories, come down to one tiny gesture? Our marriage ended over a necklace from Greenwich Village, but of course it was more than that.

Soon after that the day came when she ordered me from the Upper West Side apartment. Where to go? What to take? I had to escape the city; a confused weekend in Connecticut with Rose and William Styron: "God, you look awful!" The mirror betrayed a complexion sallow as parchment, rings under the eyes like coal-black blisters, and I was developing a wicked little rash about the neck, what we once called *risin's* in Mississippi. Now we were in the deepening maw of divorce, a desolate subterrain all its own. The lawyers, of course, took over — mine a breezy man, cynical and unfeeling, hers hard and professional and unmitigating. Neither she nor I were mavens of heartbreak, and the wound and disarray of "the lawyer phase," as experts of marital rift chose to call it, were as mean and excruciating as anything I had ever known. I felt I was all beaten up. I feared I was losing not only my beloved son, but my pride and dignity, most of my money, our dog, and all the books it had taken me three years to compensate Blackwell's in Oxford for. The nadir came one wintry night in a dark, cold basement apartment I had just rented downtown. The movers that day had brought a few items of my furniture there, and the utilities were not working, and by candlelight I rummaged through an ancient bureau that had once been my great-grandparents', and I found there a few forlorn mementos of a marriage: a few surviving letters from her, even then shriveling at the edges, party invitations, a menu from the *Ile de France,* some of our little boy's toys from Christmases past, a photograph of the two of us holding him for his first glimpse of the Statue of Liberty.

It took me a long time to acknowledge she was truly gone. It was like death, but worse: She was not dead. I tried diligently to consign her to oblivion, but it did not work. I still loved her. There descended on my poor betrayed spirit a bizarre, enveloping jealousy, an acid sexual envy, tortured images of her with other men. The mounting carnage in Vietnam, its headless gluttony and cataclysm, only reinforced my indulgent fever. After the divorce I did not see our ten-year-old son for two months, because I did not trust my bitterness, the things I might say. The first weekend he eventually came to spend with me, he rang the bell to my new apartment, and when I opened the door he stood there with a shopping bag full of gift-wrapped objects. "Hi, Daddy," he said. "I brought you some presents." When I opened them, they turned out to be *my* Sandburg's *Lincoln,* all seven volumes of it, which he had selected to purloin from my own lost library. Was it an act of forgiving? At least I got my Sandburg back. I was forced to give up our farmhouse in the country, the one we had put so much of ourselves into, and loved so much. I locked the front door behind me one day and never went back.

I became a weekend father. You saw hundreds of these wretched fellow creatures with their offspring on Saturdays in the Central Park Zoo, or F.A.O. Schwarz, or the penny arcades in Times Square, or the big movie houses along Broadway or Third Avenue, or Lincoln Center at Christmastimes for *The Nutcracker,* or the old Palisades amusement park in Jersey, all trying to be solicitous, as if to make up for something. I recall the two-headed cow at the Palisades, David Rae and I staring at her for long moments in her pen as the music of "The Lord's Prayer" drifted over the scene. I always felt unbearably sad for this poor pathetic figure, surely having to do with my own sadness, even if she did evoke assuaging memories of a two-headed black female gospel singer rumored to have lived on Brickyard Hill in the hometown of my boyhood, one head soprano, the other alto. In Woody Allen's film *Manhattan* he and his young boy wore identical sweatshirts while playing basketball in city playgrounds on similar weekends: "Divorced Fathers and Sons." On some Saturdays we journeyed up to Baker Field to see Columbia play football against gridiron behemoths the likes of Lafayette, Lehigh, and Brown. We watched Tom Seaver pitch an opening game for the Mets in twenty-degree weather and modest sleet. We saw movies such as *Yellow Submarine, 101 Dalmations,* and *The Green Slime* and in a movie house off Times Square sat through all fifteen installments of the old *Batman* serials of my own childhood in the crazed Batman and Robin mania of that era, coming out bleary-eyed and partially blind into the light of day for hot dogs and sauerkraut from the streetcorner entrepreneurs. We watched late-night television and ordered from Chicken Delite. We spent many hours in my deserted office, where he idly pecked away on typewriters while I read manuscripts. Many were the Saturdays he and I would devote all day, breakfast to midnight, to Madison Square Garden, never leaving its splendid interior cosmos for so much as a moment: first the bowling alley, then lunch in the Stockyard, then the Knicks in their penultimate glory in the afternoon for Bradley, Frazier, Reed, Debusschere, and Barnett, later a boxing match in the Felt Forum, followed by a comedy act of Bill Cosby or some other rising star, then dinner all over again in the Stockyard. And when I safeguarded him the next day to a cab on those poignant Sabbath twilights and he left me, I felt unbearably guilty and bereft and alone.

One day he was to meet me in my office at an appointed hour. George Plimpton had arranged to take him onto the field at Shea Stadium an hour before a ball game and introduce him to all the Mets and Cardinals. I waited and waited but he did not come. When I telephoned, it was she who answered. I had not cleared the arrangement with her, she said. She was teaching me a lesson. But to meet the *Mets* and *Cards?* I prayed revenge all over again on my *bête noire,* the shrink. After that I would not talk to or communicate with her for years.

A month or so after my divorce I was in the St. Moritz with a young woman from out of town whom I had once known. The greatest snowstorm in a quarter of a century descended on the city. It lasted the entire weekend. From the windows of the room the view of Central Park far below in that incredible blizzard was singular to behold, a frighteningly magnificent panorama of the surging elements. All of New York was closed down by this stunning act of nature. Late that Sunday night I had to return to my magazine office thirty blocks away to work. The subways were not running. It had just stopped snowing and the plows were not out yet. Fifth Avenue under its mound of snow was utterly deserted. It was bitterly cold. Abandoned cars were everywhere, obscured like big grotesque white anthills in their blankets of snow. As far as the eye could see there was not one moving vehicle, nor was there a single other person out and about. I began walking down the middle of that hushed and ghostly thoroughfare. The only sound was my own footsteps on the hardened snow. It was the most ethereal feeling I ever had in my life, and I suddenly felt tears. I was consumed with shortcoming and loss, and the tears froze on my cheeks. As I trudged step by step southward on this night, the whole city lay there before me, this city that I adored and honored and feared as much as any American provincial all through the years ever loved and honored and feared it, all phantom-like now and still.

With divorce one gives up a whole way of life — friends, routines, habitudes, commitments. Who gets the friends? Who gets the dog? Who gets the furniture? You are on your own again, and in subtle territory, and for a while your most fiendish habits may worsen. I was in the seizure of the utmost dysphoria, what a complex man like Winston Churchill in his most suffering moments called "the black dog." I found myself taking a dozen or more Valiums a day. Then I told myself I could not *afford* to be deranged. I had a demanding job, after all, and not an unimportant one, and scant choice but to function. The problems of real day-today life were easier to deal with than the imaginary ones; I willed my own salvation. I flushed my insidious Valiums down the toilet.

For the longest time I thought I could never love again. I was wary and afraid and remembered too much. Yet as the days slowly pass, on into the years, you discover you *can* love again, and that, of course, is a whole other story, to be considered in these pages. But I shudder now to think what my girlfriend of that subsequent time had to live with — and not merely the intolerable bitterness and spleen she was forced to share — for in the nature of it we all subconsciously compare our later loves with the first, no matter the wreckage and flaw.

I still sometimes ponder the pain I must have caused my wife, the selfishness and doubts: *her* side of the matter. Of course it was not the headshrink I compelled myself to pursue that faraway Manhattan dusk, for he was only conduit and symbol. I do not mind if he rewrites Freud and makes a million. In those inevitable moments of great ill temper, we damage what we cherish. All the time we must somehow grow from the sinews of our own experience, learn to conduct ourselves a little more compassionately — for what is intelligence if not the ability to cope with the recurrences of one's existence?

There remains the incontrovertible burden of lost and damaged love. Finally, I have learned how difficult love is, how hard to achieve and sustain, no matter who the person or how felicitous the circumstance. How could I have known then of the psychic hold she would have on me for the rest of my life? It was like the psychic hold of the city itself in all its loves and hates and passions and dramas. Across the years, I would think of Celia, and remember her.

~ Elaine's and Other American Peregrinations

12

THE PLACE FOR many of us in the New York City of the Sixties was a restaurant called Elaine's. The unfaltering Plimpton first brought me there in '65. "This is going to be your hangout," he presciently warned, and my friends and I attended frequently, although I did not become an arch patron of these riotous and nimble quarters, to the point of receiving considerable of my mail there and negotiating various magazine assignments on napkins there, until I was a bachelor again. With the trauma of destroyed love and divorce, one desperately needed a haven from parched sickly introspection.

With my divorce, I had the wisdom to abandon the glum and dispiriting basement apartment downtown and to take an efficiency apartment on an upper floor of the old Vanderbilt Hotel directly across East Thirty-third from my magazine offices, located so auspiciously that I could get from apartment to workplace in no more than three or four minutes, and less even than that when the elevators were prompt. This apartment had a table at a window overlooking the nineteenth-century regimental armory down on Park Avenue. I could work on it into the evenings on manuscripts and correspondence, or I could remain at the office long after everyone had departed, getting home in that brief portal-to-portal time in those lonesome days for what more often than not was a TV dinner. There were nights, especially on weekends, as New Yorkers would readily testify, that one had to get out into the town.

Along with the magazine office, Elaine's became in many aspects a second home. Often I would even hide at a corner table and read manuscripts there. Why not? Didn't Hemingway write his Michigan stories in the Closerie des Lilas?

Elaine's was product and expression of the city I knew in the Sixties, its volatileness, its flair, its elusiveness, its clannishness, its hunger for company. No social nor literary history of the city in those years by the canny scholar of 2050 A.D. could ever be written without it. There were distinctive forerunners to it for writers and poets and playwrights and journalists. There was Chumley's on Bedford Street in the Village with its speakeasy origins, its blazing fireplace and wooden tables and dust jackets lining the walls from the books by the authors who came there in the Twenties and Thirties: Fitzgerald and Hemingway and O'Neill and Edna St. Vincent Millay, and rumor had it that Joyce himself had worked on *Ulysses* at a corner table — a watering spot too for the writers of the Fifties, including Jerry Salinger, before he made initials of his Christian names. There was the White Horse on Hudson Street, also in the Village, another informal and sometimes raucous social locus for writers in the city, where they sang rebellious Irish songs; Dylan Thomas was said to have had his valedictory drink there before he collapsed and died in St. Vincent's Hospital up the way, and Vance Bourjaily held a writers' group there in the Fifties. And there was Bleeck's in midtown for the *Herald-Tribune* and *Times* crowd, back in the era, as one of its denizens remembered, when there *was* a *Trib* and before the *Times* people stopped living in Manhattan.

But there had never been any place quite like Elaine's. New York then seemed much like an enormous semi-private club, and this was the clubhouse, the small town in the throbbing metropolis, the urban enclave, giving one the warmth and togetherness of the small town: in the years of the Sixties "a men's club for the literary lonely," as Jules Feiffer called it. If the rich establishment titans could have their clubs, why couldn't we? We were more exposed than the Century, and younger, and knew the rash times better, or at least knew them more graphically. This was before many of the recognizable celebrities and the show business wizards came there to be seen, for it was largely a place for serious people whose calling demanded they spend the most productive hours of the day alone, and who craved the stimulation of the Manhattan night.

I suppose I should confront at the start the cybernetic scoffing of a place like Elaine's in my New York days, and the aura encompassing it. Not a few of my compatriots subscribe to the notion that writers and artists really should stay at home in a kind of cloistral hush, or live out their creative days in basilicas in the tundra. They certainly should not compromise their hard-earned talent and solitude by spending too many moments with their fellows, who at best are a competitive and contentious and paranoic species and will only wreak straightout havoc, or more calibrated degrees of destruction, on their brothers and sisters in the unlikely calling; one artist can never learn anything about his craft from another one anyway. There is a certain substance, of course, to this misgiving, and I robustly defer to it depending on the artist. In my time in the city I never once saw Eudora Welty in Elaine's, or Walker Percy, or Shelby Foote, to mention a few Southerners, or Saul Bellow or Bernard Malamud or Isaac Bashevis Singer, of urban-dwellers, but I did know some very good ones in there. Flannery O'Connor would not have come to a spot like this, bless her memory, and probably not William Faulkner. But Faulkner's own daughter once confessed he liked, for instance, the *Hollywood* scene more than he himself ever made out, and despite his hermetic reputation and apprehension of literary company, when he was lonely in New York City or Beverly Hills he spent a great deal of time with fellow writers he enjoyed — Dashiell Hammett, Nathaniel West, John O'Hara, Frank Sullivan, Dorothy Parker, Corey Ford, Lillian Hellman, Budd Schulberg, Irwin Shaw, Marc Connelly. Understanding something of Bill Faulkner, I know he would have admired and trusted the Elaine of Elaine's, if not Elaine's per se. From what I know of them, the young Hemingway would have come to the place if it had existed then when he was out of sorts in the town, and Fitzgerald, and Steinbeck, and for that matter Dreiser and St. Vincent Millay. We were *here,* and young, and people were lonesome in the city in the Sixties. Marriages came and went in a thundering metropolitan herd. There was a need for comradeship and talk, and sometimes, lest one forget, for free meals. And one was, after all, an editor of a magazine, and magazines published writers and journalists, and it was damned fun besides.

Elaine's last name was Kaufman. She was born at 140th and Amsterdam, the daughter of Russian Jewish immigrants who owned a dry-goods store, and grew up on Sutphin Boulevard in Queens. She was a voracious reader, and when she finished high school went to work at a Woolworth's, next at a second-hand bookstore on Forty-second Street, and finally as a waitress, during which time she managed a restaurant at Bleecker and Thompson in the Village. In 1963 she bought for $11,000 a shadowy, austere Austro-Hungarian bar surrounded by brick tenements at Second Avenue and Eighty-eighth Street in a tenuous and unfashionable German and Irish neighborhood. Jack Richardson, then stony broke and writing the best book ever written on gambling, which may have been why he was broke, came upon the place not long after it opened. He remembered hookers at the bar arm-wrestling for boilermakers, a jukebox blaring polkas and German marches from the days it had been a venue for Bundists from Yorkville up the street, and Irishmen off work from a nearby brewery singing, brawling, and passing out on the floor. One of Richardson's first sights of the new doyenne was of her gingerly stepping over the prone Irishmen while waiting tables. She tried to make a traditional Village restaurant out of these surroundings, with checkered tablecloths and tin ceilings and eventually *Paris Review* posters donated by Plimpton, and a menu of squid salad and veal parmigiana and pasta and calamari and fried zucchini and scungilli. Her first part-owner and waiter was a red-haired Irishman, gregarious and a fighter, who brought in a pretty wild crowd himself.

Elaine was a large woman of equal largesse, thick eyeglasses with thick black rims, amply bosomed, a tough, resourceful, gentle woman in a tough, resourceful, ungentle town. She relished jokes and gossip and was a saint, with the irascibility of the good saints, but she was only a saint to those she loved. As for the others, she could sniff out iniquity as some can the lines of a race-track greyhound, and in these moments she was not in the least saint-like. As Hemingway said of Sylvia Beech, an equal patroness of writers and artists in the Twenties on the Left Bank, no one that I ever knew was nicer to me. "Whom the gods adore," Irwin Shaw would write in an affectionate memoir, "they first make plump and equip with a curly smile, a twinkling, welcoming eye in which, almost hidden, lurks the steely calculation of a riverboat gambler and the nerve of a cat burglar. The gods free their favorites, in this case Elaine, from all sentimentalities of democracy, and by instinct furnish them with the invaluable arbitrary snobbish gift of choosing favorites, relying only upon their own taste in such delicate matters." She did possess the steely calculation, and eventually acquired that reputation among some around town, and likely under circumstances would have made a successful female wrestler on the Dixie mud-wrestle circuit, but she was never just the lady of the manor. There was a certain shy, nearly tender delicacy to her, in her quiet talk, her affectionate hug or motherly caress, a vulnerability that only a few of us knew, vulnerability in her face and in her smile, the origins of it surely somewhere over on the misbegotten reaches of Sutphin Boulevard, and I grew to love her for that vulnerability and for her tenderness.

On an early call to her new establishment, as she stuffed the paltry evening's profits into her bosom, and ignored the chanting, fighting Irishmen all around, sometimes as they did abruptly expiring in the middle of a chorus, Jack Richardson counselled her on how she might save her struggling business, and later vowed the authenticity of this worthy exchange:

> "First," I said, "you need some sensitive types in here."
>
> "You mean fags?" she asked, her face colored by a gentle blush.
>
> "No," I answered, "I mean writers."
>
> Elaine greeted this proposal with a quaint Jewish obscenity, so I quickly explained to her the relevant virtues of my profession.
>
> "What would you say to some steady customers who don't have to get up in the morning and can therefore be plied with drinks until closing time? Who will eat anything put in front of them — and enjoy it?"

Now there was a flicker of interest in her eyes.

"Do they spend?" was her circumspect question.

"An indifference to money is the hallmark of the profession," I answered with pride.

"Okay," said Elaine, "bring me a dozen."

In the gods' arbitrary gift of choosing favorites, she chose writers. She called them her "boys" and herself "Big Mama." "I don't have any family of my own — who needs all those problems?" she would say. "I prefer my restaurant family because no matter if I have a rotten day, I know that come night I'll be in my place and it'll revive me and I'll have a good time. Those boys go through some funny things. They get in trouble and don't even know it. They're crazy, these boys, but not as crazy as they think. I gotta watch out for my boys, you know. They need me, those boys. Big Mama. Rain or shine, I'm there." And she did try to keep them out of calamity. When she sensed an ungainly or dim-witted situation with one of them, she would motion to him from several tables away, and tell him to calm himself down. But her criticisms were soft and oblique, and always ended with her own sympathetic chuckle.

One night she summoned me. "You're being too hard on that poet," she said. "It's not at all like you. He's a stranger here."

"But he doesn't write poetry," I said. "He just says he does. He attacks everybody else's poetry. I think he's a phony."

"If I had to judge every phony in this town I'd go bats. You look hungry. I'll get you some lasagna." So I went back and treated the fellow as if he were Samuel Taylor Coleridge.

When Elaine's was new, a few of the writers began to wander in late at night. Being a reader of books and a lover of literature, she was the softest touch for them on Manhattan Island. Some of the broke writers ran up legendary tabs. Jack Richardson's, it was rumored among us, was so enormous that the *Wall Street Journal* was tempted to report its accumulation on a daily basis in a box next to the Dow-Jones Industrials. It was salubrious for the ego, Larry L. King confessed to me, to go to Elaine's and spend like a rich Arab even though his telephone had just been disconnected.

"Only about twenty percent of the writers I met there proved to be assholes," he would remember. "This is much more tolerable than the national average." With alimony and child support, I myself once had debits of more than $2,000. "I owe you money, Elaine," I said. "Pay when you can," she replied. "I ain't complaining." To my knowledge she never once hectored anyone to collect, even in those days when her commerce was marginal at best.

Nelson Aldrich lived in the neighborhood and was among her maiden clientele. So was A. E. Hotchner. Plimpton came on his bicycle, locking it up and propping it at the entrance, the Jacques Tati of Second Avenue. Tennessee Williams, no connoisseur of the city, was there in the early days with his sardonic wit and repartee. I only had one exchange with the Mississippian Tennessee Williams, who was surrounded one night by admirers and sycophants. "I'm from Yazoo City, Mississippi," I said. "Well, I'm from Columbus, Mississippi," he replied. "Yessir, I know." "So you're from the Delta," he said, "a profligate place, the Delta. Very profligate. It's a wonder you survived." Eventually the regular clientele was a roster of some of the finest writers of the generation, who came there with or without wives or girlfriends. The proprietress looked over the women carefully. If she did not like a particular woman, and judged her too mean-spirited or philistine, Elaine presumed her to be exploiting her boys, some of whom were so broke they had nothing to exploit.

There was frequent talk in these buoyant transpiring evenings about money and royalties, or which New York publisher at the moment was paying book advances that a man could live on, and in such moments Elaine's resembled less a literary salon than an animal auction. The best table up front was the writers' table, where they could invite anyone they chose to sit down. This is not to suggest that all these hardy souls descended on these unprepossessing premises at the same time — how much propane will a propane cylinder bear? But they might drift in every three or four evenings or so, and get to know each other and to talk also with some of the painters and composers. With an exception or two, the movie producers did not start coming in till later, and when they did it was to seek out the writers. A lot of jabberwocky there? Yes, indeed. A hothouse? Of course it was, and who would deny it? But it was more companionable and civilized than most places one might have been in New York City at night in those times, and a lot safer too.

After a while Elaine began to collect the jackets from the books written by her favorites and framed them and hung them on a wall, just as the proprietors at Chumley's in the Village had done a generation before. She would often have a little ceremony with the writer when she put up the jacket, and buy him a bottle of champagne. I was sitting there with Ed Hotchner and Halberstam and Elaine one of these nights when Hotchner asked her why on earth she really liked writers. Well, she answered, they thought a lot, and were funny and smart, and were right out front with their feelings. "They like to stick together," she said, "because they're all under the same strain of working on their own against a blank piece of paper. But they don't talk about writing, because they've had that all day long, so they turn their minds to other things. And they keep the same hours. What good's a saloon for stockbrokers who watch the *Today* show while they're getting dressed?" The only writer I ever knew her to have a feud with was Norman Mailer, which lasted a long time. The clientele speculated on the origins of this monumental schism, almost papal in its intensity: was it temperamental? Ideological? Was it reconcilable? Should the United Nations, after all only thirty city blocks downtown, be called in?

Given the frothy brew, it was confounding, especially considering the nature of the times in both city and hinterland, that there was so little violence. I was once witness to a venomous lovers' quarrel at the bar. I believed they had both visited their psychoanalysts that day, who had given them conflicting advisements; the man rushed impetuously into the night, and in no time at all a garbage can crashed through the big plate-glass window, showering the front table, happily unoccupied, with its spray of wicked shards. The same glass was cracked a second time when a displeasing drunk entered the door and began taunting Bruce Jay Friedman and his *confreres;* the interloper was so resoundingly smitten that his head shattered the unfortunate window again. On another occasion Mailer and Jerry Leiber had placed bets on an arm-wrestling contest between two of their fellows. Tempers erupted and Mailer tried to strangle Leiber, but in the sweep of the days this, too, was not considered portentous.

In those days Elaine's was as much a sports saloon as anything else, and the worries of the Sixties, including even Vietnam, were often subsidiary to the New York athletic scene, as if people wished to put aside their concerns for the country for a while, especially when the Knicks and the Mets were beginning to win. For the hardened and habitual patrons a famous movie actress sweeping in with her lapping retinue was trifling, but when Walt Frazier of the Knicks entered one evening in a fur-collared coat and flowing silk scarf with a scintillatingly beautiful woman on his arm, he could have been the Prince of Wales. Once I brought into dinner a young man named Gerry Moses of Yazoo City, Mississippi, who had been the batboy on the baseball teams of my high school days. He was now the number one catcher with the Detroit Tigers, in town for a series with the Yankees, and although Gerry Moses was a .230 hitter, to the writing clients he too was of the highest ascent, and they treated him with a grand obeisance.

"What's it really like to go up against the big league curve, Gerry?" one of the writing boys asked.

"It's tough at first," the visitor replied, "but you got to confront it."

"How do you confront it?"

"You dig in against it."

"Do you like coming to New York?"

"It's big time all right. I like the hotels. It's bigger than Yazoo City, I'll tell you that. It's bigger than *Detroit.* I like Yankee Stadium. But don't ever hit a good one to left-center. Left-center's about a mile long. I hit a good one out there yesterday and Mickey caught it like it was a little piddlin' pop fly."

Aberrant episodes often involved the Texans, who were the closest the nation had then to Australians, especially the sportswriters Dan Jenkins and Bud Shrake. I had known both of them well in Texas when they were in daily newspapering, and now they lived in the city while travelling the country for *Sports Illustrated.* I was once at a table with Jenkins and Shrake, along with two young women training to be Delta Air Line stewardesses in the time before they were called flight attendants, and Dandy Don Meredith of Mount Vernon, Texas, quarterback of the Dallas Cowboys. The stewardesses were right off a flight from Houston and gorgeous in their blue uniforms. One of them kept quoting Browning's "How Do I Love Thee?" I posed a question with a felt pen on the tablecloth to Dandy Don Meredith: "Having been a quarterback since the age of eight, what has this taught you as a human being?" "Can I answer in two parts?" Meredith asked. Then he wrote: "One, all leaders are lonely. Two, there is unexpected pleasure in continuing failure." "My God!" someone said. "You've read Ernest Hemingway." "Of course I have," the quarterback replied. "These Texas boys got me to read everything that man wrote." On leaving, one of the Delta trainees took the tablecloth off the table and slipped it into her purse to take back to Houston as a memento.

Rich Texas visitors to the city were infamous for not paying for dinner, leaving that to the Texas writers; Elaine herself was aware of this, and other malfeasances, which did not please her. Once I was with Jenkins and a group of these Texans. Several tables away were some movie stars; the visitors stared at them unabashedly. Elaine sat down with us and was in the middle of a story about a fashionable lady with a three-foot handshake. One of the Texans interrupted and asked directions to the men's room. She gestured testily toward the rear of the room. "Go to Michael Caine," she said, "and take a right."

There were sad things about Elaine's too, in keeping with the city. Gazing across at the kaleidoscopic scenes I often felt sorry for the pretty young women from the provinces new to town, all fresh-faced and enthusiastic, drawn to it by the promises of publishing and broadcasting and the theater, brought to this establishment by older men of some prominence and power, especially the ones I did not admire, trying to take advantage of them by impressing them with suavity and power. Beware, young lovelies! — even if it *is* the Sixties.

One evening I glanced across the room and saw Ingrid Bergman dining with friends. My heart skipped two beats. She was old and looked ill; Elaine later told me she had cancer. Her hands trembled slightly and she seemed frightened. I remembered her in *Casablanca,* her magnificent and tender allure, her lithe movements, her Nordic smile: "Here's looking at *you,* kid" — and as Maria in *For Whom the Bell Tolls,* and as the pale, driven beauty Paula suborned to madness by the diabolic Charles Boyer in *Gaslight.* I could not take my eyes from her. Briefly our glances met, and I turned my head in embarrassment. She overcame me with sadness, and I recalled the lines of Tennyson I had memorized in Mrs. Omie Parker's English class in high school:

The woods decay, the woods decay and fall,
The vapors weep their burthens to the ground,
Man comes and tills the fields and lies beneath,
And after many a summer dies the swan.

Woody Allen, producer, director, writer, latter poet of the city, began to frequent Elaine's, accompanied by one or another of the movie actresses, Mia Farrow or Diane Keaton or Meryl Streep, coming in with a frightfully haunted look and looking straight down at the floor while being guided to his regular table in the obscure corner he had requested near the kitchen. He never spoke to anyone in his lengthy private dinners except his companions, the waiters, and the proprietress. Sometimes customers from out of town would stand behind a column in the back room and peer out at his brooding silhouette. When his table was empty there was always a "reserved" sign on it.

I loved Woody Allen, his wonderful self-parody, his unredeeming affection for the city in all its madness and glamour and whim. Didn't he say success in New York City is mainly a matter of showing up? His Manhattan people all seemed lost, but were not people in Mississippi lost too, or for that matter Texas, although they did not talk about it so much? As different as Martians in background, I felt Woody Allen and I had many things in common. Despite its travail, why was life worth living, he would ask himself, and in his movies reply: Groucho Marx and Willie Mays and the second movement of the Jupiter Symphony and Louis Armstrong and Swedish movies and *A Sentimental Education* by Flaubert and

Marlon Brando and Frank Sinatra and Cézanne's apples and pears. In the opening of his movie *Manhattan*, "Rhapsody in Blue" soaring majestically against the city skyline, he would agonize as haltingly as this memoirist years later as he launched into a book on his exalted subject: "He *adored*, he *idolized* New York City — no, make that . . ." (Scratch) . . . "He *romanticized* it all out of proportion, for it was a great town that existed in black and white, that pulsated to Gershwin tunes, no matter the season." (Scratch) . . . "He was too romantic about Manhattan, as he was about everything else, he thrived on the hustle and bustle of traffic, and crowds in the street, smart guys who had all the angles, beautiful women. Too corny!" (Scratch) . . . "He adored New York City. To him it was a metaphor for the decay of contemporary culture. The same lack of individual integrity that caused so many people to take the easy way out was rapidly turning the town of his dreams into . . . Too preachy, after all I want to sell some books here." (Scratch) . . . "He adored New York City, although to him it was a metaphor for the decay of contemporary culture. How hard it was to exist in a society desensitized by drugs, loud music, television, crime, garbage. Too angry!" (Scratch.) And he would start all over again.

I wanted in the worst way to talk with Woody Allen about New York City, and what was happening in the nation out beyond the Jersey Palisades that he might not know about, and would he write something for my magazine, and did he really cry during *Gone with the Wind?* "I'm going to go over and talk with Woody," I said to my companions one night. "I adore the little guy." "No, you're not. Don't do it. He'll cut you dead." And so I never did.

Even the far-ranging Plimpton himself, who knew more Americans even than David Halberstam, had never exchanged a word with Woody Allen until one memorable evening he would remember in much detail. The circumstances were not perfunctory. A gentleman named Jerry Spinelli of Philadelphia had bid for and paid more than four hundred dollars to the educational television station's auction there to spend an evening in New York with Plimpton. Plimpton pondered what to do with Mr. Spinelli and his wife — shoot a little pool, perhaps, and then take them to Gallagher's Steak House, and get them on an early train back to

Philadelphia. But while Plimpton and Mr. Spinelli, a thin shy young man, shot a desultory game of pool at Plimpton's house, Plimpton's wife, Freddy, learned from Mrs. Spinelli that her husband was writing a novel, rising at dawn to work on it before going to his office, and returning to it again night after weary night. The writing was not going well, and on the most benevolent impulse Mrs. Spinelli, when the Plimpton evening was announced on the television, entered the highest bid to help her husband make a New York literary contact. "Oh Lord!" Plimpton said when his wife took him aside and informed him of this, and that Mrs. Spinelli had withdrawn most of the money from their modest savings to pay for it. "We'll have to go to Elaine's," Plimpton said, hoping it would be an evening when some of the crowd was out, and it was. The Plimptons and Spinellis entered the premises. I was sitting with Irwin Shaw and Winston Groom when Plimpton introduced us to Mr. Spinelli. We exchanged pleasantries. Moving slowly from table to table Plimpton presented the visitor to William Styron, Kurt Vonnegut, James T. Farrell (Plimpton later admitted he was not sure it was James T. Farrell, but said so anyway), Gay Talese, and Bruce Jay Friedman, who in turn introduced their companions to Mr. Spinelli. Plimpton and his party were now approaching the Allen table. Since Plimpton had noticed several other literary personages available for introduction, his instinct was to adhere to protocol and pass up that undefiled table, but then he delicately pondered Spinelli's four hundred dollars, the depleted savings account, the unfinished manuscript of the novel. From our perspective several tables over I said to Shaw and Groom, "My God! He's taking Mr. Spinelli to Woody Allen!" Plimpton said: "Woody, forgive me. This is Jerry Spinelli, the writer from Philadelphia." Woody looked up. "Yes," he said, with doleful eyes. "I *know,*" then returned to his chicken francese.

In the years to come, long after I had left the city, Elaine's would breed the image of snobbishness, celebrity-seeking, social-climbing, and the Hollywood hordes. But my comrades who remained, the ones who had come when the German marches and polkas were still on the jukebox, and the drunken Irishmen on the floor, thought this unsporting. Even after the enormous prosperity of this improbable institution, Elaine herself remained true to her original friends. "The power patrons," she said, "they come, they go, but the people I was involved with mainly were the boys."

I have an old photograph before me, a big black and white, taken for one of the glossy women's magazines, Elaine surrounded by her "Sixteen Favorite Boys." Here we are, sitting or standing, looking somewhat insouciant: John Barry Ryan, Lewis Lapham, Bobby Short, Bill Styron, Bruce Jay Friedman, Nick Pileggi, Bob Brown, Jean-Pierre Rassam, Buzz Farber, Jack Richardson, Christopher Cerf, Dave Halberstam, Arthur Kopit, Jack Gelber, George Plimpton, Gay Talese, myself. That was nearly a quarter of a century ago as I write, and how young we are! — and that picture brings back everlastingly for me the sunniness and camaraderie of Elaine's and its funny invisible spirit.

I came back into the place recently after many years, and she gave me an ebullient hug, and then the motherly caress reserved only for those unlikely boys of summer, and we resumed the same conversation which must have broken in midsentence one late night a very long time ago. The boys still come back in, she said. Many have remarried younger women and are fathers of small children. "They're all on their second litters now," she reported. Not long before his death Irwin Shaw wrote: "The plaque on Second Avenue will finally read, THIS WAS THE PLACE." To that I myself would only add, "She knew us, and understood."

I long to capture the mood, the feel, the look of the nation out beyond New York City and Elaine's as the Sixties mounted to crescendo. Perhaps it is coincidental that the three of its societies I knew the best, Mississippi, Texas, and New York, were in some ways also its most violent. The Nixon election came aglitter with his pledge of reconciliation, but this did not last very long. The early promises of withdrawal and pledges for the South Vietnamese to fight their own war, called "Vietnamization" by Nixon, led secretly to the widening of it with the massive Cambodian bombings. The Great Society was in rubble, and many quarters felt the end of hope and the beginning of a resigned and embittered desperation. There seemed a fatalism inherent in the Nixon Presidency, as if real power had resided in the Right all along and even the center could not hold. Buttressing this was the gnawing reaction of the white lower-middle class against black rebellion, welfare programs, and student protest. With the abandonment of his nonpartisanship and his lacerating counterattacks on activism and dissent, Nixon found his point-man in Spiro Agnew, who addressed himself on the evenings' television to "ideological eunuchs" and "parasites of passion" and "nattering nabobs of negativism" and the "effete corps of impudent snobs who characterize themselves as intellectuals." The activist Todd Gitlin recalled the demonic disposition of the moment:

> The once-solid core of American life — the cement of loyalty that people tender to institutions, certifying that the current order is going to last and deserves to — this loyalty, in certain sectors, was decomposing. Not even the extravagance, the confusion and sometimes moral dubiousness of the opposition could keep the schools and the army and the family from losing their grip on the young. The liberal-conservative consensus that had shored up national satisfaction since 1945 — the interwoven belief in economic growth, equality of opportunity, and the Cold War — had fallen afoul of black revolt and Vietnam, and it was as if once the keystone of the arch was loosened, the rest of the structure teetered.

The campuses themselves were an unerring reflection of all this, and I often visited them in those years to lecture — about Vietnam, and contemporary writing and journalism, and race relations — and to find out what was going on, because I felt that an editor of a national magazine ought to get knocked around a little. The protests were growing more aggressive and widespread, and regional institutions which not long before had been sedate as the Methodist Epworth League were caught in the turbulence. This was the time of the disruption of classes and college administrations and, increasingly, of the bombings and arson. The night before I was to give a lecture at Washington University in St. Louis the ROTC Building had been dynamited. The action was such a *succès de scandale* that on the early evening of my lecture the campus seemed all but battened down. Eight people turned out in the auditorium and I suggested we retire to the nearest saloon to drink beer and talk, which we did.

"I'm not happy over the bombing," one young man said. "But I think the authorities got exactly what they deserved."

"Well, *I'm* happy about it," another student said.

"What if people had gotten hurt?" someone asked.

"They would've deserved it," he replied. "They didn't have any business being in the building in the first place."

Adalbert de Segonzac, the American correspondent for *France Soir,* wrote a piece for *Harper's* about his visits to the American campuses. The things he was told were identical to the words I was listening to also. The young people did not want to contribute to an impersonal, increasingly distant society rooted in the acquisitive urges. "The old values of your generation no longer have any importance to us. We aren't pining, as our fathers did, for automobiles, television, or other amenities of life. We are raising our sights higher."

"But I agree with that," I would often say. "And I'm not all that older than you anyway."

"Older enough," one young woman said. "And a member of the Establishment."

I rented a car in Memphis, where I had been talking with students at Memphis State University, to drive that time to Washington University in St. Louis, just to reacquaint myself with my favorite American artery, Highway 61, which begins on Tulane Avenue in New Orleans and pierces the heartland all the way to Thunder Bay, Canada, with its distinctive character and passion and history long before Bob Dylan memorialized it: Blues Highway, Freedom Highway, Great River Road. I was alone with my musings behind the wheel, absorbing the eternal river in its twisting and turnings at the closest horizon, and the worn concrete finger of the old original No. 61 appearing and disappearing in the grassy fields along the modern one like an ancient Roman road. I had spurned three or four hippie hitchhikers down around Cape Girardeau, but at the intersection near New Madrid stood a solitary one, a long-haired young man in T-shirt and Levi's carrying a hefty Army duffle-bag, and I stopped for him. He was twenty-one years old and on his way back to the University of Missouri after the weekend home. The talk turned to Vietnam, where he had served his year before returning to Missouri a few months previously. Even though he had not been a combatant, indeed he had been a clerk typist, he said that when he returned to college he was cursed and taunted by his fellow students, and even spit upon by one young woman. "That's when I let my hair grow long," he said. Some of the returning combat veterans were treated fiercely. "They were pretty screwed up anyway," he said. "I guess they went over there thinking it would be like a John Wayne movie, and they had a really bad time of it. I felt sorry for them. The closest *I* came to a Purple Heart was when my little finger got tangled up in the typewriter keys."

Everywhere I went I saw these dilemmas, heard young war veterans complaining that coming back was as hard as combat, and of course the profound agony over what was the right thing to do: whether to leave for Canada or declare conscientious objection or join the National Guard if you had influence or find an exemption somewhere or go ahead and serve, each emblematic of a generation living at the edge. I felt very much for all of them. Years later, the election of 1992 would emphasize for all the stark contrast between President George Bush's World War II era with its clear absolutes and Bill Clinton's generation and its wrenching moral gropings over Vietnam. The future President Clinton's best friend at Oxford University, a Rhodes Scholar from Spokane, refused to serve and became a fugitive from justice. He eventually returned home and later committed suicide.

If you were in Boulder in the Sixties, it has been observed, you probably don't remember. It was an epicenter of drugs. I stayed in a couple of dorms there, where there was also considerably more hard drinking than there had ever been even at the University of Texas in the 1950s. "Relevance" was a major word. As at many universities, posters of Allen Ginsberg, who had survived from Fifties beatnik to Sixties champion, adorned the walls of dorms and coffeehouses. The campus *tableaux* in all their panoply were archetypical of those years, flamboyant hippies and protesters of more serious mien in juxtaposition with radiantly immaculate Young Americans for Freedom carrying Barry Goldwater's *Conscience of a Conservative* and Ayn Rand's *Atlas Shrugged* and placards proclaiming "Stamp Out ADA" and "Better Dead Than Red." In these times even Chapel Hill, that most beautiful and serene of campuses with its resonances of Thomas Wolfe and the more secluded and bucolic Southern days — "it seemed to Eugene like a provincial outpost of great Rome; one felt its remoteness, its isolated charm" — was mightily brushed by the Sixties' virulent clashes and diversities. Here one day I struck up a conversation with a young student wearing a "Get Out of Vietnam" T-shirt and tattered khakis. He had observed me looking up at the big statue of the Confederate soldier just off Franklin Street. "That guy's outmoded now, don't you think?" he said to me.

Three or four times I ran into Abbie Hoffman in his busy campus travels: this former pharmaceuticals salesman-turned-revolutionary noted for such puckish pranks as tossing dollar bills from the gallery of the New York Stock Exchange and gleefully watching the stampede of traders rushing to pick up the money, or selecting three thousand souls at random from the New York telephone book and sending each of them marijuana cigarettes with directions on how to smoke them. A most unlikely revolutionist he was with his ginger wisecracks and savvy one-liners and antic gyrations, but he was a high-strung and effusive presence wherever he went and easily rivalled Ginsberg as an icon of the restive middle-class young, and one could not help but like him. Encountering him walking with a small group on one campus or another in those years I introduced myself. "You're the one who publishes Mailer," he said, eyes diligent and aflash above his scruffy black beard. "Hey, man, you're not all bad." It was Berkeley in those times that was still the great outpost of disaffection, the goblin to the blander decencies, and as I walked one day beyond Sproul Plaza, down Telegraph Avenue, I saw all around me what Marshal Frady had seen and described here for *Harper's*, the ragged jean-shorts and sandals, bearded Ezekiels shouting from the Old Testament, heads shaved and faces dabbed in paint, the slapping of drums and tinkling of ankle bells. Mario Savio did not speak much anymore, I was told — burnt out already by the Sixties, for to me and countless others Berkeley was everything the decade was, and more.

I heard, too, the rhetoric of revolution from nattily dressed Ivy Leaguers. I was once invited by David Riesman to speak to his huge sophomore class in sociology at Harvard. The students hissed me when I made a remark against violence, a little less shrilly when I espoused the First Amendment, applauded my remarks on the war. I spent a couple of days there later with our valorous *Harper's* contributor Larry L. King during his tenure as a Nieman Fellow. The Harvard *Crimson* was beginning to print the word "fuck." When outside police invaded the Yard to quell a demonstration, the circumstances of that bust had radicalized the students and polarized the faculty. Later three hundred students seized University Hall. One midmorning King and I strolled through Harvard Square, a scene which he soon most accurately described in our pages, as Frady had Berkeley:

> . . . packed by hairy wrecks and braless butterballs hawking their wares — Fem Libs, Black Panthers, SDSers, Weathermen, nihilists, hedonists, devil worshippers, and unspecified crazys all proclaiming The Only True Salvation; chanters of Hare Krishna, Hare Krishna, Krishna / Krishna / Hare Hare, wearing their peach-colored togas, with shaved heads and rattling tambourines. Agents of bug-eyed spiritualists, peace marches, and coffee houses thrust their documents into his hand, while teenyboppers from South Boston and juvenile runaways from Indiana made their ersatz Harvard poses. Bellbottoms and miniskirts. Pot smokers and panhandlers. Green-eyeshadow gals and anticosmetic feminists. . . . Jivers and schemers and round-the-clock dreamers. Merchants posting notices proclaiming Absolutely No Bare Feet Inside. Through it all wandered occasional gray old faculty heads wearing the tweeds and ties of another day, sometimes muttering to themselves.

The students at Gettysburg College in Pennsylvania had numerous activists among their number, but they seemed less volatile and aggressive than at many other places. Could this have been because of the haunted and tragic ground which abutted their campus? The nickname of the athletic teams there was the "Bullets." I stayed with a college family who every year planted a large vegetable garden in the back of their house, where they frequently dug up mini-balls and shell fragments; recently they had found a rusty old belt-buckle with "CSA" on it. The chairman of the history department took me on an afternoon's tour of the battlefield, my first visit to that most American of terrains. Late that night, against the park regulations, I drove my car over there and got out. I had the place all to myself. It was springtime and the grass was heavy with dew. The fireflies were out, and rabbits and squirrels bounced haphazardly among the monuments and artillery pieces. In a spooky half-moon I wandered around Little Round Top, Big Round Top, Devil's Den, and the Wheatfield, then paused at the crest of Cemetery Ridge and gazed across at the rounded green valley where the Charge had been, and its dreadful harvest of death. A handful of Mississippi boys in the first wave had made it into these final embattlements, but they had not lasted too long, and I remembered the lingering fealties and funny contradictions of one's boyhood, and history arrested and suspended for me in that one hushed moment before that majestic and dismembering assault. The quiet earth before me left me breathless with lonely sorrow and understanding. I thought of the nation now in that year of 1968, the terrible brevity of its attention spans, and what this heuristic ground must have meant to it, or not meant to it at all.

Suddenly, from around a bend, came a car, its blue lights flashing. It came to a halt. A park policeman got out. He examined me from a distance with a flashlight.

"What are you doing here?" he demanded. "It's midnight." Did he think I might be the last surviving Mississippian, still tarrying here on Cemetery Ridge after all the years?

"I don't know why I'm here, officer. It was compulsive."

"I'm supposed to take you in, you know."

"Well, I'm giving the commencement speech at the college tomorrow. Can you let me off on good behavior?"

"Okay, okay," he said brusquely, yet not without a trace of

amusement. "But try not to come in again after dark, will you?" I was about to get in my car when he addressed me again. "It happens all the time," he said. "And it's always Southerners. Why always you Southerners?"

"But I'm an American now, Officer," I replied. "I promise I am," and after a whimsical and rather tender silence we both laughed.

At far remove from the city was Texas, where I had come to maturity as a zealous and embattled young editor, and which provided its own perspective on the nation. The prospect on the Mall and the Drag at my old university was not so lucid nor full-bodied as Berkeley or Harvard Square, yet still no one could so much as have imagined in my own era the miscellany of liberated humanity there now. I sensed little had changed, however, in the old country boys from the lost little sun-parched towns of the Texas vastness, the prairies and steppelands and arid leas and valleys, who skirted the Fellini scenes with a phlegmatic yet vaguely importune disdain. These heirs to the same boys I had known in the 1950s who watered down the Baylor or Texas Christian marching bands with firehoses from their dormitory windows on football Saturdays, or wandered the tunnels under the campus in the nighttimes changing the mechanism which controlled the clock on top of the Tower so that it struck sixteen, or twenty-four, or thirty, or spied on parked cars in the bosky groves and terrified the vulnerable lovers by circling around these vehicles while chanting like Comanche Indians, seemed to me as stolid and impervious to the dissonance of the new decade as their predecessors of my youth would have been. In America some things do not change.

There was a canoe trip down the Rio Grande with old Texas friends, many of whom populated my *Texas Observer* days, politicians and writers and their wives and girlfriends, one young woman among them named Ann and destined one day to be Governor of Texas. It was Ann Richards, talkative and fun-loving, who chided me for brushing my teeth in the waters of the Rio Grande, dutifully proclaiming I had lost all insight on reality in my regal perch in the cultural capital, and that the Rio Grande despite its placid and unruffled beauty was now rankly polluted with chemical wastes and a veritable taxonomy of feces. The dusky sunlight filtering surrealistically into the tall, ancient Boquilas canyons, the echoes from the other canoes resounding for miles it seemed, a fire from the live oaks, whiskey neat and in tin cups, the florid Texas talk, of the nation in its agonies and Lyndon and the war and Nixon and politics, the Lone Star rhetoric: one legislator "as red as a fox's butt during pokeberry season" and "missing a few dots on his dice," a rich reactionary oilman eventually to be elected Governor "dumb as a bucket of rocks," so dumb that when the man disclosed he was taking Spanish lessons, one of our number announced that soon indeed he would be "bi-ignorant." In this mischievous yet idyllic journey down the lonesome old river dividing one culture from another I was suffused anew with my affection for Texas. "The country is most barbarously large and final," William Brammer wrote in *The Gay Place.* "It is too much country, boondocks country, alternately drab and dazzling, spectral and remote. It is so wrongfully muddled and various that it is difficult to conceive of it as all of a piece." Living as I was in New York now, I remembered the bitter clash of interests in this Texas land of my youth, the new freedoms conflicting so acutely with the old restrictions and suzerainties.

Strangely, much of these Sixties journeyings were crystallized for me in, of all unlikely places, Grinnell College in Iowa, where I and several others, including Martin Luther King, Jr., had come to give talks and to receive honorary Ph.D.s. I always liked Iowa, the neat farmhouses surrounded by a few trees, the vast empty sweep of the land. ("Is this Heaven?" Shoeless Joe asked Kevin Costner in *Field of Dreams.* "No," he replied. "It's Iowa.") Grinnell is a small, isolated, distinguished institution, and I was there for three days or so, and they brought a great many contemporary things together for me. It was both valuable and affecting to see in all the compact directness of a small town and a small college just how much the spirit of the era had settled so into the heartland.

The Grinnell people had Ralph Ellison and me staying in the home of a chemistry professor and his family. I had come to know

Ellison well in New York. I sometimes dined with him and his wife, Fanny, in their apartment in Washington Heights, or on soul food in the Red Rooster in Harlem, and my young son David Rae would sometimes visit them after school, to walk their big black Lab named Tucka in Riverside Park, or to listen to Ellison's jazz records. He was a solidly built, handsome man in his mid-fifties, an Oklahoman who had attended Tuskegee to study music in the 1930s, a warm and generous companion. His *Invisible Man,* that towering tale of a young American black and the brutal experiences that affected his naive idealism, had just been voted by some two hundred American writers, critics, and editors under the sponsorship of the New York *Herald-Tribune* the finest novel of the two decades since 1945. One saw little of the anger and rage of that book in Ralph personally, although I had sensed it was not easy for him. He owned a car, which many New Yorkers did not, to drive around the city to avoid the insults of white taxi drivers. "If Ralph were any angrier," James Baldwin had observed of him, "he could not be alive." However, the wild humor of some of the novel's pages, among the funniest and most nightmarish in American literature, were also part of his private composition; he was often full of laughter, and ironic funny stories, and there was a twinkle in his eye at such moments, and a good feeling for all things in their passing. I thought him a very great man, and also a friend, yet I always sensed in his core an ultimate self-protective distance breached by only the very few. "I'm a novelist, not an activist," he had said. "But I think that no one who reads what I write or who listens to my lectures can doubt that I'm enlisted in the freedom movement. As an individual I'm primarily responsible for the health of American literature and culture. When I write I'm trying to make sense out of chaos. To think that a writer must think about his Negroness is to fall into a trap." For the 1960s these were gallant words, and risky ones.

Ellison and I were to give a joint lecture in the Grinnell College auditorium, and he and I were working in separate rooms on our remarks. An hour or so before the lecture I heard a knock on my door, and he stuck his head inside. "Morris, let's see if we can't find us a little whiskey." This seemed a good idea. The chemist and his family were not there, and we rummaged the house. Finally, in a cabinet under the kitchen sink, we discovered one lonesome bottle, half-full, of cooking sherry. "Well," he said, "between cooking sherry and nothing, I'll take cooking sherry," and poured out a couple of tumblers. The abominable sherry was a mere fillip for what was to come. In the questions after the lecture the students were aggressive in wishing to expose all the hypocrisies of the day: Vietnam, racism, the corruption and remoteness of college administrations. They were especially hard on Ralph Ellison, who responded calmly.

The next morning I was to talk informally at a coffeehouse the Grinnell students had designed for themselves near the campus and called "Ex Loco Parentis." Since Ellison had nothing planned, he went with me. The walls of the coffeehouse were decorated with posters displaying the clarions of the age, and photographs of the Beatles and The Grateful Dead and the Black Panthers and the ubiquitous Allen Ginsberg. I liked the free mood of the place and said as much. One young man in particular, however, had been stalking me in every lecture and seminar for the last two days, challenging my credentials, my politics, my magazine, and my accent. That morning he was back again on the edges of the gathering. He stood up.

"I don't trust anyone over thirty," he shouted. "What do you think of *that?*"

I hastily contemplated what I did indeed think of that, for I had been asked it more than a few times on the campuses. "I'll tell you what," I contrived to reply to my efficient young antagonist. "I don't trust anyone *under* thirty."

"I thought so. So why don't you?"

People under thirty are too self-righteous, I said. They don't care for history or literature. They're all wrapped up in themselves. I also didn't trust anyone *over* thirty, I continued. They're too materialistic, caring only for the superficial things, and are nearly as righteous as people under thirty.

"How old are *you?*" the young inquisitor demanded.

Lying by the breadth of two years, I said, "I'm thirty." From the rear of the room, where he was drinking coffee with students, I heard from the author of *Invisible Man* a wild Oklahoma guffaw.

Our last night there three or four of the other participants and I were invited to a late party in the apartment of some students. In cast and temper it was a mold of the decade. It was Saturday, and a good crowd of young people were there. There were candles in candlesticks on the floor, where several students were sitting, one of them playing folk songs on a guitar. Sitting in an easy chair was S. I. Hayakawa, semanticist and future U. S. Senator, diminutive and flamboyant and sixtyish, elfin almost, and dressed in a colorful shirt with a tam-o'-shanter on his head: he was less than a year from becoming nationally known, in calling out the police as president of San Francisco State to quell students' attacks on classrooms and administration buildings and in personally ripping out the wiring on the students' loudspeaker, as "the samurai in the tam-o'-shanter," and a soon-to-be hero of Governor Reagan and the petulant Right. On this evening at the Grinnell apartment, however, he seemed anything but: flourishing his glass of wine he was making witty and good-humored declarations to the young hosts. He rose from his chair and joined the youngsters sitting on the floor.

Sitting at a nearby table talking with other students were Ralph Ellison and Fred W. Friendly, president of CBS News, Edward R. Murrow's old comrade and collaborator. He was a lean, tall, gray-haired figure of great energy, and I overheard him conversing with the young people about the possibilities of television, about its failures. The students were complaining to him about all the commercials on TV, and the influence of the advertisers. He was volubly agreeing with them. The students liked Mr. Friendly.

I was seated on a lengthy sofa. To my right was a student who, as with all the others, had introduced herself only with her first name. She was Felicia. To my left was Marshall McLuhan, and the contrast between his public persona and his private personality was singular. He looked a little subliminal himself. He was tall, slim, graying, in his late fifties, lackluster and frayed as an old mackintosh; the new world figure of "the medium is the message" and "the global village" and the computer and the electronic revolution just now reshaping civilization seemed shy and vaguely uncomfortable on this collegial night. I had earlier heard him in a campus seminar, where he was given to colorful, even bombastic overstatements, some of which I failed wholly to comprehend, but now he was quietly talking with me about magazines and their financial problems. I was about to tell him of the very first time I ever saw television, in the Sears-Roebuck on Main Street in Yazoo City: Muscles Upton of the hapless St. Louis Browns striking out on a slow sweeping curveball in the man-made snow. Momentarily a student came over and literally sat at his feet, however, and soon the young woman Felicia and I began talking. She was taking a course in American drama and had been reading *Cat on a Hot Tin Roof.* How did she like it? Not very much, she said: it was about a dull, ineffective Southern redneck concerned with job security.

I was considering how best to respond to Felicia's assessment of *Cat on a Hot Tin Roof.* But there was the loud roar of a motorcycle outside, and then suddenly and peremptorily the door to the apartment burst open, and in came a big, rousing figure, a young black man in his mid-twenties in a black leather jacket and a black beret. He stood there for a moment surveying the scene. Several of the students rushed toward him and amiably surrounded him; he accepted their salutations without expression. The young black had just come all the way from Chicago for the party, it was ascertained, and now one of the hosts fetched him a beer and began guiding him around the room introducing him to the guests: first S. I. Hayakawa, then Fred Friendly, Marshall McLuhan, and myself. He did not shake hands with any of us, and he looked me over with a gloomy sort of disdain. Then he was in front of Ellison. He was soon joined by another black.

The two blacks got into a vehement argument with Ellison about the ending of *Invisible Man,* in which the protagonist retreats to anonymity in his cellar. The young black men told Ellison this signified giving in to oppression rather than fighting it. Ellison was defending his ending.

Suddenly the young man with the beret who had come in from

Chicago on the motorcycle said: "You're an Uncle Tom, man. You're a sell-out. You're a disgrace to your race."

As Ellison stood there, wordlessly at first, a silence fell on the room. Some of the others were craning to watch. The whole set of his features was transmuted, the muscles of his body tensed. For one horrible moment I thought I was going to have to step between them. It would have made headlines in Mississippi, a white Delta boy trying to break up a fight between a Black Panther and a black American writer.

When Ellison spoke, his words were tight and clipped. He jabbed with his finger, "I resent being called an Uncle Tom. You don't know what you're talking about," he said. "You don't know anything. What do you know about my life? It's easy for you. You're just a straw in the wind. Get on your motorcycle and go back to Chicago and throw some Molotov cocktails. That's all you'll ever know about."

A black Grinnell student from Jackson, Mississippi, Henry Wingate (years later to be a U.S. district judge) and an admirer of Ellison's, was one of the hosts. "I represent Grinnell," he said, "and it's time to break this up." Ralph had had some drinks. He turned to young Wingate and repeated, "I resent being called a Tom." He put his head on young Wingate's shoulder and began sobbing, "I'm not a Tom, I'm not a Tom."

Shortly after that we left. It was late. The chemistry professor and his family had long since retired, and Ralph and I sat out on the front steps. I wondered inanely how Marshall McLuhan had fitted the passing *contretemps* into the medium being the message.

"How are you?" I asked.

"Hell, I'm fine."

"I'm sorry about that."

"Why be sorry? I've heard that kind of thing for a long time. I'm used to it," and we just sat there for a little while listening to the great expansive encompassing Midwestern night.

~ Loves and the Island

13 LOVE WILL COME AGAIN, but in circuitous paths.

My one-bedroom apartment across East Thirty-third from my magazine on the seventeenth floor of the refurbished gallant old Vanderbilt Hotel was greatly favored among my male companions, who in no time at all considered it by right theirs on demand for their innumerable afternoon assignations. I will not name names, but they included a roll call, the long gray immutable line, of literary America. Since I was keeping, or trying to keep, ritualistic daytime office hours, I docilely acquiesced, a blunder of colossal proportions. I began to feel not unlike Jack Lemmon in *The Apartment*, for among these friends, who would sneakily arrive at the *Harper's* office at all daylight hours, the doorkey to my bachelor quarters would in time become more popular than I myself ever was. Belittling this expression of Christian charity, some of them would go so far as to suggest that the apartment be a little cleaner next time around, and would I put in more cashew nuts and beer and wine, and next time Heineken's perhaps rather than Schaeffer, and in bottles rather than cans? I was acutely grieved.

As Gershwin said: They're making songs of love, but not for me. The memories of my now ex-wife, and the tenacious emotions of estrangement, were still consuming, for there was something about the finality of divorce that evoked in one a curious sort of puritanism. After a while there was a fling with a young woman from the Midwest, an Elaine's regular working for one of the newsweeklies, and one night only with a movie actress leaving the next day for shooting abroad who said, "You really can't believe you're with who you're with, can you?" then after that the abysmal transaction of waking in the morning with some achromic young New York woman whose name you could not recall, or women named either Stacy or Tracy, one could never be sure, with prowling urban apartment cats named Raffles or Sigmund or Fyodor or Pharaoh who seemed poised to leap upon you and gouge your eyes out with their rapier-like claws, and once a girl from Chicago with a flat face and flat nose who, if she had grown up with you in a small town of Dixie, would have had the nickname "Mutt," and if all this sounds sexist to the later generations I can only beg merciful absolution because in the insufferable heart of me that was the way I felt.

After a while to my good fortune I grew to know a young Manhattan woman precisely my age, darkly and stunningly handsome and rich and good-hearted and extraordinarily "well-connected" as they would have said in New Orleans or Charleston or Mobile, and of the fun and adventure to agree with fine acquiescence, to cite an example, to dine with me for purposes of voyeuristic curiosity at a substantial midtown Japanese restaurant on December 7, the twenty-eighth anniversary of Pearl Harbor, and who on glancing about at the ingratiating waiters and proprietors and Nippon clientele tartly observed, "Do you think they're *contrite?*" One wintry day she took me upstate to meet her friend Gore Vidal, who was living at the time in a graceful old mansion on the Hudson River, where we sat in a half-darkened study drinking wine, the prospect from the windows of the half-frozen Hudson outside, broad and stolid under the grim, frosty skies, and silent like a hibernating serpent. Vidal had large dark eyes and graying hair and was a magnetic figure with his caustic and charming wit. He even advised me that he had cousins, mostly named *Gore,* down around Chickasaw County, Mississippi. For a long time he sat on a couch and told stories about his two adversaries and arch-enemies Truman Capote and William F. Buckley, Jr., this disquisition so pointedly acerbic that I considered myself glad on that waning Hudson Valley's afternoon not to be *his* enemy.

I thought I was growing then to love the young woman, and to this day still believe I was. But again guilt itself, pernicious and indwelling guilt, sooner or later would intervene, because she was married and with young children, and wished the marriage to work. There I was once more, left with America's oldest magazine — a most capricious and seductive mistress, my real love? — and with the companionship of the fellows, and with the wistful yet sedative promise that someday I would persuade some ambitious Ph.D. person, at Berkeley, say, or Ann Arbor, to contrive a sociology dissertation: "Southern WASP Men and Yankee Jewish Women: Syndrome and Apotheosis in Post-Jungian U.S.A."

I met Muriel for the first time at Elaine's, of course. It marked the beginning of a long relationship, somewhat inconsistent at times, and not always incandescent, but it lasted off and on for several years, one of those unlikely couplings that, as we age, make better and more rational sense in hindsight than it might have at the time, though what on earth does love have to do with being rational? — and I honor now those days.

She had light brown hair, blue-green eyes, a narrow-bridged nose, her slender face in profile uplifted in an odd, almost haughty gaze, and then, contradistinctively, a riotous grin and giggling laughter, a slouch of the shoulder, a long gliding gait, and slight toss of the head, a Manhattanite to the deepest core, irreverently bright, educated at Barnard, a founder of the American painting and sculpture department at the Metropolitan. Her father had established a sardine factory years before on the coast of Maine which had made the family rich, but beyond that she was the divorced wife of an exceedingly wealthy Irish-American from the West Coast much older than she whose money derived from timber and other enterprises, and the settlement had not been spartan. On a wall she had a picture of herself when she was twelve years old, taken at her brother's *bar mitzvah,* a picture that haunted me so with her dark brooding gaze and an air in repose of such vulnerability and expectancy and gentleness that I told her I would write a little story one day about her called "The Girl in the Bar Mitzvah Photograph," and this I suppose is at last the story.

Muriel's cultured metropolitan friends more or less tolerated this upwardly mobile son of the South, although her mother and brother and cousins were unfailingly warm and generous. That family also included through marriage Princess Elizabeth of Yugoslavia, a relative of the pretender to the throne of Yugoslavia, so that various strains and offshoots of dispossessed European royalty were always drifting through her household, and we once had a drink with the pretender himself, throneless and debonair, the only king, pretender or any other, I ever called by his first name. Many years later and in another place I saw a movie entitled *Someone to Watch Over Me* about a young detective from Queens called upon to guard a wealthy and beautiful Manhattan woman who had been the only witness to a Mob killing, and while I was watching this film I sat upright and said to myself, "My God, that's Muriel!" — and in her looks, her clothes, her worlds of art and music and the *haute* New York culture she was stunningly reminiscent of her, and the reader has by now likely perceived who the detective from Queens in that context reminded me of. I suppose, in the old flow now of the years, that I watched over her, the fragile beauty of the girl in the *bar mitzvah* picture, just as she watched over me, although I guess neither of us could ever be sure, for it all had to do with both time and the city in their passing.

Muriel had a refined and educated Upper East Side accent, but when vehement or angry or excited this was a flimsy and even reluctant overlay on the strident and lucid and enduring urban Jewish modulations as they inevitably broke through, and I cared for her the most when the voice of the city, of the sardine princess, triumphed, however so tangentially. I loved her dear, kind passion, the private times when she seemed almost like a girl of the South, as if she wished momentarily to get away, away with the hotheaded Jeffersonian goy, and she did, yet always to return to her own world and its wants.

She had a four-story townhouse in the East Sixties, in a neighborhood of other perfect townhouses and brownstones, and children in private-school uniforms on the sidewalks, and nannies with baby carriages, and hired retainers walking suave and coiffeured city dogs, and toney tucked-in basement restaurants of fine deferential aspect — one of countless similar semi-protectorates set down in the great amorphous bosom of the city of that day, all of this not wholly but at least titularly removed from the whirring clank and rattle and incoherence of Lexington Avenue right up the way. It was a finely furnished house but comfortable and uncloying, with old family photographs on oval mahogany tables, and an air of knowing and urbane civility, and Mozart and Beethoven flowing from some hidden speaker. Often I accompanied her to the art gallery openings with all the champagne and Sixties music and psychedelic polka dots dancing on the walls, flashes of diffuse light across the encircling patrons as in filigree, and sometimes one of the great and magnificent institutions like the Guggenheim with its vertiginous vistas and ample lobbies — women in sheer black stockings gleaming in the light, and dangling earrings and old wonderful cameos, and long satiny gloves and floor-length coats. She knew everyone in this city *milieu* — Columbia intellectuals, art critics and dealers, museum curators (her vital and gregarious cousin Allen Sven Oxenberg ran the American Opera Society), contributors to the more lofty and harmless of the literary journals, some of the older *New Yorker* writers, as well as the fine artists themselves such as Willem de Kooning, Jasper Johns, Saul Steinberg, and others, and since she was a *saloniere,* the outlander appropriated for a time something of that world, of its genius and insouciance and haughtiness and indiscriminate opprobrium. Quite a number of Muriel's coterie did not know their own country very well, and more or less viewed the rest of the nation out beyond the Jersey Palisades with a rather patronizing regard, an appendage to and afterthought of what they had wrought for themselves here: the perfect city in an imperfect time. Their paragon misgivings often centered on the South. There were moments when one of such a gathering, ever so charmingly condescending, might well have started playing "Dixie" for me on a Stradivarius, as the Manhattan impressario does for the Carolina football coach Wingo in Pat Conroy's *Prince of Tides,* after which Wingo nearly throws the Stradivarius off the penthouse terrace.

To Muriel a person who was especially distinctive and intelligent and complicated was, in her words, "highly evolved," as indeed was she. The composer Jerry Leiber captured something of her background complexities in a popular song he entitled "Muriel Oxenberg Murphy, I'm in Love with the Sound of Your Name," which was on a few of the jukeboxes in the town in those days. She could be funny. Once on a rainy afternoon she found herself sharing a taxi from in front of the Metropolitan to downtown with Kirk Douglas, to whom she turned and asked, "May I do something?" and the actor replied, "I know, touch the cleft of my chin, so go ahead," and forthwith she did. One day as the two of us strolled through a lovely cemetery on eastern Long Island she tripped and almost stumbled over a small tombstone set not very high off the ground, then stooped to read the name. "Huh!" she said. "I'd wondered why he never called again." She had a nine-year-old daughter named Julia, who attended Nightingale-Bamford and whom I loved very much. For me that little girl was *lagniappe*. How on earth had this small, clairvoyant, mischievous conspirator entered my existence? She was one-half Jewish and one-half Irish, conspiratorial and zany, tender and brilliant, very pretty and irreverent, and one could talk to her as if she were an adult, until all of a sudden she was a child again. Young Julia and I would often sit and talk about New York City, and magazines, and the hazards and wants of all of it, and the land and loves and the Sixties themselves, and in her precocious understanding, even then, she was a remarkable companion, and almost contemporary, as certain kids were in those days. She and my son David Rae eventually became friends too — the "new siblings" of that flowering epoch of divorce.

Muriel had a French maid, who often moonlighted behind the hat-check counter at Le Moal, Norman Podhoretz's commissary; she also had an informal chess club and spoke French to the maid and sometimes on the telephone or to the chess people. I brought Larry L. King of West Texas to Muriel's one day. "I don't understand a damned word they're saying," he said. "Why don't they speak a little English? For all I know they're making fun of me." After a few drinks, in retribution, he began speaking pig-Latin.

The salon gatherings included numerous Western and Eastern Europeans, who frequently used Muriel's quarters as a stopping-off spot in their ceaseless wanderings in search of the Big Green currency. At one time or another some of their number stayed in the small rooms and garrets of the top floor; when especially in force they slept sideways in groups on the beds. They were frequently as surly as they were disputatious. Despite their castigations of the United States as the most violent society in the world, at Muriel's international *soirees* they and their whole combative *ouevre* gave new and valuable comprehension for me to the word "Balkanization." After dinner they would remain in the dining room while the Americans retired to the parlor. From there we could hear them quarreling in a half-dozen tongues, these Serbs and Croats and Czechs and Slovaks and even a pontifical Rumanian or two, joined sometimes in this dissonance by an occasional contentious Frenchman or Italian or Greek. We Yanks, pacific as kittens, sat there with our coffee absorbing that thunder of spleen from the adjoining chamber, and the specious soliloquies that trailed off unresolved, then burst forth all over again in renewed vituperation. Halberstam or Frady or Corry or King might be sitting there listening with me — should we have summoned the Swiss Red Cross? "I'm sure glad we got our own Civil War over and done with," King observed on one such evening. One of our group accosted an agitator when he came into our room to fetch a brandy before returning to the fray and said: "Pardon me, boy, is this the Transylvania Station?" And through it all Muriel Oxenberg Murphy, who in her golden heart really did believe in bringing people together, wafted gently and serenely, oblivious to any hint of global disintegration.

It was the beginning of the age of "living together" there in the city, and she and I established a bond in simple things: vintage double features (*Key Largo* and *Ninotchka*, for instance, or *Mr. Smith Goes to Washington* and *It's a Wonderful Life*, or *Public Enemy* and *I Was a Prisoner on a Chain Gang*) on weekends beginning at ten in the mornings at the Thalia on the West Side, and progressing into the afternoons at the New Yorker on Upper Broadway, and then moving on down to the shadowy little cinemas of the Village. One Christmas Eve of chilled wind and snow I descended to a discount mart at Park and Twenty-eighth and bought her a new stereo for her records, and not finding a cab on this holiday twilight of the elements carted the burdensome package a dozen blocks beyond Grand Central before I found one, briefly accosted on this journey by a tipsy streetcorner Santa Claus, and her daughter Julia was waiting for me in the foyer of the townhouse, and we secretively concealed the offering in a downstairs alcove for the next day. That night I took mother and daughter to a college basketball game in the Garden, the Louisiana State Bayou Bengals versus the St. John's Redmen as I recall, neither of my Manhattan girls having ever seen a real basketball game and hence much taken with the ambidextrous felicities of LSU's Pistol Pete Marovich: "Ah just *luv* that Pistol Pete," young Julia said in a put-on Southern drawl, "droopin' socks an' everythin'." And then on to a Mexican spot on Second Avenue for a Christmas Eve enchilada dinner, and solicitations for the new year coming.

I have memories of waking in the mornings at Muriel's house to the dulcet echoes of pianos from the music school across the back garden, Mozart or Tchaikovsky or Mendelssohn, the notes softly floating through the open windows, redolent for me yet, reminding me of my mother's piano as I awakened as a child, and of time itself and the dearness of Muriel's friendship and love, her loyalty and belonging, her unselfish caring for me, and the brilliant and capricious life of the city we together shared. As with the Comden and Green words from *Auntie Mame,* "Your heart is from Tiffany's too."

Muriel had a big sprawling house on eastern Long Island — "the South Fork" — a hundred miles from the city which she claimed to have purchased from the proceeds of her wedding ring. It was near a village called Wainscott, on a placid inlet not far from the Atlantic. The South Fork was a settled place touched with the past. We often went there on weekends. I had discovered the area by accident two or three years before, from the back of a chartered bus, with people from *Harper's* going to Montauk for a business meeting. In a lethargy that day, I glanced out my window. Things flickering obliquely before my eyes brought me awake: lush potato fields on the flat land, village greens, old graveyards drowsing in the sun, clapboard houses, ancient elms along the broad streets, a flock of Canada geese overhead, and far in the distance the blue Atlantic breakers. The flat, verdant potato fields would always remind me a little of the Mississippi Delta, the potatoes even having much the same growing season, but without the Delta's blood and guilt. I knew then, as the heart tells you such things, that I would come back someday for a long time. I would learn that the summer influx from the city distorted the area's true character. In the "off-season" it was still a rural place then with a quiet village life. You did not have to go to the ocean every day to remember it was there, for the roar of it was never far away. On the drives out the early stretches of the Long Island Expressway there were often the funeral processions from the city, going out to where there was still empty land to bury people, the hearse heaped high with flowers if it were an Italian family from Brooklyn or the Bronx. I grew to love eastern Long Island, for it was one of the loveliest terrains in America before it began to be encroached upon. Even then, in the summers, one could see grown men wearing red shoes without socks and silk ascots about the throat and parrot-green sports jackets and white flannels: New York show-business people, and Wall Street brokers, and trust-funded suburbanites with Rolls Silver Clouds, and Upper East Side psychoanalysts with aqua BMWs. Once I spotted Terry Southern and Dennis Hopper, speeding by in a white Mercedes ambulance.

While I was on a week's vacation one of those summers, my mother, Marion Weaks Morris, visited me on Long Island from Mississippi, daughter of an older South, widow, church organist and teacher of the piano. She lived in the house of my childhood with my grandmother, where they viewed the television each night, and all she could talk about was Dick Cavett. "He's so cute and smart," she kept saying. "I don't know what we'd do without Dick Cavett. The whole town *loves* Dick Cavett."

Dick Cavett then had the most urbane late-night talk show on national television, in the same time spot as Johnny Carson. I had been on the program three or four times, because I lived and worked only a short ride from the ABC-TV theater in the West Fifties, and often when a scheduled guest dropped out at the last minute the producers called me. That may have been one of the reasons my mother adored Dick Cavett. Richard Schickel in our own magazine wrote of him: "Dick Cavett . . . is quite obviously the most intelligent new television star. He is obviously also a decent sort. He has good manners, asks reasonable questions, and actually listens to answers. In short, he converses with his guests instead of interviewing them. He also does the funniest monologues in the business, and he and his producers have shown a willingness to move beyond the customary limits in booking guests." His 1960s activist melange had included, among others, left-wing crusaders like Mark Lane and Jane Fonda, members of the new women's liberation movement debating Hugh Hefner of *Playboy*, Janis Joplin talking and singing, and Stokely Carmichael and Black Panthers delving into racial oppression in America. Cavett himself could indeed be funny. His ideal male guest would be "a combination of John Wayne and Oscar Wilde — a man who could kill Apaches with epigrams," and the ideal female guest "a combination of Raquel Welch and Oscar Wilde." On Long Island that week my mother persisted in her adulation of Dick Cavett. I would be talking with friends in a restaurant about some new book or another, or some national issue, and she would interrupt. "Did you see Dick talking about the Marx Brothers?" or "Wasn't Dick funny talking about termites?" or "Didn't Dick have a good description of Mr. Nixon's nose?"

The time had come, as I feared it would and must. Cavett, a Nebraskan, was married to the actress Carrie Nye, and Carrie was from Greenwood, Mississippi, the craziest town in the Delta, fifty miles north up Highway 49-E from my hometown. She was three years younger than I, and I had not met her until my days in the city, where I had found her a source of good-humored cheer. She and her husband had a Long Island house, designed by Stanford White, on the bluffs above Montauk. I telephoned Carrie Nye, explaining my mother was visiting from Mississippi and that I had a problem.

"I know. She's a fan of Dick's and wants to meet him," Carrie said.

"How did you know?"

"I just know." And she suggested we drive up the following Sunday for a lobster lunch.

In hindsight I wish I had waited until the Sabbath to tell my mother. She is now long-ago dead, buried under a mimosa next to my father on the last great sloping hill before the coming of the Delta, but when I told her I thought she might expire on the spot of a coronary thrombosis. "Dick Cavett! What will I *say* to him? What will I *wear?*" She bought a new pair of stockings. She got a hair-do. She even went to a dentist and had her teeth cleaned. On the telephone I heard her telling the neighbors back home. She also called the *Yazoo Herald,* which ran a story: "Marion Morris to Meet Dick Cavett." Sunday arrived and she was nervous. She changed shoes four times, and as we drove east on the Montauk Highway she would gesture out the window and say: "Look at that bird!" or "Look at that telephone pole!"

When we arrived at the grand Stanford White dwelling, Carrie Nye graciously greeted us. Dick was upstairs working on a monologue, she said, but would be down soon. My mother was now so agitated that her ears were red, and she had lost one of her shoes, and the hostess, born of the Delta and comprehending such regional mysteries, assuaged her by showing her a few of the nautical furnishings. The three of us were sitting on a sofa when suddenly Dick Cavett came in, shortish and mischievous and bright-eyed with a Dutch-boy cap on his head.

"Oh, Dick!" My mother rose full height and went over and hugged him.

"Hello, Mrs. Morris."

"I have to ask you something straight off. When you're out and around somewhere, do people come up to get your autograph?"

"Yes, ma'am, they sometimes do."

The tone was set, but with a portion or so of *vin blanc* my mother calmed down considerably, as Cavett told her cool little tales, about some of his TV guests, including the aged Chinese-American actor Richard Loo he had interviewed recently who had played the Nippon villains in such wartime films as *First Yank in Tokyo* and *Purple Heart.* "What is Fred Astaire *really* like, Dick?" A little later he invited her on a tour of the house, and a few minutes afterwards Carrie Nye and I overheard them from an adjoining chamber. My mother was calling her old spinster neighbor, Ethel North! "Ethel, guess who *I'm* putting on the line?" "Hello, Miss North, this is Dick Cavett." A pause. "Yes, it's me. That is, I *think* it's me."

Here one Long Island weekend afternoon in those days I found myself with Scottie Fitzgerald, divorced and in her fifties, daughter of Scott and Zelda, who through mutual friends had asked me to drive her around the vicinity, for she was searching for landmarks of her mother's forebears, named Sayre, and the Sayres were among the first settlers here. I myself was just learning the neighborhood, and the two of us cruised about the farms and beach roads and villages, among the oldest in the nation, and soon enough we found "Sayre's Path" in Easthampton; she took notes but was diffident, and said little. That evening, at dinner with our friends, after drinks Scottie Fitzgerald said she wished to apologize. For what? I asked. "For being such a poor companion today," she said. "I'm always afraid I'll disappoint people. They only remember me as the cute little girl in the picture by the roadster with my mother and father."

Her father, indeed, had called it "this riotous finger of island," meaning the area of East and West Egg closer to the city itself, Gatsby country, and the South Fork here was indeed on the precipice of becoming riotous, although that was still in the future. Only later, beyond the purview of this memoir, would I come to know and spend time with some of the nation's finest writers who would choose out of love for this land to live here: Peter Matthiessen, Joseph Heller, Jean Stafford, Shana Alexander, Kurt Vonnegut, Jr., Wilfrid Sheed, Betty Friedan, Budd Schulberg, John Knowles, Craig Claiborne. But two among others I got to know in this period, one of whom would become as close a friend as I ever had.

Truman Capote had a house out here, hidden behind tall hedges, close to the ocean in Wainscott, only a mile or two from Muriel's. I had met him in the city through Bennett Cerf, and once had a quiche lunch in his apartment in UN Plaza, but always saw more of him in my time on Long Island. He was so often alone.

One day I am strolling up the sidewalk on the main street of Bridgehampton on a Saturday afternoon. An enormous Buick with a small man, so small that his nose barely rises above the dashboard, as in the "Kilroy Was Here" drawings of World War II, stops before me. "Hop in and let's ride around and *gossip*. I can't wait to tell you about my conversation at lunch in Le Côte Basque with Princess Radziwill yesterday."

He gestures dramatically and pays little attention to the road. We are around the block and toward the ocean. Finally we are travelling in long widening circles about the dunes and potato fields. Truman is telling me of his social life in Manhattan, a brilliant, perfervid monologue touched with flamboyant flourishes. Now he is talking of Bennett and Phyllis Cerf — some party for a U.S. Senator — and Babe Paley in the Four Seasons, and a tryst in a New Jersey motel between a WASP female socialite and a mobster. And a lunch in the Plaza, I think with Katharine Graham, and who is having an extramarital affair with whom in the interstices of the Upper East Side, for he was nothing if not a savant of all such matters.

"How old were you when you wrote *Other Voices, Other Rooms?*" I interrupt.

He pauses over the dashboard. "So very young," he says. "Oh so very young and brilliant."

He negotiates the turn at Church Lane. He tells me of his latest recipe for quiche. "Oh, Willie," he says. "How naive you are! Your simplicity! The things I could tell you!"

I liked Truman, and for whatever reason, he liked me. I do not know if this mutual affection was because we were both small-town Southerners in a place where there were so few of us to be found. It may well be so; the small-town South never left Truman, though it always seemed subtly at war with his cosmopolitan instincts. When I first got to know him, I suspected he had given too much of his heart's substance to those cosmopolitan instincts, to a style of living and a company of companions about whom he cared too much, a company that chose to turn upon him in his twilight time.

He may well not have agreed. Though he was very small, and he had that high, shrill, lispy voice, touched by the South, that was as distinctive a voice as I ever heard (there is no way to mimic the way he talked, although even those of us who cared for him tried when he was not around), he claimed he was impervious to bullying. The other children never bullied him when he was growing up, he said, because he had the most wicked tongue in Monroeville, Alabama; the adults he later seemed a child among likely never bullied him for the same reason.

His voice came from his past as an orphan brought up by old-maid cousins, from his life as the kid who started writing and getting drunk on wine at age twelve. The immemorial Christmas morning in Alabama was an indelible part of him, as was the dual hanging in the state prison in Kansas he captured in *In Cold Blood.* These were the two poles of Truman's art — observing himself and observing others.

A middle-aged woman with purple hair from Alabama once came to our table in a restaurant. "Mr. Capote, I read that book *In Cold Blood.* I just have one question. Did you personally know those two *murderers?*"

"Madame," he said, "did I *know* them? I lived with them for seven *years.*"

I cannot help but believe that both these poles had much to do with his having been raised in the ornately polite society that was so often found in the old small-town South, a society that rewarded you well for keen observation and encouraged a child to listen. Truman did listen. He could hear what people said, and what they meant, and then get that on paper in a clear and clean way that escapes most writers. Other writers could not help but envy in Truman that which, if he had been a singer, might have been called his purity of tone.

But that purity may well have been a curse as well as a charm. When I grew to know Truman on Long Island, I wondered if perhaps the keenness of his observation had begun to wear on him. What he could put on paper was never quite as true as what he could see, and so there were long periods in which he published little, and the subsequent constant unmet promise of *Answered Prayers.* He could talk what he saw, could keep the audience at bay with the wicked intelligence of his tongue, but though he may have archly realized that all literature is gossip, he knew as well that all gossip is not literature. As he got older, he found it harder to write, he once told me, because his standards were too high. It was easier when he was twenty-five, but now he expected too much of himself. For all his fame from conversation, Truman realized he was a writer. But he was a writer who had to meet the hard standards of an acerbic critic whose last name was Capote.

Those of us who cared for Truman had something of a proprietary feeling for him. I think we felt his extraordinary tenderness and self-destructive vulnerability, and we worried a little for him, for in those years he often seemed lost and afraid. I drove him home from Bobby Van's saloon in Bridgehampton a number of times. One heard the roar of the ocean from his house. He would sit in an enormous sofa much too big for him. One afternoon of snow and high ocean winds he brought out an unopened pint of seventy-five-year-old bourbon that he said he had bought at an auction in the city for $300. When I took a sip, I could feel it in my toes. Truman drank most of it, and it enhanced his stories. But as the stories wound down, he would sink into his sofa, a small man, alone. "I have too many houses in too many places," he would complain then, and he would number his various properties on his fingers. When I admired one of his paperweights on the coffee table, he said: "Isak Dinesen gave it to me. It's yours. Please." I refused. "If not, never speak to me again." He gave wristwatches to people he trusted, he said. Why not paperweights?

I had first met James Jones in the city the evening he told Ted Kennedy I was not the bartender. He and Gloria and their children lived in Paris but were spending several weeks every summer on eastern Long Island. They rented a ranch-style extravaganza in the woods out around Three Mile Harbor. There was a swimming pool where Jim taught other people's children, including my son, how to dive. In between these sessions Jim watched "Star Trek" on television, and New York Mets ball games which he said he missed in France. They threw a huge party for the birthday of their daughter Kaylie (soon to become for such things my late-in-life goddaughter, because she chose me) which was one of the most unusual parties I ever attended. They hired a group of Shinnecock Indians to perform skits. The Indians did so, getting very drunk in the process, and finishing their act with the most mindless dirty jokes ever told at a children's party: "Chief Bowels won't move. Teepee full of shit." One Indian fell into the pool and Gloria had to jump in wearing a new pink dress to pull him out.

I had known much about Jim Jones from a distance. When I read *From Here to Eternity* in college I was moved by its power. It was one of those American first novels which in youth touches you with a sense of discovery. It evoked for me the timely yet timeless quality of an era, suspended there for an instant before that morning in Schofield Barracks in December, 1941. I knew he had grown up in Robinson in southern Illinois, the son of a father who killed himself and a mother he hated — a tortured and lonely childhood. I knew too he had made a lot of money and owned a house on the Île St.-Louis where the Americans in Paris congregated, with plenty of poker games and hard drinking. And barroom fights with cracked ribs and broken teeth to show for them, and cocktails on boulevard St.-Michel at twilight, and afternoons at the track. I knew also, from mutual friends such as the Styrons and Irwin Shaw, that he was beloved by many people and that he had a beautiful, no-holds-barred wife.

I did not know then, but he told me later, of the time he was discharged from the Army in '45 after months in hospitals, with a damaged ankle and not all that good in the head, when he went to the mountains around Asheville, North Carolina, because he had been absorbed by Thomas Wolfe, and rented a cabin from a farmer and drank corn whiskey in solitude and ate new potatoes and green peas and green beans to try to get over the war. The combat in Guadalcanal had been bad enough, but he was all alone relieving himself behind a rock by a ravine when a half-starved Japanese soldier came out at him from the jungle, and after a struggle he had to kill him with a knife, and then he found the family photographs in the dead man's wallet; for a time he refused to fight again, and they put him in the stockade and busted him to private. Nor did I know that he came to New York City after Carolina and wrote a novel, then went to the Scribner's office on Fifth Avenue and Forty-eighth Street with the manuscript in a box tied with string and demanded to see Maxwell Perkins because he knew Perkins had been Hemingway's and Wolfe's and Fitzgerald's editor. The receptionist said Perkins could not see him. He was adamant — if Perkins would not see him, he would goddamned sure take his book somewhere else. The receptionist, possibly frightened by this stranger with the feral eyes, more likely than not smoking a cigar and carrying his knives in his ubiquitous satchel, ushered him back to Max Perkins. Perkins did not like the novel all that much but was taken by a paragraph in a later letter about how his next book would deal with life in the pre-war Army, and gave him a $500 option to write what became *From Here to Eternity,* which Jones eventually did in various trailer camps around the country. I had always been curious that a man so intensely American, from that border-region America which had produced Mark Twain and Theodore Dreiser and Sherwood Anderson, a man who had written about the beauty and restlessness and promise of America, had chosen to live in Europe for so many years. The jacket photos had given me the impression of a somewhat pugnacious and snarling fellow, someone who was not to be trifled with. Although I was very much part of the literary life, I will admit I was in awe of him before I got to know him, nor could I ever have predicted he would become close as any brother. He was one of those elemental figures in American letters, a man's man who knew life the hard way and wrote about it — about valor and grief and friendship and adversity — a man who knew what he was talking about. I was to learn that beneath the rough exterior was a profoundly cultured and feeling man, someone who could cry while reading Yeats.

He had a gruff voice, and slow emphatic gestures. Of someone who had recently come out with a war novel, he would say, "Looks to me like he got all his stuff about combat from *The Cambridge New Modern History of Man,*" and then draw on his cigar and giggle, and draw on the cigar again and giggle some more. He was zealous about his big cigars, which he got circuitously from Havana, and he never offered one to anybody he did not like. If someone declined the offering he would say, "Then I'm damned sure glad I didn't waste it on you." He had an almost heroic patience for all kinds of harmless fools and mountebanks who approached him, and with his baseball cap atilt on his head would ask them questions in his low, growling tones about their hometowns, families, and personal histories. He could not abide pomp or phoniness, however. Once a talkative New Yorker went on and on to him about how culturally barren the Midwest was. Jim responded with the enlisted man's contemptuous "Sir?" and when the fellow departed, said: "Now there goes a city hick."

As for his wife, Gloria Mosolino of Pottsville, Pennsylvania, John O'Hara's hometown, her family was in the rackets, and one of her uncles was the model for the bootlegger in O'Hara's *Appointment in Samarra.* Living in New York before she met Jim Jones, introduced to him by Budd Schulberg, she wrote a novel which was never published, did a little acting, and was the stand-in for Eva Marie Saint and Marilyn Monroe in some movies. Apropos the scene in *The Seven Year Itch* where Marilyn's skirt blows high, Gloria said, "When the legs look good, they're mine." "Mainly I was a writer fucker," she once said to me. "There was a group of us — writer fuckers." A player of the horses, a card shark, a drinker of booze, a reader of literature, a judge of character equal to her husband, she was touched with mischief and just as unpredictable. She also had a way, in moments of drama or tenderness, of coming out with things she did not intend to say. One day in the Russian Tea Room I was with Jim and Gloria when they ran into an old acquaintance and asked how he was doing. Not too well, the man replied, and went on to tell them he had terminal cancer. She wished to say how sorry she was, but somehow the words came out, "My God! Better you than me."

In that first summer on Long Island, Jim had just finished his not very adroit novel set in the Parisian student revolt of 1968, *The Merry Month of May,* from which I nonetheless wrangled a magazine excerpt. I was also trying to persuade him to return to Schofield Barracks and Honolulu to re-live his Army days, to see how things had changed there. But he was already back to his novel *Whistle,* which had obsessed him for years, the third book in the war trilogy beginning with *From Here to Eternity* and *The Thin Red Line.* One evening we were leaving Muriel Murphy's house in my car to bring home some Chinese food. "What kind of driver are you?" he asked. I was a good driver, I said. Why did he ask? "Because I don't want to die before I finish *Whistle.*"

Jim's eternal search, as he once wrote, was for "some nice quiet dimly lit old infantryman's dream of a bar somewhere." That place for him was a saloon named Bobby Van's, an angular structure on Main Street in Bridgehampton with dark panelling, Tiffany lamps, and old fans suspended from an undistinguished ceiling, a long mahogany bar, and from the back the flickering of candles on small booths and tables covered with red tablecloths. He loved that bar, enjoyed sitting right at it stirring vinegar and a dab of mustard for his hamburger and talking books and writers and passing the time of day with his admirers. We already knew then that he had congestive heart disease, of which we knew he would die in only a few years. I was well aware that he was in a struggle against time with *Whistle,* on which he was beginning to work several hours a day. But we never talked about his condition back then, only other and sometimes smaller things, such as how to season a piece of beef with dill, or plumbing or aluminum siding, or why he would never live in New York City again because he had already served his stretch. One day in Bobby Van's, Jim in the baseball cap smoking his cigar, a man paused with us to chat. "I'll be seeing you, Jimmy," he said in departing.

"I hate to be called Jimmy," Jim said. "I wouldn't name a dog Jimmy."

"How would you like to be named Willie?"

"That's okay. People will think you're a sprinter, or maybe a running back."

Eventually we started visiting places with our sons, including the Civil War battlefields around Virginia. One of our stops was Antietam, the bloodiest single day's fighting in that war, some say the bloodiest in the history of mankind up to then. The men on both sides, Jim told us from his reading, were caught in outdated formation by the fire of deadly weaponry, new and old. They fell in rows. At Antietam, Jim remembered, they were firing cannon almost point-blank, two cannonballs attached with a long chain, and when fired the chain would extend and cut rows of men in half.

It was a day of heavy mists and rain, and there was ominous thunder way off toward the blue mountainous skyline. Jim wore a slouch hat and walking boots and tarried in the cold wind with a pair of binoculars.

"If we'd been living then and been here, we'd probably have fought against each other," I said.

"Yeah. I guess that's true."

We remained there a long time. He was a lonely figure in his slouch hat, standing there in the middle of the Sunken Road. We returned with the boys to our motel in Harper's Ferry. Jim left us and went back to the battlefield in the rain and stayed until dark. He returned to the motel room soaking wet.

"Why did you go back in this weather?" I asked.

"I don't know," he said. "I guess there are certain places a man has to be alone."

We decided that we would someday take our boys on another trip: first to Robinson, Illinois, to which he had not been back since '57, then the trailer camp in Memphis where he worked on *From Here to Eternity,* then on down to Yazoo City, Mississippi. It was a trip we never made.

The Joneses eventually moved permanently to Long Island from Paris, but that was in the future. Jim said he wanted his children to go to high school in America.

I wish good old fine Jim Jones had been in the vicinity of New York City, rather than in Paris, France, in the next many months. I always wanted to know what he thought about things. He would have advised me about matters occurring for me in the magazine business, and I would have been a fool not to listen, because the man and his work were all of a piece.

~ Apex

14

IT IS A JANUARY FORENOON of '69, all Manhattan chill and dazzle. The winter sun brilliantly dapples the shards of ice. The remnants of yesterday's snow are in the branches of the little trees in the traffic islands. Park Avenue on such a day is all rapture and possibility. Over on Fifth Avenue the noises in the street belong to me, and all the windows in all the stores with all their metropolitan riches. I am the editor of one of the most respected magazines in the history of America, and the most long-lasting. The best writers will write for us and not for the money. *Harper's* is what this town calls "hot"; I cannot help but remember that *Esquire* citation in '63 of its being "Squaresville." It is the kind of moment that I have come all my life for. We are making a difference in the way the most powerful civilization in the history of the world perceives itself, the sexiest, richest, most self-conscious society ever conceived. I have at my touch the best and the brightest. Is not Halberstam, at this very moment, writing for us on that subject, but with a certain irony? What killer idea will be pursued today? Everyone who matters wants more. Why has Jack Valenti of Hollywood called to have dinner at the "21" Club tonight? What is shaking in D.C.? Whose cage should be rattled? I am on my way to lunch in the Plaza with Seymour Hersh, who has an important story to tell. Or is it Styron, who will describe the Polish girl with the Auschwitz tattoo he knew just after the war in Flatbush? Or Lizzy Hardwick, about going home to Kentucky? Or Vermont Connecticut Royster, editor of the *Wall Street Journal?* Or the precocious tycoon with Macmillan who wants to talk about something? Or Joan Didion fresh in from L.A.? It is a fine day for Fifth Avenue. In my pocket I have tickets for *Fiddler on the Roof* and front-row seats for the Knicks and Lakers. The Knicks are winning, the Jets are winning. Has not the fabulous Broadway Joe Namath told everybody the Jets will beat the Colts for the big prize? And the Mets — yes, the *Mets* — will take it all this time too. What was the gossip at the party at Plimpton's last night? Who has fallen out with whom over whom? Owners of the magazine are lying back in their luxury, and not at this moment too bothersome. This is my moment. And way back in the last of one's mind, still fresh as sun in the Hill Country, the days at Texas and the people and events that trailed after that all the way to the White House, and down in Mississippi some old ball park is baking in the counterfeit spring's sun. . . . The carriages are waiting at the Sherman statue by the Plaza to take the wide-eyed tourists on spins through the park, and in the Palm Court now the ensemble is playing Gershwin, of course "Rhapsody in Blue." Two tables over: Otto Preminger and Gene Tierney, bent low over daiquiris. Had I not given a toast right here last week at the banquet for Professor Galbraith, proclaiming we pay him five dollars more per article than we pay Professor Schlesinger? These are the New York days, the fabulous and limitless and halcyon days, and I think we will surely be young forever.

In the zenith of those days I loved going out to Garden City to watch the magazine press runs, always remembering Turner Catledge's tales of the old hand-fed press on the *Neshoba Democrat* in contrast to his *New York Times* press runs later and my own times on the *Yazoo High Flashlight* and the *Daily Texan* and *The Texas Observer*. And there were auxiliary demands. Fred Friendly wanted me to leave the magazine business and go into television news. On the David Frost TV show a drunk French actress was unable to perform, and I was *it* for an hour and a half, and had not Frost included the conversation in a book of his favorite interviews? And always there were the young people, caught so in the torrents of the Sixties, who not unlike Ann Baxter in *All About Eve* congregated about us in the Empire Chinese. Bill Clinton of Hope, Arkansas, was only one of the bright young provincials who wished to mingle with the *Harper's* crowd, coming into the office as they did from wherever, aspiring writers, and otherwise, and looking to you for advice and encouragement, caught up too in their first Manhattan glitter, and revering you, and there was a responsibility to it. (And hard responsibility not fulfilled, as in the inevitable rejection letters to future distinguished writers, such as the young Mississippian Richard Ford, who years later on a balcony in the French Quarter brought out two or three of my rejections and read them aloud to me.)

It was therefore, for all such as this, not unhealthy to be roundly tested at the apex from time to time, to be reduced a notch or two by the elemental challenges, as at an exceedingly high-level breakfast one morning at Arthur Schlesinger, Jr.'s.

Professor Schlesinger had arranged his meeting to introduce a handful of influential New Yorkers to Senator George McGovern of South Dakota, who just then was looking ahead to the possibility of running next time for the Democratic Party nomination for President, to let him talk about his plans and credentials and to answer questions. The meeting was at the unholy hour of 8:15 A.M. Schlesinger's brownstone was on the Upper East Side, and I caught a cab uptown. In front of the house I paid the cabdriver, opened the door and got out, whereupon I stepped full foot into a substantial pile of fresh dog shit lying there in the gutter, so copious that it immediately consumed the bottom and one whole side of my left shoe, and was, indeed at that very moment, oozing down into one of my socks. The malodor was, to say the least, obstinate. The taxi had already departed and I was left there considering how best to proceed. I did not have a handkerchief, but I was fortunate to spot a small deli up at the corner. As I walked toward it the excrement, which possessed the creamy consistency, say, of overcooked mashed potatoes, began squishing in my shoe, a soft but not negligent whish, like walking in wet mud in the Mississippi Delta after a thunderstorm, the water rising under your footfalls like a modest little suction pump, and making similar uningratiating noises. Nor was it comforting when a uniformed nanny pushing an opulent baby carriage sighted my shoe and said, "*Ooo-whee!*" or when a small retinue of schoolchildren in Dalton coats pointed at the shoe and laughed. I entered the store and as quickly as I could bought a small box of Kleenex, paying for it and retiring from there before the proprietor had time to notice the tracks I was making on his floor.

There are no public benches on the cross streets of the Upper East Side, so I sat on a curb and began wiping off the emulsive substance with the Kleenex. It was not working too well. For one thing, the dog shit was making its way into my fingernails, and, in addition, was dripping deeper into the shoe. I removed the shoe and noticed that the droppings had by now soaked into the porous cotton fabric of the sock. I must say in my own defense that nothing like this had happened to me since grammar school. I had never been much for expensive socks, even in our cultural metropolis, and was disappointed to learn that this sock had no resistance whatever to alien substances. If the sock had been purchased at Bloomingdale's, and hence silk, rather than from the counter of the little dry goods store on East Thirty-fourth, the inchoate roughage would have merely formed a thin skein on the bottom, rather than intruding into my naked foot, and inevitably down to the toes. At the matrix of national editorship, I silently pledged to be more unstinting with my apparel in the future. I did the best I could. I should make it plain that I have always loved dogs, but this one had to have had the girth of a medium hippopotamus, and my sentiments in that moment about dogs were at best ambivalent. In this graphic yet unavoidable scatological exegesis, I cannot begin to convey my schizophrenia of the moment: on the one hand the sense of responsibility I felt for my beleaguered nation by hearing out the ambitious Dakota Senator, and on the other the contrasting state-of-the-art ooze in my toes. I left the befouled Kleenex in the gutter and dropped the rest of the container on Professor Schlesinger's doorstep before ringing the bell. A maid let me in the foyer, and I walked upstairs to the dining room.

The room was a small one, and I was greeted there by the host, as well as by the Senator from South Dakota, by Bob Silvers of the *New York Review of Books*, by Professor J. K. Galbraith, by Alan Jay Lerner, who wrote *My Fair Lady*, and by two or three other significant New York men I did not immediately recognize. "Pleased to meet you," George McGovern said on shaking my hand, and I immediately noticed that his nostril began to twitch. While Alexandra Schlesinger and the maid were preparing breakfast in the adjoining kitchen, everyone sat down. Schlesinger began a few introductory remarks about McGovern and the Presidency. I have mentioned that the room was relatively small. This was the wintertime, and it was also overheated, almost stuffy in fact, so that the heat would have hovered heavily on the olfactory glands even under the most salubrious of circumstances. The odor from my shoe rose and mingled with the smell of scrambling eggs. I dared not so much as cross my legs, remaining as stationary as humanly possible while nonetheless trying to hide my shoe behind the leg of a small table. The author of *My Fair Lady* began to sniff audibly, so too did the editor of *The New York Review of Books,* and in time even Professor Schlesinger, in the middle of his informed disquisition, had a vaguely distasteful expression. I began to discern the others surreptitiously looking about the room, yet avoiding one another's glances as if this simple expression of quizzicalness might imply some guilt by association. But I could see it in their eyes. After Schlesinger finished, McGovern began talking about his chances to be President of the United States. He was a very sweet and friendly man, a sober and sincere man, with an honest religious voice. "There was nobody nicer or cleaner than George McGovern in the city of Chicago," Norman Mailer had described him in *Harper's* during the '68 Convention, and it was this very aura of cleanliness which I found the most threatening, because every time he took a breath after a remark, or declaration, it seemed to me his whole lower lip quivered and trembled. Now even Professor Galbraith was secretively appraising everyone in that little chamber. I discreetly shifted position and tried to hide my left shoe with my right. That, likewise, proved not efficacious. At last I knew I had to do something, and to do it fast. As casually as possible given the conditions, I rose while McGovern was still talking and walked over to the host, requesting the use of the telephone in the kitchen to contact my office, explaining it was our deadline day. Then I dialed my secretary, Judy, speaking to her in a loud voice that could be heard in the next room about some complex and nonexistent technical problem. "Have you lost your senses?" she asked. "You're talking gibberish." I hung up and wrote a note. "Arthur — crisis at my magazine. Must leave immediately," and asked the retainer to take it to Professor Schlesinger. Then I hastily, and in tiptoeing disgrace, sneaked down the stairs, out into the mercifully fresh and free outdoors of the Upper East Side. Later in the week I described the happening to Larry L. King. "You loony!" he said. "Don't you realize the moment you left, everybody knew who the damned culprit was?"

Such were the hazards of responsibility in the great city. And there were others as well, of more existential application.

We were now into the Nixon years.

I once made a horrendous mistake concerning Richard Nixon. Many years have passed since then, but this unconscionable misjudgment still goes around in my head.

I had met Nixon in '58 in Oxford, England, when he was Vice-President. He was touring England and we invited him to address the American students at Rhodes House. He was certainly charming enough, and before an inevitably unsympathetic audience largely of Rhodes Scholars acquitted himself well, prompting one to acknowledge his gift for resilience. He was obviously an intelligent man, which somehow surprised me. I only considered him all the more dangerous. After lunch in one of the colleges, where he spoke to me of his high regard for Senators Eastland and Stennis of my native state, Mrs. Nixon led him into the back rooms to greet the kitchen help. "They always seem to appreciate that," she said. Nixon would cast a bizarre, tragic shadow over our American day. As with most young liberals of the era, I could never stand him, nor most of what he stood for, and it was that deep personal antipathy that did damage to my professional judgment as an editor.

After his defeat by Pat Brown in the California gubernatorial race of 1962 — "You won't have Nixon to kick around anymore" — he eventually moved to New York. Few would have predicted in the mid-1960s that he had his eye on the White House again in '68. Yet he became a familiar figure in those years around the city, springing out of limos in front of the great hotels, socializing at the grand and proper parties. Sometime in '67 one of his friends and key advisors, Raymond K. Price, phoned me to have lunch in the Yale Club. Ray Price was five or six years my senior, Yale and Skull and Bones, and noted among the cognoscenti as a masterful writer of the big sweeping political oration. He said he wanted our conversation held in confidence. His employer, he said, had been seriously pondering the absence of any relationship between the United States and Mainland China. (In those times we all still called it "Red China.") Nixon thought the time might be coming, Price said, for detente, and the American people should start being prepared for this possibility; only a conservative leader, it was of course implied, could get away with anything like that. *Harper's* was fast becoming a widely read magazine. Mr. Nixon was earnestly considering a major article, or a series of articles, on a new relationship with China, and they had *Harper's* in mind.

I did not say as much, but I did not want Richard Nixon in *Harper's*. Nixon himself subsequently telephoned, as charming as he had been in Oxford, and seemed open and accessible. Then Ray Price called again to say he was setting up a small dinner with Nixon in the apartment of a friend, where we could talk. I told him I could not come but wished to send David Halberstam. They did not think much of that, and the matter was dropped.

I never pursued Nixon on this project. His watershed article, which in no small measure helped pave the way for the mammoth transformation in Sino-American relationships during Nixon's Presidency, appeared in *Foreign Affairs*. In my failure to respond with interest and enthusiasm I violated one of the bedrock responsibilities of the editor: never let personal hostility obstruct the broader perspective. Not many months before he became President, I had had the rare chance to get to know, or at the least to have private glimpses into, this elusive and enigmatic man, whose very image cast itself on a generation and more. It was one of the two or three largest mistakes I ever made in my life as an editor, and more important, a great loss for *Harper's*.

Crucial to the coalition which elected Nixon in '68 were the blue-collar and recently white-collar voters in the suburbs and urban neighborhoods, and farmers and World War II veterans — "Reagan Democrats" many would become — who had supported LBJ in '64 but now felt that the core issues of the economy, education, and health care in a moment of prosperity and consumption were secondary to what they deemed a frontal attack on old American values: drugs, sex, hair, dress, language, music, devotion to country, law and order. "America, Love It or Leave It" became a slogan of this supposed new day. Nixon himself had said he wanted to win back the young people, but soon hundreds of thousands of them were retreating to a cow pasture around Woodstock, and when "hard-hat" construction workers took to assaulting anti-war demonstrators in city streets, it was not long before Nixon was congratulating them and calling the student activists "bums." "Politics," Henry Adams said, "is the systematic organization of hatreds," and this was not an inappropriate assessment of that moment.

"Perhaps the trouble with America in the late Sixties," Halberstam wrote in *Harper's*, "was that reality, though slow, was too often catching up with us." Their traditional constituency in tatters, the Democrats were suffering far more from the turbulence afoot in the country than the new Republican administration. To me the declining months of the decade, reaching some dreadful culmination with the killings at Kent State in '70, were as agonizing as '68 had been. Janis Joplin was singing, "Freedom's just another word for nothing left to lose." The British writer Jan Morris, living in New York City then, said that its atmosphere "often felt to me like a city battened down, all its brilliance, savagery, misery, and brute force precariously held in check" — an ironic but truthful qualification hovering above one's own personal acme.

The Nixonian promises of domestic tranquility did not last very long. As a candidate Nixon had cited a secret plan for American withdrawal from the Vietnam abyss, but despite the sixty-five thousand troops removed from there in 1969 the war was more entrenched and insoluble than ever. Less than three months into his administration he began the secret bombings of Cambodia while expanding the air war in North Vietnam. In March, in what had now become the lengthiest war in the nation's history, American deaths exceeded Korea's. The national divisions caused by Vietnam were sharper than they had ever been, split almost precisely down the middle on whether the United States should get out. By the end of the year the American death toll was more than forty thousand.

To me one of the most terrible things about Vietnam was the cynical policy of continuing to sacrifice lives while the policymakers themselves, Nixon and Kissinger and the others, were in agreement about subtly "winding down." In 1969 most young men of draft age were well aware that the United States had given up on any prospect of winning that war and were fighting for what Kissinger himself called "negotiating strategies." Lance Morrow, who perceived this decade as sensitively as anyone, would later write of those boys who did not wish to die in an unfathomable and already relinquished cause:

> To go there to fight at that late stage meant joining a demoralized army that was sometimes fragging its officers, smoking dope, and avoiding enemy contact where possible. . . . After deciding in 1969 to withdraw from a hopeless cause, Richard Nixon and Henry Kissinger allowed 18,000 more Americans to be killed so that, bizarrely, the snarling and bleeding American could exit from Vietnam with sufficient style, an illusion of credibility.

Perhaps Kissinger should have been over there in combat with them. Could one have imagined him, two dozen hand grenades strapped to his circumferential midriff, shouting as John Wayne would: "Come on guys — let's get them gooks!"

Strikes and takeovers continued to paralyze campuses around the nation. In November a quarter of a million demonstrators marched in Washington carrying mock coffins bearing the names of Vietnam dead. One of the great paradoxes was that as more and more Americans were concluding they wanted an end to the war, if the opinion polls of the day were to be believed, in increasing numbers many of the same people deplored and distrusted the organized anti-war movement itself. In this atmosphere Nixon's speeches oscillated between high statesmanship and strident clarions, relying faithfully as always on Vice-President Agnew, who sooner or later would reveal himself as the low-priced crook he really was, but who persisted now against the "malcontents, radicals, incendiaries, and civil and uncivil disobedients," and the campuses themselves and their *engagés* as "circus tents or psychiatric centers of over-privileged, under-disciplined, irresponsible children of well-to-do blasé permissivists." Quieter methods, however, brought more effective results. The Nixon administration, backed by the FBI and the CIA, pursued the New Left with wiretaps and undercover agents and felony prosecutions, which inevitably led to its famous "enemies list" of anti-war moderates. The burning cities, too, and the intensifying revolutionist stance of the Black Panthers, continued to bring the Asian violence home. At the Chicago Seven trial, the Panther leader Bobby Seale was ordered bound and gagged. Police raided the Panthers' office in Chicago and killed Fred Hampton: In the months to come, consistent with Nixon's law-and-order mandate, the FBI sought to eliminate the Panthers as an active force through a systematic campaign of killings and jailings.

At the height of its strength and activism, with SDS hounded by these concerted official tactics, the movement itself began to splinter into self-destructive factions, the most extreme of which, the Weathermen, consisting of some of the same idealistic political reformers of the earlier, more innocent Sixties, opted for explosives. The objects were usually university ROTC buildings, federal buildings, induction centers. As a suggestion of the times, the *New York Review of Books* published on its cover a diagram of how to make a Molotov cocktail. On the day after the townhouse on West Eleventh Street in New York City where the bombs being made accidentally exploded, with three dead and others vanished, I went down there to look at it; the acrid smoke, the riven hulk of the dwelling, suggested to me a frightful juncture. As the news had spread in America's media center of what was being manufactured in that townhouse, Todd Gitlin noted "the toll of an ending, the subliminal sense that what blew up was not just three people but the movement's innocence and its larger logic."

Yet more than anything else, it was Kent State that marked a dreadful turn in the national psyche. One of our secretaries, who had been listening to the radio, came into my office crying: "Now they're killing children!" The Kent demonstrations were part of broader campus protests stemming from Nixon's announcement of land assaults into Cambodia. Not long before that, in foreboding counsel to "my friends in the academic community," Spiro Agnew declared: "The next time a mob of students, waving their non-negotiable demands, starts pitching bricks and rocks at the student union — just imagine they are brown shirts or white sheets and act accordingly." Kent State itself was a relatively placid middle-class Ohio school with little tradition of protest, but the ROTC building had been burned down two days before and the students, including young women, taunted the National Guardsmen with rocks and obscenities. Thirteen students were shot, four of them killed: none of the dead an activist, one in fact an ROTC cadet, and there was the appalling John P. Filo photograph of a girl wailing over a boy's body, of textbooks soaked in blood. The thirteen tragic seconds of May 4, 1970, were catharsis and epitome of the whole age, white youngsters shooting down white youngsters, its nightmarish montage vivid to this day. After Kent State more than a million students went on strike on 450 campuses. (Ten days afterward the police in Jackson, Mississippi, fired three hundred bullets into a dormitory at Jackson State, a black school with a civil rights history, killing two students and injuring twelve, but blacks bitterly noted Kent State had received all the attention.) And after Kent State many of the same universities closed early and the students, moderates and militants alike, went home. When the schools opened again in the fall, they were quieter than they had been in years; confrontation itself was slipping away.

Our magazine, I believe, reflected much of these national realities. The magazine was a pastiche of diverse pieces, and clear delineations among political, social, economic, and artistic stories as manifestations of the period were impossible, as they should have been, for even in its divisions the Sixties somehow blended things together.

The role of the editor-in-chief of a magazine like *Harper's* was a combination of the tangible and the instinctual, as most such editors past and present would likely testify. The daily, most concrete aspects, of course, involved choosing the writers and subjects — the general *themes* — and getting the contributors on deadlines. Since in our case we did not have formal editorial meetings, more often than not Bob Kotlowitz and Midge Decter and I would sit down a couple of times a week, usually at the end of a day, and see where we were, and what we needed. We might be joined by whoever of our stable of contributing editors was in town at the moment, and often by our art director, and toward the end of the month by our production person. My own most zealous possession was the tentative monthly editorial list, which we were constantly juggling, depending on how writers at the time were progressing on pieces under assignment, and balancing that with our "inventory" — pieces and stories and poems already in galley proof or about to be. I myself always made the final decision on manuscript submissions and how much further editing might be required, but this also was part of our informal consultations. Kotlowitz and Decter and I did all the actual editing on manuscripts accepted for publication. We also had to keep an eye on the production schedule, layout, covers, art work. Too, "query" letters from various writers suggesting articles had to be dealt with, promptly if possible. And there were always piles of manuscripts to be read and decided upon, and more telephone calls than any normal human being could ever handle with civility.

There was also the matter of keeping an ear out for things among writers, agents, publishers, and a broad range of people, what certain good writers around the town and the country were working on at a given time, what they had remarked to someone or other that they might want to do, what was *moving* them. Who were the young writers and journalists we should know about? What were their interests? What likely or unlikely subjects were we neglecting? It was always important to peruse the other magazines, including the "little" journals. The *New York Times* was a wealth of information; occasionally the small, buried away item on page 36 from somewhere out in the nation carried the germ of a major magazine piece. A key was matching the right subject with the right writer, and with the very best writers this invariably involved persuasion, if not cajolery. The core of an editor's responsibility forever remained his relationship with writers and his trust in them, for the simple reason that a magazine depends on writing, and do not let anyone tell you otherwise.

One of my own most gratifying moments in a month's work was making out the final table of contents from the best we had on hand. For in these funny private moments this was the juncture at which all of it seemed to come together. But this private reward had its inevitable qualifications: no sooner had you finished an issue before you had to start afresh on another. This often brought moments of panic: better goad such-and-so to get his big article in ahead of deadline. "What the hell's our leader [lead article] for *next* month?" Kotlowitz might drift in and ask, for one of the magazine editor's most singular incentives was uncertainty.

The editor-in-chief in the nature of the position represented the magazine before the public, and given the fact that *Harper's* was trying to succeed as a vital and diverse American voice at such a moment in our history I felt it part of my mandate to give even more frequent speeches before significant forums, especially college campuses. And since our monthly newsstand sales around the country were often meaningful signals, I tried to make myself accessible to the press and to radio and TV concerning especially important pieces.

The things that tried me the most were the telephone, and getting to the office early, and our five-week "lead time," but there were genuine lasting joys in eliciting the writing and in the final issues, and the truth of it is I really was working all the time, maybe too much. I never could turn off from *Harper's*. It was my blood, and to this very day my blood churns in its memory, and I will feel forever that old incorrigible churning.

There were other specific aspects of the job, *ad hoc* and elusive, that came with the working day, deadline crises, personality clashes, a dozen niggling details, but these seldom fit any philosophical overview. Yet in the end, I judge, the heart of the editor's calling, for me at least, came down to instinct, and hence was glandular: as with the hitter going after the fast-breaking curveball, the most crucial decisions and commitments were dare-taking and instinctual, and I am unable to define them now, as then, because I have no earthly idea of their sources.

Running the magazine likewise involved considerable commingling with fellow editors in the city of the day, from whom one could always learn a great deal. One of the most distinctive of these was Cass Canfield, Sr., chairman of the board of the publishing firm of Harper and Row.

Cass Canfield was seventy years old and had joined Harper & Brothers more than forty years before. He was the epitome of the Eastern patriciate, Groton, Harvard, Oxford, the Sorbonne, a tall, slender man, totally bald, with an aristocratic mustache, modest of expression in the worldly Eastern speech, yet a singularly wry and witty figure who, despite his reputation and demeanor as paradigm of the old-line New York gentleman-publisher and as friend and editor and acquaintance of more members of the American Establishment than any man I ever knew, had a keen sense of mischief and adventure. He was intensely proud of *Harper's Magazine* as a symbolic parcel of the historic old publishing house, and he was a vigorous devotee of the First Amendment, often calling me with ideas and counsel, and taking me to lunches at the Century where he relished introducing me to his commanding and estimable old companions of Wall Street and the publishing houses and the governments and the thickets of the law who knew with much exactitude where the national skeletons lay hidden. The Century was a looming, imposing structure on West Forty-third with a broad marble staircase, at the bottom of which the Negro porters greeted you by name before you went upstairs with Cass Canfield, Sr., there to be met by various of the members, some of whom were robust and in the hardy prime of their establishmentarian tranquility, others of whom resembled the cartel men in Chaplin's *Modern Times.* I was once told I was one of the youngest members in the annals of the august Century Club, but I had odd feelings about the place, and seldom went there alone, preferring to be there with people like Cass Canfield. Once Cass even took me to lunch at the Four Seasons with Svetlana Alliluyeva, for he was her

American publisher. Even in a plain brown dress and without a trace of makeup or jewelry she was much better looking than her daddy, whom I remembered less from his heroic World War II poses when we were allies than from the demonic portraits favored in our public prints after Yalta. I admired the way Cass Canfield handled her volatile personality and discourse, which was mainly by letting her wax and wane. She called me "Mr. Marcel." Had she confused me with Proust? Throughout this meeting, as happened to me all the time in my inordinate city juxtapositions, I conjured equally striking images: in the case of this unusual woman sitting next to me, of her and her father's associates watching helplessly as the diabolic, saturnine, chain-smoking old tyrant choked to death in his bed in the Kremlin. Or conjuring, too, my own childhood back home, and what my approximate response might have been if on watching a Movietone News in our frayed little theater on a wartime evening in 1944 of Stalin conferring in a Ukraine snow with his generals, Henjie Henick had turned to me and said, "You'll be having lunch with that man's daughter in a restaurant called the Four Seasons in New York City one day a long time from now."

There were frequent contacts, too, with fellow editors of other, vastly wealthier publications than my own. Turner Catledge, head man of the *New York Times,* was a born-and-bred Mississippian from the ingrown and tragic and impenitent hills of Neshoba. He was in his late sixties when I got to know him, having run the *Times* for more than fifteen years and before that one of its frontline political and domestic correspondents, in and out always of everything pertaining to the *Times,* and if Gay Talese's best-selling volume of that august institution, *The Kingdom and the Power,* had a hero, it was Catledge, who gave it new cohesion and spirit — sometimes in rather devious moves, someone said, "without leaving any fingerprints." He had begun his career as a threadbare teenager on the weekly *Neshoba Democrat,* and one of his tasks was to operate the old humpback press, into which he would feed newspapers at about five hundred an hour, then turn them over for the other side. By his later estimation of printing time this process would have taken his Sunday *New York Times* roughly 165 years.

This compound of the urbane and the outback was one of Turner's singular charms, and beneath his courtly and suave veneer lay a very complex and resilient and savvy and resourceful son of Mississippi. This was our bond, and as late as 1966 I almost went to work for him. He was a big, imposing presence around the town in his finely tailored suits, in the lounge of the Algonquin, Bleeck's, the Century, as if he had just emerged somewhere from a Turkish bath, or a tête-à-tête with a President, and he never ever forgot a name. He never lost his Mississippi accent, either, and at the dinners at his penthouse apartment with five or six other guests he entertained us with his outlandish Dixie tales. One evening he took Theodore H. White and me into his study and proceeded to deliver a fifteen-minute mimicry of a Senator Bilbo oration so realistic and true, replete with the gestures and pirouettes, that it almost made my hair stand on end with my memories of having heard Bilbo in the flesh as a boy on the courthouse lawn of Yazoo. "I wanted to bring you back to my den for this," he told White and me. "It might scare the people in the parlor." His dogged and colorful down-home narratives usually came after a few sour-mashes, and he had some good New York stories too, and his later memoir *My Life and the Times* never began to catch the circumlocutions and byzantine asides and the good breath of whiskey in his spoken locutions. One day, for instance, as he relished describing the episode in conversation, using the accurate and flavorful accents, he got a highly literate letter from a gentleman somewhere in the Midwest who told him he read the whole Sunday *New York Times*, every word, every page, each week. The man cited the precise hour the *Times* reached him on Tuesday, and the precise hour on Friday he finished reading it. He had written to inquire if there could not be a second Sunday *Times* to occupy him from Friday till Tuesday. Catledge was so fascinated that he wrote the man back. Shortly he received another letter, this time from a doctor, who reported the man who had written the letter was one of his mental patients who had been assigned to read the Sunday *Times* as therapy.

In the hearing of blasé New Yorkers Turner and I would discuss in large detail the people from my hometown he had known at Mississippi A & M, where he had worked his way through by serving meals in the mess hall, his descriptions of them so vigorous and glowing that I could identify their descendants of my own generation from their not dissimilar visage and character. And we often discussed the troubles in his native Neshoba, which had hurt and disturbed him. He said some of his old friends and even relations there felt he had let the town down because of the *Times'* extensive coverage of the civil rights murders. "But I felt the town had let me down," he later wrote. "Or perhaps I had just expected too much." I perceived almost from the start that he was shrewder and harder than I, and I knew I would have been better off in this city to have possessed more of those qualities. A number of my acquaintances on the *Times* were critical of his Machiavellian impulses, but his enduring legacy would reside in the way he strengthened and broadened that magnificent institution, an accomplishment, shall it be suggested, that was worthy of his lifetime, and that matters yet? Later in that decade, after Catledge had retired and moved to New Orleans, I visited him in his house in the Garden District. It was a French Regency, but as we sat in the spacious front parlor I felt oddly discombobulated. "I feel as if I've been here before," I said. "You have, sort of," he replied. He and his wife had designed this room in exact replica, down to the minute detail, of the parlor in their high-rise in New York, and had the same furnishings in the precise place also. If I too finally left New York someday, I secretly mused, would it have the same hold on *me?*

Another such editor was Henry Anatole Grunwald, the new chief of *Time* magazine. Peter Bird Martin, an editor on that journal, was among the younger people there who fervently wished, as expression of the times, that the magazine be more innovative and less imperiously conservative, including its strong pro-Vietnam position. Martin got Grunwald and me together for lunches and also wanted Mailer, who declined to come, one of his reasons being that *Time* had historically treated him so shabbily that under no circumstances would he trust them with much of anything.

Henry Luce had been dead since '67; through his magazine, Joseph Epstein wrote in *Harper's*, he had "confused more issues than he clarified, harmed more people than he helped, and contributed more to the Gross National Product than to American Culture," although to me Luce had indeed expanded the range of popular journalism to include subjects until then rarely covered by the press. After this Grunwald came along.

Henry, born in Austria, was in his mid-forties, short and round, an intellectual who had started with *Time* as a copy-boy and knew the system. As a copy-boy he rewrote mock cover stories to impress his superiors. "Once I was standing in a writer's office," he remembered, "peering over his shoulder as he sat at his typewriter. I was somewhat startled to find that the words he was typing were as follows: 'Kid, if you don't cut this out, I'll break every bone in your body.' " Grunwald left the office in a hurry, muttering as he walked out: "Cliché." He used this story in speeches, but suggested it was legend.

He was succeeding in bringing panache and responsibility to his magazine. He and his wife Beverly gave small dinners, where I privately scratched at my all-suffering neck and shoulders in an ill-fitting tuxedo rented from an Upper West Side mortician while conversing with Henry about the works of J. D. Salinger and the lead-time of monthly magazines, or with Clare Boothe Luce, serene and lovely and coolly contained in a matchless chartreuse gown, or the head of Time Inc., Hedley Donovan, looking not unlike an Episcopal rector from a diffident yet not undebonair Midwestern parish, as impeccably American Establishmentarian in background and portfolio as John Cowles, Sr., father of our magazine owner, would ever be, and who in conversation with Mrs. Luce and myself actually said the times were in flux as seldom before. "*Harper's* has changed in a way we can't, at least not now," he said. "I wish you well." I heard a lot of talk like that in the city in those days. Then, sitting on a sofa with aperitifs and the lustrous actress Ali McGraw as we discussed American writing and the latest Broadway stage, Henry Grunwald deftly presiding over the tranquil conviviality like an accomplished Viennese concertmeister, I observed the play of candlelight on the chandeliers, and on Miss McGraw's silver necklace as she crossed her perfect legs just as I remembered them from *Goodbye, Columbus.*

In these months there was fiction in *Harper's* by Isaac Bashevis Singer, Larry McMurtry, Bruce Jay Friedman, Wright Morris, André Platonov, poems by W. H. Auden, Robert Penn Warren, James Dickey, Robert Graves, John Hollander, Richard Howard, Arthur Miller, even a periodic column by the eighty-seven-year-old Igor Stravinsky on topics that included his friendship with Auden, Beethoven's piano sonatas, illness and death. Articles in a series on returning to American hometowns included Midge Decter on St. Paul, Elizabeth Hardwick on Lexington, Bob Kotlowitz on Baltimore, Fred Powledge on Raleigh, John Thompson on Grand Rapids, and James Dickey's famous poem "Living There":

Home?
Which way is that?
Is it this vacant lot? These woven fences?
Or is it hundreds
Of miles away, where I am the keeper
Of rooms turning night and day
Into memory?

In brief random sampling, there were pieces by Eric Goldman on LBJ's disastrous White House Festival of the Arts which had been exacerbated by the Vietnam question and Gay Talese's series on the *New York Times.* Pauline Kael wrote on trash movies, Richard Levine on young Jesse Jackson of Chicago as possible heir to Dr. King, Justin Kaplan on Emily Post, George Thayer on the arms merchants, Kingsley Amis on *Portnoy's Complaint,* Oscar Lewis on three generations of a Puerto Rican family, Richard Burgheim on TV coverage of Vietnam, Dean Acheson on Joe McCarthy, Margot Hentoff on Elvis's comeback in Las Vegas, Neil Sheehan on the Hamburger Hill carnage in Vietnam, James Q. Wilson on the young people of North Long Beach, Nick Kotz on hunger in America, Bayard Rustin on the failure of black separatism, Maya Angelou on growing up black in Arkansas, Michael Harrington on the decline of socialism, Peter Schrag on the first black football player in the Southeastern Conference, Joseph Goulden on travels among the Nixon "silent majority," Richard Schickel on pornographic movies, Sara Davidson on travelling with Jacqueline Susann, Jeremy Larner on the people and issues of the Eugene McCarthy Presidential campaign, Richard Pollack on *Time* after Luce, Joe McGinniss on "the selling of the President" in the '68 campaign, a series by John W. Aldridge on the young generation in America, Kathrin Perutz on teen-age beauty pageants, Jack Richardson on the joys of sex and gambling, and Tom Wicker on the details of the Nixon administration's undeclared witch-hunt, with its dark prophecy of the Watergate days of the future:

> What seems more threatening than ever is that, while they may not now be seeking a Red Spy under every bed, the ubiquitous security *apparatchiks* are out for more difficult and dangerous game — the homegrown agitator, troublemaker, and "militant" — and with far less vociferous opposition than was heard in the McCarthy catch-a-Commie-for-Christ days.

Was there some common thread to all this diversity? I pray to believe there was: good writing that related to the larger community, to the civilization, writing that aimed toward clarity and relevance and truth, and if the magazine did not always succeed in that, at least it was trying.

A brilliant poet then in his late thirties, John Hollander, joined the magazine as poetry editor, a part-time position on a small retainer, and enhanced the wit and energy of the others. Hollander was a New Yorker, Bronx High School of Science and Columbia, where he had studied under Trilling, Van Doren, and Barzun and was later a protégé of Auden; he had already published *Movie-Going and Other Poems and Visions from the Ramble,* and his enthusiasm for fine verse was contagious.

As another contributing editor, we brought in Lewis Lapham, a journalist who had been doing good work in other magazines. Lapham was a likeable, good-looking young man my age, born in

San Francisco but in cast an Easterner of the titular WASP lineage, Hotchkiss and Yale: Lapham Fieldhouse at Yale.

A young art director, Sheila Berger, began to put her mark on the issues, an added dividend to her talents being that the offices were often visited by her boyfriend and future husband Tom Wolfe in immaculate white suit and cane. The role of a superior magazine art director is to enhance the printed words with compatible visual images, inherent in the text, to help make the words themselves more inviting and alluring, to conceive of a magazine as a kind of flowing entity, to make it *look* vital and attractive, and she concentrated on such matters to imaginative effect. *Harper's* looked different, more *graphic,* which one supposes is what graphics is all about.

The magazine's handful of "contributing editors," our comrades since the experiment began, overtravelled and underpaid and complaining as always about getting too old too soon, were at their best in this moment for *Harper's,* putting in their long nocturnal hours under deadline, wishing for their words to be integral to a significant fabric, and none more so than Halberstam, as in his lengthy "The Very Expensive Education of McGeorge Bundy," about one of the smartest and most elusive figures in the American Establishment, both JFK and LBJ's national security director, later to become part of Halberstam's classic study *The Best and the Brightest* about the handful of brilliant, isolated men responsible for dispatching the nation to disaster in Southeast Asia, and the thousands of American boys, mainly poor whites and blacks, to the deaths and maimings. The policy-makers' perpetration of the war, in its lachrymose folly, amounted to the great sorrow of the generation. As early as 1961, Halberstam reported, Harvard's David Riesman had warned some of John Kennedy's closest advisors against the perils of an elitist internationalism: "You all think you can manage limited wars and that you're dealing with an elite society that is just waiting for your leadership. It's not that way at all. It's not an elite society run for Harvard and the Council on Foreign Relations." Halberstam's *Harper's* piece, the first of a series, was a study that people had been waiting for — why men so supposedly ingenious had gotten us into this tragedy — and it had a special impact because a large readership had been wanting it:

> Thus he saw Douglas MacArthur defeating his own case by his excesses, and thus he saw Joseph McCarthy seriously hurting legitimate anti-Communism by the wildness of his charges. And it was on reflection a charge that one might make against Bundy himself, that in his own intense belief in himself, in his tradition and the right of the Establishment, he would contribute to a disillusion and disrespect and alienation among the young from those very traditions and institutions which he so ferociously believed in.

And Halberstam on "Ask Not What Ted Sorenson Can Do for You" pertaining to Senator Ted Kennedy's grievous misjudgments and the death of a young woman at Chappaquiddick, in itself part of the texture of the day:

> So that Chappaquiddick would become a classic example. It was handled from the start along the lines of the Cuban missile crisis, with all the great men of 1963 scurrying to the compound with their attache cases. It was, after all, an affair which raised questions of simple human decency, and the occasion demanded candor, honesty and simplicity, not lots of lawyers who told him — and he listened — not to talk. Finally he would break too long a silence to read a statement for television on his own terms — without answering questions of reporters — the very kind of thing which Kennedy enthusiasts disliked so much in Nixon. The statement itself was of such cheapness and bathos as to be a rejection of everything the Kennedys had stood for in candor and style. It was as if these men had forgotten everything which made the Kennedys distinctive in American politics and simply told the youngest brother that he could get away with whatever he wanted because he was a Kennedy in Massachusetts. One knew, when one heard that speech, that Sorenson had written it.

Marshall Frady went down to Austin and Johnson City to observe LBJ out of power:

So now dispensed with, abruptly and totally disposed of, he is decompressing into the vast vacant spaces of south Texas — inevitably sunken at times in profound mopiness, seized by sourceless pointless after-spasms of urgency and impatience while ceiling fans murmur drowsily and flies bump against back screen doors. As he sits on his back porch in the long late-afternoon sunlight with swing-chains creaking, he unpacks his huge neglected heart only to himself about why he happens to be down here now, listening to bulls moan, instead of still up there in that oval office along Pennsylvania Avenue. . . ."

And to the angry and disaffected steel mill town of Gary, Indiana:

For these — the children and grandchildren of the Poles and Armenians and Greeks who were most of all escaping something behind them — this is what it is all for now: the neighborhoods; their own children, many adolescents, who themselves have already in their hearts renounced and abandoned it as they prime themselves for college; the corner taverns on Saturday afternoon where they may roost along the bar with beers watching the Chicago Cubs on the mounted TV. It is, in a way, a stranded population, accidentally collected here with no deep blood memory of the earth, the weathers, the past — and no way now for there ever to gather such a memory through successive generations, since any sense of earth, past, place had already been aborted here even when the first ones began to arrive.

And on to California ("But even more it seems here that America's whole terrific resistless move toward the West was abruptly concluded in a kind of anarchic distraction") and a governor named Reagan:

The feeling is like nothing so much as a consultation between the gynecologist and the relative of a patient. His elbows tucked in close to his sides, [Reagan] absently twirls and taps a pen between his fingers during the exchange, and when he is asked a question, he usually pauses to glance over to his press secretary on a nearby couch with an expression of amiable if slightly pained uncertainty before he responds with a measured earnestness. There is, in the graham-cracker texture of his voice, seriousness.

John Corry was writing on Fidel's Cuba, torture under the Greek junta, George Meany, Billy Graham, the *Los Angeles Times,* saving time too for the return of Ted Williams as manager of the Washington Senators.

Then, because he always operates that way, he started to ask questions, wanting to know if I had hunted, fished, or played sports, and whether I thought Castro was truly intelligent, and since he knew that I had been there, what was it really like in Cuba.

"Look," he said then, "you're honestly going tomorrow."

"Yes," I said.

"Great, and take your friends with you," he said.

That afternoon, when a Senator was hit in the elbow by a pitch, Ted Williams walked partway from the dugout to home plate, and stood there just a moment to see if his man was hurt. He was not, and when Williams turned to walk back a fan on the third-base line called, "Hey, Ted come on, how about a smile?" Williams shook his head, and kept staring at the ground, but he was smiling, by God, he was really smiling.

Larry L. King went back to West Texas to write about his best friend, a brilliant and loquacious trial lawyer:

The single public performance for which citizens of Odessa best remember Warren Burnett occurred when lawyers and physicians met at a Country Club dinner to alleviate tensions aggravated by courtroom disputes between the two proud professions. Perhaps the pre-banquet cocktail party ran two hours too long. When Burnett rose to deliver the welcoming address on behalf of the host lawyers, it was not the speech printed in the official program. "I have watched our learned doctor friends arrive here in their Cadillacs and their wives in precious stones and furs," he intoned, "and have observed their expressions as they considered superior secrets known only to themselves and/or God. I would like to remind our guests that

> when *their* professional antecessors were teaching that the night air was poisonous, and were setting leeches on George Washington's behind the better to bleed him, *my* professional antecessors had written the Constitution of the United States — as noble a document as known to the minds of men or angels."

As I look back, two pieces among the many gave me special pride. One was "My Lai: The First Detailed Account of the Vietnam Massacre" by Seymour M. Hersh, which stirred American readers more than any single piece we published, and that included Mailer's "On the Steps of the Pentagon" and "The Prisoner of Sex."

"My Lai" was the entire cover for May, 1970, the text covering thirty double-column pages and more than thirty thousand words. It had been more than two years since the massacre of 587 old men, women, and children by American soldiers in the Vietnam hamlet of that name in the village of Song My. "Largely through the persistence and talent of one American journalist," we wrote in the magazine's introduction, "the murders there have cast a widening shadow on our national conscience." Hersh was thirty-three at the time, a University of Chicago graduate, a former police reporter there and AP man in Washington. I never knew a great investigative reporter who did not palpitate with energy, with the hidden *possibility* in things, and Hersh was no exception. Having been tipped off the previous fall by a source in the Pentagon, he was the first reporter to interview Lieutenant William L. Calley, Jr., leader of the American Division platoon that performed the killings. In the previous several months Hersh had travelled fifty thousand miles interviewing more than fifty members of Charlie Company, the result being a thorough reconstruction of the massacre itself, and of the attempt of high military officials to conceal it:

> There were few physical protests from the people; about eighty of them were taken quietly from their homes and herded together in the plaza area. A few hollered out, "No V. C. No V. C." But that was hardly unexpected. Calley left Meadlo, Boyce, and a few others with the responsibility of guarding the group. "You know what I want you to do with them," he told Meadlo.

> Ten minutes later — about 8:15 a.m. — he returned and asked, "Haven't you got rid of them yet? I want them dead."

The hundreds of letters-to-the-editor alternated between incredulity and outrage. Many Americans not only refused to believe the story but suspected it of being an anti-war ploy. Nixon himself ordered a secret investigation of Hersh in an effort to discredit him. Official Army charges were eventually dropped against all the accused soldiers except Calley. Convicted of premeditated murder, he was paroled after serving thirty-five months of a life sentence, most of them under house arrest in his apartment in Fort Benning. At the time of our publication, Bob Bernstein, head of Random House, which would publish the book *My Lai* the following month (it won the Pulitzer), predicted to me that since in those years Americans had become so cynical and distrusting, the *Harper's* spread would sadly have little or no effect on the public. But I cannot help but believe that it did.

The other piece was "The Land of the Permanent Wave," by Edwin "Bud" Shrake, a large, tall Texan with a blunt exterior that disguised a lyric but misdoing heart. This piece was infinitely less ambitious than "My Lai," but struck a chord in me that I have never quite forgotten, having to do with how clean, funny, and lambent prose caught the mood of that moment in the country and mirrored with great felicity what we were trying to do at *Harper's.* To me few finer magazine essays have ever been written.

The genesis of "The Land of the Permanent Wave" was in itself a germane story of the magazine business of that era. *Sports Illustrated* sent Shrake down at his insistence to do a piece on the beautiful and haunting Big Thicket area of East Texas. This was about the time a Texas lumbering company was becoming a major stockholder in Time Inc. Shrake's story on timber choppers and developers ruining the Thicket was not happily greeted at *SI.* Andre Laguerre, the managing editor later to be dismissed by the money men, broke the news to the writer at their daily late afternoon gathering in the bar around the corner from the Time-Life Building where many of their editorial decisions took place. It was the only *SI* story Shrake ever wrote that the magazine would not print, and Laguerre was embarrassed. Shrake got his permission to rewrite it and give it to *Harper's*. He sat down and changed the main angle of the story from the mercenary destruction of the Thicket to his and his young wife Doatsy's travels through Lufkin and on down to the Thicket, about permanent waves and long hair in the Sixties and cowboy hats and rednecks and cops and the fumes from the paper mills.

> When I got out of the car I was assailed by another of the noxious stinks that Lufkin is distinguished for. This one came from the huge paper mill across the road. Smoke poured from the stacks and spread across the neighborhood like a fog that smelled of rotten-egg puke. The odor wrenched the stomach and made one hesitant to breathe.
>
> "If I lived around here, I'd blow up that place," I said to the man at the drive-in.
>
> "No sir, you wouldn't," he replied. "If you lived around here, you'd work there."

The two of them, Shrake and his wife, had long hair. In their convertible driving through Texas they had encountered contempt, rudeness, even cruelty. People sneered at them; the cops followed them; motels would not take them: "They would tell the Easy Rider to crawl on his bike and haul his bones out of the county, and if he moved fast enough he might make it."

> "I'll tell you something," a man said to him. "You're not such a bad fellow. I could learn to live around you, and I could even get used to your hair. But there's one thing I've got to admit. I hope you won't get mad at me for saying this."
>
> "Let's hear it," I said, having begun to be fond of the old man and finding it unimaginable that he could anger me.
>
> "Well, like I said. I could get used to your hair. But there's no way in the world I could ever make myself like your wife's hair."
>
> My wife's hair! So that was part of it too! I had assumed the hostility we had encountered in the last few days of driving through East Texas in our convertible was directed at me. But my wife had been receiving her share of it, and maybe more, all

along. My wife's hair! My wife Doatsy is young and pretty and her hair is the color of caramel; it is soft, it shines, it smells like baby soap, and it is long, hanging to the middle of her back, a glorious drop of hair that my grandmother would have been proud of, that young girls of today strive for, and that Arch could never make himself appreciate!

"I'm amazed there is a man in America who objects to long hair on a woman," I said.

I don't know what Arch thought I was calling him, but he got up and went to bed, and I could tell he had been insulted. But as I thought of the way we had been treated for the past week, I understood what Arch was telling me. As the beatniks long ago learned, out there in America hair matters, and here we were in the land of the permanent wave. The shellacked bouffants and beehives, sprayed hard as a real hornet's nest, had become acceptable at last, along with high-heeled shoes, in East Texas, where information does not readily penetrate, but the thing for a real lady still to have was a permanent wave like my mother used to come home with twenty years ago. In East Texas, long-haired women went out of mode with long-haired men, about the time McKinley was shot, and in my big-city naivete I had thought I was the only one being scorned by the natives for disregard of custom in a place where custom means everything.

A friend finally gave Shrake a cowboy hat, which he proceeded to wear. The man, who was a native of the neighborhood, congratulated him on having lived for a week in Texas long-haired and bareheaded without getting beaten with a tire iron. "With that hat on," he said, "they can see your hair hanging down, but a long-haired cowboy is likely to be a dangerous man that is best left alone." From then on he and young Doatsy, even without a permanent wave, were treated with respect, and possibly even fear.

Alfred Kazin and Irving Howe were two people who would have done any civilization proud, and any magazine, and their essays and literary criticism were among the most trenchant, and in many ways the most relevant, of the period. In these months Howe contributed pieces on Hemingway, Orwell, Dostoevski, Bellow,

O'Hara, Edwin Arlington Robinson, Gandhi, Isaiah Berlin, Herbert Marcuse, Kate Millett, and Tom Wolfe's portrayal of the radical chic of the day, and Kazin's cast included Mary McCarthy, Lionel Trilling, Stark Young, Bellow, Edmund Wilson, and Walker Percy.

Kazin was in his mid-fifties, Howe in his late forties. Both were products of New York who wrote often of the city and its varied tapestries, including the immigrant ghetto and the children and grandchildren of the first arrivals. Kazin's parents had immigrated from Czarist Russia and he was born in the tenement section of Brownsville in Brooklyn, where his father was a house painter. Howe's parents came from the Ukraine and had a small grocery in the Bronx. His first language was Yiddish, and he, in fact, was to become the greatest advocate of Yiddish culture. As with so many of the young New York Jewish intellectuals, they both attended City College, and both were destined to become luminaries among the New York and American literary intelligentsia, prolific writers and critics long noted before these *Harper's* days for their broad and humane interests. Howe, indeed, invented the phrase "New York intellectuals" in a 1968 essay. They were also outstanding teachers of literature, and had taught at various collegial venues all over the country.

"America is a country of many cultures," Irwin Shaw wrote, "some clashing with each other, some complementary, some a volatile combination of simultaneous attraction and rejection. We are in need of all possible bridges between citizen and citizen." The American literary heritage is a rich and diverse one, and the urban Jewish tradition which is a vital part of it is variegated also, and by that token Kazin and Howe were different. Alfred was more traditionalist, less ideological, with a more vulnerable personal aspect. When Truman Capote remarked in a magazine that American Jewish writers "squeeze from the same tube of toothpaste," Kazin wrote an angry rejoinder summoning the dangerous legacies of the Holocaust. Once, in a description of the American literary backdrop, he made a reference to "our mountains," to which Norman Podhoretz countered, "*Our* mountains, Alfred?" He was personally the more gregarious of the two individuals. He enjoyed the atmosphere surrounding magazines, having started out writing on the old *New Republic* among others, and while Irving was all business when dropping off his pieces and was never one for small talk, Alfred Kazin liked to linger and chat, a cheerful pleasure with his recollections of various American writers and a curiosity and interest in the personal idiosyncrasies of writers I knew, including Southern ones. "When you were growing up in the South," he once asked me, "did your father take you into the woods to hunt?" Years later he remembered Israel's "fiery, crucial, overwhelming moment" when we sent him there during the 1967 war to do an article. He wrote:

> At El Arish on the Mediterranean, on our way to the Suez Canal, I sat in a grove of palm trees looking at the clear, shining, blue-green water. Everywhere were shoes that had been thrown off by the Egyptians so they could run faster. As we toiled to the Canal through the Sinai desert with a busload of correspondents and photographers, a mild-looking little Israeli colonel hitching a ride to his encampment bitterly observed the enthusiasm with which the photographers shot every blackened, burned-out tank and truck. From the Gaza Strip to the Canal you could see hundreds on hundreds of shot-up, burned-out Egyptian vehicles. It was not difficult to picture soldiers on fire, screaming. One photographer, coming back with shots of still another burned-out tank, announced triumphantly that he had seen a body in it. The little colonel said with scorn, "May I say one word? You have seen what we can destroy. May I ask you please to notice what also we can build?"

Irving Howe seemed always under deadline, since as a leader of the anti-Communist Left in the United States, he was the editor of *Dissent.* I had known him, however, in Palo Alto when he was on a visiting professorship and, like many Jewish intellectuals and writers I would later know in New York City he had a high relish for baseball — and as also with many of them I knew who had grown up in New York, I do not think he ever forgave the Dodgers and Giants for forsaking Ebbets Field and the Polo Grounds for California. One night at Candlestick Park in San Francisco, Irving and I saw a Giants–Mets game suspended for more than an hour in the middle innings because of fog. "This wouldn't happen in the Bronx," he said.

One of Irving's notable stands in the 1960s was his consistent, eloquent position against the extremes of the New Left for what he perceived as its authoritarianism, its tendency to anti-humanism, its distaste for the norms of political liberty, and its modish and often violent anti-Americanism. On our pages he wrote of the "apocalyptic turgidity" of a Herbert Marcuse: "Marcuse has been discovered in his old age by New Left students throughout the world and, like one of those poor captive kings of African tribes, hoisted to the glory of theoretic mentor. That these student admirers read him, that they *can* read him seems doubtful — his style is steadfastly opaque. Given the temper of the moment, an unreadable mentor may be just right." On Radical Chic, including a well-attended party at Leonard Bernstein's in the city, it had become "who can say for how long, a season or even two? — a fashion among the more stylish segments of our upper classes. . . . One can't help feeling that not only was there a failure of intelligence in Mr. Bernstein's living room, but, something much more troubling, a *willed abandonment* of intelligence." And on "The Middle Class Mind of Kate Millett" and her *Sexual Politics* — "a book declaring itself to be a 'revolutionary' manifesto, presenting Jean Genet as a moral exemplum, and with the barest lilt of the eyebrow envisioning the abolition of the family" — and yet a best-seller, Book-of-the-Month Club selection, cover of *Time.* I quote Howe's concluding words:

> I recall my mother and father sharing their years in trouble and affection, meeting together the bitterness of sudden poverty during the Depression, both of them working for wretched wages in the stinking garment center, helping one another, in the shop, on the subways, at home, through dreadful years. And I believe, indeed know, that they weren't unique, there were thousands of other such families in the neighborhoods in which we lived. Was my mother a drudge in subordination to the "master group"? No more a drudge than my father who used to come home with hands and feet blistered from his job as presser.

> Was she a "sexual object"? I would never have thought to ask, but now, in the shadow of decades, I should like to think that at least sometimes she was.

On his death in 1993, *The New Yorker,* in an affecting eulogy, would faithfully reflect my own great regard for Irving Howe. He "was grief-struck by the horrors of his age, and he was determined to resist them, and he was filled with golden dreams, and he had no illusions. . . . Irving Howe was one of the splendors of American culture and intellect, and the splendor was impeccably human."

Norman Mailer remained as always indelible in these years. There were the big raucous parties at his house in Brooklyn Heights with its rear view of the Brooklyn docks and, across the East River, its intimate vista of the mighty towers of Wall Street, so compact and yet so immediate as to appear dream-like in an evening's mist, the Sixties' smell of pot wafting above the electric gauntlet of New York people: writers and poets and editors and detectives and filmmakers and actors and actresses and prizefighters. Mailer was then directing and acting in three of the most unusual movies ever filmed, bringing together a menagerie of acutely diverse individuals. In one of these he and the actor Rip Torn staged a fight which, as the cameras whirred, settled into the real item, Torn later complaining that in the wrestling which ensued Mailer tried to bite off his ear. Mailer took these enterprises with a holy-day seriousness that would have shamed a Mormon elder, and he would have private screenings of these improbable ventures for a few friends at the Leacock and Pennebaker studios in Manhattan, and during the merciful intermission of one of them he accosted me in the men's room for my opinion, and did not appreciate my judging it much too long, glaring at me for an instant in which I thought he might go for the earlobe, then grimly laughing and saying, "Well, at least you're candid."

He likewise ran for Mayor of New York City, taking as his running mate for the office of Comptroller the irrepressible Jimmy Breslin, who was once likened by Tom Wolfe to a bowling ball radiating steam. They invited me to a press luncheon at one of the midtown hotels to announce their intentions, whereupon Mailer gave a speech pledging that if elected he would lead a movement to make New York City the fifty-first state in the Union, a sovereign and independent entity with its own finances and militia. Then he solicited questions. I raised my hand. "Okay, Morris," he said, "go ahead and get it over with," and I said, "Mr. Mailer, we tried that where I came from a hundred years ago and it didn't work." Mailer rejoined, "We're not seceding, we're adding to."

In the months to come, he would do for *Harper's* one of the most controversial articles of all those years, but for now we could not persuade him to write anything. One evening in the dregs of a party at Jean Stein's, Mailer and his cousin and lawyer Charles "Cy" Rembar and Jean Stein and I were standing at the fireplace where I presented the writer with another possibility. The United States, I said, was soon to send some men to the moon. Already they were in training for this journey in Houston, Texas. Why not go down there and get to know these people and write a blockbuster article about it? Cy Rembar was amiable enough, but declared he thought the suggestion preposterous, and also demeaning of his cousin's talents. I vehemently demurred. Mailer agreed with Rembar. His strongest writings lately, he said, involved personal participation, and how could he actually participate in a landing on the moon? Suddenly, however, he grew pensive. "God, I'd love to go to the moon," he said. Did I know anyone in Washington who could pull strings? If so, he would get himself in shape and make the trip. One's editorial hunches deemed this an unlikely prospect, and the talk drifted to more casual topics. Not long after this Mailer telephoned me at my office. There was honest contrition in his words. Remember your idea about the astronauts? he asked. *Life* magazine had offered him $100,000 to go to Houston and do a substantial piece about them. He knew about our limited budget and needed the money, he said, and wanted me to know about the deal before *Life* announced it the next day. He apologized. Disappointed, yet understanding of the circumstances, I gave him our blessings. That was the background of his remarkable article and subsequent book, *Of a Fire on the Moon.*

* * *

It was part of the pattern of my life, I see now, always coming home, even at the apex. I made several trips back to Mississippi to do the *Harper's* cover story on the occasion of the magazine's 120th anniversary number. The subject would be the massive overnight integration of the public schools in my hometown.

I would have been ashamed not to be there during this, the town's critical crossroads. I felt responsible to my magazine to be there too. I had seen a small story in the back pages of the *New York Times* that the Fifth Circuit Court of Appeals in New Orleans had ordered mine and many other Southern school districts to comply with the law of the land, this fifteen years after the 1954 Supreme Court decision. Some of my colleagues did not see the importance of this event, as if what was happening there in Yazoo, and in similar places, was a mere speck of sand in the whole sweep of the American Sixties, the black urban ghettos, the deep national divisions, and at a moment when the entire notion of meaningful racial integration seemed either passé or under assault from both Right and Left, and when the continuing widespread flight to white suburbia in the North was leading to the white abandonment of the urban public schools. I begged to disagree, for I believed the Deep South, with all its failings and complexities, darknesses and bequeathed transgressions, was a symbol and crucible, and had much it could teach the nation. My old friend in my town, Harriet Decell, wife of the state senator and Harvard Law graduate, had put all this to me eloquently, and with resonances for all little towns:

> I have a consciousness that small things fit together into big puzzles and that one is responsible for one's actions and had better be ready to accept it. You get tired of getting up every day and wondering if you're being challenged by your environment. You can live in a small town and be sorry for yourself that the world passes you by — and suddenly you realize that the world isn't passing you by at all — that it's all here. We've got a lot of friends in big cities, and they seem to be beating their heads against the wall all the time. That's not so true here. One individual can affect a small town. At least you can decide what you believe and stand for it.

In my growing up there in the Fifties, and on into the early Sixties, with rare notable exceptions (and rare lonely dissident voices among whites such as William Faulkner and Hodding Carter, and James Silver and P. D. East, not to mention the courageous blacks such as Medgar Evers, Aaron Henry, and Fannie Lou Hamer) the white people of my native ground had entrusted their votes and support to anxious, marginal, visionless men, inconstant and cynical and unmanly men, who had come exceptionally close to destroying Mississippi in what could very well have been an ocean of blood. To Bob Moses of SNCC in these times Mississippi was "the middle of the iceberg" with its defiant hostilities. "Mississippi set itself up to be our destiny," he remembered, "and so it attracted what it eventually got: us." There was a story that made the rounds during the days of the Movement, told to me again on these forays home, about the black sharecropper named Ben McGee, who died at the age of seventy-five, ascended to heaven, and was immediately escorted into the presence of the Lord.

> "Ben McGee," the Lord said, embracing him in an LBJ-like hug, "I'm proud of you. We've kept our eyes on you. You've done the cause of Christianity and human brotherhood so much good down in the Mississippi Delta that we intend to send you back."
>
> "O Lord," Ben McGee said. "I'm not going back. You've never been. You don't know what it's like down there."
>
> "If necessary, Ben," the Lord said. "I'm going to have to put that in the form of an order."
>
> "If you send me back down to Mississippi, Lord," Ben asked, "will you go with me?"
>
> "I'll go as far as Memphis," the Lord replied.

Now it was half a decade beyond that, after the Kennedys and Martin Luther King, Jr., and LBJ's momentous civil rights acts, and I observed there quiet and unusual things. Black and white high school athletes, suddenly brought together with the merger, were providing the leadership for change. Kenny Graeber, infant son of my next door neighbors in my younger days, now quarterback and white student body president, even got a letter from President Nixon praising him, and so did the black student body president. The NAACP leader, a seasoned civil rights activist from Chicago, with a .38 pistol on the table as he talked with me, and Martin Luther King, Jr.'s photographs on the walls, and carbines stacked in corners — "one of the few black radicals left who still believes in integration," a Mississippi NAACP leader had told me — said he used to be anti-white. "I didn't trust the Northern white workers who came down here. But the young kids now, all over the country, are proving their commitment. Racism in the North is more complex and subtle than it is here."

I subsequently made some mistakes in my assessments: underestimating the long-range tenacity of some of the white private "seg" academies, miscalculating though not minimizing the more subtle forms of the old racism just then developing. But I would stand by my broader judgments in the anniversary number, the cover of it a photograph of a yellow bus with "Yazoo County Public Schools" on it, for in the state at large less than twenty percent of the white children deserted these public schools.

There were those who said New York City was a provincial enclave, unrepresentative then of the rest of the nation. But I had long since learned that New York, far from being an estuary of our national life, was if anything more *representative* than not. Yet it drove me back almost against the will toward my past. Growing up in the Deep South a generation before, I became aware of the life of that place as a cross section and a microcosm of my time and region, and much that was typical of humanity was there for me to judge and comprehend. What I missed that generation ago were the great exertions of the national presence, the manifestations of the relentless movement toward homogeneity and nationalization — the farthest nerve endings of America as a civilization — toward some kind of pluralistic accommodation, however fragile and illusory this might seem, among our races and peoples and our separate collective pasts. The generation of children I had watched in Yazoo, white and black, would not be so isolated as mine, for they would be confronted quite early with the things it took me years to learn, or that I had not learned at all.

As I wrote then for my magazine, they were the first white and black children in the nation brought together under the federal courts' specific doctrine of total integration, and they were intensely curious about each other. They fumbled for words to express their new feelings. Black and white, they were children of the South, Southern to the core, and in this regard they were different from children in, say, New Rochelle or Los Angeles or Indianapolis. Yet like all young people in America, as Ralph Ellison suggested, "they have been unable to resist the movies, television, jazz, football, drum-majoretting, rock, comic strips, radio commercials, soap operas, book clubs, slang, and any of a thousand other expressions of our pluralistic and easily available popular culture." They were as American as they were Southern, but it was this common bond in the South — the rhythms and tempos, the ways of speaking and of remembering, the place and the land their people knew and out of which they suffered together — that made them, young blacks and whites, more alike than dissimilar; and it was this, before it was all over, that I hoped in my heart might be some salvation — hoped, too, I was not wrong.

An Easterner, Mel Leventhal, was the principal school lawyer for the NAACP Legal Defense Fund in Mississippi during these trips of mine there, a young Jew from Brooklyn, graduate of NYU Law School. He expressed a strong love for Mississippi and believed it someday could become a "great state." He spoke, in fact, with a Southern accent and used the word "fella" when talking with you, and I was not at all surprised when he told me that as a student in New York he spent many hours at the racetracks. I had arranged to meet him and his wife at their house in a black neighborhood in Jackson, but I had been there only a short time when there was a telephone call and he had to leave for an unexpected meeting.

I sat at the dinner table with his wife. She was black, in her early twenties, quiet and soft-spoken. I thought her strikingly beautiful. She said she was a writer, her first book of poems, in fact, having recently been published. As we sat talking, her one-year-old daughter named Rebecca sat near us in a high chair. I had not heard of Mrs. Leventhal's work and asked what name she wrote under. Alice Walker, she said. Her parents had been sharecroppers in Georgia and she was the youngest of eight children. When she was a student at Spelman, in Atlanta, she joined civil rights demonstrations, she said, and then she went all the way to Sarah Lawrence in Bronxville to finish college, travelled in Africa, and began writing poems, and in '66 arrived in Mississippi and became involved in the civil rights movement with people who had been thrown off the welfare rolls and their farms for registering to vote. That is how she met Mel Leventhal, and after living in a studio apartment over Washington Square in New York they got married and moved back to Mississippi; they were the first legally married interracial couple in Jackson. Now, she told me, her first novel was soon going to be published by Harcourt Brace. The story intrigued me, especially since I myself had moved South to North: a Southern black tenant farmer named Grange Copeland who leaves his family for the aspirations of the North, but eventually returns home to a hopeful then tragic end. I told her I looked forward to reading it.

She had just had a magazine piece accepted for publication in a Southern journal, she said, and she had given it the title "The Black Writer and the Southern Experience." She gave me a copy of the manuscript to take with me:

> Southern black writers, like most writers, have a heritage of love and hate, but they also have enormous richness to draw from. And having been placed, as Camus says, "halfway between misery and the sun," they, too, know that "though all is not well under the sun, history is not everything."
>
> No one could wish for a more advantageous heritage than that bequeathed to the black writer in the South: a compassion for the earth, a trust in humanity beyond our knowledge of evil, and an abiding love of justice. We inherit a great responsibility as well, for we must give voice to centuries not only of silent bitterness and hate but also of neighborly kindness and sustaining love.

"I sometimes wonder if integration is really worth the effort," she said to me. She believed in the Southern children working it out together, but worried that all the pressures on them might finally prove destructive. We talked of New York, of the nation, of the South, of the land itself. "Can you imagine what the Delta must have been like a million years ago?" she asked. She had grown impatient of New York and the East when she was a student there, she said, and her heroine was Flannery O'Connor. To tell the truth, she reminded me a little of myself. I sensed that despite her husband's active life as a lawyer for blacks, their existence in Jackson had to have been very private and alone. "Sometimes it gets to you, the pressure," her husband had admitted to me. "Going to a movie together. Holding hands walking down the street." Only a few days before, the two of them had taken their daughter into a Sears, and everyone gathered and looked at them so intently, it nearly caused a riot.

That night, far away from New York in my homeplace beginnings, this young woman poised at the verge of her great writing career demonstrated something to her visitor that he would try hard someday to emulate, after the power and the perquisites and indeed the very reality of the city itself were gone: to try not to be afraid of the circumstances which sometimes threaten and encompass you, to observe, to feel, and to know.

We were standing at the doorway as I was about to leave. "I think you wish you'd never left Mississippi," she said. "The more I hear you, the more I believe you really want to live here."

I never saw Alice Walker again, although I read *The Third Life of Grange Copeland* when it appeared in New York and wrote her how much I admired it. She subsequently spent two more years in Mississippi, which she later said had just about driven her around the bend. Her later novel *Meridian* had to have been shaped by that experience. My memory of her on that long-ago evening is an imperishable one, of a warm, brave young woman searching her heart, searching for the words. Who was I then? Who was Alice? And why were we there?

Back in New York City, and the magazine business, there was a worm in the lilac, as there forever will be.

Our owner, John Cowles, Jr., had grown more and more impersonal and withdrawn. Far from concerning me, which it should have, in truth I rather welcomed it. Gone were the promising talks about the future of the magazine, and no more high social times in Minneapolis. I had long since known that the Cowleses and their people had a great deal of money and enjoyed having it. I had seen the deference paid to them in Minnesota, and also in official Washington, where they had once taken me to the Gridiron Dinner, that utmost convocation of the country's power elite; they had an honored table.

The Mississippi Jeffersonian hothead had not courted them. He certainly recognized that what had happened at *Harper's* was one of the singular experiments in the long history of American magazines. I believe we had succeeded in bringing together many of the nation's best writers who were dramatically reflecting the clashing American cultures of the time: the tensions and madnesses, the complexity and promise. We were pushing the language to its limits in a national journal, a journal that was iconoclastic and unpredictable and, I trust, edifying and entertaining, and all this expressive of *Harper's* more long-lasting literary and journalistic lineage. But was that enough? Or was it *too* much? What must the patriarch of that clan, the keeper of the expanding exchequer, the flesh-and-blood epicenter of the American Republican Establishment, the old Vietnam hawk, be making of that crazy experiment? Of Irving Howe writing eight thousand words at a shot on Ernest Hemingway? Of Nixonian witch-hunts revealed, and four-page *poems,* and voices merging in epiphany? Was he saying to the heir anointed, "Let go of those crazies. They're too much trouble"? Of course he was. But was the heir standing up to him? And should the editor, against all his deep blood instincts and experiences, have served as courtier? Been more cunning?

~ FAREWELL

15 WHILE JOHN COWLES, JR., remained aloof in The Land of 10,000 Lakes, he more or less turned over his purview of *Harper's* to the elusive William S. Blair, now the magazine's president and chief executive officer. In mid-1970 the magazine formally became an operating division of the Star-Tribune Company, which in fiscal 1969 had turned a profit of many vast millions. We were beginning to hear reports that Jack Fischer, the editor emeritus, now age sixty, who was still writing his "Easy Chair" column but who rarely came to the office, was openly expressing grave distaste for the magazine in the city's publishing circles for its editorial content and writers, for the whole thrust and language of it, for its anti-Vietnam posture. What we did not know at the time was that his denunciations were being taken earnestly in Minnesota. A friend in the Century Club told me he had overheard Jack Fischer at an adjoining table with John Gunther and others being unqualifiedly critical of the publication's entire substance and approach.

Co-existence between Blair and me was at best uneasy; "I've had some sense of Willie's philosophy and mine being incompatible for some time," he said later. He was a cloud of doom and pessimism. The personal chemistry between the two of us had become an evil and destructive one. I had long suspected he was undercutting the editorial side at every opportunity among the proprietors with criticisms of the writers and their writings while protecting his own flanks — a not unfamiliar and indeed hoary tale. He was often suggesting *Harper's* become more a special-interest journal like *Ski Magazine.*

It was the fecund era for executives, and Blair eventually began turning out the memos. In the recession that was generally affecting American publishing, *Harper's* circulation, which had been rising by about 100,000 in four years, had dropped from 350,000 to 325,000, roughly the same as our competitor, *The Atlantic Monthly.* Advertising lineage was on the same level as the previous year but with a strained overall budget; although the total editorial costs of the magazine were no more than $250,000, Blair proposed dismissing either Bob Kotlowitz or Midge Decter. "It should be possible to get this magazine out with one editor-in-chief (yourself), one responsible senior editor (either Midge or Bob), and one junior editor," he declared in one such memo, with other reductions in secretaries, promotion, and office space. He criticized the amount of money being paid the contributing editors Halberstam, King, Corry, Frady, and Lapham under our contractual arrangement determined by the number of stories produced, questioned their productivity, and advocated drastic change in that set-up. In my reply I supported some of these reductions (though certainly not firing Kotlowitz or Decter, who were making $32,000 and $30,000 a year respectively), defended the editorial quality of the magazine, proposed as another economy measure that my salary of $37,500 and Blair's of $54,000 be reduced one-third (this not being agreed to), and defended the money paid the contributing editors and their prolific output. In his best financial year at *Harper's,* for instance, Halberstam had grossed $20,000 by writing seven ten-thousand-word articles and another of twenty thousand words. Two others had produced more pieces than their contracts required. All were compensated more for writing for other magazines than for *Harper's.* Larry L. King was never paid more than $2,000 for a *Harper's* piece; *Life, Playboy, True, Cosmopolitan, West,* and *Saturday Evening Post* paid him much more. Among other contributors the magazine's commission for a standard article ranged from $1,000 to $1,500. However, Norman Mailer would receive $10,000 for "The Prisoner of Sex," which the business side considered would be a good investment.

It had become clear to many of us that Blair had spent considerable money on promotion and readership surveys and polls and a new assistant publisher and was quick to blame editorial when circulation diminished. The story was by no means a new one. Yet the real question underlying all of this concerned the basic philosophy about the long-range and enduring future of the publication, and what it might or might not embody, say, in A.D. 1993.

Larry L. King, whose account of what was to ensue at *Harper's* in his book *None But a Blockhead: On Being a Writer* is an accurate one, wrote: "In retrospect, *Harper's* as we knew it was doomed early on. The Nixon recession of 1970–71 caused losses larger than had been anticipated, and Bill Blair was a bottom-line business type who cared no more for literary standards than a billygoat." King sometimes enjoyed paraphrasing his fellow Texan J. Frank Dobie in saying Blair valued good writing and reportage and fiction and poetry about as much as a razorback sow cared about Keats's "Ode on a Grecian Urn." Blair once referred to himself, in talking with King, as "the boss." "You're not *my* boss," King told him. "I'm not a goddamn accountant. I'm a writer. Morris is *my* boss."

I had long before discovered that John Cowles, Jr., was not exceptionally bright, and not very strong, and that somewhere beneath his phlegmatic exterior lay reclusive yet strongly evangelical compulsions, groping and inconsistent though they might have been. His uncle Russell, a reformed alcoholic, would tell Richard Broderick of the *Minnesota Monthly* that the Cowleses were "a dysfunctional family" given to "compulsive behavior." I would not learn for a long time, however, that beginning in that year, 1969, John Jr. was becoming seriously immersed in what later would be called the human potential movement. That year he attended a clinic for executives at Menninger's in Kansas called "Toward Understanding Man," from which he returned highly excited. From there he and his wife, Sage, inevitably drifted into EST — the Erhard Seminars Training — founded by the later-discredited entrepreneur Werner Erhard, who inspired confrontational sessions conducted like boot camps with emphasis on intense emotional experiences with the purpose of stripping the faithful to the bone, tearing down their "belief systems" and their guilts, shames, and insecurities. John Jr. said later that "it was like living in a house and thinking you knew all the rooms and then suddenly discovering that there were many more rooms in the house and places you could go. The realm of possibilities expanded enormously." In addition to the EST commitment, the Cowleses eventually joined other human potential programs such as channeling, and the Skinner Releasing Technique.

Robert Gottlieb, the chief editor at Knopf in those days, who was bringing out some of the best books of the decade, once suggested to me why magazine editors were so consistently anxious. No sooner had they put one monthly issue to bed, for which they had opened a vein, than they had to start in all over again on another, which had to be better than the one before. In that sense one's monthly magazine was not unlike the cotton candy at the county fairs of one's childhood, delicious and sweet but not lasting very long. It is an occupational hazard.

A suicidal sense of perfection, not to mention the big dare, will often be compounded by personal and professional faults, as in my case. In time's perspective I see how bull-headed I was, and not a very good administrator or businessman. Midge Decter once remarked that a magazine such as *Harper's* could never make any money, but that the owners foolishly thought it could, and that I should have confronted them with that reality at the start. She was probably right, as she usually was — if I had it all to do over again, I would have said: This magazine will never make money, you have all the money you need anyway. Your corporation made so many millions last year, let's continue to put out a fine magazine and keep the losses down: let's consider *Harper's* a luster in the corporate crown. I believe I thought I was buying time, with good writing and hard work and, yes, adrenaline, but I soon perceived that time would buy nothing: our owners had become fearful of the kind of magazine our labors had created, the no-holds-barred nature of it that surely was a challenge to what they themselves believed, but gave no indication beyond "specialization" of what it was they wanted. Perhaps there should have been a wave in my petulant brain that said *stroke them,* "kiss ass," but I could not do so. I had been schooled in newspaper journalism, in which the mentors and exemplars taught young editors then never to concern themselves with writing for the advertisers, or publishing what readers wanted to read, but to print the truth; there was always Pulitzer's claim on my wall. That, at least, was the old way, and it may have been vanishing. There was also something going far back in my very blood and heritage, of the bloodkin's irascibility and defeat and dispossession, that would not allow it, my very Southern pride, and distrust of inherited and entrenched absentee wealth and what has so often sprung from it, and its absence of any real comprehension of the complexities of this nation, and in this regard I suppose I was exceedingly ill-equipped for that job. But I have never once apologized for that pride, and never been ashamed of it, and never will be, and it is just such indigenous regional pride, admirable to some, abominable to others, that might someday help redeem the greater nation.

In the retrospect of time, I cannot help but believe that what was hotly simmering near the surface of things at *Harper's* much pertained to the Vietnam war, with all that that involved. The war dominated everything then. It was both substantive and symbolic. Every argument, every idea, every policy came back to it, and the new *Harper's* group was on one side, and the old group, represented by my predecessor John Fischer, was on the other. Everything in the larger society seemed at stake. Some of that showed in the tension I observed between Fischer and David Halberstam. In his "Easy Chair" columns Jack was continuing to take a strong pro-war position. I suspected that he was going off to his lunches at the Century Club to meet with his sources, whom he valued, his old friends in government and the foreign policy Establishment, the good people who represented the Washington view that the high Americans in Saigon were telling him the truth. Then, oddly, he would bring in the drafts of his columns and ask Halberstam to critique them. David had returned from his weeks in Vietnam in '67 on *Harper's* assignment and was darkly pessimistic about the war, and he continued to write as much. He remembered that Jack Fischer kept asking him for his suggestions but never once used any. Although no harsh words were ever spoken between these two very different men representing two irredeemably different American generations and outlooks, I could tell they personally despised each other, and when Halberstam advised Jack that his premises were wrong and that he was hedging the reality of our failure in Vietnam, this was only representative of the generational and political divisions taking place all over the country in those years in homes, businesses, everywhere. "We spoke in the same language," David recalled, "but we understood nothing that the other said."

"People were doing it all over town," a character in Wilfrid Sheed's *Office Politics,* his novel of the magazine business, observed, " — in all those great morose buildings on both sides of the street, it was plot, plot, plot." It was a wizened New York circumstance, to be repeated time and again as long as there are magazines, and people who run them. John Kennedy liked to improvise from *Ecclesiastes*: "A time to weep and a time to laugh, a time to mourn and a time to dance, a time to fish and a time to cut bait." JFK also knew there was a time to keep fishing. What were being made plain to me were these alternatives:

- Fold the magazine.
- Retrench and cut back circulation.
- Cut the budget in half, and fire most of the editors.
- Make *Harper's* more "specialized."

Someone else could do these things, but I was not the man; I genuinely thought we could make it, given time, with the kind of publication we then had, which was of some importance, I believed, to the social and cultural life of the nation. Who knows? Yet it was not difficult to see the handwriting on the wall. I myself did not handle the situation particularly well, but I see now how inevitable it all was.

"The American psyche of 1970," Steve Erickson wrote, "seemed split between those who hated and loved America simply — those who questioned everything about it, even what was good and reasonable; and those who served its authority and rules so blindly that not only their imaginations but their common sense became paralyzed," and in this regard the early months of the new decade extended the antagonisms of the Sixties. In addition to the continuing generational hostility, the war, the racial violence, the broader economic affluence which undergirded even the most calamitous strivings of the 1960s was giving way to high unemployment, inflation, and recession. "Not only is there no God," Woody Allen said, "but try getting a plumber on weekends." The anti-war movement, riven with factionalism and the simple debilitating reality of the broadening war itself, was beginning to sour. The Sixties party was pretty much over, with Watergate yet to come. But when Nixon's Republicans did poorly in the off-year elections, the background was set for the increasingly parapolitical tone of the Nixon realists, beginning with the founding, subsidized by large and often secret contributions, of the Citizens Committee for the Reelection of the President, of which much was destined to be heard.

The example of the older black civil rights movement was having a passionate impact now on a yet more widespread social revolution, a broadening change of contexts: the burgeoning women's movement in particular. And paralleling this were the accumulating demands for gay rights, Indian rights, single-issue causes, and the first effective beginnings of one of the most valuable and lasting endowments of Sixties protest, the environmental movement.

At *Harper's* the good moments remained. Marshall Frady had his three-part series "An American Innocent in the Middle East," where he found between Arabs and Israelis "a collision of two ages, a blind grappling of two dialectics, two realities, each barely comprehensible to the other." Pete Axthelm's *The City Game* examined basketball in New York, and how it offered escape to its boys, and the brief glory of being a hero. (*The City Game* was one of quite a few examples of the symbiosis between the magazine and Harper's Magazine Press, which we had established early on. Herman Gollob had asked Axthelm to write a book about the New York Knicks. He responded he would like to do a book which would combine the Knicks' championship season and the story of Harlem playground basketball. We made a deal calling for the book and a magazine first-serial excerpt.) Aaron Latham wrote on Scott Fitzgerald's last days in Hollywood, Blair Clark on General Westmoreland, Joseph Kraft on Henry Kissinger, John Bart Gerald on the Vietnam wounded, Harold Clurman on the contemporary theater, R. C. Padden on Las Vegas. Fiction by James Jones was set during the 1968 student revolution in Paris. Frank Conroy in the Empire Chinese had proposed to do a piece on Charles Manson and the most garish crime of the decade; he had been unable to gain access to the prisoner and wished out of his own imaginings to delve Manson's masturbatory fantasies when thrown in jail, and this grew into "Manson Wins!" one of the most adventuresome extensions of the new journalism.

Jack Richardson wrote on the Ali versus Quarry fight in Atlanta:

> It was a Klansman's nightmare, a recrudescence of the worst excesses of the South's post-bellum years. Inceding down Peachtree Street, spiritual and legendary Southern thoroughfare, were Muhammad Ali and his laughing entourage. They moved with loose, ambling confidence along this main street of Atlanta, as though each step were a gentle appropriation of a moment in history, a casual reclamation of a cultural manner that had been kept . . . in the corners of our society for a hundred years.

John Kenneth Galbraith wrote an account of a dinner at Averell Harriman's house in New York for Nikita Khrushchev with all the American power scions there, the Rockefellers and Rusks and McCloys and Sarnoffs and Finletters — and why on earth, Professor Galbraith asked himself, was *he* there, and on leaving, a distinctly city tableau:

> Outside it was still daylight, a lovely autumn evening, and a large crowd of newspapermen and cameramen were waiting. I walked out with Tom Finletter. Several reporters sensed that we might be the soft underbelly of the Establishment and tried to pump us. We remained loyal — a sense of class solidarity is quickly acquired. But it was not quite complete. As we turned down 81st Street, Tom said, "Do you have any doubt as to who was the smartest man in there tonight?"

For several years Larry L. King had been trying unsuccessfully to write about his father. Many times I had attempted to get him to. "Goddammit, I'm intimidated," Larry kept saying. "I guess I just don't understand him well enough." I always agreed with his first point, but never his second. A couple of hours after his father's funeral in Midland, Texas, Larry telephoned me. "I can write it now," he said. The result, which Bruce Cook of *The National Observer* called "quite simply the finest piece of magazine journalism I have ever read," proved also to be one of the most widely anthologized ever:

> Now it was late afternoon. His sap suddenly ran low; he seemed more fragile, a tired old head with a journey to make; he dangerously stumbled on a curbstone. Crossing a busy intersection, I took his arm. Though that arm had once pounded anvils into submission, it felt incredibly frail. My children, fueled by youth's inexhaustible gases, skipped and cavorted fully a block ahead. Negotiating the street, The Old Man half laughed and half snorted: "I recollect helpin' you across lots of streets when you was little. Never had no notion that one day you'd be doin' the same for me." Well, I said. Well. Then: "I've helped that boy up there" — motioning toward my distant and mobile son — "across some few streets. Until now, it never once occurred that he may someday return the favor." "Well," The Old Man said, "he will if you're lucky."

Halberstam's piece "The End of a Populist" on Senator Albert Gore, Sr., and his final defeat in Tennessee because of his civil rights and anti-Vietnam stands dealt too with the son, Al Gore, Jr., who had just graduated from Harvard, militantly anti-war and not wanting to go into the Army, but faced with a big choice: to stay out and avoid the draft in Tennessee would cost the Senate one of its most outspoken doves. Al Jr.'s family told him to make his own decision, his mother even saying she would go to Canada with him:

> Young Al called an uncle down in West Tennessee who questioned him on why he was so antiwar. "I guess," he said,

"it's my Baptist religion." "I never knew there was anything in the Baptist religion against war," the uncle said. "What about the sixth commandment, thou shalt not kill," young Al answered. But the conversation had given young Al the feeling of what the campaign against his father would be like and he had decided to serve. Those who know the Senator suspect that he would not have minded at all running a campaign with a son who refused to go to Vietnam; that he would in fact have relished it — the drawing of the line, the ethic of it. Show Albert the grain, says a friend, so he can go against it.

Halberstam's explorations of the roots of the Vietnam war, of how and why we went there, continued with the career that reflected and powerfully influenced the nation's journey in the Sixties, from highest idealism and confidence to the deepest self-doubt, in "The Programming of Robert McNamara": "To say that something could not work, that it was beyond the reach of this most powerful country in the world, was to fail. He hated failure."

Two of the most striking projects in the declining months involved a pair of American originals, Bill Moyers and the undauntable Norman Mailer.

There were parallels between Bill Moyers's life and mine. We were almost exactly the same age. He was a small-town Southerner, having grown up in Marshall, Texas, near the Louisiana line, and he too had started working for newspapers as a teenager. We were classmates at the University of Texas. He was funny and a prankster, and hard-working: a forty-eight-hour week at Lady Bird Johnson's television station, and Sabbath sermons as a part-time Baptist preacher. We were different kinds of people: he less histrionic, shrewder and more pragmatic; I admired him enormously. His relationship with Lyndon Johnson, for whom he also worked, was son-to-father, but he left him during his Vice-Presidency to become deputy director of the new Peace Corps, and was instrumental in making that institution a vital force among the young people of the country. He was in Austin doing advance work for John Kennedy's trip through Texas when he heard of the assassination, chartered a small aircraft to Dallas, scribbled a note to Johnson outside the Presidential plane saying, "I'm here if you need me," which he gave to a Secret Service man, and soon was rushed aboard Air Force One. He was to remain with Johnson as a close advisor and then chief of the White House staff, where at age twenty-nine he was a principal architect of the programs of the Great Society, the high-water point of the LBJ Presidency. "I think he is a Texas-size man," Tom Wicker wrote of him at the time for *Harper's*, "in his great talent, his unflagging energy, the reach of his ideas, the depth of his dedication. There is nothing small about Moyers, including his ambition and where it may take him in the long years ahead perhaps only a Texan's imagination can conceive." Once early in his tenure Celia and I came down from the city to have dinner with Bill and his wife Judith in a restaurant near the White House. Later we walked there and wandered about the deserted and darkened West Wing, like college kids on an outing, the slender and boyish Moyers flipping a light on here and there as we explored the Cabinet room and the Oval Office and the little rooms bordering the big ones, a strange and spooky midnight stillness pervading that place of history and endurance and power. He subsequently became press secretary at LBJ's insistence, resigning in '66. There were reports that he left because of his opposition to the war in Vietnam. "I'd like to claim to have been a prophet about the war early on," he told me much later, "but I'd be lying. I paid little attention to it while I was working on the domestic programs, and when I became press secretary, I accepted for a while the premises LBJ had embraced. Things were complex in that house of gray shadows. As the war claimed our resources, the President's time and energies as well as the budget, I became disillusioned, frustrated, and ineffective, torn by loyalty to him and my inability to make a difference."

After that, Moyers was publisher of *Newsday* on Long Island, the largest suburban daily in the United States, for over three years. He had transformed *Newsday* into one of the country's most exciting papers. Among other projects, he had persuaded Saul Bellow to cover the '67 war in the Middle East, and Daniel P. Moynihan to write on the urban uprisings, and he and his editorialists defended the peace marchers and anti-war activism of the late Sixties. On a television program, when the interviewer asked me what person my age did I think might someday make an outstanding President of the United States, I cited Bill Moyers, and explained why. The next day Moyers telephoned me.

"Okay," he asked, "what do you want?"

"I want the Court of St. James's," I said.

"You're not rich enough for that. I'll give you Haiti."

Bill's patron on Long Island, much as John Fischer had earlier been mine, was the wealthy Harry Guggenheim, the controlling owner in *Newsday,* and it was even rumored in New York circles familiar to me that Guggenheim intended someday to deed his majority interest to Moyers. It did not work out that way. Guggenheim became increasingly annoyed by his protégé's "left-wing sympathies" and sold the paper out from under him to the L.A. Times-Mirror Company. The Binghams offered Moyers the editorship of the *Louisville Courier-Journal,* but he did not like horse racing and mint juleps. I had known Bill for years, and when he lost it all at *Newsday* I felt for him, for what he was going through. David Halberstam and I asked him what his plans were; he did not know. We suggested he consider travelling extensively around the country on a bus for three months or so, stopping off at wherever his impulses told him to, and write about it for *Harper's.* He agreed on the spot. This was the origin of his brilliant "Listening to America."

"Listening to America" was a forty-five-thousand-word cover piece resulting from a thirteen-thousand-mile swing across the nation — "a troubled, spirited, inspired, frightened, complacent, industrious, selfish, magnanimous, confused, spiteful, bewitching country" — capturing as few documents did the moods, fears, and accents of that day, with its portraits of college presidents, student radicals, American Legionnaires, runaway kids, street people, union rebels, junkies, country doctors, black spokesmen, unemployed executives, business leaders, hard-working cops, ordinary citizens (and also Groucho Marx) — all part of a narrative rich in humor, sorrow, and understanding. Bill was a joy to work with, funny, mischievous, curious, although I detected in him then a dejection about his own life, surely having to do with losing *News-*

day after the thrall and majesty of the White House. I felt that his confrontation with hard-core reporting changed his life. "No one really understands just how difficult it is to write, do they?" he said to Marshall Frady and me one day. The book from the experience published by Herman Gollob and the Harper's Magazine Press under the same title eventually became a bestseller.

> People are more anxious and bewildered than alarmed. They don't know what to make of it all: of long hair and endless war, of their children deserting their country, of congestion on their highways and overflowing crowds in their national parks; of art that does not uplift and movies that do not reach conclusions; of intransigence in government and violence; of politicians who come and go while problems plague and persist; of being lonely surrounded by people, and bored with so many possessions; of the failure of organizations to keep the air breathable, the water drinkable, and man peaceable; of being poor. I left Houston convinced that liberals and conservatives there shared three basic apprehensions: they want the war to stop, they do not want to lose their children, and they want to be proud of their country. But it was the same everywhere.
>
> There is a myth that the decent thing has almost always prevailed in America when the issues were clearly put to the people. It may not always happen. I found among people an impatience, an intemperance, an isolation which invites opportunists who promise too much and castigate too many. And I came back with questions. Can the country be wise if it hears no wisdom? Can it be tolerant if it sees no tolerance? Can the people I met escape their isolation if no one listens?

The people at Channel 13 in New York saw the piece, thought Moyers would be a suitable host for a series they were launching from around the country, and that was the beginning of his life in national television, for in truth it was his love of conversation that would be his greatest gift to that powerful and tainted medium. He would become one of America's freshest and most essential voices, dramatic as Edward R. Murrow, trustworthy as Walter Cronkite. "I know that trip redeemed my life," he told me years later, "caused me to want to put behind me all that establishment stuff that had reached out to seduce me at *Newsday*, and to be a real journalist. It not only helped me rediscover America, but myself as well."

To no avail we had been trying to get something else from Mailer. I called him to have lunch. He would like that, he said, but not to try to persuade him to write anything. We met at a restaurant called Spats with an ersatz Twenties motif on Thirty-third Street. After the second Bloody Mary he said, "I know you've got an idea, and I know what the idea is, and I've got the same idea." What was it? I asked. He told me, and he was right: the Women's Movement. He agreed to do it. Once again Midge Decter and I flew up to the Cape, to another wintry landscape by the water. I brought Muriel Oxenberg Murphy with me this time. Mailer had a new wife, Carol Stevens. As before, he had been working at a feverish pace. As he was finishing he said to me, "I may be handing you a hot one this time."

"The Prisoner of Sex" was the whole cover for the March 1971 issue, with the subtitle: "On women and men, liberation and subjection, the body, the spirit, and physical love." Midge wrote the introduction:

> In devoting virtually our entire March issue to "The Prisoner of Sex" — Norman Mailer's bold analysis of the Women's Liberation Movement — the editors of *Harper's* wish to assert our belief that Women's Liberation is a development of possibly very great significance to the future of American society — certainly this movement is showing itself to be a major force in the social and cultural atmosphere currently surrounding us. We believe, moreover, that no writer in America could have illuminated as Norman Mailer has the deep underlying issues raised by what may be — in the parlance of Women's Liberation itself — "the last of the revolutions." Far from being simply the preserve of an extreme or "elite" minority, as many people charge, and far from being merely the latest of the creations of more publicity, this new radical impulse to erase the body of our institutionalized distinctions as to sex touches nothing less than the very heart of our traditional arrangements for day-to-day human existence.

Our magazine from the start had amply dealt with the Movement in all its implications, and Mailer's essay confronted in all his characteristic wild humor and vitality the most mystifying and often threatening question of all: the individual and private relations between women and men — and sex itself.

"The Prisoner of Sex" issue sold more copies on the national newsstands than any single issue in the history of *Harper's*. It also proved to be my last as editor.

Now the days were winding down, the words of a sad song, to a precious few. I suppose now I knew these were waning days. Did I see the omen and refuse to look at it?

In late February, a week or so after the "Prisoner of Sex" issue came out, I went to Minneapolis for a meeting, having been the only editorial person so invited. John Cowles, Jr., and Blair were there, along with other executives. Blair read a twenty-one-page memo. The meeting lasted three and a half hours and dealt with money and editorial content, including criticism of editorial performances as they related to circulation, making *Harper's* more "specialized," and continuing the readership polls. Blair spoke at length on how the magazine had caught on only with "Eastern communicators." He advised dismissing all the contributing editors. The atmosphere was cold. Cowles backed Blair without reservation. One of the Minneapolis businessmen said, "No wonder it's such a failure. Who are you editing this magazine for? A bunch of hippies?"

The Mississippi bull-head was angry, more than he had ever been in his whole life. After the meeting I skipped lunch with the executives and booked a flight back to New York. I had some time to kill, walking about in the clean snow, white and immaculate on the streets of the clean, white, immaculate town, and went into a movie just then sweeping the country called *Love Story*, in which Ali McGraw delivered the line "Love is never having to say you're sorry," and then died, aptly matching my own mood.

On the long flight back it all came to a head for me. I knew in my deepest being I could no longer stay with the magazine, for this would involve acts of both public and private humiliation, not to mention the danger to the sturdier traditions of *Harper's*. In New York, against the advice of some of my friends, who counselled leaving room for compromise, I mailed my letter to Minneapolis. My statement to the press read:

> I am resigning because of severe disagreements with the business management over the purpose, the existence and the survival of *Harper's Magazine* as a vital institution in American life. My mandate as its eighth editor in 120 years has been to maintain its excellence and its courage. With the contribution of many of this country's finest writers, journalists, poets and critics, I think we have succeeded.
>
> It all boiled down to the money men and the literary men. And as always, the money men won.
>
> The article in our current issue by Norman Mailer has deeply disturbed the magazine's owners. Mailer is a great writer. His work matters to our civilization.
>
> I have given eight years of my life, four of them as editor in chief, to help make *Harper's* true to its finest traditions. I leave *Harper's* with an honorable conscience. It is at its most vital. It matters to the nation as it seldom has before. My resignation grieves my heart, but I am leaving as a protest against the calculated destruction of *Harper's*.
>
> All writers, editors and journalists who care passionately about the condition of the written word in America should deplore with me the cavalier treatment by business management of America's oldest and most distinguished magazine. This is the saddest day of my life.

The only point I would alter in that statement was on the Mailer piece. It was not central to the issue, only part of it, less at that moment substantive than symbolic. As for the rest, many years have passed since then, and in the nature of things few except the surviving participants really remember or care, and there has been many another editorial crisis in that city in time's long interval, though none nearly so lucid and emotional and direct. Rereading those words now — in a place far away, on a yellowing clipping from the *Times* — strangely overcomes me anew with the emotion and the fear of that long-ago moment, as any of us who has experienced similar moments will know and remember, for other people I loved suffered from them too. But to this day I will hold to them — because despite everything I was right.

Not long ago, the passions of these events muffled but still very real, a couple of my colleagues of that time and I, in the spirit of rounding out the story, pondered the question of John Cowles, Jr., of what had happened with him, and to a remarkable degree we agreed. A magazine taking off on a journey like ours, especially given the nature of those years, has a limited amount of powder it can use, no matter how successful "Steps of the Pentagon," or "My Lai," or the Bundy and McNamara profiles, or "The Prisoner of Sex," or the others. What the magazine was cumulatively demonstrating was that Cowles could not really control us, and that this began to work systematically against us.

By coincidence on the noon of the morning I mailed my resignation to Minneapolis, another of the endless happenstances of New York, I had a lunch appointment with my competitor, Bob Manning, the editor-in-chief of *The Atlantic Monthly,* down for the day from Boston. He was a very fine editor, and in our lengthy yet not unfriendly *mano a mano* we had gotten together occasionally over the years, just the two of us, to compare tales and complain of ownership and feel each other out, like old managers long around the hardball circuit. He consoled me in my melancholy. I apologized that lunch would have to be brief, since Bill Bradley of the Knicks had invited my son David Rae to work out with the team in Madison Square Garden and I had to meet him there. "God, I'd love to go with you," my rival said. "I like Bill Bradley. I've got an appointment with Dean Rusk at the Century."

Later, in the big deserted Garden arena, I idled on a front row and watched David shoot free throws with Frazier, Reed, and Debusschere. I was just then losing everything I ever wanted, I was thinking, and I was suffused now with a terrible sorrow and guilt and shortcoming, the sorrow and guilt and shortcoming of the headstrong, emotions that would never leave me for many years — and also with waves of the most tender memory. As the echoes of the bouncing basketballs resounded to the arched roof high above, and my son weaved a fast-break with Barnett and Bradley, I thought of my own father not long before his death on gray winter afternoons long ago, stopping on his way home from work to watch our high school team practice in our cramped little gymnasium in Yazoo. I half-expected him now. I would have wished to talk with him. Down on the basketball court, the practice was over and all the Knicks had retired to the lockerroom except Bradley, who was at the free-throw line giving David instructions. Immersed in my thoughts, alone in my conjurings in that grand and empty palace, I barely heard the footsteps coming my way. Suddenly the editor-in-chief of *The Atlantic Monthly* stood before me. "I cut Dean Rusk short," he said. Then, pointing to the two figures on the court, he asked: "Say, which one's Bradley?"

Later that day I had my last appointment as an editor, among the bizarre and notable hundreds of those years in all the city's wide-swept settings, and this one was with Gore Vidal, who had phoned in an agitated mood and wanted to have a talk. I had resigned my official position, and I had nothing else to do, so what the hell? Vidal and I met in the King Cole Room of the St. Regis, just down the hall from the little bar where Bill Styron and I had convened that distant afternoon when he had just finished his novel and conversed with the Englishman who had had tea with Hitler. I had not seen Gore Vidal since the winter's day at his house on the frozen Hudson River, and his vehemence, which at the moment seemed boundless, was over Mailer's "The Prisoner of Sex," which he had just read and judged, on a number of counts, outrageous. "Break my icy exterior," Vidal had once said of himself, "and beneath you'll find ice water." He wanted to do a long rebuttal to Mailer and, lame duck though I was, I said why not? Besides, I enjoyed sitting there listening to his brilliant, amusing, dyspeptic critiques of the New York intellectual life. I suppose one could have done much worse than go out of the New York days *tête-à-tête* with Gore Vidal.

George Plimpton had been assigned by *Sports Illustrated* to cover the Ali-Frazier fight at the Garden that week, the first heavyweight championship to which he had ever been assigned, and he remembered sitting at ringside only seconds before the first-round bell with his notebooks and pens feeling very nervous. This had been billed as the Fight of the Century and the tension, Plimpton recalled, was extraordinary; a man a few rows down had just been carted off with a heart attack. Suddenly Norman Mailer came up and knelt next to Plimpton in the aisle. Plimpton could barely hear what Mailer was telling him: "George, we've got to get to John Cowles. Willie Morris has just resigned." Cowles had been Plimpton's roommate at Harvard. Plimpton remembers Norman's urgency, "as if he half-expected me to rush out to the nearest pay phone to call John Cowles." Plimpton replied, "Oh, God, Norman, I don't think I can do anything about this right now."

Any irrational thoughts I might have had about my resignation not being accepted, and for a brief time I actually must have thought it might not, were soon dissipated. The resignation was quickly announced without explanation by the Cowles organization. I learned of the acceptance from William S. Blair's secretary — "Oh, I'm so sorry you're leaving us." At the *Harper's* offices both Halberstam and King angrily confronted Blair with having told the *New York Times* that the magazine's contributing editors were overpaid and had not produced the number of pieces called for in their contracts. King had agreed on Blair's suggestion to confer with John Cowles, Jr., about the future of the magazine, and when Blair told other colleagues that the proud Texan was staying on, King called him a son-of-a-bitch and demanded he admit to having lied. "All Blair would admit was 'a misunderstanding,'" King wrote later. "I roundly cursed him, said I would have nothing to do with him the rest of my life and forbade him ever to speak to me again." That evening, in a party at Muriel Murphy's, I watched helplessly as King, sobbing and raging, delivered a kick to an antique chair, which shattered into many little pieces.

Shortly after that, there was a bitter, edgy meeting with John Cowles, Jr., who flew in from Minneapolis, and the other editors, Kotlowitz, Halberstam, King, Corry, Frady, John Hollander, and the newest addition, Lewis Lapham. Three of the number later described the event to me. Midge Decter had already resigned;

telegrams arrived from Arthur Miller and William Styron. Lewis Lapham, who had not been with the magazine very long, went to Halberstam and said he wanted to be with them. David advised him that there was going to be blood over everyone and that he ought to stay as far away as possible, but Lapham told Halberstam and the others that the magazine had been the happiest professional experience of his life and that he wanted to support them.

The meeting began late at night and lasted three hours. The setting was the St. Regis, "in a chandeliered suite," the sweet-tongued Frady later noted, "that would have fair served for treaty-signing ceremonies at the Congress of Vienna, complete with a pageantry buffet of DeMillean splendor and various waiters and attendants padding about." Larry L. King said, "We were treated as buck privates in the rear ranks — lucky to escape court-martials," and that the event reminded him of the film clips of General MacArthur accepting the surrender of the Japanese on the *U.S.S. Missouri*. With the editors lined up in front of him on straight-backed chairs, from a yellow couch Cowles spoke at first from a prepared statement concerning the publication's decline in circulation and said that William Blair would be promoted to publisher, effective immediately, and that *Harper's* would go in "new directions." He spoke of readership survey polls showing the magazine should try something else, and that market and readership research should determine the stories the magazine should undertake. Larry L. King said, "If you can find one single goddamn self-respecting writer worth the ink of his by-line who'll work on terms like that, John, I'll kiss your ass till your nose bleeds." Halberstam asked Cowles to define the new directions the magazine should pursue, and what he was specifically objecting to, suggesting it was "the hottest book in the trade." Cowles replied, "A magazine can't live on favorable press notices and dinner party conversation." He added, "Much of it bores me." Halberstam reminded him that he had pledged the editors five years to turn the magazine around, that in response from readers they had done so, and now he was "pulling the rug." Larry L. King would later write in *None But a Blockhead: On Being a Writer*:

Cowles said he just couldn't give it more time, that the magazine had become a cross to bear and that his father had urged him to sell it or padlock it "because it simply isn't worth the trouble." This cavalier dismissal of a magazine we loved and that had an honored history and tradition in American letters infuriated the brotherhood. We began to shout of money *Harper's* management had wasted in redesigning the magazine's binding, in remodelling Bill Blair's offices, in commissioning useless readership surveys, in buying *The Reporter's* circulation for huge sums when that magazine folded and then doing nothing to keep that circulation. Junior Cowles was offended that a scruffy bunch of writers would presume to question his business acumen, and the air grew chillier within the St. Regis.

The dissenters offered to find financing to purchase the magazine. It was not for sale, the owner replied, and William Blair would remain in charge and choose the new editor. The editors backed Bob Kotlowitz for that position. Cowles responded that Kotlowitz was on Blair's list, but added that he was sure Muhammad Ali was also. "Either we were speaking in Chinese and he was listening in English," Halberstam described the session to the newsweeklies, "or we were speaking in English and he was listening in Chinese." Cowles began enumerating all the things he disliked about the magazine. Halberstam asked him if there was anything he liked about it and he said, No, there was not. "That, of course, was it," Halberstam remembered. "We had poured everything we had into the magazine for a long time. We had *lived* that magazine, we were justifiably proud of the product, the response on the part of the readers and our professional peers was exceptional, and here he was giving us a vote of no-confidence."

A strange thing happened. Lewis Lapham switched sides and began agreeing with the owner. Yes, he said, polling readers to ascertain what they wanted was a great idea. "His behavior," Halberstam recalled, "stunned us all."

John Corry said, "All right, John, are you telling us that the magazine will change but you won't say in what direction, and that

Blair will remain in power?" Cowles replied, "Yes, that's pretty much the case." With that Larry L. King stood up. "Then fuck it, there's no reason to stay here. I resign," and stormed out of the chamber, followed rapidly by Kotlowitz, Halberstam, Corry, and Hollander. Marshall Frady, often gentlemanly in the manner of Ashley Wilkes in *Gone with the Wind,* stayed behind. He remembered: "I thought Cowles, who seemed a rather amiable and mild-mannered if somewhat simple-witted chap, could somehow be *reasoned* with. Which I was effusively trying to do, until I heard a bellow from the hallway, *'Frady, get on out here!'* I mumbled to Cowles, 'Scuse me now. I'm with them,' and bolted on out." All of them subsequently resigned. The only one who stayed behind was Lewis Lapham. (Lapham became the new managing editor, replacing Kotlowitz, and in due time would be editor-in-chief. He told someone that it was during the meeting in the St. Regis that he suddenly realized he could have the entire magazine.) Someone said to Hollander, the poetry editor, "This bunch of owners won't care much for poetry now." In his letter to Cowles Bob Kotlowitz said he was leaving because "the heart has gone out of the magazine" and because he did not think Blair should have the authority to pick a new editor-in-chief.

John Fischer was brought back as interim editor. He immediately sent out a memo. What *Harper's* needed most, he said, was articles about the future. "We don't need articles about dead people. We don't need criticism of Henry James, or Proust, or William Dean Howells. We don't need articles about defeated politicians. We don't need nostalgic reminiscences of childhood. We need material about people who are on the way up, not on the way down."

As such things happen, the mass walkout was a media event. *Saturday Review*: "In issue after issue *Harper's* writers put their own lives on the line in passages of personal revealment and commitment [and] provided pieces of penetrating journalism." *Boston Globe*: "one of the very best magazines ever published in America." On and on. And none more touching to me, in these dreariest moments of my life, than the words of my colleagues and collaborators to the press. Midge Decter: "I cannot believe that in a country of two hundred million people — even during economic recessions — there isn't room for a good magazine like *Harper's.*" Norman Mailer: "This is the most depressing event in American letters in many a year because *Harper's* had become the most adventurous of all magazines." Dave Halberstam: "Cowles did not understand what the excellence of the magazine stood for. It was an editorial *tour de force* with limited financial resources. He did not know the value of what he was sponsoring." He added: "We were a band of brothers."

The last day in my office, a Sunday when no one was there, I lingered for a long time at my old desk, remembering in the strange quiet the burnished morning of spring those years ago when I had sat there for the very first time with my youthful hopes and memories. In this moment I thought about my colleagues, and how proud and gratified I was that they had stood up to the magazine and for themselves and for me — but had I let *them* down?

I had to give a speech that night to the University of Texas Alumni in New York, and in the solitude I sat down and wrote it, a defense of my old student paper the *Daily Texan* against its most recent bouts with the censors. Later, at the alumni meeting in the Princeton Club Bill Moyers was to present me with a Texas Longhorn Award. "We have gathered together tonight," he said, in tones more sonorous than his youthful Baptist sermons must ever have been, "to honor a truly distinguished, gracious, and eminent American." He paused. "And after we finish with that, we're going to give a prize to Willie Morris."

Marshall Frady came back up from Atlanta on a special mission. He had journeyed to a Civil War shop at Kennesaw Mountain, where he bought a cavalry saber which had belonged to a young officer from Corinth, Mississippi. He had taken a flight for New York with the saber unsuccessfully disguised in bulkily wrapped butcher's paper, and it had taken, he reported to me, "no inconsiderable exertions of elaborate explanation to get it aboard the plane." A blizzard had settled over the northeastern coast, and the plane was diverted to Baltimore, and he had made it into Manhattan by train. He presented the handsome saber to me with a fine flourish of rhetoric at our same old table at the Empire Chinese. As the snow flurried on the darkened Madison Avenue outside, we talked of writing. Finally he had to leave. We shook hands, and then he, too, was gone.

Everything in life I have known to be true has come to me as a paradox. To me in this moment the most aching irony involved a reversal of the deepest emotions: almost overnight years before I had suddenly felt myself a "New Yorker," and now, just as swiftly, the city became large and hostile again. This, too, is a very American phenomenon, not an unfamiliar sensation to the many among us who arrive from elsewhere and appropriate the city's glitter and promise and then, sooner or later, confront in full, last measure its stalemates and subjugations. The magic and wonder and challenge give way, as sometimes they must in the miscreance and adventure of life, to pain and loss and reality.

"The city arouses us with the same forces by which it defeats us," Alfred Kazin wrote in our pages in those years. Even Scott Fitzgerald, lyricist of the New York splendor, came to the misgiving that the city had eventually blighted and devastated the people he knew from the Midwest, and that in the end it was "unreal, a mirage, and distinctly treacherous." Perhaps I too had not had the patience or the staying power for it. The burning passion had given way to the uneasy suspicion that I was now all emotionally burnt out. The high whining screech of the garbage trucks on the turbulent thoroughfares, the casual taunts and gesticulations on the streets, the whole jarring thrust and parry of that teeming life, served only to mock me now, and even the lights of the skyscrapers seemed dim and craven. All this, I suppose now, as with the very Sixties themselves, had something to do with a loss of innocence. I never picked up a *Harper's Magazine* again, sometimes even averting my gaze when I saw one on a newsstand.

One thing I did know was that after nine years of hard work on a publication, I was left with little money, departing the city, just as I had first come to it, more or less broke. Job offers came, of course. I thought about newspaper work again and other magazines, but I had had my organizational summit. I had given all of myself to my magazine, and I felt there was nothing else comparable for me in an institutional way. I even responded to a telegram from Sargent Shriver and met him for lunch in the Four Seasons, where amid the wordly consonance of the midday trade among the same tables where I had so often entertained writing people we talked lovingly of his brothers-in-law Jack and Bobby Kennedy, and he wanted me to go to work writing speeches for Senator Muskie of Maine, who was about to seek the Democratic nomination for President so he could run against Nixon. But nothing came of it, and I knew anyway it was really about time to go.

So I packed my stuff and moved out the hundred miles to eastern Long Island — the South Shore — the vicinity I had grown to love, and settled in a wing of a sprawling old house on an inlet of the ocean. It is an axiom of existence that people will drop you. Also, that it is exceedingly human to be curious about, and even to enjoy, the travails of one's fellows, for the simple reason that this takes one's own mind away from one's own sorrows and failures, but not for long, since one's own troubles will sooner or later win out again anyway. Nonetheless, normally the least paranoic of creatures, I imagined that half of Manhattan Island in that transitory instant was reveling in my headstrong, self-inflicted exile. I felt like the old horse set out to pasture must have felt, the fine white horse who had walked round and round in circles ten hours a day pulling the beam that provided the power for the presses of Harper & Brothers Publishers in the last century, who in retirement continued to walk round and round.

The South Shore is a place of bleak and procrastinating winters, of long nights and silences, and there was immense snow on the ground. In the snowy solitude I surveyed the frail wreck of ambition. The telephone never rang. I missed the perquisites and attentions of high station. It was strange to wake up in the morning and have no place, no office, to go to, no salary to pay the bills. I had come to New York with a heart full of stars and hopes, and to have gone so high so fast, then down in a moment, was more than I had ever bargained for, as if I had somehow lost my reason for existing. I gazed interminably out the window upon the hushed landscapes, the frozen inlet, the Canada geese in V formation, trying to put things into some larger piece. To try to figure out anew who I really was, and to begin molding from this another life, was baffling and mysterious. Perhaps our greatest personal strengths, I see now, also entail and embrace our greatest weaknesses, and that we somehow have to reconcile these old secret human dichotomies through time, play them off against each other, comprehend them, seldom wanting others, even those we love the most, or those who love us, to recognize these weaknesses, but they come out sooner or later anyway, and that is likely just as well. I tried to explain to my son David what had happened, but in the moment I was not completely sure myself. "It's okay," he said. "I think I understand. Let's go to a ball game." I talked with Bill Moyers, who had been through the same himself. He reminded me I was thirty-seven years old, and to remember that I still owned a typewriter. I was not so much frightened as bereft.

From the bookcases I pulled out three books: *Huck Finn, Moby Dick, Go Down, Moses.* I had not been truly lonely in a long time, and it hurt. I took long walks in that sequestered terrain, past a derelict concrete pillbox or two built against the Nazis in the previous war, to the sand dunes in the snow and the desolate winter beach, the gulls and scurrying little terns, and as far as the eye could see the gray wintry Atlantic breakers. A lone fisherman said to me, "Take a boat from right where we stand and head due east and the first landfall is Portugal."

Was it my fault? Should I have always just been a writer, and never tried the editor's role? Should I have compromised with the owners? Had any of it been worth it? Hundreds upon hundreds of letters came from the magazine's subscribers, often eloquent, including a wonderful one from Cass Canfield, Sr. I tried to answer some of them, but there were far too many, and after a while I gave up. I do not even know where those letters are now, probably in a dusty corner of an abandoned attic in eastern Long Island.

A man has to search for the hope in the hurt. "In reality, nothing is as bad as it seems," Mary McCarthy once wrote, "or in logic ought to be," and the same emotions of a future Kenny Rogers tune kept going around in my head — "Got to know when to hold 'em, know when to fold 'em, know when to walk away" — and after a while I sat down and started writing a children's book, about childhood and adventure and frightening things in the South many years ago. Muriel, her daughter Julia, and David came out from the city on weekends. In front of the roaring fireplace, the snow again falling on the frozen pines and inlet, I would read to the kids what I had written that week.

"Go on," one or the other of them would ask when I finished.

"I can't," I would say. "That's all I've got for now."

"What happens next?"

"I don't know, but I'll sure find out."

Why would the hurt and anger and guilt, the tangible and continual sense of loss, last so long, so far into my adulthood? Someday I would know. My magazine was a living thing to me, and leaving it was like death. And it was palpable and inherent and symbol to me of its place: ineluctable town, sinew and fabric, of youth and dreams.

~ SOUTH TOWARD HOME

16

ALL THAT WAS a long way from where I now live. As it does, the world took a couple of turns. In 1980 I returned to my native ground out of blood and belonging, as others among my fellow American writers had, for in this civilization still there are injunctions which sometimes tell you it is best to be getting on back before it is too late.

"The writer's vocation," Flaubert said, "is perhaps comparable to love of one's native land," and there are moments as I age that I feel I should never have left it, but stayed with it, in all its cruelties, fears, and hopes. If it is true that a writer's world is shaped by the experience of childhood and adolescence, then returning at long last to the scenes of those experiences, remembering them anew and living among their changing heartbeats, gives him something he could easily otherwise lose, a physical relationship to the significant events of his own past.

Here I was back again in the sweet and deep dark womb of home. The eternal juxtaposition of my state's hate and love, the apposition of its severity and tenderness, would forever baffle and enrage me, but perhaps that is what I needed all along. I would never deny the poverty, the smugness, the infectious cruelty which have existed on this soil. Sometimes I cannot live with its awesome emotional burdens, its terrible racist hazards and human neglects, sometimes I can, but these forever drive me to words. Meanness is everywhere, but here the meanness and the desperation and the nobility have for me their own dramatic edge, for the fools are my fools, and the heroes are mine too. Do not think that even in the poorest commonwealth of the Great Republic the acquisitive American urges are not still in flourish; down here the merchants perform their own television commercials, and the undertakers do also. The merchants sound like undertakers, and the undertakers sound like merchants.

For ten years or so I wrote books and articles and was writer-in-residence at Ole Miss, and pray the reader to be titillated that subsequently one of my students, at age twenty-five, got $450,000 in advance money on her first novel. To this day I am half a Yazoo boy, half a cosmopolitan man, and most of the time, as in New York, I still do not know which. I like certain things about home that would not happen in many other places, as on the morning a black state trooper pulled me to the side of the highway and told me my inspection sticker had expired, and also my license plate, and demanded my driver's license. From the rearview mirror I saw the black trooper examining the driver's license on the way to his patrol car to radio his headquarters, but abruptly turning on his heels and coming toward me again.

"Mr. Morris, are you the writer?"

"I'm afraid so, Officer."

"Then have a good day," he said, and handed the license back to me.

Disney was filming a movie of the children's book, *Good Old Boy*, I had written in the wintry snows of Long Island those years ago. The director asked me to come down to Natchez to coach the Hollywood youngsters on the Southern accent. I was sitting at the bar in the hotel in late afternoon while the cast was still out shooting. Suddenly I felt a tug on my arm, looking down to see a mischievous ten-year-old in blue jeans and a navy-blue baseball cap.

"Are you Willie?" he asked in a Southern California tongue.

"Yes I am."

"Where've you been, Willie? We've been expecting you for three days."

"Who are *you?*"

"I'm *Willie.*"

Watching the filming of the L.A. boy playing me, and the others acting my boyhood chums such as Henjie Henick, and my long-departed mother, father, grandmother, grandfather, and great aunts, and even a Hollywood dog portraying my Old Skip, was *déjà vu* of the most impressive kind, and exceedingly strange. They were ghosts for me in sunlight.

There were other moments: standing in an eerie dusk in the red earth of Neshoba County on the exact spot where the three young civil rights workers had been murdered in '64; writing a book in a lonesome cabin on the green and serpentine back stretches of the Bogue Chitto River; following old No. 61 — the "Freedom Highway" — from the Delta to New Orleans; suppers in Mississippi-Greek tavernas with Eudora Welty; renewing friendships with people I had grown up with; observing the white-and-black Ole Miss Rebels from the south end zones. An afternoon in my familial village of Raymond, when the town dedicated a historical marker to my patriarch, at which my son and I spoke as great-great-grandson and great-grandson, David's prefacing his words by confessing to being "one-half Yankee," the aged president of the United Daughters of the Confederacy later patting him on the knee and tremulously saying, "Young man, it's not *your* fault you're one-half Yankee." And one bizarre evening, inexplicable to this diehard great-grandson of Democrats, finding oneself up from home at the small round head table at a state dinner in the East Room of the White House with the President of the United States, the Queen of Jordan, the coach of the Chicago Bears, and Little Orphan Annie.

There was the moment, too, I found myself driving in a Delta twilight toward a warm new love. All around in this twinkling of serenity and happiness and fulfillment were the landmarks of my own beginnings, the cypresses in the mossy ponds, the dwindling woods, the little hardscrabble towns of my youth, the interminable flatness in the burnt orange glow. She was a Mississippi Delta girl ten years my junior, of good beauty and disposition and finesse, and a kindly and percipient heart and a sense of laughter. And she had written the history of Yazoo County! She was warm-spirited, and touched the lives of many people, cared for the lingering landscapes and memories, adored Christmases, wished for snow in

Mississippi then though it never came, always had a flourishing, pungent cedar for a tree. Her father had survived the fighting in France as an infantry captain, a Bronze Star and two Purple Hearts, and came home to see his daughter for the first time and carried her into the backyard, and her first words to him were, "Daddy, see the moon?" When we drove through the Delta she had a gift for spotting egrets perched on cows' backs out on the flat dark earth, and solitary hawks in the autumnal trees, and once in Birmingham she wished to visit the grave of Paul "Bear" Bryant. Who can explain such enigmas of belonging and love, especially when they come late? In her backyard, on dewy spring nights, we listened to the supple, beguiling Mississippi mockingbirds in their eternal rhyme; who would ever kill a mockingbird? We were married. I inherited a pair of companionable and inspiriting stepsons, and she named our three white cats, a mother and two irascible offspring, Rivers Applewhite, Spit McGee, and Henjie Henick, after my kids in the children's tale. Against all expectation the inveterate dog-lover and feline misanthrope grew to love these capricious, exasperating Mississippi cats, and soon became their valet, butler, and menial in daily and permanent indenture.

We live in Jackson, the funny old overgrown town where I was born, only forty miles from Yazoo, and one windswept gray forenoon not long ago we stopped at the Yazoo cemetery. I practically grew up in this graveyard, and as children we came here for picnics and games, wandering among the graves on our own, with no adults about, watching the funerals from afar in a hushed awe, and I believe that was when I became obsessed not with death itself but with the singular community of death and life together — and life's secrets, life's fears, life's surprises. I return here whenever I can, for there is a lot of sky here, and quiet, and its familiar stones and its last sloping hills before the coming of the Delta envelop me with stability, and help me reflect on my own life and where its mysteries have taken me, as the dispirited Roman legionnaire must have felt on re-entering his cherished outpost after foraging the forlorn stretches of Gaul. William Faulkner said that perhaps after death we become "radio waves," and I can stand here in some preternatural stillness amid the elms and junipers and magnolias and absorb everything of these people I once knew. I often think here of how each generation lives with its own exclusive solicitudes — the passions, the defeats, the victories, the sacrifices, the names and dates and faces belong to each generation in its own passing, for much of everything except the most unforgettable is soon forgotten. My mother and father are buried here, and so someday will I be. I cannot think of a single spot in America so far removed for me from Park Avenue and Thirty-third Street.

We entered the gate at the old family section and took the customary turn at the abandoned goldfish fountain. Close by was a new grave with its fresh mound of flowers. "I'll see who it is," JoAnne said. She got out of the car and walked to the grave, and I watched her from the distance as she stooped over it. Then she returned. "Henjie Henick," she said.

We had been out of the state for a couple of weeks, and it was odd, and sad, to discover the death of an honored childhood comrade in this way. Could it be a hoax, of the kind Henjie and I ourselves had perpetuated long ago on unwitting victims in this very cemetery? Was he himself in this moment hiding behind a tree laughing at me? I was taken aback by the depth of my sorrow for Henjie. I remembered how as children we pulled a string of tin cans up the boulevard to celebrate the Normandy landings, the basketball goal in his backyard down the alley from mine, the night we left the Dixie Theater in abject terror halfway through the ghost movie *The Uninvited,* the high school days when we played "Taps" on our trumpets for the Korean War dead in this cemetery and flipped a coin before each funeral to see who would be at the grave and who would play the Echo since neither of us wanted the scenes of grief at the grave — remembered too his letters of support to me in New York over the many years. Strange how of all the Yazoo boys it was Henjie who became the best of them all. I knew that my grief for him was grief for myself, and for mortality, and for all of us who have shared childhood and growing up in settled places before we went away, and got older. He had stayed, all along running his father's auto parts store at the same familiar foot of Main Street while I was doing my multifarious New York tasks, and my national quests and assignations. "He sits in his tiny store way down at the south end of Main," a mutual friend had once written me, "amid the rubble of old family stores, like the sole survivor of a barrage, kind and thoughtful of others, a sort of gaunt and weary symbol to me of goodness surviving decay." Little arcs of fallen leaves swirled wantonly about as I stood now before his grave, feeling all the years, as if everything had finally come full-circle.

My *Harper's* comrades. As the record would amply testify, they went on to greater (and, yes, even more lucrative) things. Bob Kotlowitz moved to public television and for WNET would produce, among other successes, *Brideshead Revisited,* Dickens' *Hard Times, The Magic of Dance,* and *The Sleeping Beauty,* win Emmys, and write critically acclaimed novels, including *Somewhere Else,* which won the National Jewish Book Award. His son Alex also became an author, writing the classic *There Are No Children Here: The Story of Two Boys Growing Up in Urban America,* likely deriving the inspiration for it from the basketball I gave him at his bar mitzvah. Not long ago Bob wrote me from up in the country of Columbia County, New York, where he spends half his time:

> That already says something of the New York of today. There is no literary world, no music world, none of that, really, just a lot of clashing social activity, mainly built on money and celebrity or access to both. As for the rest, they've disappeared into the orange heart of California, moved to London, dropped out, or just quietened down. No one seems to come to New York anymore with the hopes that you and I had, those inflated Balzacian ambitions to meet the great ones and become one of them.
>
> But the years at *Harper's* were wonderful ones, summing up everything that made New York special. When the magazine blew up, while John Cowles languished in Minnesota, as only the rich can languish, I felt a terrible sense of loss. It was grievous. It took years for me to come out of it, and for a while I thought I might never find or repair the loss.
>
> I also read more than ever, more slowly, too, more carefully, and certainly more respectfully.

Dave Halberstam's big, significant books on a broad tapestry of America and the world would continue to be commercial and critical successes. Larry L. King would write his books and plays, including *The Best Little Whorehouse in Texas,* which allowed him to purchase a mansion in Washington, hire nannies for his children, and subsidize their riding lessons in Virginia. What would his old West Texas daddy say? Midge Decter stayed active as a prolific writer in highly conservative causes. John Corry would remain a foremost journalist. Herman Gollob of Harper's Magazine Press would go on to become one of the most respected and resourceful editors in book publishing. John Hollander, the poetry editor, would continue to write his distinguished verse, and become the A. Bartlett Giamatti professor of English at Yale. Marshall Frady, in his words "after passing for a time into the electronic Philistine bondage of television," has returned to writing. "It was a season, no matter how increasingly distant," he would recall, "in which I've continued to live and against which continued to measure what I've been doing ever since. Though one didn't altogether suspect its magic while in the midst of it — it's been as if it's only taken on its full Camelot aura in retrospect, as so often we only fully realize things when they're gone."

Many of the other contributors still alive were doing valuable work. Bill Styron's novels would forever be among the nation's best. Norman Mailer would remain a brilliant and forceful influence in the literary and social life of the nation. Recently I caught him on a national television interview for his thousand-page novel *Harlot's Ghost,* and from far down in Jackson, Mississippi, heard the familiar voice, "Let me make one more remark before we go on to reincarnation, which I really want to talk about."

My former wife Celia married a mutual friend of ours, and divorced again. She would become a respected feminist and writer. As I was working on this book she wrote me:

> I went just this past weekend to the wonderful house in the country. I was in Connecticut and the dogwood was out, so I got a powerful urge to see the grandest dogwood there ever was, the one in our front yard. It looked pathetic — whether because this

> is its personal off-year or whether it's not too long for this world, I don't know. But everything else seems to have enjoyed a natural evolution. The house is intensely lived in and looks much the same as in our time. The crimson king maple I planted is a great flourishing tree, a real treasure. The crabapple out the big picture window is glorious. It all was graceful and touching and intensely real to me. I'm thankful we had that place, if only for a little while.

My son David Rae, signal, talisman, hero, and friend of those, and all other years, would graduate from Hampshire College, get a master's from the University of Minnesota, and become a talented photographer, sometimes searching the old, tragic landscapes and the varied people of Mississippi for his material, all the while still loving the Knicks and Mets. "I was just a little kid then," he muses now. "But I still consider myself a child of the Sixties: distrust of politicians, a certain kind of personal cynicism about the fate of the world, Vietnam, Watergate as an extension, a sense of rebellion, a belief I can make a difference."

William S. "Bill" Blair, I was told, eventually went to Vermont and put out a magazine there, I hope with a ski emphasis.

Harper's would try a number of editors-in-chief. I am not certain if John Cowles, Jr., arrived at his "new directions" for the magazine before selling out in 1980 to a nonprofit foundation with right-wing inclinations.

John Cowles, Jr., himself, after selling off the magazine, would be summarily ousted from the helm of Cowles Media in 1983 when the family enterprise went into deep decline. The dismissal was performed by the board of overseers' seven outside directors, all of them Cowles relatives. The reasons for the dismissal, it was widely described in the press, including in much and graphic detail his homestate *Minnesota Monthly,* were multifold, involving the loss of $25 million on a newspaper they had bought and then folded in Buffalo, and also personal: John Jr.'s reclusiveness, his inability to deal with people, his highly public involvement in the fringe commitment groups like EST and Primal Screaming, his new enthusiasm for motorcycles. He retained, however, a substantial percentage of the voting stock: "Still worth untold millions," the *Washington Post* reported. For a time he would indulge in other interests, including a degree in agricultural economics, before he turned to aerobics. This, in turn, led to nude dancing. In the early 1990s John Jr., now sixty-one, and his wife, Sage, sixty-five, toured twenty-five cities of the country with a group performing "The Last Supper at Uncle Tom's Cabin/The Promised Land," which ended in a flower-power manifesto with what one reviewer called an "apotheosis in the buff." When the troupe reached the nation's capital for a performance at Lisner Auditorium, Cowles, in a story headlined "The Nude Paper Man," told the *Post:* "The nudity, I think, is simply a metaphor for getting rid of the unimportant barriers between people and stressing what may be the simultaneous similarities and differences among people." To others he noted, "Older people are past the mating mode, and they know who they are." Cowles's son said, "They're having the time of their lives." I myself least of anyone would denounce dancing buck naked in a chorus line, and am not faintly interested in whatever the rich do in diversion from being rich, but I suppose, in faithful service of the New York days, I should bring out the old rubric, "Water rises or falls to its own level." John Cowles's sister said, "We all believed that they should follow their dream."

As I remembered this past in the cemetery of my childhood, and the people who shared it with me, I realized anew just how much I, as with so many of the others, was a product and expression of the Sixties, and how deeply I remember the words of those times, and the passions, the fears, the loves. There is the fragment of a later tune, "Whoever thought the Sixties would be called 'the good old days'?" Certainly not I, nor most others of all persuasions then. In the early 1990s criticisms of the young Sixties generation were hardly rare, for instance, among the post–Baby Boomers of the nation. "It's a big old garbage barge of a generation," a thirty-one-year-old campaign advisor close to Bill Clinton would declare, "and we have had to clean up after it — the drugs, the greed, everything." I myself endorse something of this retrospective emotion, for not a few of the people I know today from that generation are, in middle age, of narcissistic heart and entrepreneurial disposition, who seem to have learned little from their own generational history, or care, even as they make good money off the Establishment they outwardly deplore. But few can doubt that those fateful years would affect the American society for a very long time to come, that the inward scrutiny of the era raised imperishable collective questions about the nature and substance of the society itself, questions that likely would never go away.

With all its flauntings and sufferings, its nihilisms and extremes, its self-righteousness and self-absorption and contempt for honest disagreement, its casual and careless and methodized violence, the decade was still a time of immense pristine hope and idealism, the last the nation would have for many years: a *mood,* no matter how naive and later destructive it might have become, in which young people believed they owed something to each other, often across racial and class barriers, and to the fragile physical environment of the earth, and that they were morally compelled to try to make a difference in human rights, civil rights, free speech, democracy, tolerance of personal idiosyncrasy and sexuality and ethnic diversity and personal freedom of choice, and to decry the human cost of heedless foreign imperialism. These would be enduring legacies for the better angels of our nature.

The interim years would be at such incalculably far remove as to seem of another civilization altogether. Are we to blame the memory of the tumult of the Sixties for the cultural reaction which followed? The succession of emphatic Republican victories as the other party lost much of its traditional constituencies in a numerically diminishing electorate amounted to a remolding of the national psyche, as if the organized society were reverting to the most retrenched and nascent 1920s without the flappers and bathtub gin and Scott and Zelda. Beginning with the Reagan revolution of 1981, perhaps the greediest and most cynical years in our history as a people, the acquisitive ideology so decried by the Sixties' rebellions achieved its full fruition: the aggrandizement of self-indulgence and consumption and private pursuits in the name of getting "government" off people's backs, the slashing of half the taxes on the rich while cutting social programs for the poor and desperate to the point of ruin, the Wall Street high rollers, the accumulating tension between minority rights and majority values, the private schools and protected suburban enclaves, the mounting poverty and the decline in real wages, the cascading drop in education and housing and health care to Third World levels, the rich man's officious emphasis on "family values" while the poorest families were in helpless disarray, the soaring national deficit, the growing permanent "underclass" in this nation, the ascending entrenchment of conservative ideologues in the federal courts including the highest one, the watering down of civil rights and the racial divisiveness inspired in the highest quarters of power, the persistence of — and indeed dramatic increases in — joblessness, drugs, violence and despair in the urban ghettos, and in the small towns, and suburbs, too. For these were the years, Russell Baker observed, "when 12-year-old girls in New York are having babies before breakfast and dropping them down garbage chutes on the way to school" and "schoolteachers are being fired by the truckload because voters prefer ignorance to taxes" and "the country is turning into a congeries of feuding, selfish, fearful tribes." And finally, there was the nearly unbridgeable contrast with the young people of the Sixties: the rigorous conservatism of the modern-day campuses as I personally observed them, the mercenary smugnesses of them, the absence of any real interest of many of these young in literature, in history, in ideas, in *language* itself beyond the argot of television, the computer, and the corporation.

Somehow, from the perspective of home, I perceive my country more clearly than I ever did from New York, having to do, one surmises, with isolation and quieter moments and the maturity of age. We have witnessed the swift and nearly apocalyptical end of international communism and the Cold War, and how will America react to that? Our civilization has always been tenuous, but even now I can feel the beauty and power and promise of it, its older and deeper instincts. In many aspects, as we reached 1993, the generation that had once challenged the Establishment had become the Establishment. As we approach the *fin de siècle,* I recall Professor Schlesinger's Hegelian tides in our history, the coming and going and coming again in cycles of retrenchment and vitality.

Is this protean, unpredictable, malleable, bifurcated, and sometimes frightening nation slowly approaching another such crossroads? Is something fine of the Sixties coming back someday? I look forward to knowing.

It is always difficult to try to see one's life whole. Yet in the admonition of the Mississippi blues song, "No pain, no gain." All of what I have described in this memoir was a small eternity ago, and I see now that, as with much of life, this has really been a little long-ago tale, not about politics, or history, or publishing, or a place, but about time passing, and about the allies and adversaries who were with me on that passage. So many of my friends of those days are dead now, and others have gone their own way. In the course of an existence, people move in and out of one's life. Often we do not know the *whereabouts* of those once dear to us, much less what they are feeling or remembering. Close relationships oscillate between tranquility and destruction, between fire and ice. Old fidelities wither and love dies as the lovers go on living. There are a few small islands of warmth and belonging if we are lucky. That is how I wish to remember the best of those times. In a speech to old Northern veterans in 1884, Oliver Wendell Holmes said, "I think that, as life is action and passion, it is required of a man that he should share the passion and action of his time, at peril of being judged not to have lived."

And always, throughout life, there remains for me the city itself, in memory and mirage, for the city is still part of my dreams. "There is never any ending to Paris," Hemingway wrote of his youth there, "and the memory of each person who has lived in it differs from that of any other." So, too, I with New York. As I stood that day at Henjie's grave, I was reminded of something indefinable and faraway, some wisp of mysterious belonging, some lambent whisper somewhere in the long-ago breast of the city calling to me, and I knew now I could return.

I have not been back in many years. The old, arduous, magnificent town is touched for me with youth and death, and forever imbued with an uncommon maze of feelings, some felicitous, others premonitory. I am a little wary of its incontrovertible burdens. There are old, buried apprehensions here. Perhaps I gave too much of myself to it, and it to me: a most ambivalent contract, American in its unfolding. Not long before I have come across, in an attic in an old house in Mississippi, a box containing a few idle and tattered mementos of those years — the official program of a Mets World Series match, another of a Knicks championship game, the menu of a Century Club ball, the magazine's 120th anniversary issue with the Yazoo County school bus on the cover, a faded photograph of Halberstam and King and me at the corner of Park and Thirty-third, a desk calendar and datebook for 1964 with scribbled notations for business lunches and appointments, an Elaine's menu circa 1967, a worn baseball belonging to David Rae, invitations to parties and dinners. I am returning this time to come to terms with that past.

It is A.D. 1992. Summer has fallen on the penthouse roofs and the park, and the heat shimmers in misty mirages off the asphalt and stone, and it takes only minutes for one's incumbent New York adrenaline to begin pulsing again, as if that old protective kinetic suction so requisite to daily sustenance here has been lying dormant all these years, waiting only to be summoned once more. And just as swiftly the wariness, too, returns, the attenuated Manhattan guardedness: don't bump into anyone, look around you, don't take anything for granted, acquired instincts which have never really deserted one from the setting of those days. On one of the nights I am here, there are ten homicides, including five teenagers and a cabdriver.

There is more garbage. The traffic is more torrid than ever. The homeless are ubiquitous: "Help the Homeless. Read the *Street News*." Even here in Murray Hill there is the surreal aspect of a Third World city. Yet there are more limousines by far, moving like armored titans down the inchoate thoroughfares, their flushed windows obscuring the voyagers inside, isolating them from the ruined vistas of the streets. The steam still pours upward from the sewers as if the world underneath were an inferno. My city friends always disparaged me for sidestepping these intransigent manholes as if they were minefields, yet one of them reported not long before that a series of exploding steam pipes had showered carcinogenic asbestos into apartment houses all over town. I was right all along.

It is extraordinary how *sound,* not unlike smell, brings back so much of past moments to those of our species. It is the noisome cacophony which envelops me on this waning afternoon and evokes in a rush the memories of those days: the multifarious vehicles and grinding motors and jackhammers, and sirens and "boom-boxes" and edgy berating of a thousand horns, the rumbling subways, the yelps and peals of the hastening crowds, merge mightily into an accumulating diaphanous discord so breathtaking that one cannot help but feel he is in the presence of some elemental phenomenon of near geologic propensity. Most American cities have their distinctive sounds, San Francisco the echoes of its boats' horns, New Orleans its music, but the ceaseless clamor of Manhattan rises in synesthesia, and for me on this day is a deep blazing crimson. And the human beings themselves wafting through this miasmic current, in their inconquerable miscellany, recall Calvin Trillin's reckoning that ninety percent of the people walking the sidewalks of Manhattan would be interviewed in any other town, and the other ten percent arrested.

I am in my old neighborhood, the Murray Hill vicinity, where I once lived and worked. Like my own unprepossessing village of Dixie, but from different corporalities, every streetcorner here holds a memory. The minuscule restaurant on Thirty-fourth Street between Madison and Park where I lunched alone that November Friday forenoon in the moment John F. Kennedy was killed is now a Greek Laundromat. The Irish bar on Lexington where an off-duty policeman slugged me on the jawbone that night for toasting Lyndon B. Johnson in my grief is now Kalustyan's Mid-Croatian Grocery. The tiny coin shop on Thirty-third where I often paused after work to buy my little boy a Lincoln penny or a buffalo nickel now houses a *Psychic Advisor Espirite.* At Fifth and Thirty-fourth the regal retail establishment B. Altman where I shopped at Christmas for my wife and child is derelict and shuttered. The seemly old Harper & Brother's red-brick edifice at 49 East Thirty-third where I first went to work is a Hebrew bookstore. Down at Park and

Twenty-eighth the Belmore Cafeteria, whose proprietor was my landlord and where every cabdriver in lower Manhattan, it seemed, stopped for coffee, has disappeared from the earth, now a dazzling twenty-five-story apartment building, and the site of the gaunt and improvised little apartment behind it where my family and I first lived is a courtyard for the high-rise. The treacherous, surreptitious tunnel at the intersection of Park and Thirty-third out of which vehicles whipped at uncanny speeds to run down and dismember pedestrians crossing unaware against the red light is still there, however. To this day there is no warning sign at the tunnel, so that the terrible breath of adventure at this intersection seems as vibrant as it ever was.

Our magazine was at Two Park, a stone's throw from this disputatious crossing, that stolid 1920s building with copious lobby and high ornate ceilings in the art deco mode, and that is my destination now. Instinctively I take the elevator to the same old floor, turn right down a lengthy corridor, then left toward what had been the main doorway.

It is an import-and-export establishment now. A forbearing receptionist permits me to wander the quarters alone. They are surprisingly unaltered. The grander offices and more inauspicious cubicles and rambling hallways sometimes ending unresolved in impromptu little cul-de-sacs leap out in buried recognition. It is as if I have barely left at all. As I wander about I remember my contemporaries among my colleagues, for their presence here is everywhere: their laughter, their mischief, their comradeship, and there is the phantom click all around me of their vanished typewriters.

I have one vivid recurring nightmare of the city, fluctuating only in merest detail. It is late afternoon of a midtown summer, not unlike this one. I am irretrievably lost somewhere in this neighborhood. I cannot find the subway. The longer I search for it, the more disoriented I become. All around me are the hostile people. None of them will help me. Soon a fog descends, and the very landmarks of the city itself are obscured, and I wander away into an early gloom.

So, too, with my dreams of these offices. My dreams of these quarters have been prolific, varying in detail but not very much in substance: stacks of manuscripts yet unread, deadlines unmet, and in the deep swirling shadows there is an ambience of neglect in these dreams, guilt and failure and tender regret. One such dream recurs again and again. I have returned to here from some long, enigmatic journey. At first the premises are hushed, eerie, deserted. It is unclear to me where I have been all these years. I enter my office. My old desk has been taken away. Nearby are the piles of soiled, unread manuscripts. I begin to read them, but there are so many. Suddenly ghostly figures appear before me: the nervous specter of John Fischer, whom I once loved, Catharine Meyer, Kay Jackson, and then a line of faceless secretaries. I realize they are all dead. "Where have *you* been?" one of them asks. "We've been waiting for you. We gave your desk away." Unfamiliar young executives look in on us. One of them in an immaculate pin-striped suit and an Ivy League tie makes light of my shabby green turtle-necked sweater. I look down at the sweater. It is flecked with scrambled-egg droppings! In one such apparition Henjie Henick emerges from the shadows to help me read the manuscripts. The monthly deadline is approaching, he warns me, and I have been remiss. In another "Dog" Brewer, football coach at the University of Mississippi,. and "Mississippi Red" McDowell, flamboyant sportswriter, suddenly appear to usher away the dead. No matter the *denouement,* the aspects are the same: the turtle-necked sweater, the deadline, the manuscripts, the ghosts, and the loss.

I leave the office building on this day, stand briefly before the menacing intersection. There is one last spot I wish to visit in the vicinity, a spiritual pilgrimage of a kind, for in truth I have been putting it off: our gathering spot, the Empire Chinese Restaurant. Dusk is falling on Murray Hill as I reach Madison Avenue and cross Thirty-fourth and make my way to that honorable site. And there, suddenly, it is.

I could have collapsed in my tracks of a sundered heart. Steel gray shutters cover the windows. On the front facade the letters "Empire Chinese Restaurant" are faded and peeling. There is an enormous "For Rent" notice on the shutters. I approach the front doors and peer through the glass. The interior is dark and bereft.

Even the bar is gone, and there are rows of piled trash on the floors. I close my eyes to absorb the vanished voices. Is that Norman Mailer in the shadows there? Bernard Malamud? James Dickey?

Standing in solitude here in the avenue's grand discord in the dying twilight, hearing again in the mind's imaginings the merging consonances of the Sixties, I indulgently reflect on all that has transpired with one in the many years he has been away from this spectral place: the successes, the failures, the joys and sorrows, the loves and friendships come and gone, the catastrophic whims and transmutations. I have always more or less believed in some anodyne kind of Deity, even at my most agnostic, having to do in some measure with one's own especial origins, but mine, as in Wallace Stevens's "Sunday Morning," is a God of transience.

We live in an old chaos of the sun,
Or old dependency of day and night,
Or island solitude, unsponsored, free,
Of that wide water, inescapable . . .
And, in the isolation of the sky,
At evening, casual flocks of pigeons make
Ambiguous undulations as they sink,
Downward to darkness, on extended wings.

In these days' wanderings in the city the direst of recognitions began to spring in my poor psyche that I had not made the slightest ripple on this place, for New York somehow obliterates you, and especially the outlander. Yet I conceded, too, that I had once dwelled here, and that the prodigal metropolis had taught me much about myself, and about America. I have not forgotten how much I loved this town and the awe in which I held it, and the love and awe and ambivalence come back to me now, that they may yet consume me. But hey, old town, I gave you a run. "Only the days are long," it was the histrionic John Barrymore who said, "the years move on hidden wheels." At first I thought my modest return would be about growing older, about youth lost, and youth's forfeited opportunities, but I see now it is really about the complexity of remembrance. What I was looking for all the time was me, and I was not there.

~ Acknowledgments

I wish to thank those people, too numerous to list here, who provided valuable reminiscences and read the manuscript for accuracy. A number of my former colleagues and collaborators were generous in corroborating facts and broader truths, making me remember all over again how marvelous they had been to work with.

I would have been lost without my unfailing typist and friend, Ginger Tucker. Susan Blumenthal, Valerie Walley, Tom Verich, John Evans, Carol Cox, Clarence Hunter, and Betty Power were especially helpful on research and facts. Eve Yohalem, editorial assistant at Little, Brown, was gracious and indispensable on all matters. Thanks as always to my faithful agent and comrade of thirty years, Sterling Lord.

Above all, I shall forever be grateful to Fredrica Friedman of Little, Brown, one of the great editors of America, who was committed to this story from the beginning, and whose unwavering counsel, encouragement, and friendship in these many long months make this book an act of true collaboration.

W. M.
Jackson, Mississippi 1993

~ Index